MATERIALS & METHODS
In Adult and Continuing Education

EDITORIAL ADVISORY BOARD

Dr. Dewey A. Adams
Professor, Vocational Education
Ohio State University

Dr. George F. Aker
Director, Educ. Management Systems
Florida State University

Dr. Luther H. Black
State Director Adult Education
Dept. of Education, Arkansas

Dr. Laurent R. Broussal
President, *San Francisco Community*
College District

Dr. Beverly Cassara
Dean, School of Graduate Studies
University of the District of Columbia

D. Stuart Conger
Director, Occupational & Career Analysis
Canada Employment & Immig. Commission

Dr. Gordon Darkenwald
Associate Professor, Adult Education
Rutgers State University

Dr. Eugene E. DuBois
Professor of Education
The George Washington University

Dr. Donnie Dutton
Professor, Adult Education
University of Arkansas

Dr. Richard A. Etheridge
Professor, Adult Education
Mississippi State University

Dr. Stanley M. Grabowski
Professor of Education
Boston University

Dr. John Hartwig
Consultant, Adult Education
Iowa State Dept. of Education

Shirley Heymann
Coordinator ABE Division
Phoenix Union High School System

Dr. Leonard R. Hill
Chief, Adult & Community Education
State Dept. of Education, Nebraska

Dr. Malcolm S. Knowles
Professor Emeritus
North Carolina University, Raleigh

Dr. Burton W. Kreitlow
Professor Emeritus
University of Wisconsin, Madison

Dr. James R. Layton
Professor of Reading
Southwest Missouri State University

Dr. Howard N. Lindskoog
Counselor
Community College, Juneau

Dr. Rosalind K. Loring
Associate Provost, Extended Education
University of Southern California

Dr. McKinley C. Martin
President, *Coahoma Junior College*
Clarksdale, MS

Dr. Howard H. McFann
President
McFann-Gray & Associates, Inc.

Dr. James W. Miller
Director, Div. of Federal Assistance
Ohio State Dept. of Education

Dr. John A. Niemi
Professor, Adult-Continuing Education
Northern Illinois University

Dr. William M. Rivera
Associate Professor, Adult & Extension Educ.
University of Maryland

Dr. Wendell L. Smith
Dean, Continuing Education/Ext.
University of Missouri-St. Louis

Dr. David C. Wigglesworth
President
Technical Research Associates, Inc.

CHAIRMAN EDITORIAL ADVISORY BOARD
Dr. Paul H. Sheats
Professor Emeritus
University of California, Los Angeles

MATERIALS & METHODS
In Adult and Continuing Education

Editor

CHESTER KLEVINS

ASSOCIATE EDITOR

EDGAR M. EASLEY

KLEVENS PUBLICATIONS Inc.
Los Angeles

Copyright © 1982 by Klevens Publications Inc.

Printed in the United States of America

All rights reserved. No part of this book may be reproduced or transmitted in any form or by any means, electronic or mechanical, including photocopying, recording, or by any information storage and retrieval system, without permission in writing from the Publisher.

Klevens Publications Inc.
P.O. Box 143, Canoga Park, CA 91305
(805) 944-4111
(213) 884-0593
(213) 340-1021

Library of Congress Catalog Card Number: 82-83766

TABLE OF CONTENTS

I. **INTRODUCTION & PHILOSOPHY**
   ROBERT N. WORTHINGTON
   Current & Future Status of A & C Education 1
   ROSALIND K. LORING and PAUL H. SHEATS — Basic
   Considerations of Materials & Methods in CE 11
   MALCOLM S. KNOWLES and CHESTER KLEVINS
   Historical & Philosophical Perspectives 15
   JEROLD W. APPS
   Developing a Belief Structure................................. 25
   GENE C. WHAPLES and JAMES W. MILLER
   The Political Process 33
   PHYLLIS M. CUNNINGHAM
   Status of Women 43
   ISRAEL "IKE" TRIBBLE
   Continuing Education in the Department of Defense 52

II. **ORGANIZING EFFECTIVE PROGRAMS**
   1. **STANLEY M. GRABOWSKI**
      Approaching Needs Assessments 60
   2. **DEWEY A. ADAMS and SAMUEL D. MORGAN**
      Advisory Committees 66
   3. **ARNOLD NORED and ELAINE SHELTON**
      Competency Based Adult Education 74
   4. **EDGAR M. EASLEY**
      Community Based Organizations 82
   5. **EDWIN L. SIMPSON**
      Program Development: A Model 92
   6. **WILLLIAM M. RIVERA, HILDA PATINO,
      and RALPH G. BROCKETT**
      Conceptual Framework for Program Development 99
   7. **LAURENT R. BROUSSAL**
      Education for the Handicapped 106
   8. **DAVID A. PETERSON and PATRICK KEANE**
      Education for the Aging 113
   9. **NORMA B. BREWER**
      Tailoring Vocational Education to Adult Needs 123

III. **CURRICULUM DEVELOPMENT**
   1. **D. STUART CONGER and DANA MULLEN**
      Life Skills 132
   2. **RICHARD S. DEEMS and JOHN HARTWIG**
      Career Counseling 144
   3. **LOUIS H. REEVES**
      Computer Based Training in Industry 151
   4. **PATRICK O. COPLEY, DARRELL G. ROUBINEK, JAMES R. LAYTON, DALE G. RANGE, and GEORGE McNINCH**
      Implementing & Evaluating — Reading 155
   5. **RALPH G. BROCKETT, ROGER HIEMSTRA, and PATRICK R. PENLAND** — Self-Directed Learning 171
   6. **BEVERLY B. CASSARA**
      Participatory Modes 179
   7. **LEONARD NADLER**
      Cross-Cultural Education 187
   8. **DAVID S. ALEXANDER**
      Back to Basic Skills 197

IV. **TEACHING-LEARNING PROCESS**
   1. **BURTON W. KREITLOW**
      Adult Learning Patterns 205
   2. **RICHARD A. ETHERIDGE**
      Conceptual Approach to Teaching/Learning 212
   3. **MARY JANE EVEN**
      Adult Instructional Model (AID) 222
   4. **CARROLL D. BROWN, PATRICIA TERRELL, JAMES R. LAYTON**
      Holistic Learning 235
   5. **GERALD D. BAILEY and ROBERT E. SCOTT**
      Learning Feedback — Effective Teaching 247
   6. **HUEY B. LONG**
      Teaching-Learning Through Discussion 260
   7. **LINDA H. LEWIS**
      Preferential Styles — Cognitive Mapping 268

V. **HOW TO**
   1. **JONATHAN McKALLIP**
      Use Volunteers Successfully 278
   2. **GORDON G. DARKENWALD**
      Keep Your ADA 284

3. **HARLAN L. POLSKY and EDGAR M. EASLEY**
   Helping Adults Get/Hold Jobs 291
4. **GOLDA BOCKBRADER, LEONARD R. HILL and
   SHIRLEY HEYMANN** — Use Non-Paid Professionals 299
5. **RICHARD S. DEEMS and JOHN HARTWIG**
   Career Planning — Job Getting Skills 308
6. **SALLY BREW**
   Decision Making Techniques 317
7. **McKINLEY C. MARTIN**
   Be a Better Teacher 323
8. **AHNAL M. CRIEGO de GAMARRA**
   Identify & Teach the Non-Literate 328

VI. STAFF DEVELOPMENT
1. **ROBERT A. FELLENZ, GARY J. CONTI and
   DON F. SEAMAN**
   Evaluate: Student, Staff, Program 335
2. **MARK H. ROSSMAN**
   Self-Assessment 346
3. **JOHN A. NIEMI and SUSAN IMEL**
   Information Retrieval Systems 360
4. **EUGENE E. DuBOIS**
   Human Resource Development: Expanding Role 371
5. **JACK A. SUMNER and DAVID C. WIGGLESWORTH**
   Organizational Development 378
6. **WENDELL L. SMITH, GARY A. EYRE and
   JAMES W. MILLER**
   Join Your Professional Organizations 384

VII. FUTURE IN A & C EDUCATION
1. **GEORGE F. AKER and JACK L. GANT**
   Illiteracy Eradication: A Future Model 390
2. **MAX E. JOBE**
   Career Change: A Never Ending Process 397
3. **EUGENE E. DuBOIS**
   The External Degree: A Viable Alternative 403
4. **DAVID C. WIGGLESWORTH and DAVID G. GUELETTE**
   Technology & The Future 409

EDITOR'S PREFACE

We are now in our second decade of the MATERIALS & METHODS series. It has been a very gratifying ten years for your editor and his staff. We have witnessed many advances in the field of adult and continuing education. The professionalism of our educational field has finally been recognized and we must continue to make every endeavor to continue and to improve this status.

The acceleration of change in the world has become a mandate to the adult population that education must be continuous and relevant so that they might keep abreast of our ever-changing industrial and social world. A very positive directive of the Editorial Advisory Board of *MATERIALS & METHODS* was "to keep this series of books always relevant to the needs of the reader and consistent with current thinking." Therefore, following this edict, a series of questionnaires was sent to our colleagues and subsequently many gratifying and helpful responses were received. Many of the most active continuing adult educators gave of their time and effort to reviewing and suggesting subjects and materials for inclusion in the new book, *MATERIALS & METHODS in Adult & Continuing Education;* in this process many new authors were also recommended. For this, we are most grateful!

These recommendations were then submitted to the new Editorial Advisory Board for final approval. The Board chose those areas which they felt would meet the basic directives of relevancy and need. A very special thanks to the Board members.

A debt of gratitude is owed to all those who gave of their expertise and time to make this new volume a reality; especially the authors! We would be remiss if special thanks were not given to Malcolm Knowles, John Niemi, Dewey Adams, Stan Grabowski, Jim Layton, Beverly Cassara, George Aker, Stu Conger, Bill Rivera, and many others who gave added time and encouragement to the fulfillment of this cooperative project.

A special acknowledgement must be tendered to two erudite men, Paul Sheats and Edgar Easley, without whose special talents for guidance and positive work, *MATERIALS & METHODS in Adult & Continuing Education* would not have been completed.

It is sincerely hoped that this book meets the requirements of the readers. The authors were asked to write on specified topics in their field of expertise. They were requested to prepare material from the practitioner's point of view, if possible, and certainly with their own definitive ideas in mind. The authors have met our needs and requirements. If they have also met yours, then please thank them for a job well done. If you have some other thoughts about the book, I alone must bear the final responsibility and will be pleased to discuss any and all suggestions to better meet the needs of our community, Adult & Continuing Education.

> Dr. Chester Klevins
> President
> City University Los Angeles

Current and Future Status of A & C Education

Robert M. Worthington

*Assistant Secretary for Vocational & Adult Education,
United States Department of Education*

Education in the United States, from primary through adult and continuing education levels, reflects generally the values, beliefs, and priorities of the society. Today's post-industrial society, based on rapid technological change and instantaneous communication, demands continuous lifelong learning as a necessity for individual and societal survival.

Yes, learning never ends, and during the last two decades of this century adult and continuing education will be in the forefront of a massive expansion of adult learning. By 2000 A.D. the population of this country will be dominated by persons in their middle years. The National Center for Education Statistics reports that by the year 2000 the largest age group will be 30 to 44 with the to 64 age group following closely. Nearly 60 percent of our population will be over 30 years of age.

Evidence is clear that adult education is growing at a 12 percent per annum rate compared with a 2 percent growth in elementary and secondary education. Adults in this country are looking more and more to adult education as a means for the individual to solve immediate problems. Technological advancements coupled with social and economic changes create growing pressures on individuals. These pressures in turn fall as a challenge to adult and continuing education and its educators. Clearly the educational market of the future lies with adults.

The 1960's and 1970's brought many changes in the entire realm of education, with some of the most dramatic changes occurring in the field of adult and continuing education. Those years saw a rapid growth in the Federal contribution to education. Numerous categorical programs were funded with equity and access as the foci.

During that period, also, Federal involvement began in adult basic and secondary education — a program enacted through the Economic Opportunity Act of 1964. Some of the major successes of that program, now authorized by the Adult Education Act (Public Law 91-230, as amended) are—
— All 50 States and the Insular Areas participate in the program and have personnel responsible for adult education. In 1965 when Federal funds became available less than a dozen States had viable programs and identifiable adult education leadership.

— Now more than 100 institutions confer advanced degrees to an increasing number of adult education scholars and practitioners. In 1965 only about 14 major institutions of higher education conferred the doctorate degree in adult education and less than 500 people had earned it. None of the institutions focused on adult basic education.
— Enrollments in the federally assisted adult basic and secondary education effort have grown steadily to over 2.2 million in 1982. Only 37,000 adult participants were served in 1965. This Federal/State/local endeavor has provided educational opportunities to more than 20 million educationally disadvantaged adults in its 17 years.
— Federal contributions over the 17-year term total over $1.1 billion. (Federal support for program operations in 1982 was $100 million.) State and local matching funds have added over $600 million in the program's 17-year history.
— The majority (81 percent) of the participants are less than 45 years of age.
— Hispanic and Black participants comprise 43 percent of the total enrollment.
— Over 54 percent of the participants are women.
— There are nearly 56,000 State and local staff involved in the adult basic and secondary program. Local teachers comprise 79 percent; paraprofessionals, 10 percent; counselors, 4 percent; State and local administrative and supervisory personnel, 7 percent.

(The preceding participant data are tabulated from State reports for 1982.)

Adult education programs provide open learning. Participants may enter or exit at any time depending on their needs, aspirations, and the availability of instructional programs. Not all participants desire to complete a specific level of instruction, rather they enter adult education classes to meet a particular personal objective. Over a third of the early leavers in adult basic and secondary education indicate that they left because they had met their objectives.

These programs employ a full range of learning methods. Adult learning is a way of life and need not be restricted to formal schooling. It occurs through a variety of means and methods depending on the circumstances of the individual, his needs, and his environment. Some circumstances lend themselves better to competency-based instruction, while some do not. In rural areas, home-based instruction has proved very successful. And urban areas find special adult learning centers to be beneficial. Satellite programs on the islands and in Alaska may be more appropriate than in urban areas. The important thing is not the method used, but that learning takes place.

The instructional approach for teaching adults with limited education is especially critical. An assessment of the adult basic and secondary education program was supported by the Department of Education. That assessment was reported in 1980. In the study, 47 percent of the teachers indicated that they mostly individualize their instruction. Another 19 percent mainly work with participants in small groups. Sixty percent of the teachers indicated that they frequently tutor participants. Grouping of participants with similar problems or interests was reported by 47 percent of the teachers.

Millions of adults have earned secondary school equivalency diplomas or certificates based on their performance on General Educational development (GED) tests. Many of these attended federally assisted adult secondary education programs. A State is limited to 20 percent of its allotment for use in secondary programs. GED tests are widely recognized as a valid means of determining secondary school graduation equivalency. All States use the GED tests as the basis for issuance of secondary school equivalency credentials. These credentials are official documents and are widely accepted in the same manner as regular secondary school diplomas for meeting secondary school graduation requirements for employment, admission to apprenticeship and other training programs, and admission to colleges and universities. During 1981, 804,813 persons took the GED test, and 490,000 were GED recipients. Since 1977, the volume of GED testing has increased by almost 80 percent. The average age of 1981 examinees was 25.1 years, and more than 36 percent of the 1981 examinees were 19 or younger.

These achievements are outstanding. But the best data available indicate that we are just holding even on the problem of functional illiteracy among adults. And that is not **outstanding.**

In 1975, the federally funded Adult Performance Level (APL) project reported that one out of five U.S. adults was functionally incompetent. Projected to 1980, this means that some 26 million adults are functionally illiterate and an additional 46 million do not function proficiently. Thus a total of 72 million adults in the United States have real difficulty in dealing with the variety of demands placed on them by our society. More specifically, 52 million adults are functionally incompetent at computation; 26 million have writing difficulties; 40 million are unaware of their legal rights; 34 million do not read well; 35 million do not know how to utilize community resources. Also, fully one third of, or 50 million, U.S. adults have not completed secondary education.

With these educationally disadvantaged adults, we must add the 850,000 teenagers who drop out of secondary school each year and the 400,000 immigrants arriving yearly. In recent years between 100,000 and 150,000 refugees have been added to those needing educational services. Many of these immigrants and refugees need to develop literacy skills as well as English language competence in order to be able to function in U.S. society. The number of adults entering society each year who need basic education or secondary instruction is approximately equal to the 2 million people who are currently receiving services.

Even more dramatic than the statistics on participants in adult basic and secondary education are those based on the broader concept of adult education. According to the National Center for Education Statistics, more than 21 million persons 17 years old and over participated in **organized** adult education courses or activities in 1981. That figure represents almost 13 percent of the total adult population in the United States.

Other highlights from the survey are:
— Nearly 54 percent of the adult education participants were under the age of 35; 12 percent were over 55 years old. The heaviest concentration (35 percent) of participants in adult education was in the 25 to 34 age group; approximately 20 percent of the total population in this age group took one or more adult education courses in 1981.
— Approximately 56 percent of all adult education participants were women. Among women participants, over 70 percent were working at a job, 20 percent were keeping house, and the remainder were either looking for work, going to school, or retired. Almost 96 percent of men participants were working at the time of the survey.
— The largest group of participants in adult education were professional and technical workers, who comprised over 30 percent of those taking adult education courses. Clerical workers (18 percent) were the second most likely group to have taken an adult education course.
— Over 42 percent of adult education participants had family incomes greater than $25,000 compared to only 31 percent for the population. As the level of family income increased, the rate of participation in adult education also increased; from 6 percent for those with family incomes less than $7,500 to nearly 19 percent for those with incomes greater than $50,000.
— Over 90 percent of adult education participants were at least high school graduates compared to 70 percent for the total population. Persons having five years of college or more were most likely to have taken a course in adult education; over 31 percent of this group participated in 1981. Conversely, only 2 percent of persons with less than a ninth-grade education took an adult education course in 1981.
— The majority (72 percent) of participants in adult education lived in metropolitan areas. The South had the most participants in 1981, over 6 million. Fewer than 4 million participants lived in the Northeast United States.
— Job-related reasons accounted for 60 percent of the courses. Nearly three-fourths of the courses were taken by participants who wished to improve performance in their current jobs.

Adding the domain of independent learning, investigators find that almost every adult undertakes learning through a deliberate effort to pursue a skill or a knowledge objective in any given year.

The preceding statistics and success items are certainly definitive evidence of one fact — adult education is alive, well, and growing!

And in the preceding decade and a half, Federal assistance has supported continuing education. Nearly every college and university now has a continuing education division and many have degree programs especially for adults offered at times and places convenient to adults. This effort was led by programs authorized under Title I of the Higher Education Act.

Title I offers an incentive to postsecondary institutions to make their services more readily available to previously unserved groups such as the handicapped, minorities, the elderly, and adults who live in isolated rural areas.

In 1973, 25 States supported projects to improve the accessibility of postsecondary offerings to adult learners. By 1978, all States were actively pursuing this goal.

Title I encourages the development of statewide networks to provide potential learners with information about the availability of continuing education offerings and financial aid, and to assist adults in assessing the appropriateness of programs to their interests and abilities.

Many States support projects that use broadcast media, instructional technology, and mobile learning centers to bring services to new groups of learners, especially to those who are geographically isolated from postsecondary programs.

In 1980, the two population groups who are least likely to be involved in post-secondary programs — the elderly, and those who have never before participated in a college-level activity — received substantial attention from the Title I program. More than 22 percent of the Title I participants were 55 years or older, and 43 percent had never attended college.

No Federal funds are available currently for Title I purposes. However, its accomplishments have stimulated institutions to modify their traditional credit-degree offerings and to direct their resources to serve the educational needs of new groups of adult learners.

Other Title I activities by postsecondary institutions assisted:
— State and local planning boards, private voluntary agencies, and citizen groups to identify and address such community needs as planning more efficient use of natural resources, improving schools and housing, and preserving unique cultural traditions;
— Community leaders and members of civic groups to understand demographic changes and trends and develop plans for accommodating these forces in ways which will improve the economic and social life of their communities;
— Courses, conferences, and consultative services related to such issues as unemployment, improving productivity and job satisfaction of the workforce, maintaining the competence of professional and technical manpower, and improving the operation of small business;
— Professional associations, business and labor, and government agencies to create mechanisms for identifying learning needs and resources, and for planning and delivering appropriate training activities;
— Activities designed to broaden citizen participation in the development and implementation of public policy, with particular emphasis on helping women and members of minority groups to acquire skills and information to increase their involvement in government decision-making;
— New organizational linkages and developing programs which use the combined resources of higher education, business, labor, and community-based agencies;
— The creation of new procedures to enable the participation of a broad array of continuing education providers and users in developing and implementing educational policies; and

— The creation of new mechanisms for sharing information about continuing education and training resources and reducing the duplication of program services.

Thus we readily see that education is a major activity of our adult population. Even with the successes and accomplishments, much more must be done to ensure individual and societal survival in our post-industrial society.

We must bear in mind that education in general is facing some dramatic changes in the immediate future. From a Federal perspective we are in a transitional period — between the expansionary federal role in education during the past two decades and the most constricted world of the eighties. Political realities and the administration's plans for economic recovery will have a major impact on education at all levels. Rightly so, education must bear its fair share in the reductions of inflationary Federal spending. In the long run, constantly rising costs are more detrimental to education than the projected spending cuts. In the near-term we must make certain sacrifices to help put the country back on the track toward economic recovery.

In the Department of Education we are giving close attention to the administration's overall position on public education. Central to this position is the return of operational authority — and indeed, most judgment calls — to the States and localities; in other words, to phase out Federal instrusion into day-to-day educational matters and to redefine the Fereeal role as one of "support" or "honest brokering."

There will also be a renewed emphasis on instructional content and quality. These changes will be orchestrated through consolidated and block grants, which will ultimately lead to the "New Federalism Initiative."

One of the first major vehicles for this change is the Educational Consolidation Act of 1981 — the Chapter II portion. That Chapter consolidates 28 elementary and secondary education programs into block grants with quite generalized educational resources to State and local educational agencies. Individual program funding is left to the discretion of the individual States. Many of these consolidated programs relate directly to the education of adults. Examples are metric education, consumer education, law-related education, libraries and learning resources, community education, career education, and basic skills. We are just beginning the first year of operation under this new authority. Statistical data have not been gathered to indicate the extent of instructional activities related to adult education. However, we do anticipate a sizeable portion of the more than $400 million appropriated for this consolidated effort to be used to enhance education in basic skills areas.

Another consolidation effort, now pending before the Congress, will also have an effect on educational programs for adults. This legislative proposal supports adult basic and secondary education as part of a vocational and adult education consolidation. The purposes of this proposal are to increase flexibility, reduce costs at all levels of government, and redirect Federal support to focus on the role of adult and vocational education in local, State, and national economic development. Adult education would benefit from a minimum of 13 percent of the funds. More States would have the discretion to use additional funds for adult education programs depending on the needs and priorities of individual States. This serves to set the stage for the New Federalism Initiative.

Under the New Federalism Initiative, responsibility for adult education — and for vocational education — along with their funding sources would gradually devolve to the States. This action is slated to begin in 1985, with the final turn-back to the States not occurring before 1989. In the interim, considerable Federal leadership will be exercised to ensure a smooth transition to complete State control of adult and vocational education.

A related priority at the initial stages of New Federalism will be to develop a permanent, self-sustaining State capability for leadership and technical assistance. As government spending recedes at all levels, State educational officials will be the focal point for technical assistance to local schools and non-public providers during the second half of the 1980's. This cadre of State leaders will serve as catalysts for regional and national contributions to solving such widespread problems as economic development, development of a work force skilled in the latest technologies, development and dissemination of effective methods and practices, improved utilization of private sector facilities, and the pursuit of excellence in vocational and adult education.

You no doubt have noted reference to the private sector. This is a significant departure from past policies: This administration sees **the private sector** as being much more important to the total educational enterprise than any other recent administration. The adult education program has moved in this direction through the expansion of its delivery system that was called for in the 1978 amendments to the Adult Education Act. We must make use of all systems and facilities, whether they be in our schools and colleges, in business and industrail plants or establishments, in churches, in town halls, in hospitals, or in the kitchen of a rural home. This is not unfamiliar ground, for adult education is certainly a leader in this respect as more and more adult learning takes place outside of the traditional public school setting.

Adult education is being asked to help alleviate pressures placed on individuals as a result of technological advancements. Great strides in fulfilling that mission have been made — and more are on the horizon.

While technology creates new demands for educational services, it counters with new opportunities for the improvement and delivery of these services. New information technologies will boost the capacity of educational providers to meet new demands. They include direct broadcast satellites, two-way interactive cable, low-power broadcasting, personal and hand-held computers, television, video discs and video tape cassettes. Many of these devices are already being used effectively in education and training programs. They have been found to be cost-effective, versatile, and adaptable to use in a variety of educational settings. In addition, they may be particularly suited to extending educational opportunities to persons previously denied access. Examples include those who are elderly, disabled, and geographically isolated. Some institutional barriers to the use of these technologies — high initial cost, lack of quality programming to use, and the dearth of local personnel with adequate training in their use — must be considered. However, there is not doubt that information technology will be increasingly used for educational purposes for both youth and adults.

Education has been one of the great success stories of American society. The founding fathers saw education as indispensible to a democratic society and planted the seeds of a vital system of public education in every community and state. A century ago, as the nation began to take giant steps forward in its industrial and agricultural development, the Morrill Act (land grant colleges) and then later the Smith-Hughes Act and amendments (vocational education) brought into being a great partnership between education and economic development. Through vocational education, career and professional education, and the service-oriented public universities, educational institutions became indispensible in providing the educated manpower, the basic knowledge, technology and extension assistance necessary for a modern economy. All of us are the beneficiaries and the heirs of this achievement!

Our careers have been spent in a climate of growth, achievement and optimism. consider the changing climate, but do not put aside that deep sense of pride in what has been accomplished. But we live in a fast changing world and must be prepared to make the kinds of adjustments our predecessors made a century ago. This is a time of accelerating cultural change that impacts all individuals, that impacts all institutions, and that impacts the total society. To keep our own lives intact, to keep the institutions vital and useful, and to keep America strong and productive are challenges few were prepared to meet. I do not need to remind you, the reader, that the notion of terminal education is obsolete. But most would agree that some of our schools and colleges are still basically organized to provide a terminal education. Lifelong Learning has a foot in the door, but clearly, education must become more future-oriented than it is.

One of the highest priorities for adult educators is to reverse the rate of decline and get back the high road to productivity. It is clearly the highest priority of this administration. One of the opportunities for educators, and especially adult educators, lies in the rediscovery of the human aspect of productivity. Having emphasized capital-intensive high technology as the best route to successful economic competition in the post-war era, the idea that **people can** also make a difference was often forgotten. But it is back on the top of the agenda. As *Fortune* suggested, some months ago, we must all learn to "work smarter."

Clearly, education must help the citizenry to develop the understanding attitudes, values, motives, and commitments necessary to realize all our goals in an effective and realistic manner. If everyone needs to learn to "work smarter," it is essential they also learn to "live smarter." Getting and keeping it together is a new task, not only for young people, but for all of us throughout the lifespan.

Assuming this assessment of the changing context of the 80's is correct, then what is the basis for the decline of both basic and higher education in the perception of business leaders, politicians and the citizenry-at-large? Americans expect their schools and colleges to prepare people for better jobs and careers and for the good life. Given the economic and social realities, educators become natural targets for the disappointments and frustrations of the people. But it is high time for all people, and especially educators, to understand that our schools and colleges were built on the foundations provided by family, church and community. Qualities of hard work, inventiveness, risk-taking, team work and the capacity to delay present pleasures for future reward must be augmented and reinforced in all classrooms.

Clearly there is a nostalgia for a simpler and more coherent past. But there is no point in looking backward except to gauge future accomplishments. If adult educators are to meet the challenges and opportunities of the 80's, the citizenry must be prepared to understand the new realities, and each individual must be persuaded to accept a new level of responsibility for his/her own development, for the development of their communities, and for the development of the economy.

How will these goals be accomplished? Here is a three-part strategy — which I proposed to the attendees at the 1981 National Adult Education Conference in California:

1. **First, every citizen needs to understand the changing context of the 1980's.** I believe adult educators must join with others in orienting all Americans to the changing context of their lives. We have begun to understand the economic realities, but we have yet to understand the scope of change in our personal lives, our families, our churches, and communities. Once these are also understood, the imperative to take hold of our lives in a self-directed manner and to actively engage in the additional tasks of personal, family, community, and economic development will become clear.

2. **Second, all the institutions involved in the learning and development process need to make those adjustments necessary to support the citizenry as they engage in tasks of personal, family, community, and economic development.** While this is an obvious assignment for educators in the nation's schools and colleges, it is not for them alone. Clearly, we need to become more effective. Churches and other community agencies can play a strengthened role. The workplace is increasingly a learning environment. Indeed the growth of human resource development programs in the corporations is based on a developmental premise that goes well beyond the formal educational institutions. Adult educators must seek a piece of the telecommunications action to extend their missions in assisting the citizenry in their personal, family, community, and economic development.

3. **Third, once the institutions come to some common understandings of the emergent realities and the tasks, we must develop a much improved strategy for working together at local and regional levels.** Many of us will remember that school, family, community, and church used to work much more closely on behalf of shared objectives. That old tradition-based system is gone, to be sure. But it is both possible and essential to rebuild

the system once we all understand what we have to do. I am not talking about the mechanisms we tried in the 60's to coordinate a host of institutions. What I am talking about is voluntary cooperation among institutions who work for common and shared understandings and commitments to make the development process work!

This proposed three-part strategy does not require a super-organization! It does not require new institutions! And it does not require new resources! **It does require a new understanding and a renewed commitment to direct our resources and energies to new and emerging conditions and tasks.**

The busines investment in "human resource development" has anticipated the expansion of education from cognitive and skill training to the affective, interpersonal and organizational dimensions. Notions of adult development through the various stages of living are stretching our concepts of education. Increasingly, Adult Basic Education is carried on in a developmental framework with proper attention to the other contexts of living. Parent, consumer, and self-care education stretch the present model in other ways. The rediscovery of the church congregation as a "learning community" is another recent and happy development. So is the fact that public libraries, museums, botanical gardens and other cultural institutions are making renewed efforts to reach and serve adults better.

Adult and continuing educators truly have a once-in-a-century opportunity to revitalize our institutions and to provide new dimensions of service that are desperately needed by the larger society. Now the time has come. We must ensure that all Americans **live and work smarter!**

Basic Considerations of Materials & Methods in CE

Rosalind K. Loring

Associate Provost for Extended Education
University of Southern California

Paul H. Sheats

Professor Emeritus
University of California, Los Angeles

First, note that this third edition of *Materials & Methods in Adult & Continuing Education* is going to press as many changes are occurring in the field. Not only are adult educators continuing their search for new populations and new students within familiar populations, but there are growing numbers of administrators and instructors participating for the first time. Additionally, each institution's managerial decisions regarding the program, functions, role and organization of adult and continuing education have produced such movement as to cause even those adult educators who are accustomed to change to question what should be the focus of their course or program.

Other factors such as radical and rapid shifts in the federal, local and state governments assistance in funding of many of the experimental or model programs so useful to the special needs of our students are also affecting the amount and type of program available. We could go on to enumerate other external factors but most of these are dealt with in this volume or in the public press. Suffice it to say that education of adults is as impacted as are all other institutions by the diminishing health of the economy, by changing demography (in age, sex and accelerated immigration) and by swings of political philosophy. The absence of consensus in this country as to the most effective way to organize, provide programs, oversee quality control, and plan for instructional content and methodology appropriate to the program's students is causing communication blurring as we move into the rest of this decade.

At such a time numerous questions of policy and philosophy are raised with intensity. The contribution of professional associations is critical to the resolution and integration of these challenges to accepted principles. We note that the American Association for Adult and Continuing Education has been formed from two earlier organizations (AEA/USA and NAPCAE) with the expectation that greater service to the field will be available. In fact, numerous organizations provide for various segments of the adult and continuing education field.[1] Thus far, ways of collaboration by these organizations have been discussed (and even urged), but the means for true consortium are difficult to secure.

Thus, for many professionals, para-professionals and volunteers books and other literature have provided access to information and experience which have been acquired and developed in various parts of the country. Hence — the role for **Materials and Methods** continues to be a canvas upon which the current thinking of the field is displayed.

Based on a preliminary review of chapters for the third edition of **Materials & Methods**, we realize that any effort on our part to synthesize the wide range of material in the contents would be futile. It is apparent that the central thrust of the new edition remains the same as in previous editions; namely, to be helpful to the teachers of adults in both formal and informal settings and in both pre and in-service stages of professional development.

In a book which brings together more than fifty chapters on the varied aspects of **Materials & Methods** from the point of view of more than seventy authors and co-authors, our greatest usefulness to you, the reader, may well be to suggest at least some of the basic considerations which focus the contributions of our writers.

To the best of our knowledge, no prescriptions and no sanctions were set up by the Editor to limit the freedom of the contributions to evaluate, recommend, or condemn practices or materials which the authors saw fit to express. In our view, this desirable policy of non-dictation places an additional burden upon you, the reader. Among other things, it suggests that the best utilization of **Materials and Methods** should involve selective use of chapters related to your particular interests.

Certainly, the issues and questions of policy which are discussed are legion and it is difficult to imagine that whether used as a text or reference volume the application to improved practice can be escaped. To illustrate and in no order of priority or importance we propose the following questions which are being debated now in schools, government agencies, business and wherever adult students are to be found.

CONSIDERATIONS

There is the perennial issue of creating a proper balance in concern for the rights and needs of the individual and those which are societal in nature. This country has concentrated on the individual and neglected in large part the community. Can we continue to afford this?

Nor can the practitioner escape the importance of understanding basic human needs and their impact on the teaching-learning process. Closely related is the definition of learning objectives. How do we identify the students' objectives versus the teachers'?

Must we choose in the decade ahead to concentrate on the improvement of literacy, quality of life or problem-solving skills? Can we also upgrade our skills as teachers in using new knowledge and new technology? Can we be successful if we do not?

What additional research is needed to give us the knowledge to better solve current problems in the field? When should research methods and designs be primarily quantitative — when qualitative? Do we have the proper safeguards for the privacy and well-being of those so studied?

What are the criteria for selection and establishment of sub-groups within any association's membership to meet the special needs of the aging, the handicapped, illiterates, workers in the armed services and the culturally deprived? How can we maintain a unified, active and influential national view of adult education and at the same time meet the special needs of subgroups within our several organizations' memberships?

Are there societal goals for adult education which are so important that mandatory continuing education for some can be justified? If so, what happens to our long-time commitment to voluntary learning and freedom of choice for the learner? And what of the needs of society and the citizen as consumer for quality of education at every level?

This raises a closely related concern. Some practitioners express concern for the rapid growth of informal, non-formal, largely autonomous learning groups. How can quality control over environment for learning be assured? Should it be? Again, what are our responsibilities to the consumer?

There is ample evidence in the diversity which characterizes the rather representative sample of professional thinking in adult education in this volume that there is implied a strong commitment to the principle of cultural pluralism. How can we provide this and yet continue to build a nation unified in basic principles of democracy? Or, should this be the concern of educators of adults? And if it should, then where and when do teachers and administrators plan to produce this result?

SUMMARY

It is apparent that the third edition of "Materials & Methods" is not an "answer" book, nor is it merely a tract calling the practitioners of adult education to a new crusade. Based upon our own experience, we would describe the diversity of views and approaches to adult learning represented in these chapters as one of our richest resources for professional action in the years ahead. From diversity can come unity, from faith in people can come the driving force to a better society, from mutual trust, regardless of race, sex, age or educational attainment, can come the reaffirmation of our search for the common good. In this search we can ask our readers to join!

REFERENCES
VOLUNTARY ASSOCIATIONS WITH ADULT EDUCATION CONCERNS

American Association of Community &
Junior Colleges
One Dupont Circle, N.W.
Washington, DC 20036

American Assocation of University Women
2401 Virginia Ave., N.W.
Washington, DC 20037

American Society for Training and
Development, Inc.
600 Maryland Ave., Ste. 305,
Washington, DC 20024

American Vocational Association, Inc.
202 N. 14th St., Arlington, VA 22201

Association of Continuing Higher Education
Univ. of Tenn., 451 Communications Bldg.
Knoxville, TN 37996-0341

Association for Continuing Professional Education
Montclair State College
Upper Montclair, NJ 07043

Association of Independent Colleges and Schools
1730 M St., N.W., Suite 600
Washington, DC 20036

B'nai B'rith, International Commission on
Adult Jewish Education
1640 Rhode Island Ave., N.W.
Washington, DC 20036

Canadian Association for Adult Education
Corbett House, 29 Prince Arthur Ave.
Toronto, Ont., Canada M5R 1B2

Church Women United
475 Riverside Dr., Room 812
New York, NY 10027

Coalition of Adult Education Organizations
NRTA/AARP, Inst. of Lifetime Learning
1909 K St., N.W., Washington, DC 20049

Institut Canadien D'Education Des Adultes
506 est. Ste. Catherine, Suite 800
Montreal, Que., Canada H2L 2C7

Institute of Lifetime Learning (NRTA-AARP)
1909 K St., N.W., Washington, DC 20049

Laubach Literacy International
1320 Jamesville Ave., Box 131
Syracuse, NY 13210

Literacy Volunteers of America, Inc.
404 Oak St., Syracuse, NY 13203

National Academy for Adult Jewish Studies of
United Synagogue Comm. on Jewish Education
155 Fifth Ave., New York, NY 10010

National Association of Educational Broadcasters
1346 Connecticut Ave., N.W.
Washington, DC 20036

National Association of State Universities &
Land Grant Colleges
One Dupont Circle, N.W., Suite 710
Washington, DC 20036

National Association of Trade and
Technical Schools
2021 K St., N.W.
Washington, DC 20006-1077

National Community Education Association
1201-16th St., N.W., Ste. 305
Washington, DC 20036

National Council of Churches of Christ
in the U.S.A.
475 Riverside Dr., Room 880
New York, NY 10027

National Council of State Directors of
Adult Education
Adult & Com. Ed. Div. State Dept. of Educ.
Jefferson City, MO 65101

National Council of Urban Administrators
of Adult Education
Glen Cove Public Schools
Dosoris Lane, Glen Cove, NY 11542

National Council on Community Services &
Continuing Education
C.S. Mott Com. College,
1401 E. Court St., Flint, MI 48503

National Home Study Council
1601 Eighteenth St., N.W.,
Washington, DC 20009

NTL Institute for Applied Behavioral Science
P.O. Box 9155, Rosslyn Station, VA 22209

National University Continuing Education Assn.
One Dupont Circle, N.W., Suite 360
Washington, DC 20036-1168

Public Broadcasting Service
PTV-3 Adult Learning Service
475 L'Enfant Plaza West, S.W.
Washington, DC 20024

Reference & Adult Services Division, American
Library Assn.
50 E. Huron St., Chicago, IL 60611

Society for Public Health Education, Inc.
703 Market St., Ste. 535
San Francisco, CA 94103

Historical & Philosophical Perspectives

Malcolm Knowles

Professor Emeritus, North Carolina State University, Raleigh, renowned author in adult education.

Chester Klevins

Editor, Materials & Methods in Continuing Education
President, City University Los Angeles

Lifelong Learning has a role in developing the potential of all persons including improvement of their personal well-being, upgrading their workplace skills and preparing them to participate in the civic, cultural and political life of the nation.
From the preamble to the Lifelong Learning Act passed by Congress in 1976.

The concept of lifelong learning is accepted in most every country and culture throughout the world. Education is no longer construed as something which children need in order to get ready for life. Rather it is embodied in the total constellation of living — requiring all people to learn new skills, and new attitudes and behaviors so they may better meet their survival needs. Adult education (lifelong learning) can help provide a better quality of life for people here and throughout the world. Those educators fortunate enough to be involved in adult education have a responsibility to try to make its benefits available whenever and wherever possible.

According to many experts in the fields of both economics and education, it will be necessary for every adult to return for reeducation or retraining from three to five times during his/her lifetime, in order to maintain working status. This will be required because of obsolescence or technological changes that will occur in the labor market. As a result, all persons, professional and nonprofessional, will need to follow this pattern in order to stay abreast of his/her field of endeavor. This then is expected to place a severe load on adult and continuing education.

Adult education is, or ought to be, a highly political and value laden activity. When individuals are involved in education they tend to expand: their awareness of self and environment, their range of wants and interests, their sense of justice, their need to participate in decision-making activities, their ability to think critically and reason rationally, their ability to create alternative choices of action, and, ultimately their power or control over the forces and factors which affect them — this is political action.

Lindeman pointed out that democracy is a —
conception of sovereignty founded upon the assumption that ultimate power can only be safely trusted in the hands of the people, a conception of human equality based upon the assumption that basic human needs are similar and that these needs will be more readily satisfied through democractic rule than by any other method of governing, a conception of human relationships which moves ideally from exploitative and mechanistic patterns towards mutual and organic patterns, and finally a conception of the interrelatedness of all varieties of human experience.[1]

Lindeman also stated that social action is only justified when the force behind it is democratic and this means that it must be dervied from intelligence and reason — a task involving adult education.

The Essentiality of Adult or Lifelong Education — In a recent report of the President's Advisory Council on Adult Education,[2] it was stated that we cannot afford an educational system that is predominantly child-centered. It would be too expensive. Adults, not children, are making the decisions that affect all functions and actions of our government. Adults, not children, are responsible for our productive output — or lack of it. Adults, not children, are confronted with the decisions of parenthood and decisions which determine the quality of family life and the quality of education for children. Adults, not children, are challenged by environmental or political problems that threaten all future generations. Adults, more than children, are faced with the increasing cost of living and a stagnant economy.

For these reasons, adults, even more than children, need relevant and pertinent education **now.** They need access to learning opportunities which will enable them to effectively gather and analyze the information necessary for attaining higher order solutions to increasingly complex problems. Adults also must have opportunities for individual and shared learning experiences that will foretell the consequences of alternative decisions which have to be made now and each day thereafter. They require learning experiences to enhance their ability to contribute to the business of a free society; to resist the influence of mass persuasion and propaganda; to avoid stereotyping their fellow men in negative ways; to develop an open and inquiring mind — a mind free of prejudice and premature closure to new ideas, life styles and values; and to expand their unique potentials for economic and social development, for creative leisure, and for self-actualization. Adults who have dropped from or have been overlooked by our formal educational system and who usually represent the proverty stricken and the functionally non-literate need especially designed practical basic education to more effectively function as workers, parents, responsible citizens, consumers, users of leisure time, and continuing learners.

The increasing number of older citizens need specially designed education to enable them to lead more meaningful and satisfying lives, to supplement their incomes through part-time or second or third careers and to contribute to the improvement of our communities. Middle-age workers need dynamic learning oppportunities to train and retrain for the fast changing requirements of occupations and professions.

Local social, political, and economic institutions need educational opportunities for their constituents that will help facilitate orderly growth, planned change, and continuing renewal. Community residents need opportunities to create a learning society capable of intelligent self-renewal and change.

BASIC ASSUMPTIONS

The following assumptions are proposed as a basic philosophy to assist in designing the form and function of adult and continuing education:

1. The United States has a wealth of natural resources, physical resources, and a multitude of organizations and agencies — public, private, and voluntary. But its two greatest resources are: first, its people with no known limits in their abilities to develop, to grow and learn, and to solve probems; second, its capabilities to create new knowledge and technology through education and research.
2. Nearly all of our major problems and issues are the result of human action and decisions or inaction and indecision. These problems being of human origin can and will yield to human actions and resolutions. Such problems include: failure of our educational system to appropriately respond to the needs of many children and youth; widespread adult illiteracy, poverty, crime and delinquency, drug abuse, pollution, environmental decay, malnutrition, broken homes, inadequate housing, mental illness, overcrowded cities, inequality of opportunity.
3. Given the knowledge and desire, adult educators can effectively address these major problems and substantially and continuously assist in improving the quality of life of the citizenry through democratically directed processes of planned change.
4. While education by itself cannot solve all the major social, economic, and environmental problems, its provision in adequate and effective forms is crucial to the solution of any or all of them.
5. The creation of a self-renewing and learning society is more than solving problems. It is conceiving and attaining desired futures; it is fostering and nourishing the potential interests, abilities, and constructive aspirations of each individual throughout his/her lifetime.
6. Improving the quality of life and living should afford all our citizens at every station and stage of life the opportunity to maximize their potentials to the fullest extent of their abilities.
7. The quality of our lives and the lives of our children and the usefulness of our social and organizational structures (today and tomorrow) will depend heavily upon the ability to create and maintain viable networks

for adult education — for it is the adult, not the child whose decisions and actions define the nature of our environment — ecologically, politically, economically, socially, culturally, spiritually.
8. People, whether gainfully employed or not, need and want a life's work, need to feel a sense of contribution and meaning in what they do and require multiple career opportunities.
9. People want to learn to live more cooperatively and at the same time be more self-reliant — as individuals, as families, as neighborhoods, as communities, and as a nation. They want the opportunity to individually and collectively affect the decisions and forces that shape their lives.
10. All education should become more individually need-centered, reality-based, problem-focused and functional in contrast to existing lock-step, discipline-based, and overspecialized schooling which assumes that nearly everyone should learn the same thing, at the same rate, during the same time, in the same way.
11. Learning and living (working, leisuring, socializing, creating) should become more fully integrated wherein we cease the early "sorting" for vocational training for some and academic education for others. Instead of maintaining separate educational systems for those who work with their hands and those who work with their heads, we should recognize that most people need to be able to do both, and that all people need to better be able to think critically and reflectively, and that all of us need an opportunity to stay current and become updated in terms of our skills and competencies.
12. Finally, opportunities and patterns for learning should become more varied and flexible — with easier access to and exit from our educational agencies.

GOALS AND ROLES

In examining the foregoing assumptions about our nature, problems, and goals (as individuals and as a society), it seems as though our philosophy should be based upon the concepts of the "learning society," a society that recognizes change as its most constant variable and that determines and directs the nature of change primarily through widespread citizen participation in an ongoing stream of educational activities.

Such a society would create an environment wherein the community itself becomes the educational agency or network, wherein the full range of public and private institutions (schools, colleges, stores, churches, local government, industries, universities, parks, zoos, museums, broadcasting services, correctional centers) are interrelated to maximize their educational utility and impact.

The philosophy of adult and continuing educators will no doubt continue to adjust to the fluxing needs of its clientele and to the moving parameters created by the communities of our world. The task for us as adult educators becomes one of delineation and clarification of our roles in creating the

Historical & Philosophical Perspectives 19

"learning society." Some major goals or roles might be:
1. Learning never ends.
2. The immediate reduction or elimination of adult illiteracy is attainable.
3. A powerful thrust toward lifelong learning can be sustained.
4. Pluralistic education emphasizing individual initiative and/or self-directed learning fosters maximum human development.
5. Non-traditional study and alternative learning systems for lifelong education lends legitimacy to individual lifelong learning.
6. Preparing the instructor to assume the role of facilitator or resource person allows maximum use of technology and systems engineering.
7. People matter — not institutions and things. Everything must be done to meet the individual and/or group need of potential students.
8. Equal educational opportunities and equity of access to instruction must include all adults thereby fulfilling the demands of a democratic society.
9. There is a continuing and continuous demand for more education by adults. Adult educators must become cognizant of these demands and prepare to meet these constant needs.
10. The rapid advancement of technology and educational communication is far greater than our willingness or ability to use this special technology. By the year 2001 adults everywhere will take all kinds of courses at any time of the day through the use of electronic media. Knowledge will be offered worldwide through "standard accredited knowledge kits," including print and electronic media.
11. Development and use of new techniques for measuring accomplishments and competencies of adults more accurately measures "real learning."
12. Vigorous exploration of new skills, new attitudes, new careers, and personal life strategies guide students towards self-survival in this every-changing world.
13. The move towards alternative ways to deliver education institutionalizes other educational delivery systems. Eighty percent (80%) of adult learning goes on outside of institutional auspices according to Stephen Brookfield, Director of Research, National Advisory Council of Adult Education, United Kingdom. More than fifty percent (50%) of adult Americans conduct some form of self-directed learning project each year.[3]
14. Adult education has an awareness that the adult learning process is measurable, somewhat predictable, and has a style different from other educational processes and that respects human experiences, and thus builds upon this knowledge.
15. The feelings of aliveness and excitement in adult education that is not found in more conventional areas of education solidify through the interaction of adult professionals.
16. Awareness that learning has a high priority in present day American society, and that adult educators can capitalize on this through

networking, cooperative and joint ventures, and assuredly, through taking a position of leadership.

HISTORY

As we read the history of our country and discuss the philosophy of our forebears, we see many consistencies with today's philosophies, particularly in the area of adult and continuing education. Education was to unleash the power of the masses to create and evolve new thoughts and ideas; to plan new inventions; to create new industries; to continue to educate and reeducate our total people. Then, as today, there were those for and against the philosophy of mass education. In 1821, Daniel Webster supported proportionate taxation for public education. Many newspapers opposed this revolutionary principle of compulsory equalization; on the grounds that the equalizers, "pulled down what was above and never worked in reverse." Horace Mann called the American idea of free and "access for all" education the "great equalizer" of our society. Publicly financed mass education was eventually copied by most of the modern countries of our world.

Jeffersonian democracy, the key to our educational system, proposed for all, without regard for social and/or economic status, a continuing education as the beginning of "an insurrection of science, talents, and courage against rank and birth." Benjamin Franklin in 1770 wrote to Samuel Johnson. "I think with you, that nothing is of more importance for the public weal than to form and train up youth in wisdom and virtue. Wise and good men are, in my opinion, the strength of a state; much more so than riches and arms, . . ." Government has since become a major and influential part of our educational process — its philosophy and its history.

The forefathers of our country reiterated these thoughts. George Washington in his final speech promulgated the ideas of "diffusion of knowledge through government supported institutions," and Jefferson in 1820 stated, "I know of no safe depository of the ultimate powers of the society but the people themselves, and if we think them not enlightened enough to exercise their control with a wholesome discretion, the remedy is not to take it from them but to inform their discretion by education." Jefferson sued for continuing education as the major concept of our new democracy. His ideas of education as well as government were considered revolutionary. He considered education the instrument that would give to the "common" man the tools for self-governance and self-realization. Education was to be used to challenge the old ways — not to carry on the old traditions. His was probably the first call for relevance in education as he observed, "I am not fond of reading what is merely abstract and unapplied immediately to some useful science."

The greatest legal document in history, the Constitution of the United States of America, guarantees to all equal rights and equal opportunities, which includes equal educational opportunities. Two hundred years later we are still attempting to bring into being these concepts of the founders of our country.

Education is a driving force that moves men to act; to gain power; to dominate the environment. Throughout history those men who would control society, cultures, and institutions, have controlled education. In a government of sovereign people, education must be in the hands of the people and needs to be **continuous**. **Adult and Continuing Education** is a bulwark that allows free men and women to retain their sovereign power.

Historically the education of man was direct and simple. Imitation was the major educational method. Education, as a natural and continuing process, has been prevalent since the very genesis of man, for humanity has always found it necessary to adapt to a change in external stimuli.

The early settlers of our country used the *Book of Psalms* as the basic educational material. Men and women taught one another to read the Psalms. Many children were taught to read with the same material. General education came about through observation, trial and error, and the exchange of experiences.

One of the earliest of continuing education centers was the Junta, formed by Benjamin Frankin in 1727 to provide for weekly discussions. Josiah Holbrook's Lyceum (1826) brought a series of lectures, concerts, and other continuing education programs to the New England area and eventually to many other states.

Free Library — The free library was one of the greatest boons to education to emerge from this period. The first free town library was established in Peterborough, New Hampshire in 1833. Supported by a municipal tax, it became a model for all such town libraries. By the beginning of the Civil War, the free public library had become an integral part of American culture and education. The movement continued to grow, with the assistance of such men as Andrew Carnegie who, between 1881 and 1917, donated more than 41 million dollars for the building of public libraries.

Between the end of the Civil War and the beginning of World War I there was an acceleration in both form and substance in continuing education. In the summer of 1874, a pan-denominational normal school for the instruction of Sunday school teachers was instituted at Chautauqua, New York. Shortly thereafter it broadened its spectrum of subjects for the benefit of those who desired a summer program of general education. As a result of the increased demand for a winter continuation of the summer course, W. R. Harper, a past director of the Chautauqua Literary and Scientific Circle and first president of the University of Chicago, directed the development of correspondence courses desgined to fill this need. Correspondence courses, under various auspices, were soon in abundance; public acceptance was overwhelming. University extension, the next important step, quite popular at first, entered a sudden decline until 1906 when the extension division of the University of Wisconsin imbued it with new life by offering courses encompassing more mundane subjects: economic, social, political, cultural, moral, as well as agricultural training.

The emphasis in adult education prior to World War I had been primarily remedial, an effort to make up the educational deficiencies engendered by lack of sufficient schooling. However, in 1919 a report by the Adult Education Committee of the British Ministry of Reconstruction marked the beginning of a new era in both British and American adult education. The essence of ths report was . . . adult education is a permanent national necessity, an inseparable aspect of citizenship, and therefore should be both universal and lifelong.

Modern Era of Adult Education — The modern era of adult education, dating from 1919, may be divided into three periods of growth, each with its particular characteristics and advances.

The first period, that from 1919 to 1929, was fraught with the spirit of idealism. Adult education was seen as the means of bringing about social reform, reconstruction, and progress. In 1920 the Department of Immigrant Education of the National Education Association was established, and in 1924 it became the Department of Adult Education. Numerous other agencies were also organized, the most important of which was the American Association for Adult Education in 1926, for it marked that point in history when adult education became publicly defined as a distinct field of social practice.

The second period (1930-1946) was a time during which it was felt that the country could be better served if the ideals were modified to that which could be judged realistic. The articles by professional adult educators of the time appealed for more specificity in definition and subject matter.

The third period, which brings us to the present, began in 1947. It is at this time that we find a movement toward professionalism and institutionalization; and the period is further characterized by an expansion of graduate programs in adult education. There were also formed at this time the Commission of Professors of Adult Education and the National Seminar for Adult Education Research. The Adult Education Association of the U.S.A. was formed in 1951 because of overlap of interests of the Department of Adult Education and the American Association for Adult Education.

After World War II the reliance on lectures and print media gave way to newer forms of instruction such as films and other audiovisual aids, demonstrations, field trips, dramatic techniques, and case study.

In addition to those philanthropic foundations which have rendered important financial support (Carnegie, W.K. Kellogg, Ford, and Mellon were among the largest contributors), the government has also taken a positive attitude, and has supported that position with agencies, legislation, and financial assistance. The formation, in 1965, of the Bureau of Adult and Vocational Education — as a part of the U.S. Office of Education — within which was created a division of Adult Education Programs, was one such action. Several pertinent legislative acts were passed during the 1960's, among which were: the Manpower Development and Training Act of 1962; the Vocational Education Act of 1963; the Economic Opportunity Act of 1964; the Adult Education Act of 1966 and its subsequent amendments.

Landmark legislation affecting all of American education became official on October 16, 1979 when President Carter signed Public Law 96-68, establishing our nation's first Cabinet-level Department of Education. He moved swiftly to implement the new law by nominating Shirley Hufstedler, a highly-respected Federal appeals court judge from California, as the first Secretary of Education.

Subsequently, T. H. Bell, as Secretary of Education, began decreasing the size and impact of the Department of Education as mandated by the then incumbent administration. However, many leaders in education feel that the overriding needs of education are so great that a cabinet-level Department of Education will be continued.

ANDRAGOGY

In order to fully understand the definition of, and the philosophy behind adult and continuing education, long standing misconceptions must be corrected. Pedagogy — a misnomer when applied to adult education — has been the term used to describe all education, and to an extent this is correct, for the term implies a leading out, a guiding along the paths of knowledge. However, the word taken literally from its roots means the leading of children, the implication thereof being that the learner is guided within a rather rigid system. This cannot, rationally, be applied to adult education. A basic problem with pedagogy is that most teachers have known only how to teach adults as if they were children, and, since adults are almost always voluntary learners, they will quickly disappear from learning experiences with which they are unsatisfied. A more explicit and realistic term which may be applied to adult education, is *andragogy*. From its root, it denotes the leading of man; or the art and science of helping adults learn. Yet, it is more, even, than that, it is the helping of human beings to learn; for education is a continuing process, one which begins at birth, and ends only with death.

An international definition of adult education was propounded in 1966 at a meeting of twenty-six educators representing eight countries. Their conclusion was that . . . adult education is a process whereby persons who no longer attend school on a regular and fulltime basis (unless fulltime programs are especially designed for adults) undertake sequential and organized activities with the conscious intention of bringing about changes in information, knowledge, understanding, skills, appreciation, and attitudes.

It would seem as though the above definition was as much a delineation of the purpose of adult and continuing education as it is a definition. The two do, at points overlap, but the actual purpose of continuing education is founded on a much broader basis. This is, the job of continuing education is to help people understand the rationale or order and security in a world of rapid change, and to build their goals realistically in fitting terms, and to help people understand their problems, discover the resources which are available to them, and find the way to solve their problems and to reach their goals under current circumstances.

The boons of technology are many, wonderous, and varied; but the havoc it has brought into the lives of some can be expressed in one word — unemployment. When a man's skill has been taken over by a machine, he may feel that he has come to a dead end. However, if he is willing to be trained or retrained, to change and to adapt, continuing education offers a new beginning. It is within the realm of continuing education to assist a man in the solving of a problem of this nature. This changing world has brought American culture to the state where it depends upon education to make its civilization operate successfully. It is up to those involved to develop an understanding of the situation in the unemployed; to offer guidance; and to make provisions for the retraining of the technologically unemployed. The functions of adult and continuing education in this specific situation, as in the field as a whole, are definite and necessary to the common good.

SUMMARY

Adult education is continuous, essential for growth, and impacts upon all facets of American life. As the field of Adult and Continuing Education grows, basic assumptions and goals and roles have evolved. The assumptions cover a broad spectrum from the belief that problems are the result of human behavior, to peoples' inherent desire to contribute to the worth of their communities. The roles are varied. They include the continuity of educational experiences, changed perceptions of the student/teacher relationship, and that more and more adults tend to view adult education as a survival technique.

Historically, adult and continuing education began with the American republic. Much of what had transpired in churches, lodge halls, and cultural societies were forms of adult education. Free public libraries served a distinct purpose in providing mass participation in this field.

The present era has seen a move towards professionalism and becoming more aware of the individualized problems of our adult population. Underlying a whole new focus of adult education is andragogy — helping adults learn.

REFERENCES

1. Gessler, Robert, Ed, *Selections from the Writings of Edward C. Lindeman: The Democratic Man.* Boston: Beacon Press, 1956.
2. *A Target Populaton in Adult Education,* Report of the National Advisory Council on Adult Education, Washington, DC, 1974.
3. Material has been drawn from the following:
   Talk delivered by George F. Aker to Conference on *Economic and Social Perspectives on Adult Illiteracy,* Orlando, FL, March 16, 1977.
   Swap Shop, NAPCAE, Washington, DC, Feb. 1975.
   Phi Delta Kappan, Phi Delta Kappa, Bloomington: Sept. 1980, May 1981, April, 1982, Sept. 1982.
   Chronicle of Higher Education, April, 1982.
   Lifelong Learning, AEA, USA, Washington, D. C., May, 1982.
   Bulletin: National Center for Educational Statistics, U.S. Department of Education. Washington, DC, August 17, 1981.

Developing a Belief Structure

Jerold W. Apps

Professor of Adult Education, University of Wisconsin, Madison; author of several books on adult education.

Too often the adult educator is so busy "keeping up" with everything he or she must do that little time remains to consider the foundations for decisions and actions. Many adult educators begin to feel like rudderless ships. They are tossed "to and fro" by whatever new fad blows their way.

In those agonizing moments alone, when the phone stops ringing, the adult educator often thinks disturbing thoughts: What do I want to accomplish? Do I really believe in what I do? Do I trust my decisions?

Requests from students, superiors, and often the public at large frequently bombard the adult educator. There are several alternatives:
1. Try to meet all demands — work evening and weekends — avoid taking a vacation.
2. Rely on expediency. From the power figures in the particular agency or institution, learn what is "acceptable" programming. Then carefully follow such a pattern.
3. Copy a peer's programming approach. What worked for a peer will likely work for someone else.
4. Utilize ad hoc programming. There is enough to do just meeting day to day responsibilities: teaching a class when asked, talking with prospective students, writing reports, answering the phone, answering letters. Programming will take care of itself. No sense worrying about it.
5. Analyze your beliefs about adult education programming and let such beliefs guide your action.

A Belief Analysis Process — An assumption is that adult educators hold many beliefs that serve as a basis for their programming. Some of the beliefs may contradict each other and some may have inadequate bases of support. The adult educator may not be aware of some of the beliefs he holds, and in some areas of adult education, the adult educator may hold no well-formulated beliefs.

Four phases are included in this belief analysis process:
1. Identifying beliefs held about adult education — that is, beliefs about the adult learner, about the purposes for adult agencies and institutions, about the teaching-learning process, and about the role of the adult educator.
2. Searching for contradictions among beliefs held.

3. Discovering bases for beliefs. These bases include sources of beliefs and evidence that supports beliefs.
4. Making judgments about the bases for the particular beliefs held.

The analysis does not proceed step by step, for several parts of the analysis may occur simultaneously. As the adult educator seeks consciously to recognize beliefs held, contradictions may become evident. Also when identifying beliefs, the adult educator may consider the bases for his or her beliefs, and concurrently, he or she may judge the validity of these bases for beliefs.

Beliefs — What is a belief? A belief is a statement of what a person regards as true or factual.

Order of Beliefs — Bem[2] discusses **zero order, first order,** and **higher order beliefs. Zero order beliefs** are held by a person without his being aware of the belief. Believing the seasons will change each year is a zero order belief held by most people. They accept this belief as true without being aware it is a belief they hold. Zero order beliefs are those for which no alternative is apparent. People who believe the seasons will change each year are unaware of the possibility they may not.

Accepting the truth of sensory experiences is another zero order belief. "Seeing is believing," "Show me," "I want to hear it myself," are statements indicating the importance of sensory experience. Many people do not consider the alternative that their sensory perceptions may at times be inaccurate.

In contrast, a person is aware of **first order beliefs** he or she holds. The individual can conceptualize an alternative. "All adults have the potential for learning," is an example of a first order belief an adult educator might hold. An opposite alternative is easily recognized — "Some adults may not have the potential for learning."

Higher order beliefs are usually derived by some thought process a person uses. Apps[1] suggests the following ways an individual derives higher order beliefs:
1. From a statement made by an authority whose credibility legitimizes transference from what he states to what we believe. For example, we may reason as follows —
    Thorndike said that adults can learn.
    Thorndike was a noted researcher in adult education.
    Therefore, adults can learn.
2. Reasoning inductively from our experience.
    Several adults attended a series of woodworking classes.
    These adults were able to construct a piece of furniture after the series.
    Therefore, adults can learn.
3. Building on premises that are themselves conclusions of prior syllogisms.
    Adults can learn
    Adults have many needs.
    Needs relate to motivation for learning.
    Adults might learn best when the learning situation relates to their needs.

Developing a Belief Structure

Higher order beliefs are often derived from zero order beliefs. If we believe something because we have experienced it, we are accepting as true the zero order belief that our sensory experiences are accurate.

Sources of Beliefs — When beliefs are analyzed, two sources are evident: (1) experience, (2) authority.

We have learned through experience that automobiles will transport us to work. They will give us independence when we travel and are relatively inexpensive to operate. Our beliefs about automobiles are derived from experience.

We may also believe that those who work hard will eventually be successful. Our parents may have stated this belief, both directly and indirectly, when we were children. If so, the source of this belief is an external authority — in this case our parents.

Evidence Supporting a Belief — There is a difference between source of beliefs and evidence supporting a belief. As explained above, our beliefs may be traced back to either authority or experience, or both.

Evidence supporting a belief involves those factors which influence us to continue holding certain beliefs. If we continually challenge our beliefs with new evidence, we may reinforce a belief, or discard it, or revise it. Consider the previous example about automobiles. With new evidence — increased cost of automobiles, pollution caused by autos, shortage and increased cost of fuel — we may revise our belief about the importance of autos as sources of transportation.

Belief Areas for the Adult Educator — Several categories of beliefs might be considered by the adult educator interested in analyzing beliefs:
1. About the adult learner.
2. About the purposes of adult education agencies and institutions.
3. About the teaching-learning process.
4. About the role of the adult educator.

Some authors believe the field of adult education should strive toward a common philosophy, one that all adult educators can adopt. A position can be taken that acknowledges the extension of several different philosophies within the field. Stress is placed on the individual adult educator's understanding his or her own beliefs about adult education.

BELIEFS ABOUT THE ADULT LEARNER

What do we believe about those persons who participate in our programs? We likely believe that people participate because they want to learn. We may also believe that some people participate because they enjoy being with other people. Our experience may have influenced us to believe that some adults are more highly motivated than others, that age is no deterrent to participation, and that adults want to study topics related to their own experiences.

One could list many similar beliefs. But are there more basic beliefs to consider that may help us make program decisions?

1. Do human beings have universal needs such as warmth, affection and belonging, in addition to the biological needs shared with all animals? At least two dimensions are part of this question: (a) universality of needs, (b) the relationship of biological to non-biological needs.
    First, consider universality. Do we believe that all adults share in having non-biological needs such as warmth, affection and belonging, or do we accept a position that some do and some do not? Or do some have considerably more needs in these areas than others?
    Second, do we believe that non-biological needs are as important as biological needs? Or do we believe that biological needs are more important than non-biological needs?
2. Do all humans share universal goals, such as love for beauty or desire for systematic knowledge? Do all humans seek an intimate relationship with one or more persons, search for meaning in life, or strive for self actualization? Is the concept of universal goals unique to each person, rather than shared universally with other humans?
3. How is "humanness" expressed, as distinct from "animalness"? What unique behavior distinguishes humans from other animals? Or is human behavior and animal behavior essentially similar, the difference being sophistication and complexity?
4. Where do we believe the human race is headed? Toward its ultimate destruction? Toward a time when the major problems humans face will be solved? Or will the human race continue to solve problems and face new ones without heading toward ultimate destruction or utopia?
5. What do we believe about how people relate to: (a) nature, (b) society? Are human beings basically fused with the natural world? What interacting forces exist between humans and the natural world? To what extent can humans influence the natural world? To what extent does the natural world influence humans?

Similar questions emerge about the relationships between humans and society. Do we believe individuals can influence society? To what extent? Does society influence individuals more than individuals influence society?

We may also consider the issue in terms of how an individual relates to the smaller group of which he or she is a member. For example, consider the work group in an office. To what extent can an individual influence others in a work group? To what extent can a work group influence the individual? Is it possible for individual goals to differ from group goals?

In a broader context what do we believe about the rights of society versus the rights of individuals? When does society have the right to impose rules and expectations for behavior upon the persons that make up that society? Do individuals have the right to control more of their lives? Or in a complex society such as ours, is it detrimental to society for individuals to strive for more personal control of their lives?

None of these questions are easy to answer. It is extremely difficult to conduct empirical research to locate clear answers. Many of the questions we may have already answered. Thus, we hold these answers as zero order beliefs, having never thought about an alternative to our position. Others we may have answered and hold as first order or higher order beliefs.

Beliefs About the Purposes of Continuing Education — This area relates to the more general question of what is/are the purpose(s) of continuing education. Powell and Benne[4] list two major types of continuing education: (1) developmental, (2) rationalist. The developmental type includes fundamental education best exemplified by community development and human relations best exemplified by encounter groups. The rationalist type includes such areas as liberal arts, and humanities, and Great Books. Though this rationale mixes purpose with method, it does offer insight into how continuing educators have viewed the purpose of the field.

Another way of looking at the purpose of continuing education is to consider the following questions:

1. Is continuing education the handmaiden of society? Does it share with other kinds of education the responsibility of passing on the "culture" to present and future generations? This "culture" may be the great writings of the past, or explanations of our present governmental system. It may include helping more disadvantaged people join the "mainstream" of society through adult basic education programs, job retraining and new careers. It may also include introducing people to classical music and art.
2. Is continuing education's purpose to help reform society? Should it help society modify its goals and purposes, its laws and political structures, its agencies and institutions?
3. Is continuing education's purpose to seek major changes in society such as establishing new agencies and institutions and/or seeking to eliminate certain existing agencies and institutions? As Freire[3] asks — Is it the purpose of continuing education to seek major changes in societal structures?
4. Is the purpose of continuing education to help individuals achieve maximum personal growth?
5. Is the purpose of continuing education some combination of the above purposes?

What is the relationship of continuing education agencies and institutions to other agencies and institutions in society? The rather obvious dichotomy is: (1) do continuing education agencies and institutions serve other societal agencies and assist them to meet their particular goals, (2) do continuing education agencies and institutions serve as critics and challengers of other agencies and institutions in society?

Beliefs About the Teaching-Learning Process — What is learning? Is it: (1) acquisition of content, (2) personal growth, (3) problem solving?

Acquiring content has been an accepted way to define learning for many generations. One has learned when one has acquired information. In so doing, one may also acquire a unique way to organize information in a particular content field.

Personal growth also involves content, but it focuses on relating this content to one's personal experience. Learning, then, is the integration of new information into the personal self. This integration may result in discarding some previously held information, reorganizing some information, or finding a place for new information. This description oversimplifies what may actually occur. The process, in reality, is complex and most often different for each person.

The key to this definition is the emphasis on experience. As contrasted with "learning as acquisition of content," new information must be experienced at some level. This is, the learner must be able to deal with the information as directly as possible. For example, a person might read about transactional analysis and acquire the concepts that describe the technique. So far this example defines learning as the acquisition of content. But if the person not only acquired the concepts but also participated in a group where he or she could experience the concepts, the example would describe learning as personal growth.

Learning as problem solving may be concerned with individual problems or societal problems. Individual problems might, for example, include economic problems (how to increase one's income), psychological problems (how to overcome fear), and interpersonal problems (how to relate to others). Societal problems might include inadequate cultural opportunities in a community, high unemployment rates, and inadequate transportation.

This type of learning involves solving the problem as well as individuals understanding and acquiring a problem solving process. The learner learns by doing, that is by working through the problem solving process.

Content is important in this learning approach too, but is not acquired for its own sake. It is acquired when it can be used to solve a particular problem.

The question is what do we believe learning to be? Acquisition of content? Personal growth? Problem solving? Some combination of the three? Or is learning altogether different from what has been described?

Role for the Adult Educator — What role should the adult educator play? Some will legitimately claim the role depends on the situation. But do we believe an adult educator should play one type of role more often than another? For example, should the adult educator play the role of **expert**? Should he or she be someone who commands a body of knowledge, and can translate complex information for potential learners? Or, should the adult educator be viewed as a **guide** or **counselor**? Should he or she design learning experiences which help learners learn? Should he or she help learners eliminate blocks to their learning?

The adult educator also serves as a **model** for learners, whether the adult educator is aware of it or not. Through his or her behavior the adult educator can demonstrate a positive attitude toward learning, show concern for exploring ideas in depth, demonstrate excitement about continuing learning, and show concern for learners as human beings.

Developing a Belief Structure

Identifying Beliefs — One way to identify beliefs is to analyze present behavior. To the extent our behavior is consistent with our beliefs, we can understand our beliefs from how we behave. For example, when planning a program we might pay particular attention to a governing board's recommendation about content for the program. Why did we consider the board's recommendation to be so important? What belief do we hold that influences this action? In this example, the programming approach used may be based on a belief that a programmer must bow to authority when making program decisions.

Admittedly, deriving beliefs from behavior can be difficult because many other factors may be involved. Nevertheless, an analysis of behavior can be an important indicator of beliefs held.

A number of alternative beliefs about continuing education have been presented. Thinking carefully about these alternatives may help to identify beliefs particularly in areas where the adult educator may not have well formulated beliefs, or may not be aware of his or her beliefs.

Searching for Contradictions — Searching for contradictions among beliefs is difficult but necessary. Often, while analyzing behavior, the adult educator discovers a belief implied by the behavior that is inconsistent with what the person really believes. This new information creates a tension that may result in: (1) a change in behavior to coincide with what the person really believes, or (2) a change in belief to coincide with the behavior.

For example, on the one hand, an adult educator may believe that individuals have the right to strive for more control over their lives, while on the other hand, he or she may believe the educator should help people cope with all situations as they now exist. Unless the adult educator carefully searches for contradictions while analyzing beliefs, this type of contradiction may not be evident.

Discovering Bases for Beliefs — As indicated earlier, bases for beliefs include: (1) sources of beliefs, (2) evidence that supports beliefs.

Work through a hypothetical example to see how this phase of the analysis of beliefs process might work. Assume an adult educator believes that human beings are an integral part of the natural world, that people influence the natural world, and the natural world influences people. He also believes that unless human beings come to recognize this close interacting relationship, the environment will eventually not support life.

Upon careful thinking about that belief, the adult educator may discover the source of this belief comes from authorities who have written about the topic. Upon reflection, the adult educator may remember hiking through a forest that was defoliated because of air pollution. Also remembered are experiences fishing in a polluted lake and canoeing down a polluted stream. **Thus the sources of the belief are authority and personal experience.**

Making Judgments — Likely the most difficult task in analyzing beliefs is judging the "goodness" of the bases for beliefs. As indicated above, bases include, sources of beliefs and evidence that supports beliefs.

Questions such as these must be asked:
1. If an authority is a source for a particular belief, do we value the authority? Is the authority considered competent? Does the authority have a reputation for accuracy?
2. If a source for a belief is experience, did we accurately perceive the situation experienced?
3. Is the evidence for supporting the belief accurate?
4. Is the evidence supporting the belief up-to-date?
5. Do we have sufficient evidence so we feel comfortable about a particular belief?

These are examples of the criteria that might be useful in judging the worth of bases for beliefs. The adult educator will likely want to add additional criteria for determining the worth of his or her bases for beliefs.

SUMMARY

There is a process of identifying, classifying, and evaluating the beliefs used in programming and decision-making and as professional adult educators we do not have the luxury of failing to analyze our beliefs. We are responsible to large numbers of people who look to us for leadership in developing and directing adult education programs. We have a professional obligation to these persons, both to those who employ us and to those who are our clientele, to have a solid basis for our decision-making and actions. If we are to improve as adult education professionals, it is imperative that we analyze the foundations for our decisions and actions.

Questions and Exercises

1. List four of your beliefs regarding adult education and determine the order of each belief.
2. Using these same beliefs, respond to the author's questions relative to "goodness" of the bases for beliefs.
3. In what areas, other than program planning and decision-making, can the adult educator use these techniques?

REFERENCES

1. Apps, Jerold W. *Toward a Working Philosophy of Adult Education.* Syracuse, New York: Syracuse University, Publications in Continuing Education, 1973.
2. Bem, Daryl J. *Beliefs, Attitudes, and Human Affairs.* Belmont, California: Brooks/Cole Publishing Co., 1970.
3. Freire, Paulo. *Pedagogy of the Oppressed.* New York: Herder and Herder, 1970.
4. Powell, John Walker and Kenneth D. Benne. "Philosophies of Adult Education." *Handbook of Adult Education in the United States.* (ed) Malcolm S. Knowles, Washington, D.C.: AEA, 1960.

The Political Process

Gene C. Whaples

*Associate Professor, Department of
Agricultural & Extension Education,
University of Maryland*

James W. Miller

*President, NAPCAE; Director of
Federal Assistance, State Department
of Education, Ohio*

Adult educators must be concerned about quality programs which serve the needs of adult learners. The constant pressure for building programs, and the day-to-day pressures dealing with personnel, reporting and other time consuming administrative tasks, leave little time for maintaining and increasing resources through effective lobbying. The lack of involvement of adult educators with the political process provides an interesting paradox. It is in the political arena at national, state, and local levels that the critical decisions are being made concerning resources which directly effect adult educators and adult learners. Senator James Symington placed the responsibility for legislative support for adult education on adult educators. At the 1980 Adult Education Conference he said, " . . . your task is to find a way to cause legislators to include adult education on its agenda of **must** legislation for the eighties." The nature of the paradox is that few adult educators are concerned with the political agenda; most adult educators possess limited skills in influencing the agenda; and many, also, consider it unprofessional to attempt to influence this agenda.

The immediate future should be a boom time for adult education. Changes in demographics, the job market, technology and leisure time all point to increased needs for adult learners. The high cost of illiteracy and its subsequent impact on the economy, contributing to unemployment, welfare, and crime underline the need for increased adult learning. The decline in elementary and secondary school enrollments and the subsequent availability of public facilities suggest new challenges to adult educators. The battle for increased resources may well be lost if more adult educators fail to develop those tools necessary for effective use in the political arena. Competition for the public tax dollar in the current economic climate has never been stronger. If adult education is to begin to realize its potential, then a united assertive role at national, state and local levels in the political arena must be undertaken. The choice is: (1) to guide our own future, or (2) let it be determined by others who know little of the needs of adult learners and do not understand the role of the adult education professional. Some feel that politics is a dirty game and "educators" should not become involved. For the achievement of the goals of adult education it may be the only game and it is time that all of us learned the rules of the game and the names of the players.

PRINCIPLES OF PARTICIPATION

The principles of effective participation in the political arena are basically the same at national, state or local levels. It is necessary to develop an understanding of **who** the "players" are in the power game of politics, and at **what** stages in the political process decisions can most likely be influenced. It is also vital to discuss the factors that politicians consider in decision-making and present some suggestions on how to prepare and present the case for adult education.

Know The Players — While the legislative process is not unduly difficult to learn it is important to first realize that we are not the only player in the game. This game is one of winners and losers with an occasional tie. Legislators have many different constituencies to consider and will usually hear from a variety of persons representing different agency, association, and individual concerns in regard to a particular issue. These players may come with different philosophical viewpoints.

Legislation concerned with education is of interest to a broad range of groups. Below is a partial list of those who will be concerned about legislation. The primary players are listed first; a limited list of others is also provided. The list is far from being inclusive, but it is representative of individuals, organizations, and agencies that have a strong interest in bills pertaining to adult education.

NATIONAL	STATE	LOCAL
President	Governor	Mayor
Dept. of Education	State Dept. of Educ.	Board of Education
Committee Chairpersons	Committee Chairpersons	City Coun/Co. Comm.
Committee Staff	Committee Staff	Council/Comm. Staff
Off. of Budget/Mngment.	Off. of Budget/Mngment.	City Auditor/Co. Treas.
Congress as a Whole	State Legislature	Councils/Commissions
Federal Courts	Federal/State Courts	Fed/State/Co. Courts
Parent Organization (PTA, Nat'l Coalition)	Parents Organizations (PTA, State Coalition)	Parent Organizations (PTA)
Nat'l Associations	State Associations	Civic/Fraternal Assoc.

OTHER SPECIAL INTEREST GROUPS	OTHER SPECIAL INTEREST GROUPS	OTHER SPECIAL INTEREST GROUPS
Council for American Private Education	Catholic Educ. Assoc. & Other Nonpublic Schls.	Nonpublic Schools
Dept. of Agriculture	State Dept. of Agri.	Agric. Interests
Dept. of Labor	Employ. Serv./Welfare	Labor
Dept. of Health	State Dept. of Health	City/Co. Health Dept.
Dept. of Defense		
Minority Groups	Minority Groups	Minority Groups
Private Sector	Private Sector (Retail Merchants, Chamber of Commerce)	Business and Industry

As a player in the poliltical game it is useful to know how legislators view us. Samuel Halperin addressed this issue when he wrote:

> Most policymakers are convinced that most educators simply don't understand the way the world is. In short, their initial mindset when educators come to see them is likely to be negative or at least guarded — unless you are one of that rare breed of educators who has shown understanding of the political process, appreciation of the essential role of the politician in confronting the dilemmas of a complex and contentious democratic society and, most important, that you are not 'too proud to get your hands dirty' with the less glamorous aspects of political reality.[2]

How To Play The Game — The challenge that adult educators face is how to most effectively inform and educate our political decision-makers. Researchers have concluded that some techniques are more effective than others. There is general agreement that visits in the office, telephone calls, letters, contact through other legislators, testifying at hearings and telegrams are all effective (in this order). Techniques found not effective include contact at social affairs, media, and petitions.[3] The technique selected will often depend on time and money. Not all of us can lobby full time. To be successful we must organize and work with others who are concerned about the same issues. This approach will enable each of us to contribute to the total lobby effort.

We must realize that facts and logic do not always win the game. Administrative priorities, majority and minority party positions, committee chairman wishes, committee staff bias, special interest group concerns, election year issues, results of hearings and studies, committee power plays and private sector concerns represent some of the factors affecting decisions on a piece of legislation. Trade-off and compromise play a major role in the passage of any bill. It is rare that any interest group gets all it wants. In fact Thomas R. Dye in his book **Understanding Public Policy** suggests that less than 60% of the public agree with the policies established by government policy makers.

Becoming Involved — Although few of us can become full time lobbyists, each of us can become effective players in the game of politics. Each adult educator should take the following steps as a start toward becoming an informed and active advocate for the field.
1. Join — your national and state professional association. These associations will provide a communication link and current information on legislative concerns.
2. Read — and become familiar with issues that impact on adult education. All major newspapers provide some relevant information. There are also a number of specialized newsletters. These usually can be found in the library or you may find a subscription more convenient.
3. Meet — your legislators and their staff. This can easily be done in the local area. Ask to be put on their mailing list and let them know what your concerns are.
4. Involve — your legislators in your programs. If your programs are supported by tax monies let them know how important this support is. Give them a chance to present recognition to your clientele. This opportunity will help develop an understanding of your program and will develop credibility and trust when you need to ask for help later.
5. Communicate — write often, provide information that is factual, correct, and timely. Be sure to let your legislators know when you feel they are doing something right as well as when you are concerned about an issue.
6. Visit — if you are in the capital visit your legislators' office. When you are there, sign the guest book (this will insure you are on the mailing list) and visit with either the legislator or the staff. Be friendly, constructive, and positive. If there is an issue to be discussed be sure to let the legislator know how it will affect his/her constituents. Be polite and brief — do not argue.
7. Support — candidates that represent your position should be supported with both money and time during the election.

These seven steps will enable you to become an active player in the political arena.

Where To Play The Game — Legislation as a rule moves at a slow pace. At the national level in recent years most major education legislation has taken a year or longer to pass. Protocol, tradition, power struggles, and individual egos, all contribute to the slow process of legislation. This lack of speed can work to our benefit as it provides time for our professional associations and for concerned adult educators to react to and have an impact on the decision-making process. Periodically legislation does move quickly and amendments attached to unrelated bills are sometimes made in an attempt to "slip one through." These periodic flashes of speed point out the need to stay informed and to support our professional associations' effort to track legislation for us.

The Political Process

The lobbying game is played in many arenas. Probably the most effective way to influence legislation is by working with a legislator whom you personally know and who respects your opinion. This legislator is in the position to introduce or influence legislation on your behalf. It appears that few adult educators have cultivated relationships with politicians. Thus, this pro-active position is unfortunately rarely available. Probably the most likely point of impact is at the subcommittee level. The majority of hearings, testimony (both written and oral), utilization of studies, reports, and legislative staff time is spent at the subcommittee level. This is often the first opportunity to present information through testimony. Good relationships and communications with staff are as critical as they are with legislators themselves. Often bills are drafted by subcommittee staff. Major impact on legislation can occur at this point.

Once a bill is reported from the subcommittee to the full committee, similar opportunities to present viewpoints are available but usually less time to act. As more players become involved in the full committee it becomes more difficult to impact on the process. As a bill moves from committee to floor vote opportunities for amendments are drastically reduced. At national and state level the last opportunity for change occurs during conference committee action. Here conferences will reconcile the differences in the two bills.

The message for adult educators is clear. The longer we wait to act, the more opportunities for success are reduced. Active participation in the political process is necessary and participation at the subcommittee level is absolutely critical.

Adult education needs a few good full time professionals who know the game and can be the major players. These players need to be backed by competent reserves that understand the game and can be called upon to play when necessary. Any of us may be called on to lobby in support of adult education. With good leadership from our professionals we can have an impact. Regardless of our role there are two key steps to be followed: 1) Preparation, 2) Presentation and Follow up.

I. Preparation
   A. Know the issue.
      1. What changes if any are needed? Will a new bill make a difference? Why is such a change desirable or undesirable? Be prepared to provide factual data, and explain how the issue impacts on adult learners.
      2. Know the history.
         a. If a bill has been introduced previously, why did it fail?
         b. Does the current suggested legislation solve or create problems?
         c. What information has been introduced to support the previous bill?
         d. Is there additional or new information which supports your position?

3. Review Other Impacts
   a. Is there an estimate of the cost prepared. Does it agree with your estimates? If discrepancies exist, be prepared to address them.
   b. How does the issue relate to laws and rules on discrimination?
B. Know the Committee.
   1. Know the name of the committee and the committee chairman. Also know the names of as many of the committee members as possible.
   2. It may be helpful to review which districts the committee members represent. This will help you anticipate questions arising from local needs and interests.
   3. Determine if any committee members serve on subcommittees which have expertise related to the issue.
   4. Be sure to know if your legislator is on any committees that are responsible for legislation concerning adult education issues.
   5. Know what position your legislator takes concerning the issue.

II. Presentation and Follow Up
   A. If you are writing:
      1. Be personal, don't send standard form letters.
      2. Be timely, a letter after the fact doesn't help.
      3. Be brief and to the point — one issue per letter (include bill, name, and number).
      4. Present facts and explain how the issue will affect the learners.
      5. Send a copy to your legislator when you write to other legislators.
      6. Send a copy to your nation and state association.
      7. Keep a copy.
      Writing is a low cost but effective technique for lobbying. All adult educators can become effective long distance lobbyist by taking time to write.
   B. If you are visiting:
      1. Make an appointment in advance.
      2. Visit before the vote.
      3. Know the legislator's voting record and philosophy on the issue.
      4. Be brief, positive, and constructive.
      5. Give examples and be accurate.
      6. Listen to the legislator's position and answer questions.
      7. Leave a written summary of your position.
      8. Follow up with a thank you letter and review your position. Office visits are among the most effective lobby methods. A

visit in the home district can be as effective as one at the capital.
C. If you are testifying:
All testimony should be prepared and presented in writing. An oral presentation is your opportunity to have a face to face interaction with those responsible for making decisions. Individuals may request an opportuntity to testify or may be asked to testify because they are recognized as experts. When presenting oral testimony:
1. Come prepared — know what you want to say and how you plan to say it.
2. If you are representing an organization remember to present their position not yours.
3. Stand up or take the designated seat at the witness table. If you must testify from the audience and are asked to respond to any questions as a member of an audience, be sure to stand.
4. Introduce yourself and identify your organization and position.
5. Do not read from a written statement. Summarize, paraphrase and take no more than 8 to 10 minutes to present your testimony.
6. When appropriate, use graphics — tables and charts. Remember that copies of the testimony are usually due in advance of the oral presentation. Have extra copies on hand and be sure that testimony is error-free.
7. Never assume what happens in one committee is known to members of another. Repeat all appropriate background information each time you appear.
8. Use data and examples to illustrate your points where appropriate. Remember, legislators are required to consider a broad range of issues and consequently may not be well informed about your area of expertise.
9. Anticipate questions by knowing the history of the issue and the position of committee members.
10. Give direct, sincere, and brief answers based on fact. If you are expressing opinion, acknowledge it. If you do not have the answer to a question, volunteer to get it and then provide it in writing after the hearing and before the vote.
11. Notify appropriate legislators and relevant parties in advance if you are going to recommend anything new or unexpected. Do not use a hearing to spring a surprise on a committee or the unsuspecting public.
12. Be prepared to respond to inquiries on your budgetary and staffing situation (professional and clerical breakdown, travel budget, rent, unused expenditures) and other questions concerning your operation.

13. Highlight the key issues as a part of your presentation. It helps legislators understand your position and helps them form a frame of reference in asking questions.
14. Describe your positions, issues, and concerns clearly and succinctly. Do not "duck" the issues. Make a concise statement describing central problems and your expert opinion as to how it should be resolved.
15. Do not argue with committee members. They will always have the last word. If you disagree, say so, state your case, and leave it at that.
16. Do not interrupt committee members when they are asking questions or making statements.

Coalitions To Win The Game — Coalitions can be our most effective tool in our lobbying effort. Adult education has many friends who are eager to help in the legislative process. These include, but are not limited to, adult education staff members, other educators, students, local agency representatives, business and industry representatives, the political sector (mayors, commissions, council members), representatives of other public agencies (health, labor, welfare), and representatives from the media, libraries, and churches.

It is helpful to have the broadest representation possible in speaking to adult education interests. Legislators are impressed when they hear from many different constituencies on the same issue. Of course, assistance is not a one-way venture. We must be prepared to help others with issues of importance to them. Following are suggestions for coalition efforts as developed by the California Association of School Administrators:

1. ALWAYS pick a meaningful cause to stand up for.
2. ALWAYS clearly identify the common interests of the coalition participants. Those interests will serve as the foundation for cooperative action.
3. ALWAYS be sure that all parties understand they must work for the coalition interest above their own group interest.
4. ALWAYS accept the need to forego self-aggrandizement — or even credit — for coalition successes.
5. ALWAYS identify a leader who has knowledge of, experience in, and a strong commitment to the coalition issues, and the time to devote to making it work.
6. ALWAYS grant your group's representative the authority to exercise his/her judgement.
7. ALWAYS keep communication with coalition members wide open throughout the joint effort. The troops need to know what is going on!
8. ALWAYS stay on the offensive with factual information, understanding of the legislative process, and familiarity with all issues involved.
9. ALWAYS get members of coalition organizations involved in the process at all levels. If the issue is not important to the general membership, the groups should not be involved.

10. NEVER coalesce on a weak issue that is not of vital importance to group members.
11. NEVER change or try to introduce additional interest "down the road." New and secondary items carry the potential for weakening the agreement.
12. NEVER elevate self-interests above the coalition goals.
13. NEVER expect recognition for one coalition member or leader above the others.
14. NEVER settle for leadership with less than complete commitment to stated results and without resources to see that commitment through.
15. NEVER cripple the coalition by refusing to give your representative any judgemental leeway so that he/she has to "run home" for guidance on every decision.
16. NEVER neglect to keep group members aware of changes in the coalition agreements as adjustments are made.
17. NEVER attack the opposition or react defensively.
18. NEVER leave all the ground work up to the leaders along with the planning and direction.

Other Ways To Help — As credibility and confidence in your contribution improve, opportunities to aid in development of legislation will increase. Contribution that can be made might include:
1. Drafting of legislation.
2. Analysis in detail of the strengths and weaknesses of a bill.
3. Development of questions to be used in hearings.
4. Providing rationale and language for amendments.
5. Creating opportunity for legislators to meet with local people who are interested in the legislation.

SUMMARY

Laws and the allocation of fiscal resources are determined by men and women elected by the public to represent the interests of many different constituencies.

The people representing us at all levels of government cannot do their jobs effectively in a vacuum. Elected officials depend on the support of their constituents to provide helpful information to be used in the decision-making process. They are interested in our opinions as to how they should vote on bills, which legislation they should propose and support and which bills to reject or modify. It is important for elected representatives to understand how issues and possible legislative decisions will have a direct impact on the program and the lives of their constituents.

Effective communication may be the most essential ingredient of our form of government. Elected officials communicate to the public in a variety of ways — through newsletters, speeches, debates, through reports in newspapers and on radio and television, by the legislation they sponsor, and how they vote.

Adult educators must communicate effectively and consistently to their representatives at all levels of government — through letters, telephone calls, direct personal contact, active participation in the political process, and by voting.

An adult education association must be actively involved in representing adult education interests with local, state, and federal government officials. An effective association must be careful in choosing issues that are a priority for the organization and ensuring that the majority view of association members is represented.

No matter how effective an association may be, the personal commitment of the membership is the key to enhance the credibility and clarity of the association and to provide the grassroots support necessary for success. As individuals we must be willing to spend time, energy, and resources in developing information network coalitions, contacts and credibility. Lobbying techniques that allow face to face contact produce the best results. The result will often be one of compromise developed through trade-off. Lobbying is an art not a science. To become a great artist requires hardwork and practice combined with skill and luck. The future of adult education depends on our developing individuals who are artists in the political game.

REFERENCES

1. Symington, James W. "The Right to Petition — How To Exercise It." *Maryland Adult Educator*, Volume 3, #1, 1981.
2. Halperin, Samuel *A Guide For The Powerless — And Those Who Don't Know Their Own Power.* Washington D.C.: The Institute for Educational Leadership, 1981.
3. Whaples, Gene C. and Dorothy Waugaman, "Lobby is Not a Four-Letter Word," *Lifelong Learning: The Adult Years*, Volume 5, #8, April 1982.
4. Berry, Jeffrey M. *Lobbying for the People.* Princeton, New Jersey; Princeton University Press, 1977.
5. Levitt, Morris J. and Eleanor G. Feldbaum, "Council Members, Lobby and Interest Groups: Communication and Mutual Perceptic Local Politics," *Journal of Voluntary Action Research*, 4, and 2 (1975).
6. Porter, H. Owen. "Legislative Experts and Outsiders." *Journal of Politics,* 36, 3 (1974).
7. *Plugging In To Washington: How To Communicate With Congress.* American Society of Association Executives. Washington, D.C., 1980.
8. Waugaman, Dorothy O. and Gene C. Whaples "Effectiveness of Voluntary Citizen Advocacy Activities." Paper presented at Adult Education Research Conference, Ann Arbor, Michigan, 1979.

Status of Women

Phyllis M. Cunningham

Professor, Adult & Continuing Education
Northern Illinois University; Co-editor, **Adult Education**

The Carnegie Council of Policy Studies in Higher Education (1980)[1] predicts a 23 percent decline in the traditional age (18 to 24) student by 1997. This same group forecasts an increasing participation in higher education by students over 25, women, and minority groups. One third of all college students are at least 25 years old and the number of women in community colleges is 53 percent and slightly less than 50 percent in four year colleges. The number of women 35 and older enrolled in college has doubled since 1972.

This quiet revolution, beginning in the early sixties, has provided an opportunity for community colleges, 4 year colleges, and universities to participate in broad social changes affecting not only women but also men and the institutions within society. Adult continuing educators could play an especially important role by providing comprehensive programming for reentry women and by assisting their institutions in making changes to prevent either overt or covert sexism. Responding to the needs of reentry women simply to meet institutional needs to replace clientele and generate credit hours is an alternative response which in the long run may be detrimental to a reputation for long range quality programming, a reputation which most institutions wish to have.

There are examples already which have developed in the last decade where administrators and programmers have attempted to exploit this new clientele by simply recycling unimaginative and routine offerings. There is, in this approach, little understanding of the special circumstances and problems which surround the returning women students and how their desire for more education is linked and intertwined with major value and social changes occuring in the larger society. Women's reentry programs which take these factors into account are needed by women fully as much as higher education institutions need women to utilize their capacities.

REENTRY FACTS
Facts Affecting Women's Reentry Programs — In recent assessments of women's reentry programs, it has been noted that emerging quality programs have begun to change their programming emphases. Many college administrators now recognize that the "guilded cage" phenomena, where it was assumed the reentry women were typically white, middle class, middle-aged, bored by the empty nest and seeking education for enrichment, was a totally inadequate conception on which to base programming.

The major factors which should be considered prior to developing a women's reentry program are trends regarding women as worker, women as provider, women's unique responsibilities, and institutional barriers for women reentering school.

Most women returning to school have as a major goal employment, or already employed, enhancement of career opportunities. Consider these facts:
1. During the 1970's women joined the labor force at the rate of one million per year.
2. Fifty-two percent of all women aged 16 or older are in the labor force.
3. Presently, the average woman can expect to work 34 years (average male — 41 years).
4. For women aged 25-54 participation in the work force is expected to increase to 70 percent in the eighties.

These data indicate that more women are now working and the trend is upward. The movement of women into the labor force is not always by choice but more and more is a necessity to bolster family income or as the single provider of the family.
1. In 1978 there were 8 million female heads of household, an increase of 54 percent over the last decade; 14 percent of all families are headed by a woman.
2. Two thirds of all working women are single, widowed, divorced, separated or have husbands earning under $10,000 annually.
3. By 1990, 75 percent of all wives will be working outside the home.
4. Fifty-six percent of all women in the labor force are married and living with their husbands.
5. Sixty-seven percent of all women 35 or older enrolled in school in 1978 were also in the work force.

These data show that not only are most women working and many out of need or to enhance income, but that many of these women have home responsibilities which they must carry as they prepare or retrain for work.
1. Sixty-three percent of families headed by a woman include children under 18.
2. The fastest growing segment of the labor force during the seventies were married women with husbands present and mothers with school aged children.
3. In 1978, more than half (16.1 million) of all mothers with children under 18 were in the labor force. About 5.4 million of these mothers had children under 6.
4. Full-time women workers earn 59 percent of what men earn. This wage gap is attributed in part to occupational segregation — consigning women to low-paying work.
5. The increase in single parent homes headed by women in conjunction with the wage gap has led to what is now being called the feminization of poverty.
6. There are an estimated 3 million displaced homemakers, women in their middle years (35-64) who have been deprived of their traditional role by

the loss of a spouse through separation, death, divorce, or abandonment. Seventy-five percent of these women are over 40 with an annual income of less than $5,000.
7. Minority women having a dual status may encounter double discrimination. Barriers to reentry into education on the average are greater for this group than for white women.

Institutional Obligations — At this point it should be clear that educational institutions must be prepared to provide for a very different type of student than the traditional student in a women's reentry program. Many women will be goal oriented wishing to gain a good paying secure job. Some now working in low paying jobs will seek retraining to prepare for jobs which provide income commensurate with their responsibilities. More minorities are returning to school to increase their social mobility. Many if not most of these women will be mothers and may require assistance to handle child care. Some may have husbands and children who have had little preparation for the changing role of wife and mother. This lack of preparation may place strains on both the returning student as well as the family of the student. Again institutional recognition of this problem and provision of services or referral to assist the student may be required.

Women reentering educational programs not only have special personal circumstances that often cause barriers to enrollment but the institutions/society to whom they turn for help may present barriers to reentry women as well. The greatest percentage of these reentry students are in public community colleges but the number attending four year institutions doubled between 1973 and 1978. Part time enrollment of women, most of whom are past the traditional college age has doubled each year for the past several years and between 1975 and 1978 women students aged 27 to 35 years of age rose 187 percent.

It would seem patently clear that educational institutions need this persuasive and powerful surge of women, who for whatever reasons, are seeking new opportunities and exploring differing options through reentry into formal education. However, women who have found institutions more than willing to accept their tuition check or apply for special funds created to bring them educational equity, have also found these same institutions not as willing to identify and seek to change institutional inequities or barriers.
1. Although 51 percent of all students are women only 16 percent of high level educational administrators and 26 percent of faculty are women.
2. Minority women students find even fewer role models employed in these important faculty and administrative roles than women as a group.
3. Some administrators develop and schedule programs as if reentry women were a monolithic group — thus programs of the "guilded cage" variety perpetuate the idea that reentry women are "consuming" education as a spare time hobby.
4. Curriculums, instruction, and counseling has often been shown to be sexist, yet few institutions recognize the need to provide inservice to

college personnel who either refuse to see or are not conscious of sexual bias.
5. Child care costs must be reasonable and convenient, and travel costs need to be minimized in order for many women to take college courses. Many college faculty and support personnel continue to conceptualize instruction and services as a 9 to 5, Monday to Friday activity, as if students were full time and comparatively free of home responsibilities.
6. Because reentry women are adult and many operating on slim margins of time and money, they often bring a wealth of experience as well as a goal orientation which could be served well by non-traditional degree programs which recognize experiential learning. Many educational institutions have, and without sacrificing quality, changed to meet the needs of new students — however, most have not.

Women in large numbers are and have been reentering colleges; these women are increasingly career oriented, many out of necessity of economic survival; these same students require different types of support systems. Further, it has been pointed out that educational institutions need this new clientele but changes are required to reduce barriers to participation for many women.

PROGRAMMATIC OPTIONS

Continuing educators within colleges and universities can be key people in the development of broad-based comprehensive women's reentry programs. Many women, recognizing their need for more education, yet having been away from school for some time, are not sure of either what is available or what they need. Many will want to start part time with a course close to home; some will need to have an assessment of their skills; still others may wish to have a vestibule type program which allows them to reorient themselves to career options and possible routes to specific goals. Among potential reentry students are other women who must be actively recruited because of their own self doubts regarding their ability or because of negative impressions of schooling and educational institutions. The above factors point up the importance of close community ties, extension offerings, and orientation/assessment mechanisms, all of which are logical responsibilities for continuing educators.

Recruitment — Alerting women to opportunities provided by a college requires a knowledge of the differing types of women who are potential students. Accordingly, recruitment strategies should be tied to the ability of the institution to provide for these special groups. Special populations have been identified as: minority women (Asian, Pacific American, Black, Hispanic, American Indian), single parents, displaced homemakers, older women, disabled women.

Each of these groups represent special barriers, either because of personal circumstances or inappropriate stereotyping, which must be overcome. For example, Asian Pacific women, often classified as the model minority group, are often assumed, if they are Japanese, Chinese, or Korean to be well educated and economically successful. In actuality many of this group are underemployed and some Pacific/Asian women's groups attribute this fact to the stereotype that they are perceived as being passive, content to work in isolation, and not desirous of management responsibility.[2]

On the other hand, displaced homemakers, as a group, may more often than their peers represent persons who never expected to have to support themselves or their families. Self doubt, lack of salable skills, and a paucity of knowledge regarding both the educational and work world may characterize this group. Recruitment efforts which not only inform but are directed toward addressing these barriers will have the most success.

Many of these special populations have representative community or national organizations which can be most helpful in developing programs and recruiting strategies which address the special concerns of potential reentry women. A list of such groups is available from the Project on the Status and Education of Women, Association of American Colleges.[3]

The importance of vestibule (local) programs in recruitment and retention of special populations within women desiring reentry cannot be disregarded. Many special populations may have unusually high self-doubts and/or institutional distrust to prevent them from ever appearing on campus. Orientation programs cosponsored by community groups with which the population is familiar can assist and ease reentry. Some groups have special requirements such as basic skills training and studentship skills which can be introduced through specialized off-campus formats which are then closely articulated to campus programs. One creative and highly successful venture sponsored by a California community college sent two busses into a Latino community. One bus was equipped as an informal lounge in which the women could sit, drink coffee, get acquainted, and discuss within the group options provided for them at the college. Their children could go into the second bus to play, freeing the mother from child care. Eventually mothers were studying in the bus and finally were bussed to campus for the transition to a campus program.

Assessment and Counseling — Many institutions have found that provision for a center for returning women on campus is highly desirable because of a constellation of requirements required by adult women students and their special populations. To the extent that assessment and counseling services can be provided in a place where women can gather on campus and find natural opportunities for day-to-day institutional as well as peer support, the ongoing needs for dispelling fears as well as interpreting the complexities of the campus and the work world can be met. The operation of such a center is well worth the investment according to many returning women since it represents one place on campus where women's concerns are central.

However assessment and counseling (career, financial, personal) is done, it is important that both counselors and tests are carefully screened for sex bias. Sexist attitudes found in the larger society permeate all institutions and many problems can be avoided if administrators are sensitive to the concerns of women regarding equitable treatment.[2]

Although individual assessment and counseling are absolutely basic to a women's reentry program, systematic provision through special group offerings on non-traditional careers for women, assertiveness training, preparation of resumes, interviewing for a job can assist women with ongoing concerns. Time management has been identified as an important need for returning women since many are carrying unusually heavy responsibilities at home and/or at work.

A number of studies, mostly descriptive, have been done on reentry women which provided a base for developing counseling programs for these groups. Two excellent references, one general and the other especially looking at women's studies in the community colleges, review this research.[4] The works of Hooper and Rice reviewed by Scott[5] show how important the family situation is for success to the educational efforts of women. In their work it becomes clear that women who have the support of their families, both emotional and practical, are able to better negotiate reentry into college. Assistance in this problem could be offered through group counseling or peer counseling programs.

Curriculum — Special curricular needs for reentry women are often overlooked since curriculum has already been developed for the credential or degree that most women are seeking. However, there are curricular issues which do occur. Some women believe that a woman studies program is essential in some form to properly deal with sex bias and raising consciousness of both faculty, counselors, and students on women's oppression, women's history, and women's political concerns. Although, everyone does not agree with this statement and some subject matter specialists oppose such a position, there is merit in at least considering the pros and cons raised by this concern.

There is ample evidence which speaks to past discrimination against women in educational settings (routing women away from the hard sciences and math courses, counseling women into traditional service careers, neglecting women's contributions to the study of history, science, and government, discounting women students' participation in the classroom) and in the work setting (unequal pay, limited employment opportunities, limited promotion to management and power positions). It seems reasonable to suggest that: (1) such inequities do not disappear overnight, (2) both men and women have internalized these social attitudes, (3) institutional arrangements (which are invented by these same people) suffer from inadequate assumptions regarding women.

Accordingly, either earlier or later, the importance of righting these inequities will have to be faced. Women's studies is one way of addressing these concerns. Presently over 53 community colleges have inaugurated women's studies programs while the Association of American Colleges have identified over 300 curriculum projects in mathematics, sciences, and engineering for women.[2] The least that can be done by any college is to critically assess its curriculum content, and to provide an ongoing consciousness raising for counselors and faculty on the equitable treatment of women.

Another curricular issue arises from format rather than content. Returning women were a major cliental group that non-traditional education (NTE) initiatives attempted to serve. NTE, as one dimension of their activity, attempted to find new formats for awarding credentials and degrees. From these efforts, the Council for the Advancement of Experiential Learning (CAEL) was formed and is available to help educators develop non-traditional formats to assist returning students.[6] Weekend colleges and adult degree programs are two new formats which have been added to the more accepted idea of simply extending traditional campus offerings into the community. St. Xavier's University (Chicago) has an exemplary weekend college program developed by the College of Continuing Education. In this program, women in nursing, for example, can upgrade their qualifications by attending weekend courses in which instruction from regular faculty and services of support personnel (admissions, registration, and counseling) are on campus to serve them in the same way that traditional students are served in traditional hours.

DePaul University (Chicago) developed a New School for Learning which is a free standing special adult Bachelor degree program available at three locations. Women entering this program find a competency based degree program organized for and limited to adult students which takes into account relevant competencies obtained in earlier college work or through non-formal learning experiences. This time shortened degree, depending on the amount of former learning, stresses student involvement and responsibility for designing of the educational program. Both of these programs are comprehensive programs which show major reduction of institutional barriers to the reentry woman student.

Format innovation often is accompanied by other types of innovation. Several institutions have inverted curriculum approaches to better engage adults by placing more practical courses first in the program followed by courses dealing with conceptual explanations or integrating general theories. Many non-traditional AA and BA and most graduate degrees incorporate experiential learning as a standardized method of obtaining credit and provide this opportunity through stringent evaluation of former learning or college sponsored experiential learning.

Special Concerns — Thus far, recruitment, counseling and assessment, and curriculum issues have been discussed for reentry women. These major concerns for quality in a women's reentry program can only have meaning if the program is assessable and articulates with either further training or the world of work.

Although accessibility was touched on in terms of non-traditional offerings the provision of traditional programming at hours and places convenient to working women needs to be addressed. Most community colleges have reduced these barriers by opening up their campuses in the evening and occasionally around the clock. Many universities are addressing this problem as well but have been less flexible in providing for the services of the registrar, bookstore, counseling to evening campus and off campus students.

To solve these problems phone in registration has been organized by some campuses with evening registration services available in registration periods. Flex-time arrangements for campus personnel have allowed some institutions to provide minimal if not optimal services of the bookstore and counseling department. A staffed women's center open whenever students are having classes is another way of trying to maximize reentry women students' services.

Available, accessible, and affordable child care is an additional requirement for many reentry women and one the institution can assist in providing. A child care center on campus is one option; working with community agencies or referral to community resources is another option. A third possibility is to assist women needing these services to organize themselves into developing some mutualy satisfactory assistance.

In other arrangements, consortiums of colleges and universities have developed a full-time independent women's/adult counseling center in which a constellation of services are made widely accessible and the cost is shared among institutions. Examples of such programs are the Minnesota Planning and Counseling Center for Women and CLEO (Compact for Lifelong Educational Opportunities).[7]

Articulation with other educational institutions and the world of work is one other important aspect of women's reentry programs. Since most women returning to school are preparing for work or upgrading themselves, there is a need to not only make career planning and exploration an ongoing part of the program but there is also a need to assist in job placement. The regular services of the career planning and placement office is a first step for cooperative effort. Providing for campus recruiting visits during evenings is a possible way of introducing students to potential employers. Placing students in internship positions in a job situation similar to one desired is a way of enhancing qualifications which can be placed on a resume. A job placement counselor who systematically builds relationships with possible employees and provides information and placement information to students about to graduate is another way of assisting students to find jobs. Again a women's center which regularly provides counseling and knows the students and their abilities can be helpful in assisting students in appropriate job placement. Since some women may be entering the work force for the first time, sensitive assistance in job entry is most important.

SUMMARY

The opportunities for institutions to provide strong reentry programs for women has been documented in terms of need from the perspective of both institutions of higher education and women. The special role that continuing education can play in extending courses, experimenting with format, arranging for support services, development of campus women's centers and women's studies programs, as well as lowering institutional barriers are extremely important. Hopefully, institutions of higher education will continue to develop comprehensive programs for reentry women which meet their special requirements. The ability to restructure the shape of the institution to meet changing needs of students may be the ultimate test of survival for many campuses during the next decade.

REFERENCES

1. Fisher-Thompson, Jeanne and J. A. Kuhn. *Reentry Women: Relevant Statistics.* Washington, D.C.: Project on the Status and Education of Women, Association of American Colleges, April, 1981.
2. Hall, Roberta. *Re-entry Women: Special Programs for Special Populations.* Washington, D.C.: Women's Educational Equity Act Program, Project on the Status of Women, Association of American Colleges, 1981.
3. Ibid. A list of national agencies and community groups appears in the above reference.
4. a. Elovson, Allana. *Women's Studies in the Community College. Women's Studies Monograph,* Washington, D.C.: National Institute of Education, February, 1980.
   b. Scott, Nancy. *Returning Women Students: A Review of Research and Descriptive Studies.* Washington, D.C.: National Association of Women Deans, Administrators and Counselors, 1980.
5. Ibid., pp. 20-21.
6. Council for the Advancement of Experiential Learning, Lake Front N., Suite 300, Columbia, MD 21044 (301) 997-3535.
7. CLEO, 37 South 16th St., Philadelphia, PA — 19102.

Continuing Education in the Department of Defense

Israel Tribble

Associate Vice Chancellor for Academic Support, State University System of Florida, former Director of Voluntary Education, Office of the Assistant Secretary of Defense, Department of Defense.

Continuing education in the Department of Defense (DoD) is referred to as off-duty postsecondary education. Another term frequently used is voluntary education because the military services make these educational opportuntities available and the servicemembers participate on a voluntary basis.

Voluntary education has come of age since the advent of the All Volunteer Force (AVF) in the early 1970's. The present configuration of off-duty postsecondary education in the Military Services can be most notably traced to the decade of the fifties. The 1960's and 1970's were both decades of decided program growth that has served to heighten the visibility of this military activity. The early part of the decade of the seventies saw the creation of the AVF, which spawned a new and more fertile environment for educational program growth and acceptance. Prior to the AVF, these programs were viewed by many as nice to have, but not necessarily essential. In the AVF era, it can now be effectively argued that these programs are an integral part of military activity and central to the quest for improving the quality of life for all military personnel and their family members.

Postsecondary education in the military began to receive some careful national scrutiny during the latter part of the decade of the seventies. Not unlike American higher education in general, growth increased the visibility and vulnerability of postsecondary education in the military. The Education Commission of the States (ECS) became the first to examine these programs in 1977 and found them in need of improvement. Further, the report from ECS stated that there was an important role for states to play in off-duty education and that the Military Services could cooperate.

The next national criticism was levied in 1977 by Kenneth H. Ashworth, who charged that the system was incestuous and had a tendency to offer the least demanding programs. He also expressed concern over institutions crossing into other states for the purpose of providing educational programs to the military. Mr. Ashworth felt that the regional accrediting associations were not doing enough to police the off-campus activities of member institutions, and that the states would thus be forced to take a more aggressive posture regarding the issue.

Stephen K. Bailey also, in 1979, presented the results of the visits he made to thirteen military bases in 1978 in the Continental United States (CONUS). Mr. Bailey found serious weaknesses throughout the system and felt that quality control was seriously lacking. The Department of Defense (DoD) then took the next step and sponsored a case study of twenty-five installations, both in CONUS and overseas. What eventually became known as the COPA report was released in 1980. This report corroborated many of the previous criticisms of voluntary education programs.

As a direct result of the recommendations of the COPA study, DoD significantly revised the policy directive 1322.8 Voluntary Educational Programs for military personnel. The revision reflects a new emphasis on qualitative program elements as well as a quality control system. It specifies the various roles to be played by those responsible for the quality of the programs, such as the Services, installation commanders, education services officers (ESOs), institutions, state approving agencies, and regional accrediting groups. The revised directive also requires the Military Services to issue implementing regulations to assure that the new practices and requirements are distributed to all at the installation level.

Predicting the future in any environment can be hazardous. Futurists in the military education business are not plentiful; however, futuristic thinking should be done about where voluntary education might be by the end of the 1980s and, possible, by the turn of the century. This kind of thinking requires an assessment of where on-base postsecondary education has been, where it is at present, and where it might be headed.

The fulfillment of the educational promise made to servicemembers is an important goal for the Department of Defense. Some ranking officers and others in higher education feel that there are a number of programs of questionable quality operating on military installations. It is important to examine both the positive (what is) and normative (what should be) reality of voluntary education programs, and then chart a future course that will serve the best interests of servicemembers.

There are a number of societal assumptions and realities that should be discussed when deliberating about the future of on-base postsecondary education:

1. Educaton still represents, to the vast majority of people in American society, the most direct route to a better job, economic security, better opportunity for one's family, and social and economic mobility.

2. Higher education, as an American institution, is established and possesses within it an inordinate inertia that will probably ensure its existence for many generations to come. As much as things change; they somehow stay the same.

3. Higher education will continue to be more consumer-oriented because of the financial problems that surround it and the demographic changes that will impact on the total system.

4. An education through the postsecondary level (first two years of college in particular) is perceived as a right rather than a privilege by the American polity.
5. The growth and obsolescence of knowledge will continue at an exponential rate.
6. There will be a greater acceptance of the proposition that people do learn informally (outside of the traditional school setting) as well as formally.

Military and civilian educators must examine the above assumptions and include them in any planning matrix developed for present or future programming. These assumptions form a viable framework for formal discussions about philosophy and pedagogy as they relate to postsecondary programs on military installations.

Higher Education Context — The Carnegie Council in Three Thousand Futures developed contrasting predictions of the following twenty years in higher education.[1]

One view suggests that enrollments will fall dramatically, causing colleges and universities to compete more than ever for the fewer available students, in destructive ways — including false advertising, easy academic credits, "soft" courses, and grade inflation. In response, controls will increase at the federal, state, and institutional levels. Student consumerism will lead to lower standards of academic conduct and quality. Colleges will fight new educational technology and drive it into commercial channels as a way of protecting turf.

Another view suggests that enrollments will not fall as drastically, but rather might even increase. Other students and foreign students will replace the declining 18-21 cohort. Higher education will hold its share of the Gross National Product (GNP) at 2.1 percent, thus making almost universal access possible. Faculty members will place institutional interests above their personal interests. Students will be thoughtful consumers who will demand and select the best programs at the best institutions. The private sector will lose its weakest institutions, but will emerge stronger. The job market will improve for college graduates. New technology will supplement older forms of instruction but will not replace them. The discipline of contradiction will force institutions to turn their energies to the quality of education.

Regardless of which of these predictions eventually comes to pass, there are some cautions for military on-base education — raising the question of whether it will be part of the problem or part of the solution. Whatever happens in higher education as a whole will have a specific parallel impact on military efforts at postsecondary education.

The Promise — The Department of Defense has directed that postsecondary opportunities for servicemembers shall be provided on military installations, and that these opportunities shall be comparable to those provided in the

Continuing Education in the Department of Defense

civilian sector.[2] Further, these programs should enhance military effectiveness, prepare servicemembers for upward mobility in the Armed Forces, and lay the foundation for postservice careers.

Additional purposes of providing postsecondary educational opportunities to servicemembers should be to develop their learning processes, enabling them to positively set and accomplish realistic, obtainable goals; and to promote both individual and group self-confidence while fostering a deep appreciation for freedom and equality of opportunity. These values are particularly essential in a military environment.

Given the fact that each Service and, consequently, each military installation, has a specific mission related to the defense of the United States, it is not inconceiveable that both military and educational objectives can be accomplished simultaneously. A better-educated servicemember will substantially enhance the combat effectiveness of his or her unit while either preparing for a postservice career or acquiring the advanced training needed for career opportunity.

Voluntary Education Report Card — When voluntary education and professional development education are combined, the Department of Defense operates the largest postsecondary program in the world. Since the advent of the All Volunteer Force (AVF), postsecondary programs have received a significant boost. Not only have the voluntary education programs become a higher priority at the command level, but they have also been accorded national importance, as reflected by the increasing amount of dollars made available by Congress. (See Figure 1)

	Appropriated Funds (Dollars in Millions)			
	1965	1970	1975	1980
Army	10.5	21	31.8	81.6
Navy	.5	1.3	4.3	6.6
Air Force	4.9	4.6	8.9	16.8
Marine Corps	—	—	—	1.0

Figure 1

If a twenty year analysis is made of voluntary education[3] along two variables, enrollment and cost, one can readily demonstrate significant development. For example, the Navy in 1965 had over 20,000 enrollments at a cost of $5 Million by 1970 they had quadrupled to 84,541 enrollments at a cost of $6.6 Million. The Air Force in 1965 had 189,946 enrollments at a cost of $4.9 Million, and by 1980 had doubled to 322,986 enrollment at a cost of $15.8 Million. The Army shows 201,085 enrollments for 1980 at a cost of $81.6 Million; by 1981, expenditures had increased to $107 Million, with approximately 75 percent going to institutions of higher learning who provide services and programs.

The Office of the Secretary of Defense (OSD) in the fall of 1981 directed a program review of 30 selected educational installations in the Pacific and European Commands. The review team included both the Services and the civilian academic community, representing the broadest based review ever conducted. The purposes of the visits were to determine compliance by the Services to DoD Directive 1322.8, test a conceptual model for a program review, and discuss options about the acquisition of educational services.

Preliminary findings suggest that the Services are in basic compliance with the directive. However, consistent weaknesses were found in the conduct of needs assessments. Education Services Plans (ESP) often had no relationship to needs assessments. Facilities were typically a problem throughout the commands and relief through the military construction programs did not appear promising. Command support was quite strong, with clear evidence that the programs were a priority on most installations. While voluntary education programs have clearly progressed from their position in the late seventies, improvements are still required.

The Issue of Quality Control — Quality control is a joint responsibility shared by the DoD, the Services, postsecondary institutions, the states, and regional accrediting associations. But even with shared responsibility, the proverbial buck stops at DoD. DoD has the responsibility of delineating a desired level of quality, and developing procedures and standards that will provide the necessary policy guidance to the Services for its achievements.

Off-campus quality control begins with a program operation that is consistent with on-campus practice. Central in the process is the proper administrative structure supervising all aspects of the program. Institutional processes must include built-in evaluation mechanisms spelled out in the agreements between the Services and participating institutions. In tandem with a precisely defined system of operation, careful orchestration and management by the Education Services Officer is critical; along with the commander, the ESO is responsible for all that the program does or fails to do.

The issue of quality in higher education is an elusive subject, one that is hard to define because quality, like beauty, is in the eye of the beholder. The Services must focus resources on the development of better work statements that articulate specific outcomes as evaluation measures. The evaluation of input measures is not sufficient although absolutely necessary in voluntary education. The issue of quality is a multifaceted one that requires responses from a variety of participants described above.

Directions for the 1980's — Quality control is seen as a critical issue for the 1980's with joint responsibility being shared by DoD, Services, institutions, accrediting associations, state government approving agencies and the servicemembers who sometimes get left out of the process. The 1980's should be a period devoted to the consolidation of gains, the reduction of losses and the refinement of the complex system of postsecondary programs that exists under the aegis of the DoD.

During the past twenty years, voluntary education programs in the military have made remarkable progress. But they have not assumed an integral part of the organizational and program structure in the majority of sizeable military communities. Support at the command and installation levels appears very strong, albeit follow-through is sometimes uneven. More proactive management by ESO's will insure a basic level of quality. Investigating program delivery on a systematic and regular basis, a proactive management strategy, can serve as a preventive measure. Voluntary education requires a myriad of relationships. These support mechanisms and systemic interrelationships may mean more than increased financial resources when they are well conceived and professional. The relationship of the needs assessment to the Education Services plan at each installation should be carefully reviewed to assure that the programs are not merely operating on historical precedent rather than current and future needs.

Many military personnel and civilian academics have expressed the opinion that voluntary education programs are credit and degree "giveaways." Whether the opinion is true or false may be unimportant; the fact that it is said warrants the attention of military and civilian educators. It is important to recognize the part DoD may have played in the development of such an opinion and begin to find ways to promote a different and more positive image. The civilian academic community needs to be reassured that the Services do not violate acceptable academic standards. This does not preclude new modes of instructional delivery or nontraditional ways of learning. Better communication between the sectors would enable military educators to build even more credibility.

In refining the system, on-base programs have to be carefully reviewed to determine their appropriateness in meeting educational objectives, given the inherent military constraints of scheduling, facilities, time, place, and lack of traditional resources.

Graduate study should be reassessed with respect to quality of faculty, library resources and appropriateness. Some masters level work can be effectively carried out on a military installation; however, doctoral level work is inappropriate as an on-base activity. Serious questions can and will be raised about the availability of graduate faculty, research facilities, student time available for library research and financial viability for the institutions providing graduate programs.

Voluntary education programs have experienced growing pains but are emerging as a significant force in military life and American postsecondary education. The importance of these programs to the Services and to national defense efforts cannot be overstressed. The challenge for the eighties is to refine the system and make it as academically rigorous as the traditional on-campus environment, while preserving aspects of flexibility necessary in a military environment.

REFERENCES

1. Ibid, p. 2-4.
2. Department of Defense Directive 1322.8, Voluntary Educational Programs for Military Personnel. Department of Defense, Washington, D.C., 1980.
3. According to preliminary data gathered from the Military Services by OASD, DoD, 1982.

VOLUNTARY EDUCATION FACT SHEET
(FY 1981)

	ARMY	NAVY	MARINE CORPS	AIR FORCE	TOTAL DoD
Individual Enrollments					
Basic Skills	185,428*	25,377	4,781	15,418	231,004
High School Completion	25,800	4,020	4,835	1,133	35,788
(a) Non-credit/other/Group Study	244,105	3,948	N/A	33,176	281,229
(b) Foreign Language/English as a Second Language	114,767	N/A	N/A	4,799	119,566
					667,587
Postsecondary					
(a) Technical/Occupational	142,606**	5,437	460	61,672	210,175
(b) Undergraduate	28,297	51,650	23,150	221,338	324,435
(c) Graduate	24,059	1,302	670	44,929	70,960
					605,570

*Enrollment totals include all funded sources such as Operation and Maintenance, Adult Basic Education, State, etc.
**Army's figures include lower division liberal arts course enrollments.

Degree Completions					
Diplomas/Degrees					
(a) High School/GED	17,305	1,340	1,775	3,013	23,163
(b) AA	1,917	607	192	5,065	7,781
(c) BA/BS	1,125	116	356	2,219	3,816
(d) Graduate Degrees	1,837	N/A	311	1,870	4,018
					38,778

Expenditures					
Budget Support					
(a) Personnel Costs	26.9*	3.8	.17	16.5	47.3
(b) Tuition Assistance (Partial Entitlement)	15.8	6.9	2.0	18.8	43.5
(c) Contract Instruction (100% or Partial)	25.1**	6.0	N/A	1.9	33.0
(d) Veterans Administration Support	11.4***	N/A	N/A	18.3	29.7
					153.5

*This figure represents personnel costs as reported by Army Major Commands during FY 1981.
**This figure represents those 100 percent and partially funded programs such as basic skills, high school completion and some learning center activities.
***This figure represents VA and other sources as reported by Army Major Commands during FY 1981.

VOLUNTARY EDUCATION FACT SHEET

DANTES Fully Funded Testing					
(a) GED (overseas)	25,618	15,400	3,283	1,781	46,082
(b) SAT	2,170	5,177	764	1,571	9,682
(c) ACT	1,162	1,863	242	1,145	4,412
(d) CLEP-General	24,278	25,528	3,925	22,448	76,179
(e) CLEP-Subject	13,124	6,342	255	11,807	31,528
(f) DSSTs	7,862	3,575	186	11,262	22,885
(g) ACT/PEP	816	375	3	1,163	2,357
					193,125
Active Duty Totals*					
Officer	102,578	68,465	18,145	103,308	292,496
Enlisted	671,743	468,018	169,595	460,198	1,769,554
	774,321	536,483	187,740	563,506	2,062,050

*These figures were taken from DEFENSE/81, American Magazine

1. Basic skills refers to programs that are 100 percent funded by the Department of Defense (DOD). They are designed to upgrade individual performance of servicemembers through instruction in reading, math, English, English as a second language and composition. Beyond the remedial instruction, these programs support Service occupational specialties and are meant to impact job performance. They are also seen as preparing servicemembers for postsecondary study.
2. High school completion programs are designed to provide an opportunity for servicemembers to acquire either a high school diploma or a General Educational Development certificate. These programs are seen as having a direct impact on the quality of the overall force.
3. Non-credit programs are inclusive of a wide variety of special interests. These courses range from personal enrichment and leisure activities to highly technical job related programs. They also range from being mandatory as a supplement to job specific training to voluntary.
4. Postsecondary education programs are those credit courses that lead to certificates and degrees. The range of programs conducted by the Military Services are similar to those that are found across postsecondary education in the United States.

Approaching Needs Assessments

Stanley M. Grabowski

*Professor of Education, Boston University;
author and consultant to business & industry.*

All adult educators admit that needs assessment is an important aspect of program planning and marketing, but only some agree that needs assessment is a necessary first step in systematic program development. Not all administrators are convinced that resources spent on needs assessment are worthwhile; some claim they do not have the "luxury" of time and resources, while others simply do not know how to conduct an effective needs assessment.

Needs assessment is a term used to describe a variety of functions but is limited here to its function of market analysis. As such, it is a process to determine goals and objectives for an education program. whether a new program or an ongoing one.

Needs assessments serve several useful purposes: (1) as starting points for planning, (2) to give a sense of direction, (3) to justify starting or stopping a program, (4) to modify ongoing programs, (5) to evaluate an institution's goals and mission.

The first thing one realizes about undertaking a needs assessment is the vast array of options available. Needs assessments differ drastically depending upon factors such as: the nature, philosophy, goals and values of the agency or institution; the nature of the population served; the purposes of the program; available resources for conducting a needs assessment; what the needs assessment is expected to do. Needs assessments can be simple or complex, quick or time-consuming, inexpensive or expensive, formal or informal, subjective or objective, easy or difficult.

The way needs are defined will influence the scope of a needs assessment. Needs are often used interchangeably with interests, desires, wants, gaps or deficiencies, problems, goals, and objectives. Also, needs can be those of clients or potential clients, of sponsoring institutions and agencies, and of the community, although properly speaking only individuals have needs while institutions, agencies, and communities have problems.

A difficulty faced in needs assessment is keeping clearly in mind that there are distinctions, as well as overlaps, among **felt** needs, **ascribed** needs, and **real** needs. Felt or perceived needs are needs individuals identify for themselves. Ascribed needs are those an observer determines for individuals.

Real needs are those which individuals actually have whether they or others recognize them or not. Felt needs as well as ascribed needs may be real needs, just as real needs may be felt and ascribed. There is no guarantee that felt or ascribed needs genuinely reflect "societal" or real needs however much felt needs may be "real" to the individuals.

Felt needs may be only symptons of real needs. In any case, they must first be taken care of before real needs are met. Furthermore, involving the target clients in a needs assessment psychologically disposes them toward participation in the program when it is offered. Being involved in the needs assessment gives them a sense of belonging and ownership.

Still one must be aware that individuals responding to questions about their perceived needs may not always be able to express them clearly. Some may not wish to tell everything while others may say what they think the assessor wants to hear. In most cases, it will be difficult to measure the degree or extent of the different needs expressed by a number of individuals.

PLANNING NEEDS ASSESSMENT

In undertaking a needs assessment, one ought to follow a plan which in its simplest form includes several steps:

1. Ask why the needs assessment is being done; what is the purpose for doing it, and what use will be made of the results.
2. Answer these questions to dictate the scope and methodology of the assessment. For example, one would use different approaches — to increase the number of participants in a non-credit art program; to determine whether an existing program ought to be expanded; to investigate the feasibility of starting a new program for older adults in the community.
3. Decide whose needs are to be assessed, once the purpose for doing a needs assessment is clear. Often, this step may be readily seen when the purpose is clarified — but not always. For instance, in the last example given above, it is obvious that the needs of older adults are to be assessed but, even here, the question must be specified as to which older adults — all of them, those falling within certain ages, those in a particular socio-economic status, those who are confined to their homes or institutions. At other times determining the population to be assessed is more difficult such as in the example of increasing the number of participants in a non-credit art program.
4. Decide who will conduct the assessment. In most cases one or more staff members may entirely perform the needs assessment, but there may be times when a part of it or all of it may be farmed out to an outside consultant or agency. Time and budgetary constraints will usually limit the use of outsiders to monumental projects.
5. Select the appropriate technique(s) for conducting the assessment. Part of the selection encompasses when to do it and in what sequence. These decisions are not simple inasmuch as there are many options one must

consider. The choice of techniques will depend on factors such as those mentioned earlier, as much as upon the amount of data required, the amount of time and resources available, and the expertise of the assessors.

There are numerous ways available for conducting needs assessments. Before setting forth the techniques it may help to understand the various models which have been designed. Most of the existing models cluster into six categories:[1,2]

a. **Self-fulfillment** — these models appeal to individual's interests and desires on a random and selective basis.
b. **Individual appraisals** — individuals, on their own or in collaboration with others, determine their own learning needs.
c. **System discrepancy** — deficiencies or gaps are identified between the current condition and the desired state of individuals.
d. **Diagnosis** — unmet as well as met needs are examined to determine which deficiencies would be corrected.
e. **Analysis** — a direction of improvement is determined based on the given situation of individuals.
f. **Democratic** — groups of individuals specify needs through a group process such as consensus or voting.

Data Gathering Techniques — These six general categories can be specified further into discrete techniques for data gathering. Each of these techniques has advantages as well as disadvantages which have to be weighed in deciding whether to use one in preference to another, or whether to use a combination of techniques. Below is a partial list of data-gathering techniques:

Open-ended questions.

Item check lists — Individual selects — checks off — attributes from a list.

Monadic ratings — Individual rates each item on a uniform scale such as the Likert scale.

Paired companions — Individual indicates preference between a pair of objects.

Rank ordering — Individual ranks a list of objects in order of preference.

Discrepancy analysis — Individuals select between two conditions or states of affairs as possibilities of "what ought to be."

Multidimensional scaling — Individual arranges triads into the two most similar and again into the two most different objects.

Semantic differential — Individual rates objects on bi-polar objective scales.

Q-sort — Individual sorts objects into prearranged categories with set values.

Delphi — A group of people individually ranks a list of objects, then ranks the response and regulates the process several times to reach agreement.

Individual/group interviews, both structured and unstructured.

Advisory boards.

Projective techniques such as projective questions, word associations, picture completions and role playing

Simulation — Individual is shown a prototype or solution to a need and asked for reactions.

Participation observations — Assessor looks and listens for indicators of needs among potential participants.

Traces and wearspots — Assessor looks at usage and previous patterns of participation.

Critical incidents — Critical incidents of behavior are compiled and sorted by assessor.

Expert consultants — Assessor asks knowledgeable and experienced people to identify needs.

Performance review — Employee and supervisor complete and together review performance review forms and then agree on specific objectives for the employee.

Job and task analysis.

Evaluation results of program.

Minutes of meetings.

Psychographic research — The assessor studies the lifestyles of individuals by gathering information about their psychological and behavioral characteristics as a means of discerning their needs and interests.

It is recommended that whichever techniques are employed they be verified for validity and reliability. Validity, in simple terms, asks whether the instrumentation measures what it is meant to measure; is it able to obtain what you want to find out. Reliability refers to the consistency of responses the instrumentation evokes; to what extent will it get the same responses from the same individuals if it were repeated.

In conducting a needs assessment one must choose either the entire group or population to be effected by the potential program or a sample of the group. Other than in very limited circumstances, needs assessments are done on random or selected samples of identified populations.

6. Having selected the appropriate technique(s) for the assessment, the next steps include gathering the data, classifying, analyzing and interpreting the data, and finally ranking or prioritizing the data. Sometimes these steps can be performed by "eyeballing" the data, while at other times the data will have to be analyzed by computer. In

the analysis of data, where demographic information has also been obtained, it may be advisable to use a multiple type of factor analysis for a greater richness of findings.

The raw data from a needs assessment can be analyzed initially either into clusters or directly into discrete needs. Clusters can be more believable because they gather together several needs which indicate a direction.

Whether one clusters or begins the identified needs separately, the resulting list requires sifting for "educational" needs, those which can be addressed by some kind of learning experience. Needs assessments frequently yield needs which are beyond the scope or purview of an educational institution and are best set aside or called to the attention of those in the community better able to handle them.

The refined list of educational needs may require prioritization. This can be done in a sort of mechanical fashion by relying on numerical values of the results analysis — by some kind of weighting, or by the application of criteria. The prioritization is meant to indicate the most important needs in the light of the institution's values. mission, goals, and resources. Numerical strengths of identified needs are not always the ones which ought to be considered first in implementing programs. Generally, there is a limitation on time and resources available to deal with the final prioritized list of needs; administrative decisions will have to be made in selecting the needs for translation into programs.

Successful adult education administrators draw upon as many sources for program ideas as are available and appropriate. They use a building block approach starting with the tradition of the institution and including findings from research studies reported in the literature, the results of their own needs assessments of potential participants, and their own experiences.[3]

SUMMARY
Some final observation about needs assessments:
1. Be conscious of the danger of interjecting one's own biases and prejudices into the process. This can occur at several points; the selection of techniques, the choice of the sample population, the administration or use of the instrumentation, the analysis and interpretations of data, the prioritization of the list of needs. It may be advisable to have some outsiders check your decisions.
2. Ask someone with the required skills to help you in those aspects of the process where you are weak, for example, in the analysis of data.
3. Evaluate the needs assessment process to insure adequacy of the process and the usefulness of the results.
4. Understand that a needs assessment is not final but only tentative and must be on-going, at least in the sense that is is updated periodically.
5. Needs assessment is a tool at the disposal of an adult educator; it is a way to set goals, objectives, and programs. It cannot do everything to

guarantee a successful program, but it can be a big help. Surely a program started without an adequate needs assessment is at a much greater risk of failure than one properly assessed.

QUESTIONS AND EXERCISES

Show how your own philosophy of adult education would influence your choice of phenomena as worthy of scanning in seeking program ideas.

What characteristics ought an effective needs assessment have?

In what sense can a need be said to be both prescriptive and motivational?

Show how needs assessment is an empirical process.

Discuss how the determinants of images people have about an educational institution fit into a needs assessment.

What can an adult educator do to involve the community at large in doing a needs assessment for an educational program?

REFERENCES

1. Mocker, Donald W. and Spear, George E. "Needs Assessment," In Philip D. Langerman and Douglas H. Smith (eds.) *Managing Adult and Continuing Education/Programs and Staff.* Washington, D.C.: National Association for Public Continuing and Adult Education, 1979.
2. Pennington, Floyd C. (ed.) *Assessing Educational Needs of Adults.* New Directions for Continuing Education, Number 7, 1980. San Francisco: Jossey-Bass. Devoted to needs assessment.
3. McKenzie, Leon and McKinley, John (eds) "Adult Education: The Diagnostic Procedure" *Viewpoints,* Bulletin of the School of Education, Indiana University 49 (September 1973) No. 5. Entire issue devoted to needs assessment.
4. Kotler, Philip. "Consumer Analysis" in *Marketing For Non-profit Organizations,* Englewood Cliffs, N.J.: Prestice-Hall, 1975. pp. 123-159.
5. Nowlen, Philip M. "Program Origins" in Knox, Alan B. and Associates. *Developing, Administering, and Evaluating Adult Education.* San Francisco: Jossey-Bass, 1980. pp. 13-36.
6. Grady, Sandra C. *Assessing the Educationally Related Needs of Adults: A Practical, Low-Cost Approach by a Community College in Cooperation with the Public School System.* Washington, D.C.: American Association of Community and Junior Colleges. 1979.
7. George F. and Kemerer, Richard W. *How to Assess Needs for Community Instructional Services. A Guide for Adult Education Practitioners.* Department of Educational Leadership, School of Education. Tallahasee, Florida: Florida State University. 1980.

Advisory Committees

Dewey A. Adams

Professor and Chairperson, Comprehensive Vocational Education, The Ohio State University.

Samuel D. Morgan

Associate Professor, Community College and Vocational Education, Virginia Polytechnic Institute and State University.

The involvement of citizens in planning and promoting their own education is at the highest level in the history of public education. Though the actual development of curriculum and conducting of instruction remains primarily in the hands of professional educators, many aspects of the planning process, promotional activites and the evaluation process depend heavily upon citizen interest and active participation. If society is to perfect the ideal of a "Community of Scholars and Learners," a group more likely to enhance this goal is the citizens' advisory or consulting committee. The citizens' advisory committee is one means to plan, promote and progress with respect to community and/or adult continuing education.

The Community Education Movement — Community education is much broader and more inclusive than many in the field of adult education have been willing to concede. In reality, it is far more than adult education or even continuing education when defined in rather broad terms. Certainly educational activities for adults is a major aspect of the community education scene, but many other educational endeavors are accurately included in this arena. Numerous community activities for school-age youth and children, nursery school and kindergarten activities, community educational services and business and industry consulting activities are just a few of the other types of educational efforts which appear appropriately categorized as community education.

Roger Axford described community education as "People Helping People" and suggested that a true community school program would be active in the following things:
1. Family-centered education, building individual and family strength.
2. Recreational, educational, social and vocational development programs.
3. Community study and assessment with respect to strengths and weaknesses.

4. Leadership in planning and carrying out constructive community projects.
5. Assistances for the identification and resolution of community problems.
6. Coordination and cooperation among agencies involved in the education and community services process.

The list could be extended much further but these examples serve to reveal the great variety and importance of educational activities which are included in a community school approach. They serve also to suggest the crucial role of dynamic and creative leadership as the key to successful implementation of community education. Herein lies the role of the citizens' advisory committee as one of the foremost approaches to assuring the effective involvement of a large cross section of citizens in their own education process. Among the most important values of participation by citizen advisory committees in community and adult continuing education are:
1. Stimulation of local initiative.
2. Effective use of community competence and talent.
3. Provision of effective public relations.
4. Enhancement of change and innovation.
5. Improvement and enrichment of school and community life.
6. Enrichment of adult learning experiences.
7. Improvement in public understanding and support of community education.
8. Effective inservice education of professional faculty and staff.
9. Useful in identifying and evaluating part-time teachers and leaders for educational programs.
10. Provision of a sounding body for new and radical programs and processes in adult and community education.

DEMOCRATIC PHILOSOPHY

An early consideration in the organization and use of advisory committees in community and continuing education is an examination of beliefs with respect to citizen involvement. A number of questions may facilitate such an examination:
1. What do I believe about myself with respect to meaningful involvement of lay people in educational planning and evaluation?
2. Am I secure and willing to allow others to assist in the decision-making process?
3. Do I believe the involvement of others can make a difference?
4. Am I satisfied and complacent with respect to the present adult education program?
5. Do I believe that citizen involvement can help me grow?
6. What do I believe with respect to citizen ownership and control of public education?
7. Can I accept the representative nature of our democratic republic?

8. Do I believe that citizens possess the inherent right and privilege to be involved in adult education planning and evaluation?
9. Am I willing to accept and use the advice of citizen committees with respect to adult education programs?
10. Can I be open and free to share significant problems and decision-making issues about educational programs with citizen committees?

These are rather difficult and challenging questions, but if community education planners cannot respond positively to each question; it seems doubtful that an optimum level of success in using advisory committees in community education can be achieved.

Membership on Advisory Committees — There are different shools of thought with respect to membership on advisory committees for community and continuing education programs. One school of thought would support the notion of a completely random selection process which would leave the characteristics of members to chance. A second school of thought would emphasize a screening process through which there would be control of the kinds of persons selected. Other schools of thought would employ various selection methods between these extremes in order to achieve some optimum level of randomness and selectivity.

One trend in the selection of advisory committee members appears to be ths use of a screening committee. Such a committee is representative of the population from which the advisory committee is to be selected and its members are knowledgeable with respect to those citizens from which choices are to be made. For most effective use of the screening committee, nominations are gathered from many citizens in the clientele group. From these nominations, the screening committee will choose a slate of representative candidates and alternatives for advisory committee membership. Representativeness is based upon such factors as: race, sex, age, experience, geography, expertise, interests, community relationships. Alternatives are chosen in the event a first choice candidate prefers not to serve when contacted.

Research has not provided a final answer to the question of ideal membership, but experience has enabled us to specify some of the characteristics of advisory committee members who appear to have contributed importantly to community and continuing education programming. Among these characteristics are:

1. Interest in, and commitment to community education.
2. Civic mindedness and awareness.
3. Insight and cooperativeness.
4. Willingness and time to serve.
5. Expertise in some area of human behavior.
6. Willingness not to exploit membership.
7. Constructive attitude, personal integrity, tolerance of varying opinions.
8. Commitment and caring with respect to human growth and development.

Selection and Appointment of Advisory Committee Members — Once the question of method of selection has been decided, it seems important to include two steps in making the appointment of advisory committee members:
1. Telephone, personal visit or mail should be used to determine in advance of appointment if the selected candidate will be able and willing to serve. During this process, a significant amount of information about the role of the members of an advisory committee can be shared. Such information will greatly enhance the future work of the committee member, if the appointment is made.
2. The actual appointment should be made by a high ranking official in the education organization and the appointment letter should give a few details with respect to the expectations of members of the advisory committee. There should be an opportunity for the candidate to respond to the appointment. In most cases an organization meeting of the advisory committee at which time the new member can be inducted is specified in the letter of appointment.

OPERATION OF THE ADVISORY COMMITTEE
Orientation and/or Induction Training for New Members — New advisory committee members should receive induction training or orientation prior to beginning the process of giving advice. They need to understand well their new role and the community education program which they serve in order to be of maximum assistance in the planning and evaluation process. Several resources which may contribute to orientation are:
1. A community and continuing education advisory committee handbook.
2. Minutes of previous committee meetings.
3. Copies of community studies completed in previous years.
4. Constitution and/or bylaws of the committee.
5. Current operating policies and procedures.
6. A calendar of events and specific meeting times and places.
7. A plan for committee membership selection and rotation.
8. Names and addresses of all current members and related professional staff.
9. Program brochures, catalogs and other public information documents.
10. Suggestions for effective participation in educational activities by advisory council members.

During the orientation sessions which may extend over several meetings, the professional community and adult education program planner should make clear the advisory nature of the committee. The committee may advise on policy matters, but it is always the role of a policy-making body such as a board of education to enact policy. Advisory committees can make many other contributions in addition to giving of advice. They can serve as a two-way communications link between the program and the community, defend the program before the community, help keep the faculty, equipment, program, and facilities up-to-date, assist in selecting new faculty, and assist in evaluation of the community and adult education program.

Committee Meetings — Effective advisory committee meetings are the result of careful and extensive planning. Required are leaders who are good in leading discussions and drawing out the best ideas of the group. Planned agendas distributed prior to each meeting are helpful. Reminders of each meeting can enhance good attendance which is a must for effective committee work. Real and significant problems and issues for each meeting are important. Few advisory committees will have good attendance if committee meetings have no clear purpose and issues considered are of little significance.

Advisory committee meetings need not be held often, but regular scheduling of meetings seems to enhance member interest, commitment, and attendance. Many education advisory committees appear satisfied with monthly or quarterly meetings after the initial year of operation.

Minutes of advisory committee meetings should be kept; made available to each advisory committee member and selected professionals who need to be apprised of committee activities. Members should be furnished special binders for organizing and storing materials shared during advisory committee sessions. The minutes are filed in the institution for future reference.

The selection and use of advisory committee members as officers appears to be the prerogative of the adult education professional. Many education program planners have favored the election of a chairman, vice-chairman and secretary by the committee and the use of these officers in committee planning and operation. Some favor the professional serving as secretary. Regardless of preference there appears to be merit in the operation of a new advisory committee for a substantial period of time — 5 to 10 meetings — prior to the selection of officers. Members have an opportunity to become acquainted and the selection of effective officers appears to be enhanced.

Utilization of the Advisory Committee — Successful advisory committees are most often those which have expert leadership and direction from the professional staff responsible for the educational program. More often than not, self-directed advisory committees appear to fail. As the professional staff gives appropriate guidance to the activities of the advisory committee; involving the committee in important and relevant planning, decision-making, promoting and evaluating the educational programs, the value and contribution of the advisory committee to community education increases.

Often the first task of an advisory committee may be to assist with the development of policies for broad community education areas such as: (1) adult education, (2) consumer and family life education, (3) vocational adult education, (4) public service programs, (5) general adult education. Such involvement is particularly important if general policies do not exist in written form. The advisory committee can assist in the formulation and evaluation of policy statements which can be enacted later by the citizens' policy-making board.

Faculty recruitment is of special concern to many programs which employ large numbers of part-time faculty. Such is the case where there is interest and need for the establishment of an extensive, community-wide continuing education program. The advisory committee can assist quite well with the identification and selection of part-time teachers from business, industry, and the general community.

The advisory committee can be utilized in providing public information and support for the community education program. Through the informal contacts which committee members make in the community, through the process of opinion gathering by members, and through the process of sharing program information by members of the committee with key citizens in the community, substantial communication is established and strong program support is built.

Another important process to the life of an education program is recruitment of students. Many community college and area vocational school advisory committees have made this process one of their priority functions. When business and industrial firms are well represented on advisory committees and such members are utilized extensively, the program recruitment effort is greatly enhanced. In similar manner, job placement processes are greatly improved through advisory committee activity.

Yet another vital process in each program is that of evaluation. Few other community groups have the advantage of an advisory committee in contributing to this critical process. The advisory committee has the expertise to consider the needed product; the use of the product; the educational processes through which the candidate must go; the equipment, facilities and other resources necessary to support the program of training and the changes in the economic, social, and political community which might mandate changes in the program.

Evaluation of Advisory Committees — The process of evaluation of advisory committees includes assessment of effectiveness and contribution to the program, recognition of the committee's effort in behalf of the community education program and expressions of appreciation to each member for service to the program.

Some elements which may be included in a plan for continuing and periodic evaluation of committee members are:
1. Studies and recommendations made for program improvement.
2. Contributions to public information and communications about program activities.
3. Meetings held and a record of member participation.
4. Relationships established with faculty and staff.
5. Appropriateness of committee activities, effectiveness of committee officers.

6. Development and use of committee procedures, handbook, constitution and bylaws.
7. Actual recommendations for policy changes and/or additions.
8. Visits made to similar communities and educational programs.
9. Feelings of accomplishment expressed by members of the advisory committee.
10. Appraisal of committee work by the staff, faculty, community.

Appropriate recognition of advisory committee members for their service and contribution can do much to enhance the continuing success of the committee and its value to the continuing education program. There are numerous ways to recognize and show appreciation to members. Perhaps the most desirable way is to seek and accept their advice. Other ways include certificates of appreciation, letters of appreciation, mass media recognition, names in brochures, catalogs and other publications, and invitations to program functions.

Keys to Effective Advisory Council Operations — Most would agree that the best evidence of effective advisory council operation is positive community education outcomes. If community education is available, if people are being served well, if goals are being reached, if citizens are generally pleased with results, advisory council operation is probably successful. Yet there are some other things which professional staff can do to maximize use of an advisory council and to assure most effective council input into community and continuing education:
1. Opportunities can be provided for council members to initiate and make recommendations.
2. Professionals can listen to advice and recommendations of council members.
3. Appropriate responses can be given consistently to council advice and recommendations.
4. Recognition and visibility can be given to the advisory council.
5. Professionals can lead in developing an attitude of "shared activity" or "working as a team" for the community.
6. Professionals can promote a spirit of pride in the work of the council and the community education program.

SUMMARY

Community and continuing education can truly grow and prosper if there are viable advisory councils in operation for all programs and if advice is utilized appropriately in all aspects of each program.

When the professional staff is truly committed to the advisory committee philosophy; when the committee is comprised of ideal membership; when selection and appointment is accomplished democratically; when proper orientation and induction training is provided; when committees are used for appropriate purposes; when recognition of committee service is provided; no other structure seems to do as much for efficient and effective program operation as the advisory committee. Finally, working with community and continuing education advisory committees can enhance the growth of the professional faculty and staff and can give the education leadership a sense of pride and accomplishment in their work.

QUESTIONS AND EXERCISES

1. What benefits can be expected for community and continuing education when effective advisory councils are being utilized?
2. What suggestions would you offer a program administrator who is about to initiate an advisory council for his/her community education program?
3. What does it mean to be democratic with respect to working with an advisory council?
4. How would you compare and/or contrast community education and continuing education? Adult education?
5. How can advisory committees be used to promote coordination among the various groups working in community education?
6. How can advisory council activity enhance the inservice education of faculty and staff personnel in community and continuing education?

REFERENCES

1. Adams, Dewey A. *Review and Synthesis of Research Concerning Adult Vocational and Teacher Education.* Columbus: Eric Clearinghouse on Voc. and Tech. Education, The Ohio State University, 1972. VT 014 705.
2. Axford, Roger W. *Adult Education: The Open Door to Lifelong Learning.* Indiana, Pennsylvania: A.G. Halldin Publishing Company, 1980.
3. Cochran, Leslie H., L. Allen Phelps and Linda Letwin Cochran. *Advisory Committees in Action.* Boston: Allyn and Bacon, Inc. 1980.
4. Darkenwald, Gordon G. and Sharon B. Merriam. Adult Education: *Foundations of Practice.* New York: Harper and Row, Publishers. 1982.
5. Folley, Vern L. "Some Facts About Curriculum Advisory Committees." *Community and Junior College Journal.* April, 1974.
6. Knowles, Malcolm S. *A History of the Adult Education Movement in the United States.* New York: Robert E. Krieger Publishing Company, 1977.
7. Mayer, Leon A. "Organizing and Using Advisory Committees for Adult Education." *Adult Leadership.* April, 1971.
8. Virginia State Advisory Council on Vocational Education. *Involving Advisory Groups in Planning and Evaluating Vocational and Technical Education Programs.* Virginia State Advisory Council on Voc. Ed., Blacksburg, VA, 1973.

Competency Based Adult Education

Arnold Nored

*Director, APL Project,
University of Texas at Austin*

Elaine Shelton

*Manager, APL 3-D Project,
University of Texas at Austin*

Competency-based education (CBE) is a concept that has attracted widespread attention and has expanded rapidly into a wide variety of educational programs designed to meet adult functional needs. The current CBE movement apparently originated with the publication of ten elementary models for teacher preparation. This movement developed as a process by which teacher education could be made more accountable, as a response to increasing public disenchantment with education.

Pushed almost immediately into the political arena through widespread publicity by the media, a resistance to the movement has centered far more on the issue of teacher accountability than on an examination of the merits of the CBE process. Despite this continuing controversy, use of CBE in teacher education has grown rapidly, to the extent that it is mandated in a number of states, and with other states now considering such requirements. More important is the fact that the CBE movement has expanded into many other areas of education including vocational job training, various training activities conducted by business and industry, and professional training programs conducted by universities in the fields of business education, dentistry, law, human services, and liberal arts.

The United States Office of Education (U.S.O.E.) apparently had a broader application in mind for CBE than just teacher education. In 1969 the Commissioner of Education, James E. Allen, Jr., presented the "Right to Read Program." In his introduction Allen stated that about half the nation's unemployed youth between the ages of 16-21 were **functionally illiterate**. Similar statements were made in a memorandum to chief state school officers dated April 19, 1970, in which the Director of the Division of Adult Education Programs, U.S.O.E., invited submission of proposals for a research project leading to the establishment of an adult education system based on a

Competency Based Adult Education

systematic and accurate definition of **functional literacy**. In that memorandum the philosophy for a new system for adult basic education was first articulated:

> The challenge is to foster through every means the ability to read, write, and compute with the **functional competence** needed for meeting the requirements of adult living.

The emphasis of this definition is in its final phrase, 'requirements for adult living.' These requirements must be determined by an analysis of adult living rather than the common practice of attaching a grade equivalence to them. Existing grade equivalents cannot be effectively adapted to adult needs. This is not to say that school curricula do not prepare students for adult roles, but rather it says that the format in which they are presented to school attendees are not applicable to adult learning frameworks. A system of adult education must derive its own specific aims and have its own adult based curricula, methodologies, and materials.

The obvious intent of this U.S.O.E. memorandum was to engender proposals for research projects which would be designed to identify a set of competencies on which an identifiable system of education could be based — a **competency-based adult education** system.

THE ADULT PERFORMANCE LEVEL PROJECT

The Adult Performance Level (APL) Project grant was awarded to the Texas Education Agency in the Summer of 1971. The Agency, in turn, subcontracted the major portion of the work to the Division of Extension of the University of Texas at Austin. Subsequent grants were funded directly to the APL Project.

The Project was charged with three major objectives:
1. To redefine adult literacy in terms of the life-coping skills necessary for adults to function effectively in their daily lives within the milieu of contemporary U.S. society.
2. To develop a national assessment of skills.
3. To measure adult functional competency.

Almost two years were spent reviewing the literature, conducting extensive interviews with people in state and federal service agencies, attending numerous conferences on adult needs, and interviewing undereducated and underemployed adults. The research resulted in the specification of forty-two competencies which were identified as basic requirements for daily living. These forty-two competencies, or objectives, fell within a two-dimensional framework which represented the APL Project's definition of functional competency. The APL Project defines functional competency as the application of a set of skills (reading, writing, speaking, listening, viewing, computation, problem solving and interpersonal relatons) to a set of content areas (consumer economics, occupational knowledge, health, community resources and government and law. Figure 1 is a representation of this two dimensional matrix.

APL MODEL OF FUNCTIONAL COMPETENCY

	Consumer Economics	Occupational Knowledge	Health	Community Resources	Government and Law
Reading					
Writing					
Speaking, Listening, Viewing					
Problem-Solving					
Interpersonal Relations					
Computation					

Figure 1

Once the objectives had been specified, the Project staff developed an instrument to assess these specified competencies. Performance indicators were developed, field tested, and revised before being formatted into the APL Survey. The performance indicators were not traditional test items. Rather, they reflected actual situations or requirements encountered by adults in their everyday lives. For example, respondents were asked to fill out a check, read an excerpt from an insurance policy, interpret a graph, and calculate overtime pay.

The original APL Survey was administered to five representative samples of adults 18-65 years of age in the continenetal United States. The survey was completely random so that the findings could be generalized to the total adult populations of the U.S. Approximately one out of every five persons (19.7%) of the adults living in the continental United States) were found to be functioning with difficulty (APL 1 category); 33% of the U.S. adult populaton was found to be marginally competent (APL 2); while less than half — 46.3% — was found to be functionally competent (APL3).

THE GROWING MOVEMENT OF CBAE

"One out of every five American adults lacks the skills and knowledges to function effectively in the basic day-to-day struggle to make a living and maintain a home and family." So began the official announcement of the U.S. Commissioner of Education, Terrel H. Bell, on results of the APL research. Since October, 1975 when Commissioner Bell announced the results of the APL Research, great progress has been made in the area of CBAE. By the time the final report from the APL Project's natonal survey was issued in 1977, two-thirds of the states had already decided to implement some form of competency-based adult education, almost all of them based on the APL competencies. Within the next three years, seven major state/natonal-level studies had refined, expanded, and/or modified, but basically had left intact the original APL range of competencies.

The attendant nationwide publicity soon became as critical a factor in meeting the challenge of the root problem (functional incompetency) as was the other important ingredient — commitment of federal and state moneys in funding efforts to translating the research findings into programs. The Adult Education Act was amended in 1978 to reflect a functional literacy intent for the program. Many adult education programs throughout the United States are based in whole, or in part, upon the APL Functional Competencies.

Assessment instruments based upon the APL objectives were devloped and published by the American College Testing Program (ACT).

The APL curriculum, entitled "The APL Series: Coping in Today's Society," was devloped to assure that relevance to the learner's needs exists in everything he/she is asked to learn and that what is learned can be put to use immediately. Skills taught are those which apply directly to the APL objectives: (1) writing skills are taught in the context of filling out a job application or writing a letter to a public official, (2) reading comprehension skills are improved as learners read about what to do in the case of consumer fraud or how to get the best buys for their money, (3) problem solving — knowing how to identify a problem and then choose an appropriate strategy for its solution, (4) interpersonal relations — the ability to interact successfully with social peers, fellow workers, and family members. The latter two-important skills, often neglected in elementary and secondary schools, are stressed in the APL curriculum.

Most adults who are not functionally competent (APL 1's or 2's) do not have high school diplomas. Returning to the regular four-year high school, attending a night school, or passing five tests to obtain a high school equivalency certificate (GED) have traditionally been the only alternatives open to an adult needing or wanting a high school diploma. None of these alternatives were designed for an adult who has been out of school. They do not take into account the experiences, knowledges and skills adults have acquired as the result of working, rearing a family and otherwise coping in society on a day-to-day basis.

COMPETENCY-BASED DIPLOMA PROGRAM

The APL Competency-Based High School Diploma (CBHSD) Program was designed to respond to adult needs, to recognize adult learning experiences, and to make adult education more relevant. It offers the adult the opportunity to earn a regular high school diploma for the satisfactory demonstration of functional competency. The APL Diploma Program was modeled after the New York External High School Diploma Program, but two significant differences should be noted: (1) the APL Diploma Program is based upon the APL objectives and the assessment instruments and curriculum which grew out of the APL research study and not a formal course of study, (2) the infusion of the APL curriculum makes the APL Diploma Program an instructional model in contrast to the New York Program which is basically an assessment model.

The CBHSD Program process from entry to exit is summarized in the following seven steps:

Step 1: **Counseling.** The entering client is given an explanation of all available options (return to regular school classes, enroll in night high school, GED, CBHSD).

Step 2: **Diagnosis.** If the client chooses the CBHSD Program, diagnostic evaluation determines skill and knowledge levels. Assessment findings determine the learner's placement into the APL Curriculum. A learner who proves to be functionally competent (APL 3) in both skills and knowledges is not placed in the curriculum.

Step 3: **Instruction.** Anyone scoring below a certain skill level or as an APL 1 or 2 in the knowledge areas is channeled into appropriate learning activities in the APL Curriculum.

Step 4: **Mastery.** After instruction in those areas in which the client has demonstrated weakness, assessments are readministered to verify mastery.

Step 5: **Life Skills.** Steps 1-4 reflect more traditional paper-and-pencil type assessment activities. This fifth step in the CBHSD Program demands actual performance by the client. It is required of everyone in the program. The Life Skills portion is made up of tasks which are based on each of the APL objectives. Each task calls for the application of multiple skills as they are used in dealing with real situations or problems. For example, clients are asked to demonstrate how to use a ballot, read a thermometer, use the Yellow Pages, read a map, apply first aid, fill out an income tax form, and comparison shop for groceries, for a loan and for insurance.

Step 6: **Individualized Competency Assessment.** In this portion of the program the client has the option of being evaluated in one of the following three categories:
    (a) Occupational/Vocational — demonstrating the possession of a marketable skill through either employer testimony, perfor-

mance, or a work credential such as a current state license or union card; or
  (b) Postsecondary Education — demonstrating the ability to succeed in a college or vocational school; or
  (c) Home Management/Maintenance — demonstrating adequate skills in this area as judged by a professional in the field.
Step 7: **Certification.** On the recommendation of the CBHSD site staff and local school administrators, a local high school within the adopting site's district awards its diploma to the successful candidate.

All components of the multi-faceted Diploma Program are predicated on a basic tenet of CBAE — student performance should be competency-based, not time-based. In other words, functional competency is the constant and time is the variable. Putting this philosophy into practice means that students are allowed to complete the program as quickly as they can or they can go through it as slowly as required. They are given an unlimited number of chances to demonstrate mastery. Goals, objectives and outcomes are all clearly identified. In addition, students are given credit for demonstrating present knowledge and are not specifically given instruction in areas in which they have demonstrated mastery.

IMPLICATIONS FOR THE FUTURE OF CBAE

In addition to the diagnostic/prescriptive materials, instructional materials and credentialing programs developed around CBAE objectives, CBAE staff development needs are recognized as being critically important. The APL competency-based program was the first adult education program to be validated by the Joint Dissemination Review Panel (JDRP) and funded by the Department of Education's National Diffusion Network to provide training and technical assistance to site personnel, around the country, who are interested in implementing CBAE. Since APL's beginning, two additional CBAE Programs, the New York External High School Diploma Program and the Clovis, California Project CLASS curriculum have been JDRP approved. In the past years about 20 million dollars has been committed to CBAE program development, teacher training and life skills instruction.

Research And Dissemination — This snow-balling interest in CBAE has been reflected in local and national meetings and conferences — at times becoming the major theme of the conference. The National Association for Public Continuing and Adult Education (NAPCAE) and the Commission on Adult Basic Education (COABE) have established CBAE committees. Both groups have also published journals devoted exclusively to CBAE. The importance of the CBAE movement has been evidenced even more clearly in the fact that a national CBAE conference has been held each year since 1977. Funding restraints may dictate that future CBAE meetings be held in conjunction with other national adult education conferences or be limited in their scope and frequency.

ACCOUNTABILITY

This tightening of funds should make CBAE implementation even more in demand in the next few years, as the cry for "accountability" becomes louder and more urgent. Instead of awarding credit for "seat time", students in CBAE programs are awarded credit only after satisfactorily demonstrating competency in various life-coping skills which are clearly and thoroughly specified, measured and documented. In order to implement CBAE, however, program personnel need to be aware of and trained in CBAE practices. Those intimately tied to the movement tend to lose perspective and envision the majority of adult educators as knowledgeable about CBAE. This is simply not the case. The Department of Education's Office of Program Evaluation has recently published a national Assessment of the State-Administered Program of the Adult Education Act. The report indicates that 75 percent of the teachers and directors in adult education believe that competency-based instruction has a role to play in the education of adults, but that the majority are unfamiliar with the CBAE process or are not adequately trained in its implementation. Offsetting this apparent lack of information and training in CBAE among adult educators, however, is an ever increasing wealth of publications endorsing the concept.

There seems to be little chance that the Competency-Based Adult Education movement will lose its impetus in the foreseeable future. CBAE is a process which holds much promise for a future in which educational accountability is demanded more than ever. Hopefully, more and more program administrators will recognize that their dollars will stretch much farther if they "adopt" an already established program and/or process.

SUMMARY

To use the consensual words of participants at the February, 1978 USOE Invitational Workshop on Adult Competency Education, "Competency-Based Adult Education (CBAE) is a performance-based process leading to demonstrated mastery of basic and life skills necessary for the individual to function proficiently in society." A brief historical background of competency-based education in general and competency-based adult education in particular, that demonstrates an awareness that many adults gain some competencies through daily living, has been discussed. The research objectives of the Adult Performance Level (APL) Project ushered in a new era of interest in a movement of building programs and of staff development in CBAE. The authors believe that indicators which point to a need for CBAE will become stronger in a future in which tighter funds and a growing demand for accountability are signs of the time.

QUESTIONS AND EXERCISES

1. The matrix depicting the APL Project's two-dimensional definition of functional competency was included in this chapter. There are probably an unlimited number of activities which could be used to demonstrate the application of skills

to knowledge areas. Fill in each cell of the matrix with an example of how each skill would properly apply to each of the content areas.

2. Jane Doe needs a high school diploma in order to be eligible for a job in which she is very interested. Diagnostic testing at the local adult learning center, which offers a competency-based high school diploma program, revealed Jane's weakness in reading for detail and inference and in the content areas of government and law and occupation knowledge.

The above description is of a hypothetical student. Please develop a learning prescription for Jane which would reflect a competency-based approach.

REFERENCES

1. *APL Revisited: Its Uses and Adaptation in States*, the National Institute of Education, September, 1980.
2. *Adult Functional Competency: A Summary*, March 1975, Adult Performance Level Project, The University of Texas at Austin, Education Annex S-21, Austin, Texas 78712.
3. *Final Report: The Adult Performance Level Study*, August, 1977, APL Project, University of Texas at Austin.
4. Houston, W. Robert, and Warner, Allen, R., "The Competency-Based Movement: Origins and Future, June 1977, *Issues of Educational Technology*, Englewood Cliffs, New Jersey.
5. "NAPCAE and the Commission on Competency-Based Adult Education: Position Paper," *NAPCAE Exchange*, Vol. IV, Number 1, Winter-Summer, 1981, NAPCAE, Washington, D.C. 20036.
6. *Proceedings of a National Invitational Workshop on Competency-Based Adult Education*, edited by Kasworm and Lyle, published by National Institute of Education, June, 1978.
7. Shelton, Elaine, *The Adult Performance Level Competency-Based High School Diploma Program*, Sixth Edition, Fall, 1980, The APL Project, Education Annex S-21, The University of Texas at Austin, Austin, Texas 78712.

Community Based Organizations

Edgar M. Easley

Dean of Continuing Education,
City University Los Angeles

The 95th Congress in funding the Adult Education Act, PL 95-561 made provisions for funding through State Education Agencies both community-based organizations and local education agencies (LEA). This presented a challenge to community-based organizations and to public adult education to try to formulate a cooperative existence. Community-based organizations had to develop an educational delivery system, train staff to teach basic skills, and most assuredly, provide an administrative framework for planning, implementation, and evaluation. Local education agencies face the challenge of locating CBOs, learning to network various CBOs and how to best provide unified services to the basic skills students in their areas.

The act authorized grants to states which had approved State Plans to share the cost of: (1) the establishment or expansion of adult basic education programs to be carried out by local educational agencies, organizations, and institutions, (2) establishment or expansion of adult education programs to be carried out by local educational agencies and by public or private non-profit agencies, oranizations, and institutions.

The scenario was written and the challenge was laid forth — community-based organizations and local education agencies were to work together to provide adults with survival and employment skills.

SCOPE OF COMMUNITY-BASED EDUCATION

Few think of Adult Education beyond the programs operated by local education agencies (LEA), yet, in every community there are numerous agencies delivering education and training to adults. They range from Scout Leader Training to National Guard week-end maneuvers. Some of these programs have little or no impact on the average student, some of them are specialized and cater to a narrow segment of the population, however, there are enough CBOs providing education in a typical community that their total enrollment may surpass by far those enrolled in LEA programs. If the typical community-based organization were asked if it were an adult education delivery unit, the usual response would be, "No." It will be the task of enlightened adult educators to assist CBOs to identify and strengthen their adult education

Community Based Organizations

efforts. Rather than viewing community-based organizations as competitors, they should be seen as partners — partners in serving the community.

Historically, Adult Education through the Great Depression and the development of the National Training Leadership movement had a heavy involvement with community agencies. In later years with the development of the Office of Economic Opportunity (OEO) this emphasis was renewed. Presidents Kennedy and Johnson invested heavily in community development programs, most of which had adult education components. The Neighborhood Adult Participation Programs still offer many educational opportunities to residents of low-income areas. Among those offered in a typical program are pre-employment training, utilizing community economic resources, developing and managing consumer co-ops, voter registration, housing advocacy, and tenant's rights. Soon community-based organizations began to formalize their adult education efforts and with the advent of Federal 309 (Adult Education Act) funding began to develop sophisticated programs. Notable among these were Armchair (Home) Education in Philadelphia, San Antonio Literacy Council, Navajo Indian Education Program — all operated by community organizations. With the reduction of 309 funding some community-based organizations found funding sources in the "Right to Read" program. However, with the smaller appropriations for adult education in many states, and the corresponding lack of funded base for adult education, the funding of community-based groups on a regular basis was required to insure a continuity of community services. This statement succinctly epitomizes the rationale for the present partnership of public adult education and community-based organizations. Before the advent of large urban adult education programs the only deliverer of adult education was the lodge, church, union, or benevolent society, Is it strange that today these agencies would not continue in this tradition? Whether these programs operated as solo centers (a series of programs operated by an agency), the important thing to the adult clients is that there are means of getting a valuable service — adult education.

New Focus In Community Organizations — The watershed of change in community-based organizations was the introduction of "conscientization." True, there have been politically oriented community education programs in the past, but Paolo Freire adopted much of their drive to modern times. The change that Freire introduced was using a community's problems as the curriculum. This was in contrast to previous programs which had a focus on reacting to existing problems; not the fundamental societal relationship of the community. Earlier, the community agencies of the 1930's in their joint efforts with the Works Progress Administration (WPA) made attempts to provide a "bootstrap" educational program. These programs were often aborted as they made many in the power structures of the community uneasy. Education should get us "back to work." It should not agitate. Freire opened to community-based organizations a way in which fundamental social relationships could be changed. Possibly, with the tremendous problems of the

Brazilian masses, the efforts of Freire were not in vain. The question before many is — can adult education offered through CBOs attack some of the fundamental social issues of our times? The challenge is there. It may be community-based organizations will accept the challenge. More and more evidence is appearing that CBOs are becoming engaged in developing programs that provide both education per se and education as a tool in social development. Many third-world leaders, such as Julius Nyere of Tanzania, see this as a necessity. Is this a trend in the United States? The answer is by no means evident, but it is true that the concept of community-based education serving more than educational needs has a strong group of proponents. Another new focus in adult education as delivered by community-based organizations is competency-based skills training.

Often working in conjunction with a specific job or skill in mind, this highly specialized "tailor-made" type of education appears to be well suited to some community-based organizations. In a survey made in 1980 for a NAPCAE committee it was discovered that industry is turning more and more to CBOs to organize specific industry-based training programs. The Urban League has been developing such programs for specific industries and businesses for several years.

Challenges To Community-Based Organizations — There are several clear challenges facing community-based organizations if they are to respond positively to present times:

1. Systematic recruitment is essential for programs to have continuity. To avoid being characterized as "fly-by-night," CBOs need to assess the potential student body. How many, for how long? Program goals should be broad enough to provide for a large body of potential students. The specific program may have a restricted curriculum however, this should be framed within larger program goals. Well-trained recruiters should be designated by role and have specific training in their craft. Without well-trained recruiters a program can soon run out of students. Recruiters should know the community; they should have contacts in all areas and with all social and ethnic groups. It is well to consider as recruiters persons who have worked in the skill or graduated from programs for which they are recruiting. To recruit many who are ill-suited to the program will soon discredit any CBO in the eyes of the community. Equally as true is the statement that a lack of knowledge of the community can lead to a narrow selection of students.

2. Linkage to existing public school progams will ensure that students are building on existing knowledges. Repetition of previous learning is cost-ineffective, time consuming, and possibly places a negative image in the minds of the students. Knowledge of the programs of the public education system allows for ease of student transition. It is suggested that a representative of the public schools be a member of the CBO's advisory council. Effort needs to be made to keep a constant dialogue with the LEA's leadership. With the shortage of funds facing so many local education agencies they will welcome articulation.

3. Judicious balance of activism avoids becoming a tool of political expediency. It also lends the program credibility in the student's mind as it is seen as an educational program. Students do not like to be manipulated; they want an education. A judicious balance of social action goals often best meets the community's educational needs.

4. Long-range needs assessments provide the continuity that allows for wise use of resources. Apparent needs that are short-ranged may waste an organizations resources by building a program that will have no purpose in a few months or even a year later. Needs assessments should look at periods ranging from six months to five years hence. To plan for less can destroy the community's faith in the organization.

5. The need to deliver a useful service or product challenges the ingenuity of many community planners. In fact, there is a rule of thumb that states: "Find goods or services the community needs and build a program around them." The success of sheltered workshops (where they have been successful) has come from their providing goods and services not duplicated in the community. The Urban League developed several programs which were not offered in the community, including computer technician services. These programs are continually requested to provide contractual services to industry.

6. Building a network with other community agencies is essential if community-based organizations are to best serve the community. An interagency council is preferable, but if this is not possible, an informal network can be created. Surely, the staff and director of each agency should know each other on a personal basis. One organization may take the lead in stating how broad should be the objectives of the community's educational programs. Should the goals be restricted to limited clientele, services, or areas? What are the related support services needed to implement the program? Should housing, income supplement, health care be furnished to clients?

DEVELOPING A PLAN

Developing a plan should include a clear statement of objectives. A typical plan would include a discussion of the following:
1. Is the service now being provided in the community?
2. Can these services be contracted for, and funds be received to supplement the organization's budget?
3. What is the scope of the proposed program?
4. What is the target area to be served?
5. Is the target area of sufficient size to support the program, or conversely, is it too large to be served well?
6. What are the unusual features of the area?
7. What licenses are needed; credentials for staff?
8. What community resources can be utilized without charge or with nominal fees?
9. Are there eligibility requirements for utilization of the services by community residents?
10. What are the sources for recruitment?

The community leadership is entitled to know what is proposed in the way of a CBO providing education or services. They are to be given solid assurances that the program will fill an educational need. Recent events have shown that support given to many programs was "turned off" by the community after these programs appeared to be shoddy or have little educational merit. It is wise to have most questions answered in your mind before approaching the funding source. Also, it may be prudent to establish an internal committee to act as "Devil's Advocate" and carefully screen the proposal and proposed program before placing it before the community. One such program did this by having a committee of educators review the program thus not only assuring that it was sound educationally, but helped to stem any criticism from the education community. If there is a local university nearby, use its staff to critically look over the proposed program. However, the proposal can be hampered if you request they do the work. The organization requesting both funding and community support must do its own work; develop its own program, but it can ask for critical comment, suggestions, and guidance. The public education system of the LEA does not appreciate being given a blank sheet of paper and asked to develop a program for a community-based organization. Rather, they prefer to be consulted and asked to lend assistance. After all, they will be working with the CBO in developing education in the community. In another case, a certain community-based organization asked the LEA to place several strategic persons on their planning council. As the plan was developed there was consistent and forthright appraisal of its educational merit. When the plan was finally presented, the LEA was one of the first to recommend its funding.

It is apparent that planning as a first step serves several needs; development of a total evaluation system, organizing all available resources and talents before beginning the program, and identifying strengths and weaknesses of each component. A policy followed by another CBO was to ask each related agency to assess itself in terms of the strengths and weaknesses of its input to the total proposed program. It was discovered that the limitations imposed by law on the Social Services Department made it impossible to provide client income supplement in a regular fashion. This weakness was then apparent from the onset. The organization did not promise clients what it could not deliver. Remember, do not forget that the school board, school staff, and clients themselves can give valuable assistance in the planning phase — to overlook them would be disastrous.

Stating The Objectives In Educational Terms — will ensure that the program will be viewed from the focus of education and evaluation will also be done in the same terms. As an example of stating educational terms this is an excerpt from a plan developed by a CBO. "At present, no accessible and convenient program of English as a Second Language exists for the adult residents of the Naylor Street School area. In the near future, 150 units of low or moderate income housing will be built, thus providing additional possible students. Within the same area there is a proposal to build a senior citizens convalescent home to house sixty (60) seniors" The program set forth the following educational objectives:

1. To upgrade the level of English literacy among the adult population.
2. To provide a basis upon which other educational goals may be ascertained and defined.
3. To identify problems that may arise with senior citizens attending classes with other adults.
4. To identify strengths that may arise from inter-generational educational activities.
5. To identify the inservice training needs of the staff related to the new residents and to senior citizens.

Outlining The Program — often requires a skilled person with much experience in education. Many community-based organizations do not have such a person on staff. If possible, obtain the services of one who can conceptualize the total program and give a professional touch to your program planning. Often success in obtaining funds is assured if the program is well-planned. Basically, what is needed at this point is to acknowledge that the local community will in the end decide what program it wants in order to best meet its needs. The final objectives or end-product is for the program to deliver the education that fits these needs. For this an organization must develop more than a general set of purposes; they must be specific. In the end the community is going to ask: "Did you give what you promised?" If so, they will continue to offer support; if not, they will turn to another agency or organization.

Redefining the general goals and objectives into specific program components is the best way to accomplish comprehensive program development. At this stage it may be wise to think in terms of quantitive numbers — state the number of proposed students, the budget, and other specific resources needed by the program.

There are no artibrary or mechanical bases for setting up a program. Each is unique and requires the same care and painstaking effort that is required of another. One great danger lies in trying to imitate the program of another community, though that community may have different problems and different clients. This type of "carbon-copy" program designing can be spotted quickly by a professional reviewer.

If it is the first attempt, allow six months time to develop a good program. As time goes on the staff will be more skilled and the time for program designing can be shortened. At the conclusion of the planning time, it is well to give an additional two or three weeks for review and revision. One recently funded program needed three months to secure the approval of related agencies and the LEA before the program plan was adopted. Problems were stated in the proposal so that all were made aware of the efforts being made to ensure all program components would be working together harmoniously.

The program, we have in mind, is to aid the youth in our community by providing them with the opportunity to participate and work in a vocational setting and also provide them with a facility to spend leisure time during evening hours. The university along with us, would like to see new ways of involving the youth in their programs, allowing them to work with others of their own age group and to eventually seek employment for them. We are also hopeful that the LEA will share the enthusiasm of this project by having those high school students who participate in this work program earn credit.

Can you imagine the efforts needed to satisfy all the regulations of a university or the local high school in awarding work-study credit. Yet, this was done through the patient and hard work of the community organization. This kind of program development can be done through careful planning and attention to checking with each component.

The Procedural Steps in building your plan are as follows:
1. Develop a community advisory council.
2. Direct the council to address itself to a needs assessment of the community.
3. When the needs assessment is completed, share it with the LEA, other organizations, political and social leaders of the community and from this experience choose a steering committee.
4. The steering committee should select a possible director and charge that person with the responsibility of developing a program to meet the needs revealed in the needs assessment.
5. Choose a date far enough in advance to be realistic for the beginning of the program.
6. Staff should be recruited — do not overlook retired teachers, housewives with past volunteer or teaching experience, teachers who wish to give volunteer time, students, just plain citizens.
7. Obtain the help and guidance of the local media — radio, newspaper, public relations personnel. Have them assist in preparing flyers and preparing the media presentations. Try to get at least four or five of them to provide you with additional resources; but above all, assure that they are aware of your program and that they can provide genuine assistance to it.
8. Invite the LEA to help set up the first six months of operation. If possible, secure the assistance of the LEA in assigning one of its staff to act as liaison.
9. Provide your directors with progress reports. It is critical that they know what is happening at all times.
10. Begin the program on a pilot basis.
11. Revise any plans or program objectives based on the success of the pilot operation.

Community Based Organizations

Strengthen Your Network — is an essential element at this point. One such program after six months had involved the following agencies in the delivery of services: LEA Administration Offices, University Graduate School, five local churches, Department of Parks and Recreation. Such a list can be constantly revised since various agencies and organizations expand their services or are subject to cut-backs. It is important to make sure that the network is really functional. Honest and careful appraisal of the network will allow you to know where to go for services. It does no good to have names in your network that are neither dependable nor able to deliver the required support when needed. It is important also to recognize that some agencies may drop out of your network; **you** may not serve a need for **them.** They may have shifted their focus; you are no longer one of those upon whom they need to call.

There are four separate areas of network development: administrative, staff services, client services, auxillary services. These should be clearly defined in the mind of the director when assessing the kinds of services and resources available from other agencies in the network. Each of the above areas can provide valuable assistance. Notice how carefully this agency delineated each of these functions in its planning proposal. Administrative assistance will be given by those agencies that can provide assistance in budget preparation, renting and leasing of equipment, purchasing and general program publicity. Staff service assistance will be given by those agencies that can provide assistance in negotiating with individual agencies for services, identification of community resources and recruitment. Client service assistance will be given by those agnecies that are providing employment assistance, training facilities, self-enhancement activities and childcare. Auxillary Services assistance will be given by those agencies that are providing continuing education, cultural activities, and travel services. One may disagree with the placement of several of these items, but the essential thing is that each of the areas is clearly defined.

Continuing Evaluation — is a key to continuing success. Milestones (six months, yearly) are excellent and rare opportunities to involve the total community in assessing the program's value. Several assessment strategies can be used, but one of the easiest is to assess on a simple observational basis. Few community persons are interested, nor are involved enough, to participate in lengthy diagnostic evaluations. They prefer to give their observation and make general assessments. One CBO did this by hosting a luncheon meeting to which key persons were invited. They were asked to give general impressions and several specifics as to how the program might be improved. At this meeting were several persons from all levels: staff, clients, LEA, other community organizations, political leadership. Suggestions for improvement were:
  1. Staff persons should give more assistance to recruiters.
  2. Positive effects on the community youth were observed in terms of less graffitti on the walls.

3. Notification of new programs should be given farther in advance.
4. Use the P.T.A. as a source of volunteers. (This had been overlooked by both the LEA and the community organization.)
5. Plan a culminating awards sessions for each segment of the program, rather than on a yearly basis.

This kind of feedback provides a very effective basis for future program planning, as well as gives a frank evaluation of the current program. True, this may not cover all bases of evaluation, but then the effort to be more scientific may waste the organization's resources and may not produce any more benefit than a simple evaluation. Use the K-I-S-S Principle (Keep It Short and Simple.)

Evaluation also builds morale. A truly professional community-based program will find much to applaud about itself and recognition of honorable service builds cohesive morale. Evaluation should not be a series of negatives. One of the most exceptional programs utilizing youth in training bases a good deal of the evaluation on self-evaluation by the participants. They are asked to note the positive changes in themselves as a result of the training. This has allowed the staff to find out what is really happening that is significant. As they record their accomplishments and changes for the better, they are in effect telling the program staff what is beneficial about the program. It takes little effort to later note the areas of absence from their evaluations and know that those areas may not be adding anything significant to the program.

Tuning The Budget — to reality is a process that is needed in any nonprofit community-based organization. What is the ratio of direct charges to donated services and to those services offered by related agencies? Some organizations will not embark on a program unless more than half the cost is covered by donated services and funds. If fees are charged to the clients, are they exorbitant, too small, or even necessary? How effective is the full time staff of the organization in implementing the educational program? Is more time spent in administering this program than other programs operated by the agency? One CBO tries to maintain the following ratio: 50% community organization budget, 20% from other agencies, 30% volunteers. Yet, another agency has found that it needed to have the following ratios: 75% from other agencies and funding sources, 15% volunteers, 10% organization budget.

Client costs can escalate when the staff goes beyond the scope and parameters of the proposed services. This can be prevented through a process — costs of the services divided by the number of clients served. It is true that students with special problems may increase the costs of service, but over-all costs should be fairly consistent if the previous planning is thorough. A major national community-based organization feels that it can expend $100 per year from its organization budget on each student. When the costs are significantly higher, the program is revised to limit the portions of the program that are providing excess costs. Upon examination (with the assistance of a volunteer C.P.A.) they found that the following areas were growing faster than their planned budget: (1) recruitment costs, (2) day-care costs (especially food), (3) rent. The staff went to work and found ways to reduce these costs by utilizing the services of the local Chamber of Commerce to aid in recruitment, by asking a grocery chain to donate the cookies for the day-care center, and by moving the staff offices into a church center which donated the space on a five day a week basis.

SUMMARY

Community-based organizations are a vital portion of the delivery of adult education to many communities. In some areas where there is no state funding of adult education they comprise, by far and large, the greatest segment of adult education. Increased interest and participation has created a wider knowledge of how to improve the quality of education offered through CBOs. This can be done be developing a network of organizations delivering various services on a coordinated basis to the community. Within the near future the role of the community-based organization will be well defined within the totality of adult education. Part of that definition will be defining the nature of volunteerism and how to use it professionally, as well as means to develop the professional abilities of the volunteer. Another facet of this wider definition will be the refinement of the art of administering CBOs. Complex though they may be, the administration of community-based organizations can be done by creative, flexible, dynamic, and skilled administrators. The adult educator should be willing to accept the role of the community-based organization as it is played in the community.

QUESTIONS AND EXERCISES

1. How has the community-based organizations evolved as an educational delivery agent?
2. Develop guidelines for development of an educational program by a community-based organization.
3. Using your community as a basis, develop an educational program using a CBO and have that program include some non-instructional goals and activities.
4. How can a local education agency utilize community-based organization to further its adult education program?

Program Development: A Model

Edwin L. Simpson

*Professor of Adult Education,
Northern Illinois University*

Program planning is certainly one of the most basic skills an adult educator needs in order to be effective. To those who face the challenge for the first time, adult program planning may present a minor threat. Organizing and providing adults with what they want requires: (1) identifying needs, (2) defining objectives, (3) identifying learning experiences, (4) organizing the experiences into a plan, (5) evaluating outcomes. Not until one has experienced the planning process and observed successful program planning in operation, do these simple activities take on an air of sophistication — much more than just a five step formula.

The tendency for over-simplifying the planning process is apparently based on the assumption that planning educational programs can best be represented by sequential steps — a linear model of planning. Tracing the decisions and discussions of successful planning groups however, reveals there are weaknesses in linear planning models. Although there is order in the approach, the process is not always sequential, nor is each element of the planning model parallel in functional importance.

Complexity is also increased and frustration tends to set in when planners realize, through discussion, the disparity which exists when they begin identifying intended outcomes. While one educator may expect content mastery as the intended outcome of a program, another may conceive of the same learning episode to result in acquisition of generic skills, leading to more specific learning later. The first planner is focusing on content; the second on process. Activities each planner visualizes might be quite similar, but their purposes or intentions are quite different. This only represents one side of mixed expectations. The learners themselves also may differ in what they expect to receive from a program.

Another cause of complexity in program planning is the confusion of purpose regarding level and nature of performance expected. While one program planner is aiming for minimal competency, another may have individual growth potential in the back of his/her mind as the outcome. The first expects the program to result in participants attaining basic skills for doing a specific job or carrying out a prescribed role. The other is expecting each individual in the program to develop according to his or her own abilities and interests. Linear models of planning do not recognize nor attempt to accommodate these variances in the planning process.

INTERACTIVE MODEL

A means of increasing the planner's awareness of the intricate happenings in effective planning is to present a model which more accurately represents both planning **function** and **process**. It is also important to keep the paradigm simple and descriptive so as to provide useful guidelines for practice. Rather than using a linear model as is customary, an interactive model seems a better base for effective planning.

Two fundamental differences exist between an interactive model of program planning and most linear models. The first is the acceptance that educational activities (including educational planning) do not go on in a value-free vacuum. The second is that the interactive model is based on the recognition that other functions of effective planning are more pervasive than sequential steps and actually are used more or less continuously throughout the process. Sequencing can act as normative reference points guiding and altering the direction of other sequential steps in planning and, in turn, may be somewhat modified as well. For example, such "tried and true" steps in planning, as assessing needs of learners, selecting methods and materials, and evaluating program outcomes are procedures that can be put into a logical sequence, indicating when a particular procedure might appropriately take place. However, other important functions such as crystallizing program philosophy or rationale, developing objectives, and providing criteria for reference may evolve in the process. These normative criteria directly affect the results of the sequential steps and so the steps likewise are modifed on occasion in the interactive process.

To further illustrate, the interactive planning model is conceived on the premise that program planners approach the planning process with some purpose in mind for a given program. Their principle objective is providing service to the target learning group. Through the process described by the model, initial philosophy and resultant objectives will be modified through interaction with the learning group to more nearly reach intended educational outcomes of both learners and planners.

Even programs which are intended for the achievement of very specific and narrowly defined outcomes profit from the interactive approach. For example, acquisition of a sporting skill, learning the technique of a craftsman welder, or developing the professional expertise of a nurse, all represent programs in which an interactive program planning paradigm may provide more meaningful outcomes to the adults being served.

The Model In Action — Interaction is suggested on two levels. The model first represents interaction of procedures or steps of planning with normative criteria (philosophy and objectives). The "what" of planning is compared interactively with "why" the program is being planned. As steps of planning are accomplished, frequent reference is made to purpose and goals. In the process, questions should be addressed such as, "Does what is being

Adult Education Program Planning: An Interactive Model

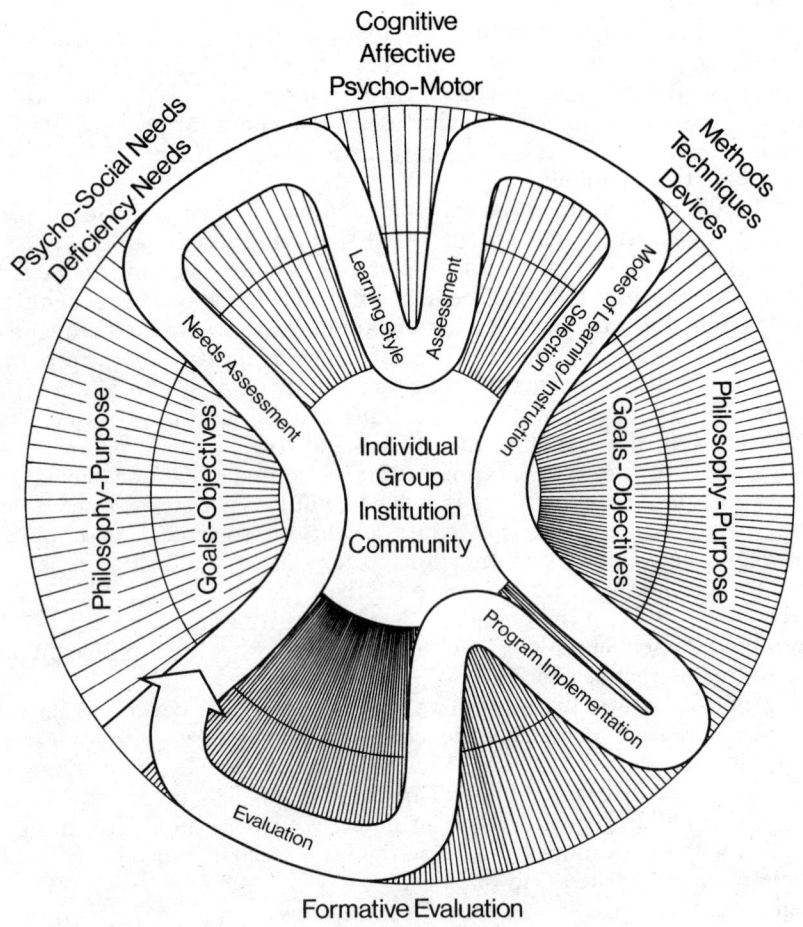

Cognitive
Affective
Psycho-Motor

Psycho-Social Needs
Deficiency Needs

Methods
Techniques
Devices

Needs Assessment

Learning Style Assessment

Modes of Learning/Instruction Selection

Philosophy-Purpose

Goals-Objectives

Goals-Objectives

Philosophy-Purpose

Individual
Group
Institution
Community

Program Implementation

Evaluation

Formative Evaluation
Summative Evaluation

Normative Criteria
   Philosophy-Purpose
   Goals-Objectives

Planning Procedures
   Needs Assessment
   Learning Style Assessment
   Learning/Instruction Mode Selection
   Implementation
   Evaluation

Figure 1

planned fit the purpose and goals for planning?" and "Should the purpose and goals be modified given assessed needs of the target learning group?" Through the dynamics of comparing purpose with intended outcomes of learning, a more effective program should result.

Effective adult planning requires some form of dialogue between those that are wanting to learn and those wanting to assist with learning. The interactive model encourages this dialogue and suggests a guideline for carrying it on through the planning process. Strategically placed at the center of the model, the target learners (participants) are systematically consulted in the planning. Learners being served may be represented as an individual, a group, an institution, or an entire community. Regardless of the form target learners represent, they act as an important reference point, giving direction for decisions in the procedural steps of planning.

PROCEDURAL STEPS

Step 1 — Needs Assessment — If the planner or planning group comes to a tentative conclusion about program philosophy and identifies initial specific objectives they hope to reach, the first step is to begin interaction with the individual, group, institution, or community representing the target learners. A result of the first step, in addition to simply "getting to know" the learners, should be a needs assessment. Depending on the group, needs may be identified on two bases: (1) psycho-social or "growth" needs, (2) deficiency needs. Psycho-social needs may best be determined through "felt" needs or "expressed" needs assessments. What the group says they want through solicited opinion indicate felt needs while what is documented in the learners' actual participation reflects expressed needs.[1] Deficiency needs may more accurately be determined from normative and comparative information. An assessment of the present level of performance or knowledge established by experts, is one method of determining deficiency needs. The other measure of deficiency is comparing the group to be served with performance of other similar groups in like programs. The purpose for education suggested by deficiency needs assessment is to "close the gap" between present performance or knowledge level and that performance which is expected. In the case of planning for individuals rather than groups of target learners, Houle has pointed out three types of learner motivation which might be considered in the planning process: (1) goal oriented need, (2) activity oriented need, (3) learning for learning sake need.[2] When appropriate, an assessment of the needs of individual learners regarding these three orientations should be part of the planning process.

Assessing Learning Style — The second procedural step is consideration of learning style or the way in which the target learners approach learning. Learning style undoubtedly is made up of many factors, including attitudes toward learning, ways of thinking, and pattern of learning behavior. Past experiences play an important part in the assessment of style. A group which has had extensive formal education or training will approach the learning opportunity differently than the group which has had little or distant school experience. Likewise, the area or field of practice in which one has learned or had professional experience will affect style of learning.

The Kolb Inventory distinguishes four learner dispositions toward learning: (1) concrete experience, (2) reflective observation, (3) abstract conceptualization, (4) active experimentation.[3] Some learners characterize their learning style as first-hand experience in which sensing is an important feature (concrete experiences). The second group view their approach to learning as a careful observation of the world about them (reflective observation). The third group of learners identify their characteristic style as systematic, cognitive, and calculating (abstract conceptualization). The fourth classification group describes their typical learning as practical, useful and an activity in which they are very involved (active experimentation). From interaction of these four style descriptions Kolb has drawn four general behavior characteristics of learners in their response to learning. Research using this inventory has produced general characteristics of learning response: accommodation, divergence, assimilation, convergence.

Cognitive style, or the way individuals process information, is one factor within the overall assessment of style which **has** received research attention. It is also an area in which some generalizations can be made about stylistic characteristics of groups. For example individuals who are field dependent tend to be more global in their approach to learning and usually are more socially oriented, whereas field independent persons are more analytic and do not require as much social contact in their learning pursuits. According to literature about cognitive field independence/dependence, subgroups within professions and fields of study differ in their method of processing information in learning. For example, psychiatric nurses are more field dependent while their counterparts in surgical nursing are more field independent.[4] Also, persons preparing for the General Education Development Test tend to be more field dependent while students in graduate school seem to be more field independent.[5,6]

Selection of Instruction/Learning Modes — The third step is selection of tools for learning — the modes of instruction/learning. Modes of instruction/learning are the methods, techniques, and devices to be used as learning tools.[7] Methods pertain to the larger organizational and conceptual considerations of planning such as use of lecture (large group), small groups, field experience, and other instruction/learning modes. Techniques refer to the instructional format of method such as lecture/discussion, buzz groups, panel discussion, or programmed instruction. Use of films, programmed textbooks, simulation games, and television are devices within modes of instruction/learning. Selection of methods, techniques and devices are made as a result of interaction between program purposes, learner needs, and learning style.

For example, if the purpose of an educational program is to inform an adult group of new developments or techniques in a specialized field of practice, a direct method of instruction, such as the lecture, may be the most efficient way of beginning to achieve this objective. However, if the unique needs of participants as practicing professionals and their dominant learning style requires concrete experience, some technique that can be used within the large group format allowing for application and "hands-on" use of the information to be shared is essential.

Conversely, if a planned educational program series is intended to raise social issues among the urban poor or to make an elderly group aware of hazardous living conditions, small group methodology, using the structure of a panel or community produced media followed by group interaction or questions and answers, should prove to be more beneficial. Given the need in this instance for first becoming aware and secondly having a chance to reflect and perhaps respond, a less direct and more informal method is appropriate.

Step 4 — Program Operation — The fourth step in the planning process may be the easiest — actually putting the program into operation. The preceeding steps having been thoroughly considered interactively, implementation should indeed be the easiest step in planning.

Step 5 — Evaluation — Continuous evaluation is an essential function of any program in order to provide information as to: (1) how well the program is working, (2) what can be done to improve it. Evaluation should answer the questions "How effective is the program?" which is a summative form of evaluation and also "What can be done to improve the program?" a formative evaluation question. The summative evaluation function focuses on the results and is usually carried out at the conclusion of the program, while formative program evaluation emphasizes development and should be conducted periodically throughout implementation of the program. Answers to formative evaluation questions are intended to be used for improving the program as it is in progress.

The summative evaluation function which unfortunately is often given most attention is intended to provide an overall picture of the results achieved. It may be determined through objectives met, activities completed, participant performance or a combination of these. Formative evaluation tends to focus on the interactive elements of program, stressing process and indicators of progress. Formative results most likely will result in reconsideration and modification of objectives and the addition, alteration, or discontinuance of certain educational activities. It is the formative evaluation function which contributes most to the interactive intent of this program planning model.

Finally, the interactive model also suggests that although planning naturally is interrupted with pauses for reflection, analysis, and redirection of energies, actually the planning process does not end with evaluation. As long as the program is operating, planning continues. Consistent with the interactive nature of this program planning model, the procedural pathway is cyclic, returning to the point it first began, to begin once again.

SUMMARY
The interactive program planning model:
1. Recognizes the difference between the function of normative criteria (philosophy and objectives) and the function of procedural steps or processes such as needs and learning style assessment conducted in sequence to effectively carry out program planning. Modification which occurs from interaction of initially identified philosophy and objectives with procedural steps throughout planning helps planners more nearly reach intended results expected by planners and program consumers (learners).
2. Is distinctive in its emphasis upon consultation or observation of the target learners during planning. Systematic reflection upon the characteristics and conditions of those whom the program is to serve is essential to effective planning.
3. In addition to the strategic procedural steps of assessing needs and styles of learning, selecting appropriate modes of learning or instruction, and actually implementing or conducting the program, interactive program planning also stresses the need for two forms of evaluation (summative and formative) to fulfill the interactive concept. Through both end-product or total-program assessment (summative evaluation) in tandem with in-progress or process assessment conducted throughout the program's implementation (formative evaluation), evaluation takes on a dynamic and generative nature which promotes continued program growth and improvement. Planning is considered a cyclic activity, never actually complete as long as the program is in progress.

Questions and Exercises

1. How does a linear model of adult program planning differ from an interactive model?
2. How are educational philosophies and objectives used in an interactive program planning model?
3. What information about the need of individuals or a community could be gained through use of interviewing?
4. What are some considerations of learning style in planning programs and how might style be assessed given an adult progam with which you are familiar?
5. What role does evaluation play in effective program planning. Give some examples of data you would collect for a summative evaluation. How would you carry out a formative program evaluation?

REFERENCES

1. Bradshaw, Jonathan, "The Concept of Social Need." *Ekistics* 37, 1974.
2. Houle, Cyril. *The Inquiring Mind*. Madison: University of Wisconsin, 1961.
3. Kolb, David, Rubin and McIntyre. *Organizational Psychology: An Experimental Approach*. Prentice Hall, 1971.
4. Witkin, Herman. *A Longitudinal Study of the Role of Cognitive Style in Academic Evolution During the College Years*. 1977
5. Loveall, Philip. *The Relationship Between Cognitive Style and Achievement as Measured by the Old and New Forms of the GED*. (Unpublished Doctoral dissertation, Northern Illinois University), 1979.
6. Donnarumma, Theresa, David Cox, and Hal Beder, "Success in a High School Completion Program and Its Relation to the Field Dependence-Independence." *Adult Education*, Summer, 1980.
7. Verner, Coolie. *A Conceptual Scheme for the Identification and Classification of Processes for Adult Education*. Washington, D. C.: AEA, 1962.

Conceptual Framework for Program Development

William M. Rivera
Associate Professor, Dept. of Agricultural & Extension Education, University of Maryland

Hilda Patino
Special ABE Program, Mexico City

Ralph G. Brockett
Adjunct Professor, Adult Education, Syracuse University

Program development refers to implementation of action, administration of concepts, promoting educational behaviors, establishment of curricular parameters and even setting up courses.[1] Looking specifically at program development as it relates to adult education, Schroeder[2] points out that the concept of program has been used to refer to the following: (1) all the educative activities available to adults in a community, (2) the total adult education effort of a given agency, (3) the educational activities designed for segments of the population, (4) the social roles with which these activities are related, (5) the nature of a specific activity.

Verner stated that the term "program" may refer to either the **entirety** of educational opportunities for adults existent in a community, the educational activities for adults carried on by a single institution, or the design of an educational activity for adults consisting of a **single** meeting or a series of sessions. Verner viewed program as a "series of learning experiences designed to achieve, in a specified period of time, certain specific instructional objectives."[3]

Similar lines of thought have been taken by Houle[4] and Knowles.[5] Houle affirmed that program is the "plan developed to guide educational activity in a situation." He proposed what he refers to as a "fundamental system" that can be used when designing educational activities. Knowles defined program as a comprehensive plan of an educational activity. From this perspective, the program development process is equal to the program planning process.

The Distinction Between Program and Curriculum — For the most part, it seems that adult educators use the term program to describe what teachers in youth education usually refer to as curriculum. Curriculum, as defined by Blishen in the *Encyclopedia of Education,* is a "statement or programme of courses of teaching and instruction . . . all the experience which a pupil has under the guidance of the school." Probably due to its pedagogical approach, the term "curriculum" suggests a pre-determined content, which is inflexible or less adaptable to adults' needs than the term program. For that reason adult educators use more frequently the word "program" to designate learning experiences that they plan to implement.

The difference between program and curriculum in terms of instructional objectives is reflected in the following quote from Verner:

> A curriculum at the preadult level is designed to provide simultaneous learning experiences for both immediate developmental tasks and for anticipated responsibilities. A program, on the other hand, is functionally related to the immediate need for specific learning. It provides learning experiences to meet new needs and expanding interests that grow out of an adult's changing role in his social setting.

Bergevin, et al, in *Adult Education Procedures,* defined program as an "educational meeting or series of meetings based on the interests and needs of the expected participants. Such an event is usually planned to achieve certain educational goals." They distinguished between program and program planning by noting program planning refers to the procedures through which the nature and sequence of future educational programs are determined. In this way "program" refers to an activity taking place in the present while "program planning" involves preparation for future activity. However, program and program planning are intimately related since planning programs and implementing them involve the same activities.

Easley viewed program development and program planning as the same, and that "program design" is a part of the program planning (development) process, which is considered both as an art and as a science. Another, more narrow, interpretation is offered by Verner. While Verner focused the concept of program planning in the design of concrete learning experiences, others believed that the program is the ultimate goal of the planning process, and this included consideration of: (1) the situation that is to be changed or improved, (2) the educational needs of the target population, (3) the planning of learning experiences designed to fulfill these educational needs, (4) the design of evaluation procedures.

In the opinion of Boshier and Peters,[6] program development must take into account the following factors: motives, needs, interests, and expectations of potential participants; prevailing social forces; community characteristics; the organization's purposes, philosophy and structure.

The boundaries of program development are not clearly enough defined to provide universal understanding of the term. Two basic points are given for consideration. First, there is no common theme linking program development with program planning. Some persons regard program planning in a broad sense, in which program development is included as a part of the total educational process. On the other hand, some use the term program development to refer to the action of developing curricula only. While still others prefer not to use the term "curriculum" because of the inflexibility that it implies and they prefer to use the term "program development" in order to designate the educational activities that take place in the adult educational arena and they do not use the term "program planning."

The second point is that the increase in the literature dealing with program development indicates that this term is crucial to adult and continuing education. Accordingly, clarification through classification of the term is essential and will provide better communication among persons involved in this field.

PRIMARY DISTINCTIONS

Some primary distinctions in the meaning of program development become possible. Program development can be viewed as the **task of planning and managing adult education activities.** In this sense, many authors identify program development with program planning and assign this responsibility to the faculty and administrative staff. The latter must assess needs, set objectives, develop topics, select appropriate resources, and assign responsibilities in order to carry out an educational program. Here, program development is used in a broad sense. It refers to the decision-making process in building educational experiences.

Program Development As Institutional Process — As an institutional process, program development is equal to program planning. In this sense, it includes general policy considerations, specific program direction and the realization of teaching/learning or educational activities *per se*. Each of these three functions — policy, direction, and realization — is performed by specific personnel within the educational institution. The relationship between these levels of program personnel is illustrated in Figure 1.

Functions of Various Levels of Program Personnel

1. **TOP LEVEL MANAGEMENT**
   General purposes of the agency;
   overall program administration.

2. **SPECIFIC PROGRAM ADMINISTRATION**
   Planning and administration of
   specific program.

3. **SPECIFIC PROGRAM IMPLEMENTATION**
   Realization of specific learning
   experiences through formal or
   non-formal "courses" (program).

FIGURE 1.

At the top level of management, the primary responsibility is the establishment of general policies, planning, and development of the agency through meeting the needs of its overall target population. Top-level management oversees programs according to the structure and goals of the organization. Their duties are referred to as policy functions since they constitute the basic conditions of program development on the second and third levels. At the second level, program administrators must decide upon appropriate strategies in order to plan, implement, and improve the specific program under their direction. Finally, staff at the realization level (third level) are the ones who actually select and implement the learning experiences that take place within the program. The functions of each level of the program personnel are further summarized in Figure 2.

The Primary Functions of Each Level of Program Personnel

LEVEL	FUNCTIONS	PROGRAM DEVELOPMENT DENOMINATION
I. Top-level Managers	General policies and overall management of the institution and its programs	Program Development Policy and Planning
II. Specific Program Administrators	General objectives of their specific program; strategies to manage the program	Program Development Direction and Administration
III. Program Facilitators	Planning and implementation of learning experiences	Program Development Realization (Teaching/Learning Process)

FIGURE 2.

Program Development as a Teaching/Learning Process — Program development refers to the activities undertaken within the educational program *per se*. These activities take place as various steps of a process. They include:

1. Program Diagnosis — Analysis of the target population, needs assessment.
2. Program Planning and Design — Formulating purposes, objectives, selecting strategies and tactics.
3. Program Implementation — Trying out the education program.
4. Program Evaluation — Evaluating program results in order to improve the program.

1. Program Diagnosis — It is essential that the teaching/learning program development process begin with the identification of who the learners are.

Although need assessment is not always considered a part of the teaching/learning program development process itself, it is a necessary requisite of all meaningful education programs.

2. Teaching/Learning Program Planning — This is the process of formulation of educational objectives and consists of translating the educational needs of specific target populations into educational objectives. These objectives can be formulated as general educational purposes or as specific goals of a planned learning experience. The program planning and design phase of the process also includes consideration of resources, personnel, methods, schedules, and other related activities.

3. Program Implementation — This is where the program actually happens. Included in this step are practical considerations such as marketing of the program; the selection of appropriate methods, techniques and devices; implementing learning strategies.

4. Program Evaluation — This concerns the specific program as well as the education agency itself. Evaluation tends to assist the individual as well as the organization in making decisions about future improvements.

Various authors, such as Knowles and Houle have refined and interpreted the teaching/learning program development process. However, the above

Program Within an Institutional Framework

EDUCATIONAL INSTITUTION

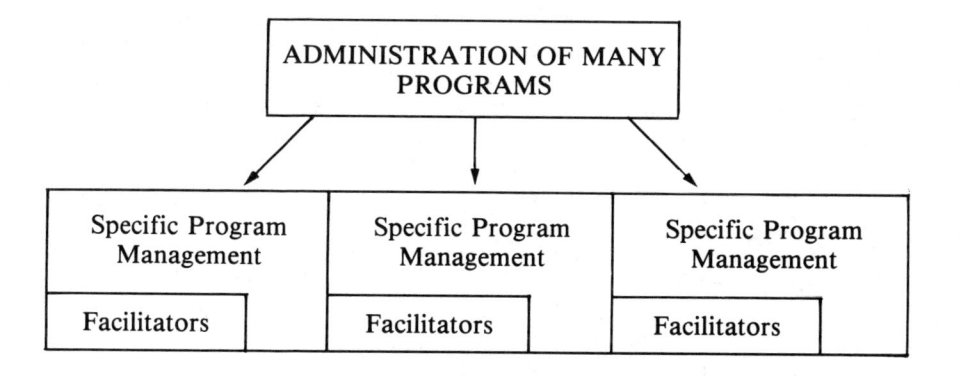

```
          ADMINISTRATION OF MANY
                PROGRAMS
         /            |            \
Specific Program  Specific Program  Specific Program
  Management       Management        Management
  Facilitators     Facilitators      Facilitators
```

FIGURE 3.

four steps emerge as basic in the development of virtually all teaching/learning programs, as well as in institutional processess of planning and administration generally.

Thus, the four steps of diagnosing, planning, implementing and evaluating programs are followed by educational agents at all levels in an agency or organization. Therefore, it is not the process of steps that distinguishes program development but rather the **level** of planning and implementation. Figure 3, in outlining how several programs may fall under the auspices of a single institution, attempts to distinguish these levels further.

Figure 3 underlines that the responsibility of top level administration extends across all programs within the institution and that specific program administration staff are responsible only for their specific programs, while facilitators are responsible for the educational activity. This is an important distinction because it has a direct effect on the vision of persons at each level. Top level adminstrators will tend to view specific programs in terms of their function within the total institution while program administrators and staff are likely to focus primarily upon the activities of their own program. An awareness of this intra-institutional distinction is critical to an understanding of program development from an institutional perspective.

SUMMARY

The term program development is central to the field of education for adults. Its multiple uses, however, have limited its usefulness, and a conceptual classification is needed. Program development can be viewed in two ways: (1) as an institutional process, (2) as a teaching/learning process. In other words, the term "program development" is differentiated by level of institutional activity rather than in terms of the particular steps involved in developing programs.

Within the institutional context, then, program development is seen to go on at three levels: (1) top-level institutional management, (2) specific program management, (3) teaching/learning facilitation. If these distinctions are accepted, the task of clarifying the term "program development" becomes one of adjectively modifying the term. A reasonable way of modifying the term might be to refer to the different levels of program development as:
   1. Institutional (or organizational) program development.
   2. Specific program development.
   3. Teaching/learning program development.

Organizational program development refers to overall planning and management; **specific program development** indicates responsibility for a particular program and its development; **teaching/learning program development** means implementation of the educational activity itself (of the courses — whether formal, non-formal or informal).

Program development as a term has evolved through the years just as adult education has evolved. It has taken on changing meanings just as the nature of the adult education process has changed. A number of thinkers in the field of adult education have proposed models in an attempt to develop parameters and a rationale for program development.

In the light of current belief, program development is an institutional process akin to program planning. Thus it requires coordinated efforts of managers, administrators, and instructors — each performing a series of functions. All in all, program development thus encompasses activities ranging from surveys determining educational needs to macro/micro evaluation of program outcomes and impacts.

REFERENCES

1. Easley, E. "Program Development." In C. Klevins (ed.), *Materials and Methods in Continuing Education.* Canoga Park, CA: Klevens, 1978.
2. Schroeder, W. L. "Adult Education Defined and Described." R. M. Smith, G. F. Aker, & J. R. Kidd (eds.), *Handbook of Adult Education.* New York: Macmillan, 1970.
3. Verner, C. "Definition of Terms." In Jensen, G., A.A. Liveright, & W. Hallenbeck (eds.), *Adult Education: Outlines of an Emerging Field of University Study.* Washington, D.C.: AEA, 1964.
4. Houle, C. O. *The Design of Education.* San Francisco: Jossey-Bass, 1972.
5. Knowles, M. *The Modern Practice of Adult Education.* New York: Association Press, 1970.
6. Boshier, R. & Peters, J. M. "Adult Needs, Interests and Motives." In C. Klevins (ed.), *Materials and Methods in Continuing Education.* Canoga Park, CA: Klevens, 1978.

Education for the Handicapped

Laurent R. Broussal

President, San Francisco Community College District; author of articles on the handicapped.

Just as the label "physical handicap" has a myriad of myths attached to it, likewise have "mental retardation" and "multiple physical handicap"; however no amount of wishful thinking can remove the real barriers these handicaps produce. They conspire to prevent "mainstreaming." Clear understanding of the nature of a handicap is essential if we are to assist handicapped adults to function in a "normal" society in a more or less "normal" manner. A working definition of "handicapped" must be identified primarily in terms of the capabilities of the person in question.

Assume that the term handicapped is a generally accepted identifier of adults who, because of some mental or physical deficiency, defect, or other aberrations, are in need of special educational considerations in order to enhance their level of achievement. Thus in spite of the exceptional nature of handicapped education, it still shares a common problem with all education: *How to make teacher-learner efforts most productive.*

The grouping of any number of people under one general identifying title creates a stereotype which is not more true for the handicapped than it is for any other group of individuals. The point is, that in relation to human beings of any kind — handicapped or non-handicapped — the psychology of individual differences is appropriate, applicable, and a valid ambience for evaluation of abilities and/or disabilities.

When students have learning disorders, the challenge of effective instruction becomes critical. Procedures adequate for the normal student may prove inadequate for the handicapped student. If teacher-learner productivity is to be enhanced, a diagnosis must provide cues for appropriate instruction and remediation. Differential diagnosis with appropriate prescriptive teaching is the key to improving the teacher/learner transaction.

Focus On Mental Disability — There is a limited amount of information on the education of handicapped **adults;** and yet, such education has been practiced for almost as long as modern adult education has existed. It has often been integrated into such programs as *Elementary Subjects for Adults, English Review, Refresher Math, Adult Basic Education, Remedial Reading,* all of which connote a gap or deficiency in the "normal" educational process. This is not to say that such courses and programs have actually been designed for mentally disabled adults, nor is it intended to convey the thought that such classes are necessarily wholly or even partly comprised of retarded adults. The logic of placement of handicapped adults into these classes makes good sense; for, after all, academically speaking, their general educational needs are basic, and these titles suggest basic content. These courses, whether or not designed for handicapped adults, have much applicability in prescriptive instruction for such students.

Neither is it surprising that education for adult handicapped probes most extensively into the area of the mentally disabled. This is not an arbitrary decision. A number of reasons suggest this priority: (1) this particular deficiency comprises the single most numerous group of handicapped, (2) there now exists throughout the United States, particularly in California, a concerted effort to extend and expand the educational services available to this group as they move into the age groups beyond elementary and secondary school levels, (3) controversy over the proper placement of persons in classes for the retarded.

Changes In Identification and Terminology — During the last decade, the care, treatment, and education of the mentally retarded have undergone major changes including the acceptance of the "normalization principle" as opposed to the previous manner of custodial care. Added to this change, legislation such as the Federal Developmental Disabilities Act and California's Lanterman Act were enacted to provide additional and augmented services for the mentally retarded.

With the changes in method of identification of the mentally retarded, came a new designation. The term "developmentally disabled" points the way to answering the needs of these people in terms of educational and training responses instead of diagnostic labels. In other words, intellectual, vocational, and social potential should be the focus of developmental attention. The result of this is a program more closely aligned to the educational and vocational needs of "normal" adults, but — at the level which best fits the handicapped individuals.

With the changes in terminology came a change in concept. The California Junior College Association (CJCA) conceptualized these changes in four (4) position statements:[1]

1. Recognize mentally retarded adults as an identifiable community that can be served by the Community College.
2. Encourage and promote existing community college programs for the mentally retarded.
3. Cooperate with other existing organizations, agencies and levels of education to provide comprehensive educational services for the mentally retarded.
4. Appoint a task force to identify models and document existing legislation and funding needs of educational programs for the mentally retarded adult and develop necessary legislation.

Tredgold,[2] over fifty (50) years ago, gave a basic definition of education that aptly summarizes this position statement: Education has a threefold object. First, it should develop and cultivate all the latent potentialities of body and mind to their fullest extent; second, it should repress or eliminate faulty modes of action; third, it should supply, if possible, such particular instruction as will fit the individual for some useful forms of work. This concept still applies after all these years, particularly so, as Tredgold was discussing this very problem of mental deficiency.

There exists today an accepted philosophical commitment on the part of public education to serve the educational needs of the total community, including the disadvantaged, the physically handicapped, and the neurologically handicapped. This commitment should be extended without reservation to the mentally retarded who are just as capable of benefiting from education, albeit — special instruction.

Consider further the conditions and educational needs of adults thought to be disabled because of limiting mental conditions. It is obvious that a most important consideration by the instructor must be that of **assessment.** A level of communication must be established, and it must be established without traumatic effect. In other words, the current level of academic and social functioning must be determined in a manner which does not frustrate nor discourage the student, but rather stimulates the student to seek further assistance and instruction. From this initial determination, the instructional process may move in one of several directions. The disparity extant in the group is one factor that determines the individualization of instruction; but, essentially, it may be generally assumed that the content will initially be a modification of basic education. Another factor is the instructor's style; however, certain basic concepts should be borne in mind relative to instruction of mentally retarded adult students. A third factor is the use of various techniques; behavior modification, social imitation and modeling. Of these, the most prominent of the current techniques seems to be that of behavior modification.

Behavior Modification — The process of behavior modification, which is suggested here, is that which has been expanded from its first successful applications in the 60's and involves operant conditioning. This technique has evoked responses most gratifying in terms of goal-oriented and specific objective-oriented expectations. It should be clearly understood that we are not suggesting the use of chemical and/or surgical interventions in order to modify behavior.

Gallagher[3] suggests that other dimensions, notably that of social imitation and modeling may be used to modify behavior patterns of the mentally retarded. Altman and Talkington point out wide varieties of possible applications for modeling with not only the educably retarded but with the severely retarded also.

A more significant and attainable suggestion in terms of retarded adults is that of curriculum modification. Two methods are pre-eminent:

Education for the Handicapped

1. The modification of large segments of an existent curriculum based upon the assessment and diagnostic prescriptions. Many mildly retarded adults can learn in regular classes if the present curriculum is modified in minor respects.
2. A plan of prescriptive teaching and prescriptive assignments. Prescriptive teaching and assignments are techniques which have built-in flexibility coming closest to meeting the special needs of special students. This particular theory is directly applicable to individuals based on individual differences requiring unique and specific techniques.

Since there is a paucity of material related to educating handicapped adults, often and inappropriately, concepts are adapted based on educating retarded **children**. In fact most of the techniques discussed and suggested for implementing adult programs have evolved from programs for children. The techniques so utilized, having been based on practical application, revision, and trial use — are usually the most viable for adult retarded students.

Vocational Emphasis — An area related to education and training, and with a fair amount of relevant information available, is that of employment of the retarded. Posner[4] reports that of the retarded adult population in the United States capable of working independently or in a sheltered situation, three times more are unemployed than for a similar group of "normal" adults. Posner cautions us that this figure should be viewed as questionable; but even if the figure advanced is incorrect, the implications of such a disparity, for education, are quite clear. We need to plan, develop, and implement programs designed to assist this group to become better qualified. In addition, we need to increase basic skills in general, and to develop individual capabilities in specific areas through cooperatively planned educational services. Lower the traditional barriers of "look alike," "do alike," "progress alike," and provide meaningful individualized instruction, in the group setting if need be, *but* provide it. Bear in mind that vocational rehabilitation in its broadest concept is a system of education and/or training. Work-study and on-the-job training are other possibilities for development of potential. Here again, behavior modification, in terms of attitudinal changes and patterns of reactive behavior, presents additional opportunities to the educator in search of a method.

A need for this primary consideration — employment of handicapped adults — is based on viewing the total spectrum of exceptionality grouped under the single identifying label — handicapped, and concomitant is the need to winnow out those philosophies, techniques, methods, and materials that provide for the most efficient use of available instructional time and talent. Finally, new legislation and strong educational thrusts at all levels and in all segments of education in the area of programs for the handicapped in general, and for the mentally handicapped in particular, lend strong emphasis to these needs.

Physical Disabilities — From the area of great need for specialized and divergent methods and materials used with the mentally disabled, consider the educational requirements for the physically disabled, particularly the wheelchair bound and the severely ambulatory impeded. The greatest help by any educational institution or system to make education more accessible to this group would be the removal of existing physical barriers, and construction and/or development of architectural aids aimed at improving accessibility to existing facilities, and, of course, at new facilities. The latter, new construction accessibility, is mandated in many states; since laws have been passed regulating such accessibility for the physically disabled in all new construction of public buildings.

Advice to Teachers — Perhaps the most valuable piece of advice that might be given an otherwise experienced instructor who has not been involved in programs for the physically impaired per se, is: After noting the physical limitations imposed on the physically disabled students by their handicapping condition, make every effort to neutralize the adverse effects of the physical environment and then **teach**. Teach exactly as required for a "normal" class. Do not be confused, misled, or intimidated by a physical appearance that is not the norm; and above all, do not let this individual difference negatively affect teaching rapport. Beyond this, we would strongly recommend, even implore, that an instructor who finds a satisfactory and rewarding experience in a teaching situation of this kind, actively promote such programs through recruitment, referral, and support of expansion of services. Bear in mind that, for the physically disabled, special program and instructors are not the vital issue; facilitation of accessibility is. Finally, the best resource for meaningful change is the handicapped person himself: for he/she, above all, knows what the major obstacles to his/her education are.

In the areas of visual and auditory defects in adults, education is geared toward compensation for the handicapping effects of the affliction. For example: Braille, mobility training, self-help, and survival training are frequently aimed at offsetting the difficulties imposed by the loss of sight. Manual communications (sign language), lip reading, combination of sign and lip reading, and developmental communications in special settings are broadly offered in the field of adult education for the deaf and, again, are aimed at compensation for the loss attributable to the handicap. All of these approaches are unique in their contribution toward the improvement and development of people who are handicapped by sight or hearing loss, and it is obvious that instructors in these fields are required to have highly specialized teaching skills. There is a bonus fringe benefit in these teaching fields and this is, that it is not only feasible, but highly recommended that deaf instructors and blind instructors be hired to serve in such programs, whenever possible. However, blind or deaf instructors should not be limited to special programs and, conversely, "normal" instructors willing to undertake the effort may find a new, exciting, and highly rewarding addition to their professional career by simply adding the skills of manual communication or Braille to their teaching repertoire.

One of the primary needs in this special field is for enthusiastic young (old) instructors who are able to teach a salable skill and who have the ability to adapt the teaching of this skill to the special needs of the handicapped. Granted that this is a difficult, but not an impossible task. If there is a commentary to be drawn from this theme, it is that failure in an attempt to be pragmatic and constructively innovative is not necessarily negative: it is an indication that even after the years of developmental educational techniques, we still have far to go. **Failure to try would be the real indictment.**

A word of caution needs to be interjected here. It is imperative that in the field of education, it is recognized that adult handicapped citizens have responsibilities and educational needs that are unique to each individual; and attempts by any agency to meet these special needs should be geared chiefly to providing experiences embodying the principle of normalization; but these attempts can not in any way absolve the educator from observing sound principles of recognizing individual differences. It is this dichotomoy between individualization and normalization (though not mutually exclusive) which causes much of the difficulty in selection and implementation of educational services for the handicapped. It is counter-productive to attempt to serve the adult handicapped as a group; and, of course, to attempt complete individualization of services is equally as questionable. The ideal educational setting for the handicapped should be a flexible program based upon an initial assessment of needs, adjustable to the adult handicapped students as they emerge and are identified, and a continual evaluation of program and student development.

Such a program design might involve one or a combination of a variety of techniques including highly specialized complex services, slightly modified regular programs, and/or completely regular programs combined with special ancillary supportive services such as counseling, tutoring, financial assistance, removal of architectural barriers, and special audio-visual aids.

Broader information for teachers of the handicapped would give greater insight into the problems confronting handicapped adults. For example, perusal of a pamphlet issued by the President's Committee on Employment of the Handicapped[5] revealed the following relevant information:

1. A New York bill recently signed into law provided that disabled people cannot be discriminated against in housing, employment, and public accommodations.
2. A young deaf person was the first, so handicapped, to be a participant in the American Legion Boy's Nation. As such, he was chairman of several seminars.
3. The Kiwanis recently awarded "The Talking Book," a widely heard non-profit, nonsectarian radio show for the nearly 20,000 blind or handicapped people in Southern Illinois and Eastern Missouri, their national radio award for the "first daily program of significant benefit to the Nation."
4. A grant was recently awarded to the University of Washington School of Dentistry to support a program for training dentists in the treatment of handicapped people.
5. The Ford Motor Company is concluding development of a wheelchair matched to a special version of its Pinto car. This marriage could become a manageable and economical system for paraplegics who use cars.

SUMMARY

With the concept of normalization and individualization, coupled with community based services for the handicapped, have come new and viable programs of education for handicapped adults. Such programs must address themselves to the individual needs of this exceptional population in terms of special education employing trained instructors possessing unique skills, and in terms of ancillary supportive services whose function it is to provide specialized services designed to bridge the gap between the handicapped individual and his ability to cope.

Continuing education and those who are involved with it are in an enormously advantageous position to give direction and meaning to programs for adult handicapped persons. The flexibility which has been a traditional hallmark of adult continuing education is the ideal educational beginning for application of the techniques and materials which have been thus far developed, and in providing a setting for needed analytical probing of new and innovative systems aimed at development of the potential of the handicapped.

There has never been another time when the needs were greater, or the resources more numerous. It remains only for dedicated instructors to become professionally involved and administrators to provide the support.

Finally, we would like to quote a California Superintendent of Public Instruction who, in 1915, advised teachers and administrators: "You are there to help folks along, not to hamper them with your official routine."[6] Paraphrased and updated: "You are there to help your students develop to their full potential: don't deprive them by what might be traditionally expected of you."

QUESTIONS AND EXERCISES

1. List any handicaps with which you have had experience and consider the adjustments made in order to be effective in relating to the individuals involved.
2. Analyze personal beliefs which you may have in regard to mental and/or physical handicaps. Identify any detectable prejudices.
3. Outline or describe techniques, special equipment and materials, or ancillary services which you might employ were you to be suddenly given the responsibility of instruction of a special class for handicapped adults of a given type.

REFERENCES

1. Position Paper. "The Mentally Retarded and the Community Colleges." California Junior College Association, 1974.
2. Tredgold, A. F. *Mental Deficiency.* New York: William Wood & Co., 1929.
3. Gallagher, James J. "Education." *Mental Retardation and Developmental Disabilities, An Annual Review.* Joseph Wortis (ed.). New York: Brunner/Mazel, 1974.
4. Posner, Bernard. "Employment." *Mental Retardation and Developmental Disabilities, An Annual Review.* Joseph Wortis (ed). New York: Brunner/Mazel, 1974.
5. "Performance." Volume XXV, No. 4, October 1974, pp 18-21.
6. Hanson, Fred M. and Shryock, Clifton. "Programs for the Educable Mentally Retarded in California Public School." California State Department of Education, 1974.

Education for the Aging

David A. Peterson
Director, Leonard Davis School of Gerontology
University of Southern California

Patrick Keane
Associate Professor, Department of Education
Dalhousie University

We are now living in an aging society. The United States has changed during this century from a nation in which most of our citizens were predominantly children and adolescents to one in which an increasingly large percentage are middle aged and older. This has occurred because widespread application of medical care, public health, and consumer protection has made it possible for virtually everyone to avoid the illnesses and trauma of infancy and to live healthy and productive lives. This is the triumph of aging; the successful culmination of the search for extended, healthy life.

In 1900 approximately three million persons were over the age of 65 in the United States (four percent of the population). Both the absolute number and the percentage have increased throughout the century so that by 1980 there were 24.5 million older people, nearly 12 percent of the total population. Their numbers will continue to grow, so that by 2000 we can expect 32 million persons in this category. However, it will only be after the year 2010 when the baby boom of the 1950's and 1960's reaches retirement age that the major impact of the aging society will be felt. By 2040, we can expect up to 20 percent of the American population to be over age 65, a total of 50 million persons.

At the turn of the century, retirement and death were closely associated. Persons tended to work until health problems caused them to retire, typically only a short time before death. Today this is not the case. The period of healthy functioning has been extended, and persons are retiring earlier. In 1900, 63 percent of those men over 65 remained in the work force. Today, only 20 percent of men in this age group are employed. This means that a whole new period of life has been created, a time after the employment years, but before debilitating health conditions require reductions in mobility, activities, and involvement. This period is often called "later maturity" and is characterized by persons between the ages of 60 and 75 who are capable of continuing all of their middle-age activities but have chosen to remain outside the work force. They are the persons seen in volunteer programs, senior centers, travel programs, golf courses, retirement communities, shopping centers, and educational programs. They are a growing group whose personal and economic resources make them a new force in the learning community.

Older persons have participated, both as learners and teachers, in instructional activities for as long as such programs have existed. The earliest education was directed primarily toward adults, and participants were individuals with available time and interest. Education, then, is not foreign to older people, but in the United States, it is only recently that conscious attempts have been made to recruit older participants and to design educational experiences which are exclusively for persons in this age group.

Education of older people is an area of study and activity which is occurring within and between the fields of education and gerontology. Studies in a variety of disciplines and professions through numerous settings and institutions have provided support for the belief that education offers much to older people. These developments are of interest to instructors, program planners, and citizens generally because they provide the hope for preventing some of the decline which often occurs in later life and the opportunity to assist older people in maximizing their potential. Success in these endeavors will have major significance for the continued employment of older persons, for their integration into the fabric of society, and for sustaining their contribution in the future. We are only beginning to glimpse the significance of education for the aged but the potential is truly great.

Since educational programs for older people are offered through a variety of institutional settings, it is not surprising that there are multiple purposes, and the results lead to quite diverse outcomes. Education may be preparation for a new task such as a job, volunteer assignment, or a new role in the family. It may be directed toward psychological growth in which the individual attempts to explore innate capabilities. Education may be a primary mechanism used to prevent physical, psychological, and social decline of the individual. Likewise, it may be used to evaluate and translate lifelong experience into insights regarding the importance and meaning of that experience. It may be the opportunity to discover meaning in the individual's knowledge and experience and translate that to a higher level of abstraction and understanding. Thus, as we explore some of the facets of this new field of educational programming, we must be reminded that diversity of clientele and program is the rule rather than the exception.

Adult Education Participation — Examination of the demographic characteristics of participants in continuing and adult education activities reveals a pattern that is already too familiar in the more traditional forms of education: the majority are relatively well-educated, financially secure, and younger than non-participants. Of these attributes, the amount of formal schooling has the greatest influence. Persons with lower levels of formal education are far less likely to participate.

The second most powerful predictor of participation is age. Only 4.5 percent of adults 55 and over participated in some form of organized adult education in 1975; statistically, the older the person the less likely he/she was to participate. One important reason for lower participation rates among older adults in undoubtedly their lower level of formal education, but age appears to act independently of other socio-economic indicators in its influence on participation.

Other factors shown to influence participation are proximity and availability of opportunities. Studies comparing different regions in the country indicate greater participation in the western states, particularly in California, than in other parts of the country. This is attributed largely to the availability of educational opportunities that are offered without charge. The greater visibility of such programs appears to have created a climate of acceptance and interest not seen elsewhere.

Data from three studies by the National Center for Educational Statistics[1] indicate a clear trend toward greater educational participation by older people in recent years. The studies surveyed educational enrollments in adult education programs by persons who were not full-time students. The original data were collected in 1969 and the survey was replicated in 1972 and 1975. Figure 1 shows that the absolute number of participants increased over this six year period as did the percentage of participating persons in this age group.

Persons Age 55+ Participation in Adult Education in the United States

	1969	1972	1975
Number of Persons Participating	1,048,000	1,363,000	1,627,000
Percentage of Persons Participating	2.9%	3.5%	4.0%
Number of Males Participating	412,000	518,000	642,000
Percentage of Males Participating	2.5%	3.0%	3.6%
Number of Females Participating	637,000	845,000	984,000
Percentage of Females Participating	3.2%	3.9%	4.3%

Figure 1

What participation statistics do not reveal is the number of persons who are interested in further learning but do not take advantage of available programs. Cross[2] noted that needs assessment surveys typically find a large number of such persons, whom she terms "potential" or "would-be" learners; nearly three quarters of the adult population expressed interest in further learning but only one-third actually participated. Some non-participators identify themselves as self-directed learners, but even those persons express interest in having outside help at some time during their learning projects. Lack of interest, then, does not appear to be the principal reason for the unequal participation rates among different groups.

EDUCATIONAL NEEDS AND WANTS OF OLDER PEOPLE

Educational needs are perceived lacks or weaknesses in knowledge, attitude, skill, or values. Generally they are determined by authorities through conjecture and the application of theory; they can be addressed through some educational intervention. Educational needs may be the result of inadequate formal education, the passage of extensive time since formal schooling was completed, social change, individual development, or a lifelong desire for personal or psychological growth.

Educational wants, on the other hand, are salient desires or preferences. Older people often express these wants in terms of content or skill areas such as learning to speak Spanish or how to knit. The vehicles for letting these wants be known are often through community groups or through institutions serving older people. Yet, preferred educational topics may be held so tentatively that they may appear to change with each whimsical suggestion thus providing little indication of the "true" wants of the older person.

Many educators have written about the educational needs of older people, but Howard McClusky's "Background Paper on Education for the 1971 White House Conference on Aging"[3] is the best known. McClusky identified five categories of educational needs. They are not the only needs of older people, but are needs which could be best addressed by instructional interventions. These categories of needs of older people are as follows:

1. Coping Needs. Needs result from the decrements which occur in aging and the absolescence of unused skill or capacity. These include survival needs, as well as those needs which allow adequate functioning in a complex and interrelated society. The survival needs are food, housing, and clothing; sufficient health care; stimulating social interactions; and consumer competence. Without these being met at a minimal level, it is generally not possible for the individual to survive or to have any surplus energy to devote to growth or altruistic activities.

Skills needed for daily functioning in a complex and interrelated society would include remedial education designed to overcome weaknesses or omissions in the formal education of childhood and youth, as well as those skills which allow for adaptation to aging and afford a higher quality of life. The functional skills are literacy education, the development of reading and writing skills, and consumer instruction. Adaptive skills might include, amongst others, adaptive health strategies, resocialization, retirement and income planning, and age stereotype counseling. Courses planned to develop these skills should be designed to help the individual deal with the daily decisions necessary for survival in a complex and challenging environment.

2. Expressive Needs. The second category of needs identified by McClusky is termed "expressive." These are needs for activity or participation which are engaged in for their own sake. The reward for involvement is intrinsic to the activity itself, and interest alone is sufficient motivation for participation. Enjoyment results from the physical or social activity, from the spontaneity involved, and from the exhilaration of new experience. For many older people time has not allowed the exploration or cultivation of all the interests they have; there has been insufficient opportunity to sample many of the possible arts, sports, and academic areas. Retirement provides somewhat more available time; so the revival of old interests, the development of long postponed relationships, and the learning of new skills is now possible. These activities are not expected to lead to a degree, a job, or higher status. They are undertaken because they are fun, or challenging, or interesting,. They allow the individual to express him/herself in a way which has not been possible during the preceding years.

Expressive needs can be met through several types of educational programming. The most evident is leisure time pursuits which result in a renewing of the individual. The preferred diversion varies from person to person depending on the interest and background of the individual. Educational experiences emphasizing creativity, such as art, music, and drama provide obvious examples of this area of educational programming. A considerable number of older people evidence interest in these areas through their participation and continued support of the arts. Their involvement may be expected to lead to increased creativity and improved self image.

3. Contributive Needs. The third category of need is titled, contributive. It indicates the altruistic desire of most people to assist others in coping with current problems and in achieving their developmental tasks. This suggests that persons have a need to give something that is of value to others. For older people the opportunity for social involvement, personal status, and increased self-worth may occur through service. This may take the form of volunteerism with local health and welfare agencies, with churches, or with government sponsored programs for older people. Whatever the avenue of their service, their resources of time, understanding, and skills can be of extensive value.

Education has a key developmental role to play in meeting contributive needs. It can be the means by which older individuals identify their potential contributions, mobilize their resources, and direct their time and service in the most meaningful manner. Education also has a role in developing and directing the contributive impulse. Without knowledge of the available opportunities for service, individuals often waste precious energy and become discouraged about the value of their contribution. The development of specific skills through an instructional program could assist the individual to more realistically assess their expectations about what can and should be achieved.

4. Influence Needs. Persons of all ages have the desire to make some difference in the general functioning of society, to affect some meaningful social change. Influence needs indicate the expectation that older people, too, will be concerned with the larger issues of citizenship and social problems; they will want to direct a portion of their energy toward these more general areas. This may be done through the typical political process, through participation in voluntary and community groups, through service organizations, or through participation in quasi-governmental structures.

Education's relationship to this category is one of identification of the most appropriate roles, development of personal or group skills, provision of social supports, and assistance in evaluating the results of the activities. Since older people typically have greater amounts of discretionary time than do many persons in their middle years, the opportunity for participation in this area is great. However, the current level of knowledge and skills may prevent optimum participation. The complexity of government programs, community politics, and bureaucratic "turf" protection may require fairly sophisticated approaches which are only available to the well educated.

5. **Transcendence Needs.** The final category of needs which McClusky identified is transcendence needs. These are needs for gaining some deeper understanding of the meaning of life, the integration of self into the larger purpose of life, the review of what a life has been, and the movement beyond the physical declines which are occuring in the individual's body. Although transcendence needs are evidenced at all ages, they are perhaps most imperative in the later stages of life since death is clearly in view and the mortality of the physical self is increasingly evident. Education here would need to encourage one to rise above physical discomfort and derive satisfaction from social intercourse and mental stimulation.

Educational Wants of Older People — Educational wants of older people are those preferences, interests, or desires which are indicated by older individuals themselves. These, of course, vary greatly from one group to the next and from one individual to another. The methodology for determining these wants is not well developed, but several means are available including mailed or group questionnaires, use of advisory committees, observation of existing classes for indications of additional interest, informal discussions with potential participants, and analysis of enrollment behavior as a means of predicting future interest and wants.

Cross[2] reviewed thirty studies of educational interest of adults. Although they included older people, they were not limited to this age group. She reported that adult learners are generally pragmatic; they wanted some visible pay off from the instruction. The more disadvantaged persons wanted vocational help from the classes. Men are more interested in job training while women appear to have more general or expressive interests. Advantaged adults indicated that the intrinsic rewards of education were their primary concern with social participation being a major reason for enrolling. One may conclude from these studies that the content is not the only or even the primary motivation for attendance for many people.

An early study interviewed persons over the age of 65 and reported that the greatest educational interests were in religion, problems of growing old, gardening, travel, physical fitness, and grooming. Other topics with high interest included psychology, managing financial affairs, history, public affairs, and foreign relations.

Galvin[4] recently reported on a survey of older persons' educational wants undertaken by several community colleges in the Los Angeles area, that coping with problems of life, health, and finance was the greatest interest, retirement preparation was second, and social development and training for voluntary service third. Categorized in another way, approximately 60 percent of this sample indicated interest in hobby and recreational subjects, health and nutrition, consumer education, and supplemental income.

Learning Abilities of Older People — More recently Cross studied the general population and reported in terms related to demographic characteristics rather than in content. Basically she reported that adults are pragmatic and want immediacy of learning application.

Determining and meeting the learning needs and wants of older people is only feasible if they are able to effectively take in new information along with changing behaviors and attitudes. While the primary ability to acquire both knowledge and skills does not disappear with advancing age, older learners may face some difficulties associated with the aging process. Verbal skills, general knowledge, and overall ability remain relatively high until very late in life. For some of them, the infirmities and inadequacies associated with old age have become a self-fulfilling prophecy, and while they learn daily from personal interaction and experiences, the notion of formal learning in a regular program is thought impracticable. For others who have progressed upward through Maslow's hierarchy of needs, having met basic physiological, safety, affection and esteem needs, there are opportunities for self-actualization not just as participants, but as planners of educational programs for seniors.

What is more important than whether older people can learn, is to determine how to design instruction for them so that the most effective learning will result. Performance on learning tasks is affected by several factors. The intelligence of the individual, the learning skills which the person has acquired over the years, and the flexibility of learning styles are, of course, key variables. There are, however, several other variables, often called non-cognitive factors, which can also greatly affect learning. These do not involve intellectual ability but nevertheless have great bearing on an individual's performance. Some of the non-cognitive factors include the visual and auditory acuity of the learner, the health status of the individual, the motivation to learn, the level of anxiety, the speed at which the learning is paced, and the meaningfulness of the material to be learned.

Four factors that greatly influence the learning abilities of older people are:
1. Interference. Learning may be inefficient if there is some interference. This can occur in several ways. First, interference can result from the conflict of current knowledge with the new knowledge to be learned; second, two learning tasks undertaken at the same time can interfere with each other; third, subsequent learning can interfere with the intended learning.

The teacher of older people could utilize this understanding by emphasizing new knowledge which will be consistent with previous learning, by minimizing any conflicts between new and old knowledge, and by helping the older person unlearn incorrect knowledge. A specific implication of this understanding is that the instructor can benefit from a familarity with the older person and the beliefs, experiences, and knowledge the older individual brings to the instructional setting. If the new information is likely to be in sharp contrast with present knowledge, the teacher should proceed in a slow and careful manner since overt or implicit resistance to the new information can be expected.

The teacher should concentrate on one task at a time and assure that one item is satisfactorily learned before the next is undertaken. If a second task must be undertaken, it should be postponed as long as possible and should be clearly distinctive so that it is possible to know when one has completed the task and is moving on to the next. Apparently, older people need more time to integrate the new learning and to rehearse it before it is well set in the secondary memory. Additional stimulation during this period is likely to result in premature forgetting or inability to adequatley retrieve the information.

2. Pacing. Laboratory studies have shown that older people perform less well when the learning task must be completed under the pressure of time.[5] Older people learn more successfully when they are provided additional time both to take in the information (presentation rate) and to retrieve the answer (response rate), although a slowed response rate appears to assist them the most. When self pacing by the older learner is allowed, the learning performance appears to be optimized.

The application of this insight from laboratory research is very direct in a teaching setting. Instruction should be self paced, or if that is not possible, should be paced rather slowly in order to provide time for both intake and retrieval. Since the lecture is a form of timed instruction, it should be structured in such a manner that material is presented, reviewed, and examined. This may be effectively supplemented by structured discussion and application which allows it to be related to previous knowledge, which offers time for consideration of the material, and which can reduce the psychological pressure of speeded learning.

3. Organization of Material. Older persons are less likely than others to spontaneously use some organizing strategies when learning new material. When investigators have encouraged older people to categorize words to be learned, scores have improved, but when the organizing strategy is provided by the researcher (teacher), then scores improved significantly. This appears to be especially true for older people who have poor verbal skill; for highly verbal older people, the weaknesses in their organizing strategies are less pronounced, so improvement is minimal with this type of assistance.

Learning performance of students, including older people, can be improved by assisting them to organize the material in better ways and by encouraging alternatives to rote memorization. This can be done through the provision of "advance organizers," aids to help the learner appropriately direct his/her attention. Many older learners have difficulty following the content because they can not anticipate what will be taught and do not see the "whole" which is being presented. It is often helpful to provide an introductory overview in which the entire lesson is given in outline form. This provides an early opportunity to see the "map" which is being followed, an insight which is especially useful for older people.

Specific examples of advance organizers include the provision of an outline of the class session, the course, or the program; sets of notes to follow; initial summaries of the content; or lists of facts, concepts, or issues to be examined. These, of course, need not be provided in written form, but when that is the procedure, it does provide a guide that can be reviewed by the learner at any time.

4. Feedback. Like other adults, older persons are assisted in their learning when they are provided feedback on their performance. Since the older individual often continues to use improper or ineffective means to address a problem solving or learning situation even after these have proven to be unproductive, the feedback is especially useful when it includes suggestions for alternative approaches.

The implications for instruction include the obvious value of allowing the older learner an opportunity to rehearse the behavior or learning under the guidance of the teacher so that corrective feedback can be provided. Since the older person typically requires a longer time period and a greater number of trials in order to achieve the desired learning, feedback on the amount of progress being made and the current level of functioning is generally of value.

As with most suggestions, negative results can occur. Older people are typically less able to accept negative feedback and to continue to do well. Since they often have less interest, greater anxiety, and lower self concept, they are likely to experience greater detrimental results from negative feedback. Thus, every attempt should be made to avoid a judgemental, critical position, and a more supportive, helpful posture should be taken whenever possible.

SUMMARY
Educational Programs for Older People — The barriers to educational participation by older people and the current limited enrollment of older people in courses and workshops does not mean that education for older adults is not a viable and growing area of activity. Public schools, higher education institutions and community agencies are all realizing the potential audience which older adults comprise and are beginning to direct their energies and resources toward this new educational population. Although much development will be required before this educational opportunity reaches the majority of the older cohort and a comprehensive set of alternative educational programs exists, the past ten (10) years have resulted in extensive expansion of these instructional services and have laid the foundation for major growth in the future. The outcomes of such programs may be less clear than are those of a professional school training of physicians, teachers, or engineers, but the societal values may be just as real, resulting in continued good health, community involvement, and personal growth for older members of the community.

Older people, then, have traditionally not been major participants in the educational system of this nation. They do have educational needs which are encouraging them to change this status. They now have the time and inclination to continue their personal growth, to attempt to solve developmental and family problems, and to understand the changes in their society and themselves so that they can prevent precipitous difficulties in later life. Thus it is possible to observe a change in the national orientation toward education;

continuing education is spreading to all ages of the population, and older as well as younger adults are discovering its value.

It is clear that higher socio-economic status, earlier retirement, better health, more years of schooling, and greater mobility are positively associated with educational participation. Each succeeding cohort which reaches age 65 has higher levels of these characteristics and consequently is more likely to take advantage of the available educational opportunities. As the need for retraining of older workers increases, as preparation for retirement education grows, and as the leisure time education for retirees expands, we can expect to witness continued growth in the numbers and proportion of older people who become students.

Questions and Exercises

1. Educational participation by older people will increase in the future. Identify at least four reasons for this occurrence and rank order them in terms of importance.
2. Good teaching of older people involves many of the same characteristics as teaching persons of other ages. However, there are several areas where older adults need special consideration. Discuss at least five of these and identify the adjustments an instructor must make.
3. Education has been viewed as being of value to youth. It is becoming of more value to all persons. Identify the five most important values of education to older persons and the five most important values to society.
4. Compare the educational wants of older people to their educational needs. Distinguish between needs and wants.
5. In considering the development of an educational program for older persons, what will be the major costs involved?

REFERENCES

1. **National Center for Educational Statistics.** *Participation in Adult Education: Final Report - 1975.* Washington, D.C.: Government Printing Office, 1978.
2. Cross, P. K. "Adult Learners: Characteristics, Needs and Interests." R. E. Peterson and Associates, *Lifelong Learning in America.* San Francisco: Jossey-Bass, 1979.
3. McClucky, H. Y. *Background and Issues on Education.* Washington, D. C.: Government Printing Office, 1971.
4. Galvin, K. et al. *Educational and Retraining Needs of Older Adults.* Washington D. C.: ERIC ED 110, 132, 1975.
5. Canestrari, R. E., Jr. "Age Changes in Acquisition." G. A. Talland (ed.), *Human Aging and Behavior.* New York: Academic Press, 1968.

Tailoring Vocational Education to Adult Needs

Norma B. Brewer

*Coordinator, Voc-Ed for the Handicapped,
Louisiana Department of Education*

Adult vocational education has been largely ignored by the field of education. Because of the emphasis that society has placed on the education of youth over the years, an educational system that is poorly equipped to reach the needs of adults has developed. The system largely ignores the impact that the accelerating rate of change has had on the lives of adults. Most adults are confronted with at least one of the following educational needs in terms of their occupations: (1) the need to update skills and knowledge in order to keep abreast of changes in their fields, (2) the need to acquire new or additional skills and knowledge in order to change fields. Adult Vocational Education should receive the staff and funding needed in order to contribute its knowledge and expertise in aiding the local community educational effort to solve the problems of both unemployment and stagnation in business and industry.

An inclusive definition of adult vocational education is almost impossible to achieve. Virtually any type of learning situation or programs in which adults participate is considered adult education, Likewise, any type of work-oriented class, workshop, or conference is considered vocational education. In an attempt to define the wide, diverse, and somewhat confusing field of vocational technical education of adults, Venn[1] stated that:

> The vocational-technical education of adults is considered by many to be a process rather than a program — a process that involves the development of the individuals for social, economic and occupational competence. It is carried on in institutions, on the job, in formal and informal situations, and elsewhere.

Bottoms[2] defined vocational education as a system that involves not only the adult as an individual, but the family and community as well. This system should strengthen an individual's ability to earn a living, a family's ability to sustain a decent life together, and a community's ability to thrive.

Two equally important dimensions are included in a recent comprehensive view of vocational education for adults: (1) assist adults to make continual career choices, to prepare for a specific job, and to progress in their work environments in a socially responsible way; (2) create a more favorable and stable community economic climate by focusing on training and service needs of employers.

In a broader context adult vocational education is defined as a process by which adults, as individuals, family members, and community participants, will prepare to enter an occupation, or upgrade or update a present one in order to benefit themselves, their familes, and their communities.

THE CHANGES IN AVE

With the advent of World War II, adults began to seek further education and training, a process that increased the awareness of the vocational education needs of adults. Some of the reasons given include:

> The obsolescence of knowledge, the rapid growth of new knowledge, the shifts in national priorities, the multiplications and complexity of social problems, and the close relationship between the application of knowledge and social progress . . .[3]

Keeping up with a vast amount of information is a problem not only for the engineer or scientist, but for all of us. Culbertson[4] described the shift in human resource requirements brought about by technological change as follows:

> Over a relatively few years, the advances of technology have created whole new industries — missiles, electronics, business machines, plastics, new forms of research. Brand new skills have been substituted for skills of traditional importance . . . New technology is squeezing the unskilled worker out of the labor market and putting a premium on ever more advanced training. Thousands of displaced workers must adjust to other industries and occupations to earn their livelihood.

Adults are participating in educational activities in ever increasing numbers. U.S. Office of Education data show that almost four million participants were enrolled in adult vocational classes in 1976. Most of these participants attended school part time. In 1976, adult education programs enrolling the most students were the trades and industry (1,191,000), home economics (764,000), and office occupations (670,000). In 1978 only 4 percent of the labor force was served by vocational education. A major indicator of the need for expanding vocational programs is the growing number of adults aged twenty-five to forty-four; in 1978, there were 53.4 million persons in that age category as compared to a projected 70.6 million in 1985.[5] Other factors as indicators for increased emphasis on vocational education include the following:

1. Overcrowding in entry level positions.
2. Flight of business and industry from many of the nation's cities.
3. Changes in technology, materials, and processing essential to the United States' competitiveness in international trade.
4. An increase in the number of immigrants entering the United States.
5. A decline in the number of small businesses created during the seventies.

6. A decrease in the quality of family life as evidenced by a growing number of family-related social problems, such as child abuse and single parent families.
7. An increase in a number of special population groups as underemployed and unemployed adults, displaced homemakers, and the elderly.[2]

AVE PROGRAMS

The need for adult vocational education is well documented. There are some excellent vocational education program in existence that serve adults.

A Typology of Vocational Education — Evans[6] divided vocational education into the following six types:
1. Job-Specific Preparation. These programs increase employability in a particular job with a particular employer. Example: a program to train people for specified job classifications for a new company moving into town. Typical outcomes: attraction of industry, increased quality of goods and services.
2. Occupational-Specific Preparation. These programs increase employability in a particular occupation, but are not designed for a particular employer. Example: a program to prepare licensed practical nurses. Typical outcomes: better working conditions and job satisfaction, higher social status.
3. Occupational-Area Preparation. These programs increase employability in a group of occupations which use similar knowledge, tools, materials or methods. Example: building trades, printing. Typical outcome: better occupational choice.
4. Employability Preparation. These programs increase employability by developing work skills and attitudes which apply to any occupation. Examples of course titles: Occupational Survival Skills, Career Exploration. Typical outcomes: greater success in work or OJT.
5. Prevocational Guidance. Through guidance activities students acquire introductory occupational knowledge and general information about a variety of work settings. Examples: industrial arts, career orientation. Typical outcomes: better educational and occupational decision making.
6. Prevocational Basic Education. Many students require basic prevocational skills before they are ready for enrollment in occupational training or other work-related activities. Example: functional or occupational literacy courses. Typical outcomes: entry into an occupational education class or OJT.

Although Evans is describing general vocational education, his typology applies to programs serving adults. The first four types, for example, draw a substantial part of their enrollment from adults who are currently employed and who: (1) desire to work more effectively in their present employment, (2) seek promotion, (3) seek job or occupational changes. The growing number of adults seeking career information is an indication of the need to provide adult prevocational guidance, the fifth type mentioned by Evans. Included in this category would be displaced homemakers entering or reentering the job market following an extended absence as well as adults making career changes. The sixth type, prevocational basic education, also serves a number of adult students who are deficient in basic skills needed to perform a variety of jobs.

Funding Categories — The six types of programs discussed generally fall into one of three funding categories: (1) programs supported by public funds, (2) programs supported by private funds, (3) programs which are cooperatively funded by local, state, federal, or private sources.

Public Funds — The programs of vocational-technical education aided by federal legislation are the largest component of the nation's organized efforts to reduce unemployment and eliminate occupational shortages. U.S. Office of Education program data show that almost 2.2 million students were enrolled in federally aided postsecondary vocational classes in the fiscal year 1976, an increase of over 250 percent from 1968.

Other examples of publicly funded programs that have been important components of adult vocational education are Comprehensive Employment and Training Act (CETA), apprenticeship programs, and training programs provided by the armed forces.

Private Funds — Business and Industry, private learning corporations, vocational schools and home study courses, have much to offer the adult who is learning new or additional types of job skills. The unique features of these programs include such things as classes of varying lengths offered with and without academic credit; objectives specifically directed toward occupational preparation with little consideration for general education; flexible entrance requirements; program planning utilizing behavioral objectives; and flexibility that allows courses and programs to be instituted in very short time periods.

Cooperatively Funded — Efforts are under way in some vocational-technical schools, community colleges, and colleges and universities to cooperate with business and industry in employee education. One such program is a cooperative venture between Northwestern State University and Riley-Beard, Inc. of Shreveport, Louisiana to provide in-plant training and education to both current and prospective workers. The co-op program offers associate degrees in metals technology, welding technology, and drafting technology; and bachelor's and master's degrees in industrial technology.[7] A project was conducted by the National Center for Research in Vocational Education to identify, study, and disseminate information about cooperative industry and state administered adult education programs.[8] As a result of the project, over 100 cooperative industry-adult education programs were identified as models for future collaborative efforts.

LEARNING DESIGNS

Programming for adults has sometimes been accomplished in a rather haphazard manner, characterized more by expediency than by planning. According to Kasworm,[9] most adult education activities have focused on short-term goals, often not by conscious design, but because of extremely diverse clientele, their overwhelming need for immediate intervention, their significant variability in skills and knowledge levels, and their intermittent participation. Adult programs have also been characterized by programmatic discontinuity, minimal resources, limited staff development, and limited research.

Knowles[10] believed that in order to design a program for adults, the technology of "Andragogy" should be used. Andragogy has been defined as the art and science of helping adults learn. It is based on the following four assumptions about the characteristics of adult learners: (1) as people mature their self-concept moves from one of being a dependent personality to a self-directing human being, (2) as a growing reservoir of experience is accumulated, this experience becomes an increasing resource of learning, (3) as the readiness to learn increases, learning is oriented toward the developmental tasks of social roles, (4) as the time perspective changes from one of postponed application to one of immediate application, orientation toward learning shifts from one of subject centeredness to one of problem centeredness.[11]

If one chooses to apply the technology of andragogy to designing a learning environment for adult vocational education, then the implication for appropriate curriculum design is clear. Adults want programs that are designed to deal with their immediate problems, that are organized to fit their own special time frame, that employ adult-oriented materials, and that utilize the knowledge that they have already accumulated. The following material concerns programs and curriculum which have been found appropriate for use with adult vocational education learners. They are:
1. A Model for Designing Teaching Materials
2. PAVE System for Utilization with V-TECS Catalogs
3. Infusion of Life Skills into Adult Vocational Education
4. A Model School for Adults in Vocational Education.

Designing Teaching Materials — While organized programs designed for the adult population have been the exception rather than the rule, there have been some developments that show promise for the future. In 1972, an educational consortium of southern states for accountability was formed under the auspices of the Southern Association of Colleges and Schools. The name given to this consortium was Vocational-Technical Education Consortium of States (V-TECS) and the sole purpose was to develop catalogs of performance objectives for many occupational areas.

Each catalog is composed of a series of tasks that the learner will be expected to perform on the job, and each task contains a performance objective, criterion-referenced measure, and a performance guide. The format of the catalogs allows for individualization and is another reason why they are excellent for use with adult learners. The following example is from the catalog for floriculture workers:

DUTY: PROPAGATION AND PLANTING OF PLANTS
TASK: Transplant seedlings or cuttings

22. PERFORMANCE OBJECTIVE:

Given seedlings or cuttings, the desired spacing intervals, growing medium, and appropriate sterile containers, transplant seedlings or cuttings. Cuttings must be handled with care and transplanted in the sterile containers in such a way that the survival rate will be at least 98 percent.

CRITERION—REFERENCED MEASURE:

Instructor will provide seedlings or cuttings, growing medium and containers. Transplant the seedling or cutting.

PERFORMANCE GUIDE:

1. Identify the cuttings or seedlings to be transplanted.
2. Fill the sterile container with medium.
3. Using the thumb, forefinger or stick, make holes in the medium into which the seedlings or cuttings are to be transplanted.
4. Transplant the seedlings or cuttings, make sure that there is good contact between the roots and stems with the planting medium. Caution: Seedlings or cuttings should not be transplanted at too great a depth, they should be placed at the same depth they were growing initially.

A V-TECS catalog might be composed of 150 tasks or as few as 50, depending on the occupational area. Some of the occupational areas for which tasks have been developed are auto mechanics, auto body, welding, carpentry, horticulture, and radio-television repair. About eighty-six catalogs have been developed by the consortium members and an additional forty-two are in process or are being planned for the future.

Utilizing V-TECS Catalogs — Although V-TECS catalogs give direction to a vocational instructor, they do not suggest teaching methods or how to infuse the V-TECS material into ongoing classroom instruction in a systematic manner. The use of V-TECS must be accompanied by inservice training of teachers. Merely to give a copy of an auto mechanics catalog to an instructor and not couple it with "how to use it skills," is a waste of an excellent teaching resource.

In 1976, the Alabama State Department of Education designed and implemented the Performance-based Adult Vocational Education (PAVE) project for the utilization of the V-TECS catalogs for adult vocational education classes. In addition to the lack of instructor time to develop course content, two other problem areas had previously been identified in programming vocational courses for adults: (1) inadequate assessment of learner competencies, (2) lack of curricula that trained adults to perform specified competencies on the job. The PAVE Project was formulated to offer relevant, job-oriented instructional content and provide for effective assessment of learner competencies. In addition, it provided a management system which was adaptive to any occupational area and flexible enough to serve a variety of individual adult learner needs.

As a result of the PAVE Project, the use of certain V-TECS catalogs was found to be successful in adult vocational classes when the instructors received appropriate inservice training. The PAVE system, a systematic approach for skills training, was developed with a PAVE guide that led both the instructor and learner step-by-step through the process.

CBAVE Plus APL — A second project utilizing V-TECS catalogs was the Competency-Based Adult Vocational Education (CBAVE) project implemented by the Adult Education Department at Auburn University. The CBAVE Project attempted to tie a systematic method of designing curriculum material, using V-TECS catalogs, to the appropriate life skills needed by the adult vocational education learners.[12] The life skills were based on functional competencies identified by the Adult Performance Level (APL) project in 1972 at the University of Texas. A model for instruction of adults based on infusion of appropriate life skills into vocational education adult training programs was developed. The rationale for the model of instruction was that learning is accomplished more quickly and efficiently when specific needs are identified. Letter writing, for example, was taught in an auto mechanics class when it became apparent that equipment and supplies would have to be ordered from a catalog. Letter writing, one of the sixty-five life skills identified by the APL Project, is not usually taught in an auto machanics class.

A Model Learning Environment — The 916 Area Vo-Tech School in Minneapolis, opened in 1972, has an open-entry/open-exit, year-round personalized vocational-technical instruction system. It now serves approximately 5,500 adults in part-time and extension programs and another 1,800 in full-time postsecondary programs. It also serves seniors on a shared time basis from the district's fourteen high schools. The facility operates twelve months of the year and houses 1,400 training stations, used nearly every day by some 3,500 different persons.

When the instructional program for the new facility was being planned in 1970, the following goals were identified:
    1. A strong committment to secondary as well as postsecondary education.
    2. A strong commitment to the disadvantaged and handicapped.
    3. A strong commitment to accountability and efficiency.
    4. A strong commitment to open entry.

There are fifty-five competency-based training programs. A total of 5,800 job tasks have been defined; 5,800 terminal performance objectives and 23,000 learning objectives have been written; and 5,800 learning guides have been developed, including individualized print and audiovisual learning materials, and performance and knowledge criterion tests. The 916 Area Vo-Tech School serves as a model for many schools throughout the country. The basic goals of the school are compatible with Knowles' andragogical theory of adult learning, which utilizes motivation and self-direction of the adult in order to design and implement an environment in which adults learn.

SUMMARY

Since World War II, adults have been asking for further education and training in increasing numbers. The primary cause for this expanded interest has been the vast increase in knowledge caused by both cultural and technical changes. Other contemporary factors contributing to an increased emphasis on adult vocational education include: (1) the growing number of adults aged twenty-five to forty-four, (2) the shift in business and industry from many of the nation's cities, (3) the increasing number of immigrants entering the United States, (4) the increasing number of special population groups such as underemployed and unemployed adults, displaced homemakers, and older adults.

Adult education within the current vocational education system can generally be categorized into six types: (1) job-specific preparation, (2) occupation-specific education, (3) occupational area preparation, (4) employability preparation, (5) prevocational guidance, (6) prevocational basic education. These six types of programs generally fall into one of three funding categories: (1) programs supported by public funds, (2) programs supported by private funds, (3) programs that are cooperatively funded by local, state, federal, or private sources.

Adults want programs that are designed to deal with their immediate problems; that are organized to fit their own special time frame; that employ adult-oriented materials; that are adult oriented; that utilize the knowledge that they have already accumulated. While organized programs designed specifically for the adult population have been the exception rather than the rule, there have been some developments that are adapatable to the adult vocational education situation.

One of these developments has been the Vocational Technical Education Consortium of States (V-TECS). This consortium has developed catalogs of performance-based objectives, criterion-referenced measures, and performance guides for many occupational areas. While the materials developed by this consortium were not designed with only the adult population in mind, the nature and content of the material lend themselves easily to individualization. Hence, these resources are useful in developing a program of instruction specifically intended for the adult who will use it. The Alabama State Department of Education designed a system for the utilization of the V-TECS catalogs for adult vocational education. As a result of this project, the use of certain V-TECS catalogs was found to be successful in adult vocational classes when the instructors received appropriate inservice training in their use.

In the decade of the eighties, many changes will occur which will result in the further refinement of adult vocational education. Perhaps different categories of adults will emerge as national priorities are examined and funding patterns change. Programs will be developed to accomodate the changes that will occur, affecting both teaching materials and methods. Adult needs will constantly continue to change and adults will be welcomed and encouraged to seek, through vocational education, solutions to the problems they encounter. Vocational education must continue to serve the needs of the individual, the family, and the community if vocational education is to fufill its role and responsibility to the growth and development of America.

REFERENCES

1. Venn, G. "Vocational-Technical Education." *Handbook of Adult Education.* R. M. Smith, G. Aker, J. R. Kidd (eds.) New York: Macmillan Publishing Co., Inc., 1970.
2. Bottoms, G. "Vocational Education Looks to the Future." *VocEd* 56 (January/February 1981).
3. Hesburg, T.; Miller, P. A.; and Wharton, R. Patterns for Lifelong Learning. San Francisco: Jossey-Bass, 1973.
4. Culbertson, D. J. "Corporate Roles in Lifelong Learning." *Lifelong Learners — a New Clientele for Higher Education.* by D. W. Vermilye, (ed.) Washington, D. C.: Jossey-Bass, 1974.
5. Golladay, M. A. & Noell, J. (eds.). *The Condition of Education,* 1978. Washington, D. C.: National Center for Education Statistics. U. S. Government Printing Office, 1978. (ERIC Document Reproduction Service No. ED 155 811).
6. Evans, R. "Reauthorization and the Redefinition of Vocational Education." *VocEd* 56 (January/February 1981): 30-34. (ERIC No. EJ 238 103).
7. Dennis, W. H. "Class at the Plant." *VocEd* 53 (September 1978): 40-42. (ERIC No. EJ 191 932).
8. Winkfield, P. W.; Granger, J.; and Moore, M. B. A Partial Listing of Cooperative Adult Education Programs. Columbus: The Center for Vocational Education, The Ohio State University, 1975. (ERIC Document Reproduction Service No. ED 122 122).
9. Kasworm, C. *Competency-Based Adult Education: A Challenge of the 80's.* Columbus: The ERIC Clearinghouse on Adult, Career, and Vocational Education. The Ohio State University, 1980. (ERIC Document Reproduction Service No. ED 193 528).
10. Knowles, M. "Talking with Malcolm Knowles: The Adult Learner is a 'Less Neglected Species'." Training 14 (August 1977): 16-20. (ERIC No. EJ 165 385).
11. The Modern Practice of Adult Education: Andragogy Versus Pedagogy. New York: Association Press, 1970.
12. Competency-Based Adult Vocational Education Project. Auburn, AL: Department of Vocational and Adult Education, Auburn University, 1978. (ERIC Document Reproduction Service No. ED 172 023).

Life Skills

D. Stuart Conger
*Director, Occupational & Career Analysis
& Development Branch,
Canada Employment and Immigration Commission*

Dana Mullen
*Principal,
Delta Methods, Ottawa*

Life Skills are the utilization of appropriate and responsible problem solving behaviors in the management of personal affairs. Problem solving behaviors include a relatively small group of behaviors usable in many life situations. Appropriate use requires an individual to adapt the behaviors to time and place; responsible use requires maturity or accountability. As behaviors used in the management of personal affairs, the life skills apply to five areas of life responsibility: (1) self, (2) family, (3) leisure, (4) community, (5) job.

THE LIFE SKILLS COURSE

In achieving its objective, the Life Skills Course provides the students with competence in the use of problem solving skills to manage their personal affairs as suggested by the terms: self, family, leisure, community, job. Although the training concentrates on behaviors, it does not discount the effects that these new found competencies have on the attitudes of the adult student toward himself and those around him.[1]

The Life Skills Course recognizes that true learning (behavioral change) occurs when the learner has: (1) a clear understanding of his goal, (2) a clear description of the new behavior, (3) an understanding of those conditions which make the behavior acceptable. The concept to these new sought-for behaviors as skills, makes a happy fit with the recognition of "learning as changed behavior." A skill has these characteristics: (1) the connotation of clarity in description, (2) a definite purpose, (3) certain standards by which people judge their acceptability.

THE LIFE SKILLS PROCESS

Life Skills training integrates the content described above and three process dimensions: (1) student response to content, (2) student use of group, (3) problem solving.

The Student Response to Content Dimension — In responding along this dimension, the student may react first in any one of its three domains: (1) the cognitive, (2) the affective, (3) the psychomotor. When students react in the cognitive or knowing domain, they might rephrase a sentence in their own words, or summarize the happenings of the lesson. If so, they might combine the rather simple act of recalling with the more complex act of synthesizing, or they might relate the discussion in a lesson to an experience in their home life thereby contrasting and comparing. Or, the students might link the items in one lesson to those in another, thereby showing relationships. Any manipulation of course content such as: repetition or recall, explanation, analysis, application, synthesis or evaluation, represents a cognitive or knowing response.

Students also respond on this dimension with affect or feeling. This affective response may occur before, at the same time, or after the cognitive or knowing response. Indeed, it may be characteristic of the disadvantaged to hold knowledge in low esteem, in which case the initial reaction might occur in the affective domain. Whatever the exact sequence, Life Skills training recognizes the affective reaction and encourages its expression and control. At the worst, unexpressed or suppressed feelings inhibit the development of behavioral change and prevent the students from facing themselves and others. At the best, expressed feelings open the students to new understandings of those around them and help them recognize that others have the same fears and uncertainties. Yet, they manage to function. Furthermore, the students soon come to the realization that the mere expression of feelings often assists in controlling them. At one extreme, they may blurt out that some things look stupid, and reject lessons by walking out. Or, they may stay, but participate passively. At the other extreme, they may speak "loyally" of the group and the activities of the lessons. Or, they may defend the activities of the course and the group against outside criticism and enthusiastically tell others what has been learned. Though such expressions of feeling and attitude demand a great deal of the instructor, students respond quickly and positively, thus helping the members of the group accept their own feelings and those of others.

When the students respond in the third category of behaviors — the psychomotor or acting category — they use their bodies: by conducting interviews, demonstrating new behaviors to others, or participating in role playing situations. The students' psychomotor responses often provide the most obvious evidence of their full participation in the activities of the lesson. Cognitive, or knowing manipulation of the content provides them with a necessary "factual" base; their affective, or feeling response to content expresses their will to face the consequences of the new knowledge; its effect on their psychomotor response represents commitment to action.

The Student Use of Group Dimension — The second dimension describes the purpose of the learning group. The students use the group to practice new behaviors. They use feedback and criticism from the group to modify new behaviors. They study individuals in the group as models for new behaviors, and use the group as a setting in which to develop skills of self-expression. The group affects its members most when they have developed a strong sense of mutual trust and an interest in helping each other through the lessons. The group provides both acceptance and challenge, and seeks an essential balance between the two: **all acceptance** reduces improvement in skills and development of problem solving capabilities; **all challenge** makes people react defensively and become more set in ineffective behaviors.

Students respond at three rather distinct levels on this dimension:
1. Students continue interpersonal behaviors which in the past have met their needs. If previously withdrawn at **a first or safe level of use,** they continue to withdraw; if previously a bully, this behavior continues; or if they in the past tried always to harmonize the group activities, this continues.
2. At the level of **careful group use,** students venture into the practice of new behaviors. They model new behaviors after those of the instructor and other members of the group. They draw attention of other group members to this new behavior, seeking support and acknowledgment. At the upper edge of this level, students try the behavior with strangers.
3. At the level of **risky group use,** students ask directly for criticism of the new behaviors, seeking to refine them and make them more effective. They give feedback to others; venture opinions which they know others in the group might find startling coming from them. They express strong feelings to other members of the group, or object to some procedures the coach has used. On the use of group dimension, students extend the range and increase the effectiveness of their interpersonal behaviors.

Students then have three levels of activity in the learning group: (1) the level of **safe group use,** (2) the level of **careful group use,** (3) the level of **risky group use.** These add to each other: behaviors characteristic of the third level do not replace those of the second or the first level, nor do those in the second level replace those of the first level. Students retain the safe group use behaviors that serve them well. To assist students in necessary learnings, the instructor encourages addition of behaviors of the more venturesome two upper levels.

The more effective the learners, the more they use all responses named in the "response to content dimension," as a consequence of this they will use more of the behavioral categories named in the "use of group dimension."

The Problem Solving Dimension — Learners could use the content group dimensions to their fullest, and still achieve none of the objectives of the Life Skills course. The complete Life Skills Process/Content Model requires a third dimension. Life Skills students use a whole array of problem solving behaviors: (1) recognize a problem situation, (2) define a problem, (3) choose an alternative solution, (4) implement it, (5) evaluate the result. Of course, each of these processes contains many sub-processes. As they mature in the course, students increase the array of the problem solving behaviors used, until ideally, these behaviors are used as the situation requires. This array of behaviors provides the third dimension — the Problem Solving Dimension. Figure 1 represents the complete process model.

The Life Skills Process/Content Model

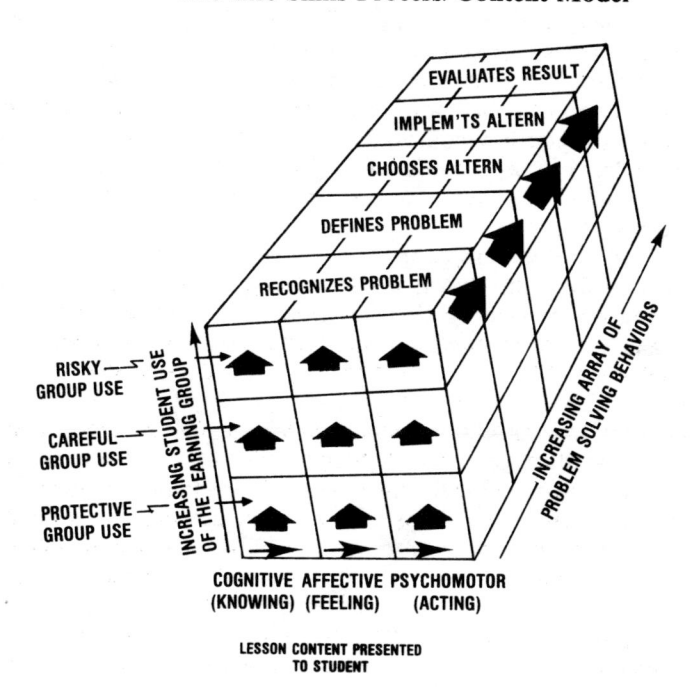

Figure 1.

THE LIFE SKILLS LESSON

The Lesson Model — The Life Skills lesson model combines techniques of counseling, learning, and skill training. The approach which the lesson model describes permits students to display knowledge and concerns about a particular problem as a first response to it. Then they seek information and practice skills which help the learners develop new approaches to its solution. They then apply these skills and knowledge to the problem as their first response to it, and finally evaluate the effect of this action.

The model requires the precise statement of each skill objective which gives direction to the students' activities in the lesson. Students work toward the achievement of the objective through the five phases of the lesson model: (1) stimulus, (2) evocation, (3) objective enquiry/skill practice, (4) application, (5) evaluation.

Application of the Model — The instructor always articulates the skill objective for the students by drawing their attention to its skill components so they know exactly what behaviors they are to manifest during the application phase of the lesson. Usually, the instructor presents the objective during the stimulus phases of the lesson; however, some lessons gain from delaying its presentation.

In the **stimulus,** the coach presents the problem. In one lesson, a film may be used; in another, a case study; in yet another, a trust exercise. During the **stimulus,** the instructor might provoke, inform, or question, Whatever the procedure, the aim is to stimulate a reaction from the students.

In the **evocation,** the coach encourages the students to express their opinions and feelings related to the **stimulus.** Using counseling techniques, the instructor remains non-judgmental, assisting the students to verbalize their concerns, to express their knowledge, and to tell their experiences. The instructor permits and may encourage the articulation of disagreements about the topic under consideration, and then uses these disagreements as a basis for the development of the investigation which takes place later in the lesson. In the **evocation** phase, the students are helped to classify their ideas and to develop fact-finding questions for investigation in the next phase of the lesson.

In the **objective enquiry/skill practice** phase the instructor acts as a teacher or guide helping the students seek out and relate new knowledge to the problem they defined. The instructor helps them search for answers to their questions and to practice new skills. The students might use video tape, or use check lists, or seek information from resource persons in the community to compare and modify their behavior.

In the **objective enquiry/skill practice** phase, the instructor arranges situations in which the students practice the skills specified in the objective of the lesson. Often, the students do this practice in a role play situation designed to resemble the circumstances in which they use the skill in the application phase. In some lessons, for example, the lesson objective requires students to conduct on-the-street interviews and to make telephone appointments. In such instances, the coach prepares the students for the use of the necessary skills by conducting skill practice in role play situations. The students use video tape feedback to modify their performances and so improve their skills.

In the **application** phase of the lesson, the coach helps students apply knowledge and skills to the solution of a problem. Whenever possible, the solution is applied in a real life situation. The real life situation changes as the course develops; in the early part of the course, students apply the skill with the learning group; later with visitors, or in the community, in the home, or in the planned simulations of other real situations.

In the **evaluation** phase, the students and instructor assess student progress toward achievement of the skills specified in the lesson objective. In some lessons, the students assess their development by means of discussion, analysis of video tape, providing feedback based on check lists, and by direct interviews with other students. In other lessons, the instructor provides each

Life Skills

student with direct feedback on his/her skill achievement. However, in the **evaluation** model, assessment of skill achievement accomplishes only part of the evaluation. To complete the evaluation, teacher and students must plan for further skill development. Often the teacher does this by encouraging the students to teach the skill to other persons; or providing for additional skill practice following the feedback; or arranging a one-to-one instructional situation in which another student, skilled in the use of the particular behavior models, instructs the less skilled person.

THE VIEWPOINT OF COGNITIVE SCIENCE

The developing discipline of cognitive science, with its fresh interpretation of the meaning of **cognitive,** provides the theoretical tools to show the interrelationships between observable behaviors and inner conceptual development.

Certain basic principles of cognitive science are particularly appropriate to Life Skills theory and practice.

1. An individual's model of the world determines the acquisition and organization of knowledge. One of the two truisms used by Life Skills as the source of its methodology is that "learning starts at the learner's current level of functioning and his understanding of present reality."[2]

The Life Skills instructor recognizes that "each individual in his group carries a unique life experience to the learning setting which affects his response to it."[2]

2. The individual's world model is organized pluralistically in domain-specific knowledge, as a set of "loosely aggregated micro-worlds."[3]

The domain on which Life Skills concentrates is the management of **personal** affairs, with particular relation to the life areas of Job, Family, Leisure and Community. The problems that Life Skills students tackle and learn to solve are all problems that concern SELF in relation to those life areas. "The course design provides the student with an opportunity and the skills to study his problems, or to put it another way, to study himself as a problem."[2]

This principle of pluralistic cognitive organization explains how it comes about that even some adults who are well equipped cognitively to deal with data from the external world may lack the skill to deal effectively with internal data. A genius in solving algebra problems may be at an utter loss in solving problems concerning himself and his relationships with other persons.

3. Knowledge is represented as "procedures" or skills" rather than as "assertions." In cognitive science, "knowing how" has superseded "knowing that" in importance. To know something means to be able to do something.

In Life Skills, learning is defined as changed behavior. The learning model alternates abstraction and application: Knowing how-to-do and doing.

4. Knowing, acting and feeling are interacting functions of each individual's world-view.

The Life Skills Process/Content Model claims that each student responds to the content of a Life Skills course on the cognitive, psychomotor and affective domains, in knowing, acting and feeling.

Cognitive Development — Recent research, according to Berzonsky,[4] suggests that all adolescents, or even adults, do not develop complete formal reasoning. "Furthermore, those adolescents who do reason formally do not do so in an all-pervasive manner; they may reason formally in some situations but not in others."

A comparison of the formal reasoning pattern with the Life Skills Problem Solving Process is instructive. That process trains students to:
1. **Recognize the problem situation.**
2. **Define the problem** — by collecting many facts; hypothesizing with the question "In what ways might . . .?"; evaluating these hypothesis with the question "Why?"; and choosing the best hypothesis.
3. **Choose a solution** — by finding possible solutions; finding criteria; choosing a solution; and predicting results.
4. **Implement a solution** — by planning how to carry out the solution and doing so.
5. **Evaluate the result** — by comparing the results of the action with what was predicted.

The inclusion of this process as a fundamental component of the Life Skills course implies that a basic need for elementary training in problem solving was identified by the program developers. In the domain of personal affairs, the typical Life Skills students seem not to have reached the stage of formal reasoning.

The implication is strong that, at least in the domain of personal affairs, the individuals who need a Life Skills course have not yet progressed from the concrete to the formal stage of cognitive development.

In the light of these comparisons, it can be hypothesized that training in the problem solving and interpersonal behaviors of the Life Skills course functions to raise the cognitive level of participants from the concrete stage towards the formal stage, in the domain of Self in relation to the external world. Life Skills students learn, as Berzonsky expresses it, to conduct "thought experiments" prior to acting and consequently to proceed in a systematic rather than a trial-and-error manner when solving personal problems.

A corollary to this interpretation of what Life Skills training does is of vital importance in planning lesson activities and presentations. Training can help an individual to pass progressively from concrete thinking to a more conceptually adequate mode of thought, but this process can only be accomplished by beginning "where the student is," that is, in the concrete mode. It is futile to present formal explanations based on a logic that is alien to the students' manner of thinking and sterile in its implications for them.

Much credit for the effectiveness of the Life Skills course, then, can be attributed to its emphasis on the concrete: observable behaviors; active involvement by the participants; physical demonstrations of abstract ideas, such as trust; concentration on the "here and now." The process of developing basic concepts is not approached from abstract theory but through concrete experience.

CONCEPTUAL GROWTH

The Life Skills Course, emphasizes the importance of gaining "self understanding." "Understanding," according to the cognitivist Moravcsik,[5] "involves having concepts." In Vygotsky's words:

> "... a concept is not an isolated, ossified, changeless formation, but an active part of the intellectual process, constantly engaged in serving communication, understanding, and problem-solving."[6]

A concept is formed as the cognitive mechanisms identify external and internal data, differentiate between them, put them in order, classify them, establish relationships between them, and integrate them into existing cognitive structures.

However, the concepts that are developed do not always reflect reality accurately. The data base on which they are formed may be weak; the information may be wrongly interpreted: the world-view into which the new information is incorporated may be colored by ungrounded assumptions. At any point in the chain of full concept formation, some distortion of reality may occur.

The importance of this point for Life Skills is that flawed concepts can play a destructive role in an individual's relations with other people and in that person's acquisition of new knowledge. If the concepts being developed out of the experiences of Life Skills training are to play a constructive part in restructuring a student's world-view, those experiences have to be evaluated critically. The new understanding that emerges from the alternating of active behavior and inner reflection has to be tested for its validity.

The skills of evaluating critically and testing the validity of claims are as necessary to mature living as practicing behaviors and elementary problem solving skills. From the cognitive viewpoint, critical thinking skills are one variety of life skills.

Two senses of the term **cognitive** have to be distinguished:
1. The thinking activity that is teamed with affective and psychomotor activity to constitute the content dimension of student response to the training course.
2. The totality of stored knowledge, or meanings, that is structured in an individual's world view and that functions in the acquisition of new knowledge.

The learning of life skills is a process of integrating sub-skills, manifested outwardly as observable behaviors, into cognitive structure. These sub-skills are successively subsumed into higher-order life skills, which in turn are manifested as observable problem solving and interpersonal behaviors of an increasingly complex nature.

In this way, the cognitive powers are raised, in the domain of Self in relation to the external world, from a concrete level to the level of formal reasoning.

PRODUCT VS. PROCESS OBJECTIVES

PRODUCT approaches view Social and Life Skills (SLS) development as a way of achieving a certain desirable **end-product;** this end-product is an individual who knows certain facts, has mastered certain skills, or perhaps has acquired "appropriate" attitudes or values. In this kind of approach, it should be possible to scale learners according to their competence or incompetence. Two of the competencies are that the learner should be able to write an acceptable letter of application for a job, and to prepare a simple meal.

PROCESS approaches, on the other hand, are more open-ended, emphasizing continuous development; goals are perceived in terms of desirable processes and potentialities (such as thinking, feeling and acting), which individuals become able to use for their own purposes. "Unlike product competencies, process competencies are never mastered, only improved."[7] In PROCESS approaches, the aim is always the development of the learning process; course content is not considered the end of learning but the means to it.

Typical PROCESS objectives are that the learner should be able to seek information and organize it into frameworks, and to see an argument from someone else's point of view.

The PRODUCT-PROCESS distinction is utilized by the British team to delineate seven models of SLS teaching.[7]

DESCRIPTIONS OF THE SEVEN MODELS

There are four **PRODUCT**-oriented models:

1. **The DEFICIENCY Model** assumes that the target population has certain basic deficiencies, which must be remedied before individuals can make progress in the kinds of study or work that are normally expected for people of their age.

   Two classes of deficiency are distinguished:
   (a) In basic skills, such as literacy and numeracy; interpersonal skills; manipulative skills.
   (b) In motivation, as the result of a poor or inappropriate self image, the image held of others, or inability to recognize needs as learning needs.

2. **The COMPETENCY Model** emphasizes "mastery," or competent performance of specific skills in pre-specified tasks for which agreed criteria of competence can be established. Using the telephone and searching out potential employers by using the telephone directory are two examples of competence aimed at in this type of program.

3. **The INFORMATION-BASED Model** assumes that knowing a body of preselected facts is the goal of SLS development. These facts may involve either **knowing how,** as in how to obtain an unemployment insurance benefit, or **knowing that,** as in knowing that vitamins are essential for good health.

4. **The SOCIALIZATION Model** aims at developing specified attitudes, values, or willingness to adjust to particular requirements in the world of work or to the expectations of society in general.

Life Skills

Three of the seven models are **PROCESS-oriented.**
5. The EXPERIENTIAL Model is based on open-ended learner activities that incorporate a range of skill and knowledge demands; in these activities the opportunities for developing particular capacities are not clearly predetermined. Organizing and carrying out a community service project, or the performance of work activities in a simulated office, are examples.
6. **The RELFECTIVE Model** aims to develop a student's ability to "pattern" experience or data in alternative ways, perceive relationships, make and check generalizations and develop conceptual frameworks.

In an academic application, students are introduced to systematic ways of tackling problems, engaging in inquiry, and other similar activities. In a personal application, the reflective process concentrates on the direct experience and activities of the participants. Usually conducted in a learning group, **REFLECTIVE/Personal** programs seek to help students develop their own perceptions of patterns and relationships and to learn certain methods of approach to problems.
7. **The COUNSELING Model,** emphasizing the importance of the affective domain, arranges for individual and/or group reflection on experiences in order to increase individual understanding and control of behavior, understanding of others' feelings and emotions, and ability to distinguish between emotional and cognitive elements, as in decision-making.

This model refers to counseling as a general teaching activity rather than as specialist therapy.

PRODUCT-PROCESS CONTINUUM

Life Skills training consists of definite and clearly stated PRODUCT objectives. The behavioral skills are competencies that can be mastered, and the "level of learning" to which they are taught in existing lessons has been assessed.

The overall program objective of developing in students the power to use the new behaviors for their own purposes, in solving their personal problems of everyday life, fits the definition of a PROCESS approach.

PRODUCT objectives, the behavioral skills are the means to an end. Each forms part of a larger, functional objective; that is, it is learned in order to be used in the accomplishment of a more complex purpose. Thus, the skill "to ask himself a theoretical question," which is clearly a PRODUCT objective, is learned not for itself but for use in solving problems. Similarly, the skill "to describe personal feelings as a result of a stressful situation" is a PRODUCT objective, a competency that can be mastered, but it is learned for use in solving problems, developing control over emotions and changing behaviors in group members.

It is interesting to position the Life Skills objectives on a PRODUCT-PROCESS continuum, according to their degree of complexity:
1. When life skills are analyzed to the most specific behaviors, they appear as competencies to be mastered, that is, as PRODUCT objectives.

2. When life skills are summarized under the category headings of problem solving skills, human relations skills, process skills, and coping skills their character as PRODUCT objectives becomes blurred. Problem solving skills, for instance, are described as those "which enable the student to set, implement and evaluate short and long term goals and resolve personal problems." That definition, which lodges control over the skills in the student, has moved closer to a PROCESS approach, which seeks to develop "certain processes and potentialities . . . which the learner is able to use for his or her own purposes."
3. And when life skills are seen as a synthesis, aimed at developing individuals confident enough to express themselves in the discriminating use of a repertoire of problem solving skills in meeting the problems of everyday life — PRODUCT has been enveloped by PROCESS.

The specific behavioral skills, which give the Life Skills program its concrete substance and rigorous training structure, are in reality sub-skills. The whole is greater than the sum of all its parts. It is as an ongoing process of moving continually to life skills of an increasingly higher order that the Life Skills program, in its totality, can best be described.

SUMMARY

The overall objective of Life Skills training is to develop a BALANCED SELF-DETERMINED PERSON SOLVING PROBLEMS CREATIVELY IN EVERYDAY LIFE.

This quality of behavior is made possible by the integration of life skills into cognitive structure and the growth of a Self concept, which leads to the formation of a coherent SELF-OTHERS IMAGE.

This Life Skills goal may not be realized during the relatively short duration of a training course. However, the spiraling process that moves towards that ideal is initiated during training. The degree to which individual learners integrate that process cognitively into their world-view determines how far they will proceed towards the ideal.

Five principles can be evolved from the Life Skills Training Course:
1. Adult education must be practical and relevant to the needs of the people.
2. Adult education must be interesting, participative, and help in creating common goals and standards.
3. Adult education must perceive the partnership between human resource development and socio-economic development.
4. Adult education must involve itself actively with groups seeking change in their lot.
5. Adult education must assist groups to define their situation, plan for action, mobilize resources, and facilitate coordination among various groups.

Questions and Exercises

Using the five (5) steps of formal reasoning give strategies and processes that would be helpful to students in a Life Skills Course:
1. In Manpower Training for disadvantaged youth.
2. At a multi-purpose senior citizen center.
3. In a new careers class for persons in mid-life crises.

REFERENCES

1. Himsel, R. *Life Skills Coaching Manual.* Training Research and Development Station. Prince Albert, Sask. 1973.
2. Himsl, R. *Readings in Life Skills.* Training Research and Development Station. Prince Albert, Sask, 1973.
3. Apostel, Leo. "The Cognitive Point of View. A Research Program. State of the Art, and Attempt Towards an Evaluation" in *Communication and Cognition,* 1977, 10:2, pp. 107-144.
4. Berzonsky, Michael D. "Formal Reasoning in Adolescence: An Alternate View" in *Adolescence,* 1978, XIII: 50, pp. 279-290.
5. Moravcsik, J. M. "On Understanding" in *Communication and Cognition,* 1977, 10:2, pp. 97-106.
6. Vygotsky, Lev Semenovich. *Thought and Language,* tr. by Hanfmann and Vakar. The M.I.T. Press. Cambridge, Mass. 1962.
7. Stanton, G. P.; E. P. Clark; R. Stradling; A. G. Watts. *Developing Social and Life Skills:* Strategies for Tutors. Further Education Curriculum Review and Development Unit. London. 1980.

Career Counseling

Richard S. Deems
*Assistant Professor, Adult Education,
Iowa State University; Consultant, Career Development*

John Hartwig
*Consultant, Adult Education, Iowa State Department of Public
Instruction; author of articles on Adult Counseling*

In a mobile, complex, technologically changing world where frequent career change is both voluntary and forced there is a growing demand for career planning services. Examples of different types of adult target populations in need of career planning service include: (1) displaced homemakers seeking the best ways to be fully independent, (2) workers caught in plant closings exploring viable job options, (3) persons in mid-life change evaluating and designing their futures. Any persons realistically planning their future can benefit from an effective career counseling program.

CONCEPTUAL MODEL FOR CAREER COUNSELING
The conceptual model was developed in order to establish philosophic parameters for effective career counseling. The parameters govern the establishment of counseling and guidance concepts for adult counseling and guidance personnel. The model is predicated on four key concepts: (1) life stage, (2) life style, (3) life space, (4) total life planning.

Life Stage Concept — A key concept in formulating effective career counseling principles involves ordering life events which define career development in a sequence of life stages. Life stages are defined as a series of psychological processes that denote the degree of individual development from the time of fantasy choices in childhood to decisions about retirement. As an individual matures, a series of life stages are experienced, each of which is characterized by unique social roles, developmental tasks, and coping behavior skills.

The developmental tasks within any given life stage are regulated by society or a subculture within that society. In a complex technological society, human development is never predictably smooth and continuous but is regulated and circumscribed by the existing mores prevalent in that society. Therefore, individuals must develop an awareness of their self concepts in relation to society if developmental tasks at given life stages are to be successfully mastered.

The life stage approach to human development assumes that a crucial dimension regulating individual differences in mastering developmental tasks is the age factor. Therefore, specific behaviors can neither be fully understood nor modified without reference to the life stage context within which specific behaviors occur.

The utility of a life stage approach for formulating career counseling objectives is predicated on the assumption that each life stage includes developmental tasks which must be recognized, confronted, and mastered if future development is to proceed to the optimum. Much of the function of facilitating human development involves assisting adults in identifying and mastering developmental tasks occurring in specific life stages. The successful identification and mastery of these developmental tasks enhances potential life planning effectiveness.

Life Style Concept — Another key concept in formulating effective career counseling principles is life style. Life style results from the unique combination of values, choices, strategies, and coping behaviors through which individuals establish unified or cohesive personal goals and strive toward self actualization.

Life style, or life pattern, is basically an individual's attitude toward life. As an adult attempts to become an accepted part of a group, it soon becomes apparent that certain behaviors have or have not helped in achieving this goal. The adult learns to avoid behaviors which hinder achievement of specific goals and to adopt specific behaviors — coping skills — which enhance goal attainment. It is the process of adopting successful coping behaviors which constitutes each individual's unique life style.

The mastery of developmental and enrivonmental tasks requires that the individual develop adequate coping behaviors. Coping behaviors are defined as the patterns used by active, effective people in dealing with biological, psychological and social demands presented by their environment. Coping behaviors are intended to establish control over the environment.

Coping behaviors that promote goal attainment and environmental control expedite ultimate mastery of developmental tasks. Therefore, mastery of developmental tasks within given life stages results in progressively greater appreciation and awareness of specific attitudes, value, feelings, choices, and strategies which constitute one's unique life style. The process of mastering specific developmental tasks becomes intrinsically rewarding because each successive mastery provides personal incentive and motivation to developing coping behaviors to master future developmental tasks. The life style process, in relation to developmental tasks and coping behaviors, provides the necessary motivation for individuals to strive toward a life goal of becoming adequate, fully functioning persons.

Life Space Concept — A third key concept governing formulation of effective career counseling principles is that of life space. Life space is defined as the totality of factors which determine behaviors of a given individual at a given point in time. It is represented conceptually as a two-dimensional space in which the individual moves (the world within and the world without). The life space contains: (1) the person, (2) positive goals toward which the person is striving, (3) negative goals which the person is striving to avoid, (4) barriers that restrict movement, (5) paths the person must follow to attain positive goals and to avoid negative ones.

The social and interpersonal interactions of individuals help define the life space in relation to their perceived environment. Each person's conception of their personal life space is dependent upon perceptions, feelings, values, and attitudes which assist in self concept formulation.

The concept of life space is more complicated than is at first apparent. It must not be confused with physical or geographical space. Life space is not the space of physical objects and real other people, but rather the perceived world of the individual. Hence, an object of which the individual may be unaware, and upon which the individual can exert no influence, would not possibly appear in that individual's life space, even though the object is physically close. Similarly, something the individual thinks is there and reacts to as if it were present, even though that object is physically absent, is within the individual's life space. For example, if one perceives they will be physically harmed by another, that perception is part of the person's life space, even if everyone else insists that the danger is purely imaginary.

The life space concept then includes the person and the behavioral environment. The environment consists of every event that influences behavior. The important points of life space are: (1) the goals an individual is seeking, (2) negative goals or situations the individual is trying to avoid, (3) psychological barriers that restrict movement toward or away from preceived goals. As an example, a student striving to reach the positive goal of being a welder, may find the lack of mathematics a barrier. Gaining self-confidence in mathematics skills enlarges the life space of this student and it becomes part of the path to follow in attaining a positive goal.

The life space concept is related to the conceptual model in that the adult counselor needs to develop an awareness of the life space constructs of the adult client. The adult counselor must then attempt to integrate those perceptions of life space, life stage, life style, and total life planning concepts.

Total Life Planning Concept — Ultimately, the career counseling conceptual model emphasizes a "total career life style planning" approach to individual development. Such a conceptual model identifies life roles and their interrelationships to an individual's total life style. The conceptual model is, in part, based upon the assumption that those who perform counseling and guidance functions need specific competencies to assist adults in identifying their personal roles and in planning those roles to fit their total life style. An approach which stresses total career life style planning will hopefully result in the preparation of adult counseling and guidance personnel equipped to work with adults in this way.

Figure 1 illustrates the model. The inner circle represents the counselor's orientation with adults. The counselor needs to be aware of a "total life planning" orientation; such an orientation emphasizes the total life roles each adult plays. The counselor should also be aware of sociological and psychological interrelationships between and among these many life roles. Each adult interacts with several roles — marriage/family, community, consumerism, religion, and others — which tend to formulate an adult's life style.

LIFE STYLE CONCEPTUAL MODEL

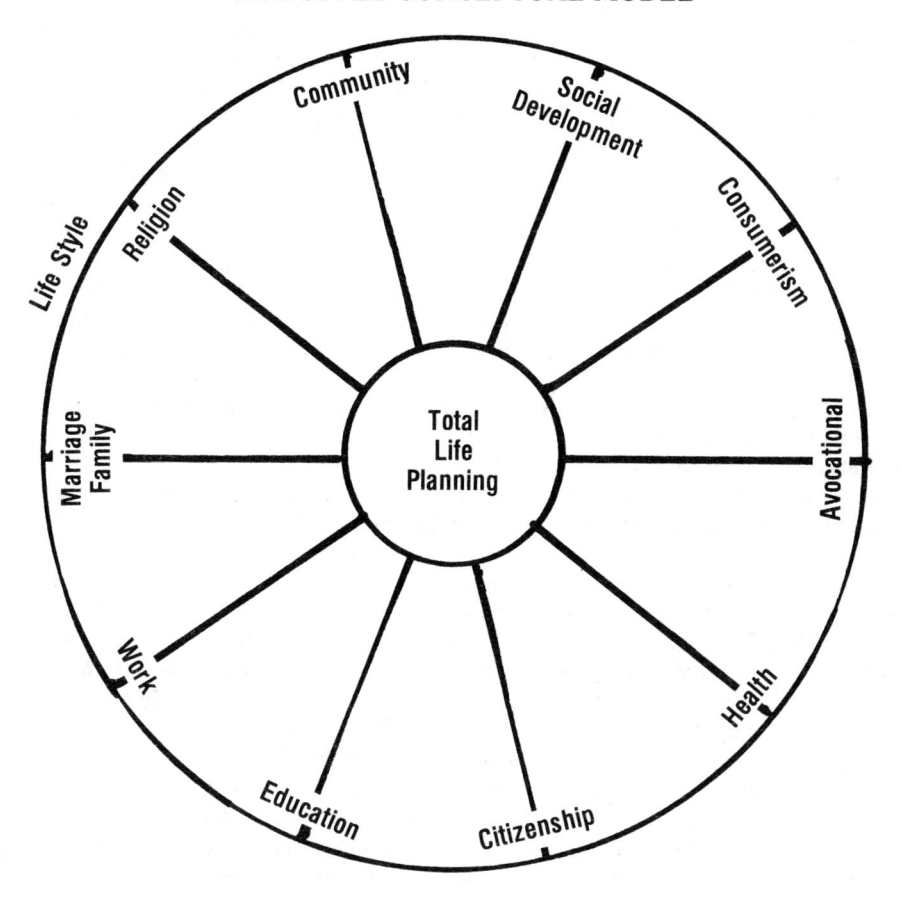

Figure 1

The lines extending from the total life planning circle in Figure 1 represent the different life roles which an adult may have. These life roles taken together comprise a life style concept represented by the outer circle of the Figure. Life roles and the behaviors produced by them are complex and interrelated. The adult counselor must recognize the complex multiple roles and the behaviors displayed by each individual.

Adult counseling and guidance essentially exist to help adults identify behavioral changes that are personally significant. It also can help adults achieve such desirable changes in a personally satisfying manner. Finally, an awareness of the conceptual model can help counselees become aware of the interrelationships among the different life roles which contribute to their own total life style. As a result of such awareness, counselees can begin to develop insight into their own self concepts. Presumably, such insight will assist an adult in making realistic decisions about oneself in relation to the larger society.

The adult counselor can use the life roles model in different ways. For example, the life roles model encompasses both the orientation of counselor and adult educator. Therefore, the total life planning model enables the counselor to synthesize the concepts of both disciplines in the process of becoming an effective adult counselor.

The fulcrum of the model is the concept that life-long learning and life-long career development are intrinsic processes in human development. Related to this concept is the "total career life-style planning" approach to human development whereby adults are given assistance in: (1) identifying their numerous life roles, (2) fitting them into a total life style. Thus, the adult counselor is, in part, a specialist assisting adults to become more self-actualized persons through a process of "total life planning." Training which emphasizes the total career life style planning approach to human development will result in the preparation of adult counseling and guidance personnel with capabilities for working with adults in this way. Thus, counseling and guidance services could be available to adults as they move through their lifelong career development. Career development is a lifelong process, and through it the counselor can assist those who are in mid-stage or transition as well as those who are making original career choices.

To be effective in career counseling for adults either as an individual counselor or as a member of a team requires certain specific behaviors. These behaviors are based upon theoretical concepts of both adult education and counseling. Adaptability and flexibility will need to be used in assisting students in career planning, yet the role statements of the counselor provide a framework in which the counselor may better assist the student. The twenty-one (21) role statements upon which effective career counseling is based are:

1. Ability to differentiate between the concepts of guidance and counseling.
2. Articulation of personal counseling theory and its theoretical basis.
3. Ability to carry out a one-to-one counseling session.
4. Ability to conduct a guidance interview to achieve a specific end.
5. Ability to structure and conduct group counseling sessions.
6. Ability to counsel with client regarding retirement and/or new career plans.
7. Ability to counsel with client regarding leisure time and avocational activities.
8. Awareness of career patterns and career change needs.

9. Awareness of various racial, ethnic, economic and age groups.
10. Knowledge of community resource agencies.
11. Ability to conduct a Needs Assessment Survey to determine adult education guidance and counseling needs in the community.
12. Ability to interact with local business, industry, and unions.
13. Awareness of problems such as alienation, stereotyping, and racial discrimination encountered in a work environment.
14. Ability to *incorporate* an adult counseling and guidance program into a general adult education program.
15. Ability to *coordinate* an adult counseling and guidance program as an integral part of an adult education program.
16. Ability to manage learning activities for counselor aides (paraprofessionals) in adult counseling programs.
17. Ability to develop a team approach with administrators, teachers, paraprofessionals, resource agencies in adult counseling and guidance programs.
18. Ability to coordinate activities related to retention of adult students.
19. Ability to establish short-term (1-2 years) and long-term (5-10 years) followup studies of adult students.
20. Ability to assist adult students in educational program planning.
21. Awareness of adult education terminology and proposal writing procedures.

SUMMARY

The career counseling conceptual model is predicated on an interrelationship among four crucial concepts — life stage, life style, life space, and total life planning.

Life stage is a series of psychological processes that denote the degree of individual development at any given age level in life. Life style is the unity that results from the unique combination of values, choices, strategies, and coping behaviors through which individuals establish personal goals and strive toward self actualization. Life space is the totality of facts which determine the behaviors of a given person at a given point in time. Total life planning orientation emphasizes the life roles and their interrelationships in the life styles of each adult.

Finally, the conceptual model's most impressive attribute is its flexibility, adaptability, and usability. The conceptual model can be applied to many diverse career counseling settings.

EXERCISE

This following exercise is used within the program described, and takes about one hour of workshop time. Participants are then encouraged to spend additional time on their own in detailing their plans before making a brief report.

Goals provide a direction, and a well-thought out goal gives a clear direction of where we want to be by a certain time.

Think about yourself, not in the present, but five years into the future. Take some time to think about where you would like to be, what you would like to be doing, and who you are with. Then, begin to write a description of yourself, as you would like to be, five years from now. Make it as detailed as possible. Describe where you live (geographical area) as well as what your living arrangements are (house, apartment); describe who you live with, or if you live alone; describe the kind of work you do, and where you do it, and why you do it, as well as with whom; describe the major events in your life of the past few years. You might want to think of what a typical-day would be like for you five years from now, if you could totally design it your way.

Persons are given instructions, and then allowed time and space to think and write. A chance to debrief and share what has been written is provided, and then the group is asked to move into the planning stage.

The only way to get where you would like to be is to plan for it. Take some time to think about what would have to happen for your description to become reality. Think first in terms of the final description, which we'll call Year 5. What are the things that need to occur in Year 5 for your description to be reality? Continue to think backward, to Year 4 and Year 3 and Year 2 and finally to this present year. What are the things that need to happen in each of those years for you to reach your goals? Be as detailed as possible.

Time is provided for persons to think, and sometimes to work in triads to help each other in detailing their personal five-year plan. Again, a chance to debrief in the total group is given before moving on to another phase of the program.

REFERENCES

1. Hartwig, John. "Counseling: A Systems Development" in MATERIALS AND METHODS IN CONTINUING EDUCATION, Chester Klevins, editor, Canoga Park, CA. Klevens Publishing Co., 1976.
2. Hartwig, John. "A Competency-Based Approach to Adult Counseling and Guidance" COUNSELOR EDUCATION AND SUPERVISION, September, 1975.
3. Hartwig, John. SKILLS FOR ADULT GUIDANCE EDUCATORS (SAGE). Portland: Northwest Regional Educational Laboratory, June, 1975.
4. Scholssberg, Nancy, and Entine, Alan, editors. COUNSELING ADULTS, Monterey: Brooks-Cole Publishing Company, 1977.

Computer Based Training in Industry

Louis H. Reeves

*Director, Program Analysis and Information,
Canada Employment and Immigration Commission*

The microelectronics era is ushering in both a new economic as well as a new educational era. Massive changes are being brought about by the technological advances in memory and logic chips that go into computers and many other electronic products which find their way into industry, the home and the school.

From an educational perspective, the work place, the home and the school will be the three prime areas for introducing the latest innovation in education — the videodisc and interactive video. In brief, we have the union of the older audio visual media systems with the new video and keyboard terminal. This union of hardware coupled with appropriate software or "courseware" has resulted in the modern educational revolution. What the printing press did for learning during the first industrial revolution, interactive video will do for the second.

Computer-aided learning systems can be developed for basic learning experiences for children who may solve relatively simple problems to the more sophisticated simulations including jet aircraft flight simulations that include enhanced realism by incorporating flight training devices which duplicate the performance and flying qualities of actual aircraft. Another example of a complex simulation would be that of a nuclear engineer who must learn how to resolve problems of normal plant operations and those of a most serious abnormal nature. It can be readily seen that training in particular skills or functions could be undertaken without affecting plant operations or without jeopardizing the health and safety of employees.

Training employees to meet the changing job requirements of organizations has been a major cost on the part of American companies. The annual investment in human resources training is estimated to be about 35 billion dollars for North America, a large part of which has been dedicated to training in government, including military personnel. To improve the efficiency and effectiveness of training and to reduce costs, many organizations are turning to the use of computers. Some measure of success has been reported within the military. A recent study by the Institute of Defense Analyses concluded that computer-based systems have reduced training time in the U.S. armed forces by 30%. Another study conducted by the Canadian armed forces indicates that computer assisted learning (CAL) courses offered time reductions of 30-60% over classroom instruction. Other smaller scale projects appear to be yielding similar results in various industrial settings.

COMPUTER BASED TRAINING

If computers and more specifically, microcomputers, are to be used for business and industrial training, training personnel must increase their knowledge of the uses of the computer in the training process directly through development of courseware using authoring languages or indirectly through working with technical support personnel to translate training objectives into computerized programs. In addition, trainers must become more aware of the potential, the uses, the prerequisites, the enhancements and the costs as well as the limitations of the software-hardware mix and their impact on the training environment.

Computers can be used to test trainees. This computer-assisted testing (CAT) can be undertaken before the training program begins for diagnostic and record purposes, during the training program to determine relative progress of individuals and the group and at the end of the program as a measure of program success on an individual and group basis.

Computer-managed instruction (CMI) would include stored information and a maintained record of trainee progress on an individual and group basis. Information on the rate of learning, time spent on each module of training to achieve mastery of content and the identification of where difficulties had been encountered along with test results should reduce much of the routine clerical work activity associated with instruction. These activities in the past have taken up some of the instructor's or trainer's time which can now be used to assist the trainee on an individual basis and to refine training programs to meet both individual and group needs.

In computer-aided instruction (CAI) the computer is modeling the activities of the instructor. The various functions ordinarily performed by the instructor in presenting and controlling the learning process are carried out by the computer. Structured exercises are designed and programmed to permit the trainee to achieve mastery of course content in a minimum amount of time.

Some of the benefits of CAI include:
1. A reduction in required training time.
2. An increase in the retention of information.
3. An assurance of uniform quality training in an efficient manner.
4. The provision of self-pacing for the practice of skills and the review of theory.
5. The identification of who was trained, the level of success and mastery of content and the time required.

INTERACTIVE VIDEO

With the development of videotechnology coupled with the microcomputer, the base for a major revolution in industrial training has been clearly demonstrated.

Traditional training media including print, still frame, motion picture films and computer-assisted instruction can now be brought together in a single medium, with the resulting features including slow motion, step framing, random access and dual sound track together with sophisticated programming that will generate a most efficient and effective training medium. High quality courseware will reflect the authoring language used as well as the human and financial resources dedicated to the development of the system. The end product will emphasize self-paced and individualized instruction. Self-paced instruction is where the learner controls the rate at which mastery of instruction is achieved. This means that the programming used allows for different rates of learning and provides for a rapid review of course content. The rapid random access feature of the videodisc coupled with indexed frames permit the learner to view any of the 54,000 frames in a matter of seconds.

Individualized instruction is achieved by programming the instructions to entry level knowledge and skills with a built-in review capactiy to ensure that any prerequisite information gaps are easily filled. It is the random accessibility of the 54,000 frames combined with quality programming that results in individualized instruction based on automatic and immediate feedback and reinforcement.

The dual sound track feature of the videodisc can either be used for two language programming such as English and French or English and Spanish, or it can also be used when two comprehension levels in one language might be of benefit to the individual learner.

SIMULATION

A simulator is a training device which resembles, to a high degree, operational equipment especially as to the layout — the display and the controls are similar to the original equipment. Simulation can reproduce a job or some elements of a job to a fairly high degree for training or testing purposes.

Recent developments in computer technology have resulted in cost-effective simulation of relatively complex maintenance tasks. In the future, relating simulation to performance should result in more training being directed to job performance skills, which in turn will emphasize the importance of measuring the trainee's performance for program and simulation modifications and for the trainee to appreciate these processes in the mastery of job performance skills.

Simulator based training systems have been built for a wide variety of "high technology" applications. Reasons for building simulators include:

1. Allowing trainees to make nondestructive errors and therefore preserve scarce and expensive equipment for operational use.
2. Providing trainees with opportunities to practice skills in situations which would be too dangerous in real-life.
3. Reducing or eliminating support costs including real estate necessary to operate equipment in real-life situations.

4. Eliminating many of the hazards to which persons and equipment are normally subjected.

SUMMARY

The world is on the threshold of a revolution in education and training. In the coming decade, millions of microcomputers will be in use in the home, the school and within industry. Through the use of appropriate course authoring languages and programs, quality individualized instruction will be available. Computerized self-paced learning programs incorporating videodisc technology developments will be a generally accepted mode of instruction. To keep abreast of developments in computer-based training, trainers need to become more involved in experimental work and they will need to devote more time to learning about the technology, its hardware and courseware.

QUESTIONS AND EXERCISES

1. What are the advantages of computer-based training?
2. What are the advantages of using interactive video in training programs?
3. What problems might be encountered when introducing computer-based training to an organization?
4. Determine the advantages and disadvantages of different course authoring languages.
5. What will the new role be for industrial trainers in the next decade?
6. What problems are associated with computer-based training?

REFERENCES

1. *Business Week,* "On-the-job Training by Computers," July 27, 1981.
2. Kearsley, G. P., "Conceptual Issues in Computer-Assisted Instruction," *ADCIS Journal,* August, 1978.
3. Menashian, L. S., "Continuing Education Resources for Electronics-Based High Technology Professionals," *Educational Technology,* November, 1981.
4. Wooley, R. D., "Microcomputers and Videodiscs: New Directions for Computer-Based Education," *Interface Age,* December, 1979.

Implementing & Evaluating — Reading

Patrick O. Copley
Dean, School of Education and Psychology
Southwest Missouri State University

Darrell G. Roubinek
Head, Department of Elementary Education
Southwest Missouri State University

James R. Layton
Department of Elementary Education
Southwest Missouri State University

Dale G. Range
Department of Elementary Education
Southwest Missouri State University

George McNinch
Chairman, Middle Grades Education Department
West Georgia College

— One out of every four students nationwide has significant reading deficiencies.
— Competency-based proficiency tests continually uncover reading problems.
— 12.5 million Americans are functionally illiterate.
— Almost one-half of the unemployed youth, ages 16-21, are functionally illiterate.
— Lack of reading ability appears to correlate positively with becoming a criminal offender.
— Media reports that lack of reading ability severely hampers the recruitment efforts of the United States military.

Adult educators are not surprised by these statements. They have known for a considerable time that many adults are in need of increased reading skills, and they are also aware that these adults need reading instruction based on the psychology of adult learning. Adults read best what is of interest to them and to attempt to use the same materials and methods utilized in elementary and secondary schools invariably leads to failure. Frustration sets in when materials are not relevant to the tasks created by adult living.

The nature of the task in teaching reading is to adjust materials to the adult student. The educator must consider the characteristics of the material; the personality characteristics and teaching skills of the teacher assigning the materials; the characteristics of the learner who is assigned or chooses to use the materials; and the consequences or outcomes resulting from the interaction of all three: the teacher, the learner, the materials.

During the 1970's many researchers explored the nature of learning, memory, and conceptual processes as each singly or in combination was related to cognitive success — especially reading performance. Other researchers investigated the nature of printed materials, the characteristics of learners, and the techniques that teachers should use to match materials to learners' needs so that the learner would demonstrate a gain in achievement.

READABILITY

When one thinks of research that has been conducted about reading, the first term that emerges is **readability** or the difficulty level of that material. There has yet to evolve a better definition of readability than the classic one written by Dale and Chall and referred to by Layton.[1] Readability has to be measured in terms of the contents of a passage and also in terms of the success students will realize. This is dependent upon the speed at which they read it, understand it, and enjoy it. Since readability is an important variable in the research, development, and evaluation of printed materials, it has been widely studied.

Readability formulas require the instructor to measure two aspects of the passage. First, the average sentence length is computed. Second, the number of difficult words are determined. Then, through mathematical computation, the readability level (grade equivalent or grade level) is yielded. There are many readability formulas available; some are easy and simple to use; others are complicated and difficult.

Readability formulas may be classified into two categories:

1. Simple Computation Formulas

The Reading Ease Formula (Flesch) — One hundred running words are selected. The number of syllables are counted. The average length of the sentences is found (#words ÷ #sentences). The results are then subtracted from constants to determine the readability level (any grade levels).

The Fog Index (Gunning) — One hundred running words are selected. Determine the average length of the sentences. Count the number of difficult words (three syllables or more). Add the two figures together and multiply by .4 to determine the readability level (any grade levels).

2. Complex Computation Formulas

Spache[2] Readability Formula — One hundred running words are selected. The average sentence length is computed. The percent of difficult words is determined by matching the words in the selection against those on Stone's Revision of the Dale List which accompanies the formula. The average sentence length and percent of difficult words are added to a constant. The sum represents the grade equivalent (for use with materials between 1.3 and 4.0 grade levels).

A Formula for Predicting Readability (Dale-Chall) — This formula is the same as Spache's except that the Dale List of 3,000 words is used to determine the familiar words (for use with materials between 4.0 and 16.0 grade levels). The reader is cautioned to use the conversion chart to determine the ranges of readability.

The Dale-Chall formula can be simplified by using Layton's[3] chart which also eliminates the need for computation and allows writers to determine the percent of unfamiliar words and sentence length to use when composing materials at a specific grade level.

3. Cloze Passages

Another method for determining if a piece of printed material is too difficult for an adult student is to convert reading passages to cloze passages. Cloze passages, according to Bormuth[4] should contain at least 250 words, from which fifty words are to be deleted. However, more than 250 words are always required. It is mandatory that the first sentence be left intact and that proper nouns not be removed. Beginning with the first word of the second sentence, every fifth word is removed except for proper nouns. Skip proper nouns and continue until fifty words are deleted. The test can then be administered to students.

Bormuth's directions are much more detailed than presented here, but these are the general directions:
 (1) The student must replace the exact words removed, synonyms cannot be considered correct.
 (2) A score below 44% correct is an indication that the material is too difficult, a score of 57% or higher indicates that the material was at a comprehensible level and that the adult learner can read the material independently, a score between those two standards is an indication that the student can read the material but will need aid from the adult educator or peer tutor.

4. Word Difficulty Considerations — To develop more sensitivity to the difficulty of printed or instructor authored materials, the following guidelines are presented:
 (1) Longer words are more difficult to perceive than shorter words.
 (2) Morphological (meaning) complexities contribute to readers' incorrect comprehension or misinterpretation of authors' intentions.
 (3) Grammatical (syntactical patterns or word order) difficulties contribute to readers' incorrect and/or inadequate comprehension.
 (4) Abstract terms that may be unknown or misinterpreted by readers lead to incorrect and/or inadequate comprehension.
 (5) Modifiers and/or pronouns placed too far from nouns, verbs, antecedents, results in incorrect and/or inadequate comprehension.
 (6) Transformational complexities (deep structures underlying kernal strings) may be above or beyond the readers background of experience and lead to poor comprehension.

(7) Shorter, single concept, concise sentences are easier to read than are longer, complex sentences.[4]

Readability measures can be an aid to all adult educators who teach in any reading-language based courses. The use of the devices is not reserved solely for teachers whose prime responsibility is to develop literacy programs. They can benefit vocational, academic, in fact all teachers of students with reading problems.

CONTENT

If the major task of the teacher of adults is to improve the students' ability to comprehend, then materials must be selected or written after the reasons for reading a selection have been established. There are two basic approaches to developing comprehension through student centered content: (1) the "content analysis" approach, (2) the "language experience" approach.

In the content analysis approach students should never be required to read for main ideas until they gain enough knowledge of details to understand their relationship to main ideas. Any time a student incorrectly identifies a main idea, the adult teacher must review the total procedure that the adult student should have used — whether the task is a literal or inferential skill.

Teachers of adult students must evaluate materials, or write them, in accordance with the purposes of the reading lesson. The ability to recognize the properties of a printed selection or the ability to incorporate those properties into a composition written for an adult student will enhance the teachig and learning that occurs. Such procedures will also allow the teacher to be in full control of the learning activity.

There are three major categories of details found in sentences, paragraphs, and longer units:

1. **Segmented details** — details that are related, but may be placed in any sequence or order. Example:

    Everyone knew that Dee was a happy woman (main idea sentence). While she worked there was always a _smile_ on her face. Often, you could hear Dee _humming_ or _singing_ a song. And the _lively_ little _bounce in her walk_ left no doubt that she was very happy.

    The underlined details could have been placed in various positions without changing the author's intent.

2. **Sequential details** — details that specify an order of importance or sequence of events. As a rule, the details occur in a specific sequence from beginning to end or may be reversed to indicate the final happening then lead to a beginning point. Often, sequential details are accompanied by key words such as **first, next, last,** but some writers prefer to present a sequence without key words, At times, some events occur simultaneously.

Example:
> Kent wanted to have the living room spotless when Linda came to visit. First, he removed all of the throw rugs. Then he vacuumed the floor and furniture. After that, Kent (dusted and waxed) the furniture. The last thing Kent did before Linda arrived was to return the rugs to their places.

3. **Merged Details** — details that are both segmented and sequential in a paragraph. At times, some of the details in paragraphs constructed this way may not support the main idea, but only add interest, continuity, or color to the story. Example:

> Dennis knew that he had less than ten minutes to reach the river; by then the raging forest fire would close the path. First, Dennis checked his pack and first aid kit. He could hardly breathe for the thick smoke. After making certain his pack and kit were complete, Dennis climbed down the ladder of the watch tower. The smoke was burning his eyes. The next thing Dennis did was to run toward the river. Trees were burning and falling all around. It was a disasterous scene. Finally, Dennis reached the river, climbed into his canoe, and headed down the river to safety.

The sequence in the example must stay as it is, or it could be reversed by allowing Dennis to retrace his movement. However, the stiffling smoke, burning eyes, and burning and falling tree references could have been placed at various positions in the composition.

4. In addition to the major categories of segmented, sequential, and merged details, there are six other subcategories of details that will form the major details:
   (1) **Specific attributes** — details that are used to describe size, color, weight, utility, length, but not characteristics relating to personality.
   (2) **Personality characteristics** — details that specify personality traits, such as happy, sad, joyful.
   (3) **Cause and effect** — details that specify happenings and results.
   (4) **Comparison and contrast** — details that specify the likenesses and/or differences found between or among persons, places, things, and ideas or thoughts.
   (5) **Emotive** — details that are intended to have a psychological influence or impact on the reader.
   (6) **Idiomatic** — details that are not to be taken literally. Devices such as slang, hyperboles, metaphors, similes comprise this area.

PARAGRAPHS

It appears simple and clear that comprehension is much more complicated than can be imagined. In addition to the major (segmented, sequenced, and merged) categories of details and the subcategories just presented, there are several formats that may be used to present the details in a paragraph. These formats and explanations are:

1. **Categorical format** — a paragraph containing a set, subsets, or more than one set of details that may be placed into categories.
2. **Associative format** — a paragraph containing information in which relationships (likenesses and differences) are shown between or among events, happenings, people, groups, things. ideas, thoughts.
3. **Procedural format** — a paragraph containing details or information in which a step-by-step, systematic procedure or process is presented.
4. **Transformational format** — a paragraph containing information that tells of a change that occurs.
5. **Implicative format** — a paragraph containing words and phrases that must be interpreted rather than comprehended for their literal meanings.

The major categories, subcategories, and formats for writing details in sentences, paragraphs, and longer units were presented as three separate categories to alert teachers of adult students to the complexities of information that must be comprehended, to serve as a guide in choosing materials, and to serve as a guide for constructing or writing materials. An astute observer will note that the three classifications are both independent and overlapping. The adult education teacher can select one of each of the classifications, combine them and use the results to choose or write a reading selection and plan a reading lesson.

CLASSIFICATION AND FORMATS OF DETAILS

Major Categories	Subcategories	Format	Rating
			EASY
segmented	specific attributed	categorical	
sequential	personality characteristics	associative	
merged	cause and effect	procedural	
	comparison and contrast	transformational	
	emotive	implicative	
	idiomatic		
			DIFFICULT

Figure 1.

LANGUAGE EXPERIENCE

Planning for the Language Experience Lesson — For the non-reader the Language Experience lesson is usually more effective in developing comprehension. The flexible nature of the language experience curriculum, the lack of a standardized or pre-organized skill sequence in vocabulary, word attack, or comprehension, requires that direct guidance in skill and material selection be the responsibility of the instructor. Since the language experience approach does not have a set learning sequence, the critical factor in success of the method is the ability of the instructor to prescribe needed skills.

Obviously, if traditional methods and materials used in reading instruction for the adult prove to be ineffective, a new or different strategy is necessary. Such a strategy should be: (1) one which the learner is capable of understanding, (2) one in which the learner will find initial success, (3) one which is interesting and motivational, (4) one that is relevant to the status or position of the adult learner. Such a strategy for teaching reading is the **language experience approach.**

The rationale for the language experience approach has been frequently expressed. Basically — the adult learner is able to take the position:

What I think, can be said.
What I say can be written by myself or someone else.
What can be written, can be read.

This approach is based on the experiences of the learner, an aspect which provides the basic strength of this creative teaching technique. Adult learners vary greatly in such characteristics as age, background of experience, ability, interests, attitudes. With the language experience approach, this variety of characteristics possessed by individual learners can be used as a source of materials which will motivate and interest the learner, as well as provide a means of sharing knowledge among the students.

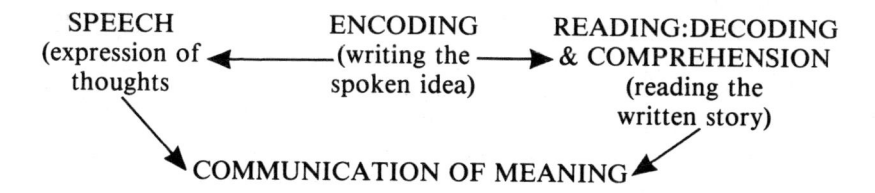

```
   SPEECH              ENCODING           READING:DECODING
(expression of  ←———  (writing the  ———→  & COMPREHENSION
   thoughts)          spoken idea)         (reading the
        ↘                                  written story)
         ↘                                     ↙
          ↘→  COMMUNICATION OF MEANING  ←↙
```

Of all the components of the communications process — speaking, listening, reading, writing — speaking and listening are the ones with which the illiterate adult is most comfortable.

The major reasons for suggesting a flexible language experience approach for the adult learner are:

1. The teacher can organize the class into learning situations that are individual, small group, and large group in order to meet the students needs.
2. The teacher can make multiple use of grouping techniques based on skills, interest, free-choice, and reading level during one session.
3. The students are not completely passive during the learning. Their ideas and feelings are presented constantly during the interaction sessions.
4. The student not only learns to read, write, and spell; he expresses himself through his **ideolect** — unique pattern of speech. Language activities build and strengthen the learner's self-concept. Either as a worth-while contributor to a group or in his individual effort, his performance is marked with visible and immediate success. When did that ever happen to him in previous schooling?

5. Through careful questioning by the teacher, the student gains skills which will transfer later to higher level comprehension and composition skills.

Language Experience Activities — Language experience is a high-success method that capitalizes on the personalized interests and goals of the adult learner. The immediate success and real goal attainment available to the adult learner tends to build lasting self-confidence. Three basic elements support the use of language experience for teaching reading:
1. The student will be more interested in the topic than in a text.
2. The student will do only that part of the lesson that is on an appropriate level.
3. The student will be successful. He will be able to read words, sentences, and whole selections with comprehension when paced properly by the teacher.

Language experience activities, if conducted properly, require five major stages: (1) Introduction, (2) Preparation, (3) Writing, (4) Culminating, (5) Extending.

Introduction — Discovering the adults' interests or needs.
Through seemingly informal interaction with a group or individual the teacher asks appropriate questions to determine:
> What interested the adults that day?
> What presentable problems were encountered?
> What jobs do the adults hold that they would like to discuss?
> What favorite or famous politician, entertainer, or other person would they like to talk about?

At this stage, the teacher is getting an idea, through divergent questioning techniques, of an extremely potent topic — What the adult learners would really like to write about.

The introductory stage is essentially a motivational period, but it is also an excellent time to explore and develop vocabulary terms and ask questions designed to stimulate divergent and convergent thinking, evaluation, and appreciation.

Preparation — For a group or individual, the major task is to decide on a topic. Once the topic has been chosen, the teacher will need to aid the group in outlining the presentation or working from a topic sentence. The beginning adult readers must never be given the formal aspects of what the teacher is doing. At all times the students must feel relaxed and unthreatened.

When topics and outlines have been decided, it is necessary to write the selection. For non-writing adults, the teacher will write the selection on the chalkboard, without expecting them to copy it. The students who can work independently should do so, but indications have been that if the discussions are lively and topics interesting, everyone wants to participate.

Writing — The teacher should ask, "According to our outline, what should we write first?"

These, being student dictated stories, should move quickly since the stage of writing has been set. Although some of the recommendations made thus far appear to require lengthy compositions, the selections should be kept relatively short. The teacher should also take precautions to keep the sentences relatively short and avoid vocabulary words which are not a part of the students' speaking and/or listening vocabulary — ideolect.

Culminating — After the selection has been written, the teacher may wish to conduct a group activity to do a word count. This can be done in alphabetical order (have students find all the words beginning with *a, b, c)*. The students' attention should be directed to the phrase patterns of sentences by drawing lines between them. The teacher should read the selection to the group. The group should read the selection; then, individual students should read it.

Extending — Once the selection has been read, and its immediate usefulness exhausted, the students should begin with other activities. A worksheet from previous compositions would be ideal. As the students do independent work the teacher should help them, but she must also make a copy of the selection.

Between class meetings, the teacher should type the selection. A pica or elite typewriter is preferred with double spaces between lines and two spaces between words.

Following the selection, exercises for word identification and comprehension should be developed. These exercises would be similar to those found in workbook materials. Contextual, phonic, and structural exercises should be included. Comprehension should begin with recognition skills before proceeding to extensive memory questions.

Developing the lesson

An adult educator with a class of twenty men (all non-readers) was charged with the task of developing their service word vocabularies and general reading abilities. The major objective of this particular lesson was to increase word knowledge and to promote structural awareness of phrases, sentences, and paragraphs. Of the twenty men in the group; only two or three had occupations other than city sanitation workers. Following a very active class discussion, the instructor asked if the students would be interested in placing a particular segment of the conversation on the board. Through a discussion, with explanations by both the instructor and the students, the following story was written in manuscript on the chalkboard.

A Dempsey Dumpster

A Dempsey Dumpster is a big truck. It is used to pick up and haul off trash. It is a tandem truck that has a hydraulic lifter on the front. It has a hydraulic packer. It will hold a lot of trash.

As this story was composed and written on the board, the teacher made the students aware of the words, phrases, and sentences as being written speech by framing the elements and rereading them orally. Much discussion was

intermingled with each sentence as it was written; every word spoken was not written. After the short time required for selection development, some questions asked by the teacher and answered orally by the students were:
1. "How big is a big truck; how many tons?"
2. "How much will it carry?"
3. "How long does it take to learn to drive one?"
4. "What is a hydraulic lifter; how does it work?"
4. "What is a tandem truck; what good is it?"
6. "Why is it called a Dempsey Dumpster?"
7. "Why do you work only at night?"

As the lesson proceeded, there were many variations possible for developing comprehension and vocabulary. There was no absolute procedure. However, major objectives may be set.

As was initially indicated, the main objective of this lesson was to develop the adult students' recognition of basic sight words. Another objective was to indicate to the students the structural elements of words, phrases, sentences, and paragraphs. Development of structural elements was partly accomplished during discussion, but needed to be more specifically reinforced by specially designed follow-up activities after the selection had been written and reread. The total group directed the teacher in marking lines between the phrases; afterwards the group, and then individuals, read the selection orally with the instructor always available.

A word count was the next step in supplying immediate word knowledge help. The word count aided in reinforcing the students' recognition of the words. Spelling techniques were introduced incidentally. The teacher directed the students in scanning from left to right, top to bottom, until all words were listed.

Word List

A	Dempsey	Dumpster	is	to	on
big	truck	it	a	off	the
pick	up	and	used	of	front
trash	tandem	has	haul	that	lot
packer	will	hold	hydraulic	lifter	

Sight words, structural and configuration clues, common word elements, consonant and vowel clusters, and phoneme (sound) — grapheme (writing) relationships were discussed.

-er—packer. Dumpster (inflectional endings)
short i—big, pick, will, it, is (vowel sound)
-au—haul, hydraulic (vowel cluster)
short a—trash, packer, tandem, and, has (vowel sound)

As the students' skills increase to mastery level in the skill area, the teacher may lead students to exercises in single consonant, blend, and digraph substitutions. The words should always be presented in context using words learned. Many exercises may be developed:

1. A __empsey __umpster is a _____.
   struck   truck   pluck
2. The big truck is used to _____ off trash.
   truck   trash   haul   pick
3. The lifter is used to _____ up trash.
   pack   pick   haul   pull

READING SKILLS

Vocabulary
word meaning: tandem
comparison: trash, garbage
contrast: Dumpster and dump truck

Synonyms
truck: vehicle, rig
big: large, enormous
trash: garbage, refuse

A Dempsey Dumpster
A Dempsey Dumpster is a big truck. It is used to pick up and haul off trash. It is a tandem truck. It has a hydraulic lifter on the front. It has a hydraulic packer. It will hold a lot of trash.

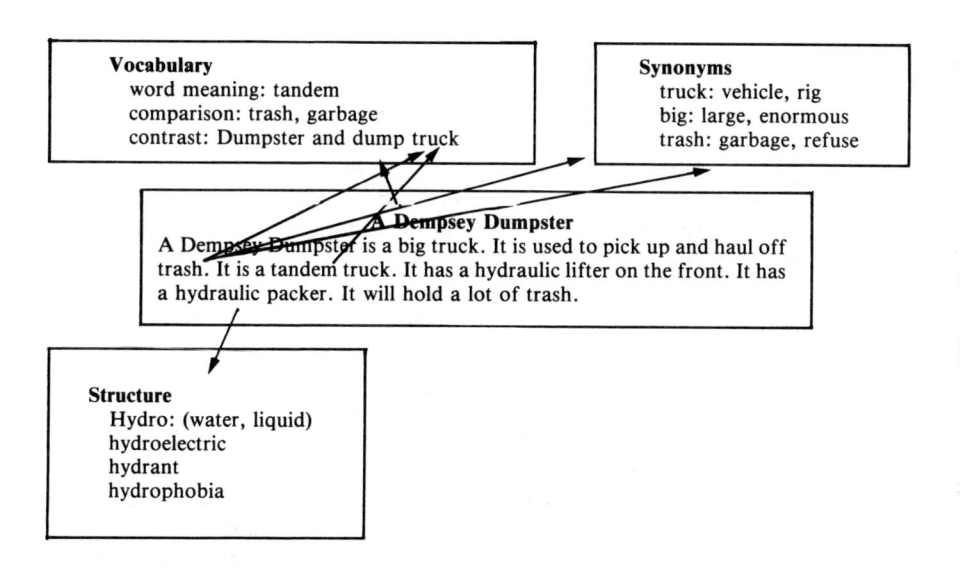

Structure
Hydro: (water, liquid)
hydroelectric
hydrant
hydrophobia

Figure 2.

The teacher worked between class meetings to prepare supplementary reinforcement activities. The selection which was written on the board was typed and exercises added before the next class period. Records were kept of the words learned by the students. As words were learned, the teacher used the words and phrase patterns to write new selections and exercises.

Naturally, language experience stories cannot serve as the total reading program, nor can the program succeed without adequate, careful planning. The personalized language experience techniques should include supplementary, independent, and group activities using other available resources.

The simplest materials construction would be one in which only one item from each classification is chosen (Figure 1), if more than one item is selected from each classification, then the materials will become more complicated. By using a single item from each of the three classifications, ninety different types of paragraphs can be written. By combining more than one item from each classification an enormous number of paragraphs are possible.

A combination of sequential details and personality characteristics in a transformational format leads to the following type of construction.

A Change in Personality

Brenda Notyal was a happy and friendly woman when she first moved to Mount King, but slowly she changed. The first event that occurred was when her home burned; she became very bitter. Next, Brenda's brother was not elected mayor and that caused her to become unfriendly with the townsfolk. Finally, when her son ran away from home, Brenda became a recluse and never went outside again.

THE READING LESSON

Ideally, the instructor should introduce the lesson to the students. A part of the introduction should contain a stimulating discussion of the unfamiliar or technical terms that may be in the selection to be read. The last item to be presented in the introductory phase would be to give the students a purpose for reading. The purpose should be based on the content of the passage which was designed from the classifications and formats chart. The questions to evaluate comprehension should reflect the earlier stated purpose. An example will be given below, based on the above paragraph entitled "A Change in Personality."

Objective: The adult students will read and be able to recall and sequence the events and commensurate personality characteristic changes of Brenda Notyal.

Introduction: Discuss the key words that are used to indicate a sequence: **first, next, later, after, last, finally.**
Discuss the terms **personality characteristics** and **specific attributes** (How are they different?).
Discuss and give examples of the words **bitter, unfriendly,** and **recluse.**

Purpose: Adult students should be directed to read the selection slowly and carefully and be able to recall the events that led to the changes in Brenda's life.

Comprehension Questions:
1. What word was used to describe Brenda's personality when she arrived at King Mount?
2. What happened to cause Brenda to withdraw from (friends) (public view) (society)? Did anything happen before that?
3. What happened (first) (second)?

Questions should be asked that are specifically related to the purposes that were set forth. One alternative to the questions that are recommended are cloze tests that were presented earlier in this chapter.

COMPREHENSION THROUGH CONTENT ANALYSIS

Very often, teachers of adults cite comprehension ability as one of the major weaknesses found among adult students, especially those students who read at the lower levels of proficiency.

When adults arrive at the education centers, it is obvious that they cannot read or read well. If they have measurable reading abilities, that is proof that they have learned to read to a degree and can probably grow in reading skill development if provided with proper guidance and instruction. The first step is to match a piece of printed material difficulty level with the students' reading levels. The next step is to ascertain that the student has the experiential background and/or conceptual knowledge (if not, the teacher must provide the background or conceptual knowledge) to understand the syntactical, semantic, and morphological nature of the material. The students must be introduced to the specific terms used in the selection, given a purpose for reading, given aid (if required as they read), and asked comprehension questions that match the purposes that were established either independently by the instructor or jointly with the students.

The adult learner has demonstrated memory ability and the ability to read printed verbal symbols for a sufficient period of time to commit the information to memory and this is almost all that is required for adult students to learn to improve comprehension.[1] Unfortunately, too many adults do not get enough practice and rehearsal periods to establish the information in their long-term memories. Usually, material is presented too briefly and too quickly and as a result, the adult students store the data in their short-term memories. That information, stored in the short-term memory, does not automatically transfer to the long-term memory, and forgetting as much as 80% of the material observed can occur within eighteen seconds after exposure.[5]

The teacher must design ways in which students can review each type of lesson daily for an extended period of time until the information is transferred to the long-term memory. A reading selection with more than six concepts to be learned and remembered may be too taxing on some students.

During the introductory step of the lesson, the student encounters what is to be learned; during the act of reading, the information is reviewed; during the questioning period, the student sees the material again. These steps will do much to ensure that the adult student stores the information in short memory and with reinforcement and rehearsal activities, daily, for a period of time will ensure storage in long-term memory.

Comprehension questions should match the purposes for reading a selection. The types of comprehension questions may also be taken from the classifications and formats chart presented earlier. There are several general categories of questions that should be used in conjunction with the information supplied in the chart. These categories are:
1. **Recognition level questions** — questions in which students are directed to find information in a selection once the selection has been read. At the literal level, the task is completed once the information is located. If an

inferential (implicative format) question is being asked, the students would underline the specific information they will use to predict an outcome or draw a conclusion.
2. **Memory level question** — memory serves as the basis for all comprehension; however, as used here, a memory question requires that a student be able to recall information explicitly stated or hold and manipulate that information to make inferences.
3. **Divergent level questions** — divergent thinking ability allows a person to seek many solutions to a problem. Initially, a divergent level question should be combined with either the recognition or memory level and a literal question using only the printed materials available. Questions such as, "How many personality changes did Brenda experience?" fit the literal (recognition or memory) type of question. When inferential questions are asked, divergent thinking must be used. A question such as, "What things could possibly happen next?" is an interpretive question requiring divergent thinking.
4. **Convergent level questions** — convergent level thinking usually requires a student to conclude a specific answer from among several possibilities generated from divergent thinking skills.
5. **Judgment level questions** — questions that require the student to place a value on actions, ideas, or thoughts either implicitly or explicitly stated in a selection.
6. **Appreciation level questions** — questions requiring answers in which students demonstrate that they can identify with the situations the characters are in and can demonstrate that they understand, appreciate, and/or value an idea, thought, or action although they may not agree with it.

By identifying the content of a piece of printed material or by writing a selection containing specific elements, providing students with specific reading materials is relatively easy. By using the information just supplied and adding that to the information about categories and formats, the teacher of adult students can generate a wide range of questions that will be very similar to those found in standarized reading and subject matter tests.

The following are categories of the types of questions that can be generated. In each question written, it is assumed that the matching reading selection will contain the necessary information for the student to answer the question.
1. **Major categories** — segmented, sequential, merged.
2. **Subcategories** — specific attributes, personality characteristics, cause and effect, comparison and contrast, emotive, idiomatic.
3. **Formats** — categorical, associative, procedural, transformational, implicative.
4. **Levels of questions** — recognition, memory, divergent, convergent, judgment, appreciation.

SUMMARY

Materials, published or teacher written, must be carefully evaluated for reading levels and content. But even if those two aspects are judged appropriate by a teacher of adults, the procedure cannot stop there. Students who exhibit problems in comprehension will not improve simply by working day after day on worksheets, with kits, and other instructional material . . . they would have arrived at the adult education center still in need of help in reading.

Adult education students are very different from elementary and secondary school students. They have extensive backgrounds, their brains and thinking processes have matured, and their reasons for being in school are unique and special.

The learning that adult students (especially illiterates) have acquired has been through auditory and visual modalities — not with complicated verbal symbols. Many of the survival skills the adults possess are mechanical and do not require reasoning abilities (knowing the cost of five pounds of hamburger and how much change is received from a $10.00 bill or the exact number of coins required for bus fare or the laundromat).

Adult students also are motivated by different variables than school children — their needs are also different. A teacher of adults must learn to match the students' perceived needs and reasons for attending adult classes to the instructional materials as well as the students' experiential backgrounds if an optimal upward gain in cognitive and academic development is to be affected.

For the non-reader a Language Experience reading prescription can reflect the skill areas chosen as important by the instructor or the student, incorporating broad categorical elements to be covered in a successful program. Basic vocabulary, selected word analysis skills, comprehension skills, and job vocabulary could be included on a prescription record sheet. Append to it the specific support materials needed for skill reinforcement.

In order to make the reading record truly meaningful, the mastered skills are "checked-off" when they are thoroughly incorporated into the functioning repertoire of the adult learner.

Adult students must also be guided to expand or diversify their immediate or felt needs and desires. If a student's major desire is to learn enough to pass the GED equivalency test, the teacher must aid the student to achieve that goal. However, the teacher must assume the additional responsibility of enticing the student to explore other areas of knowledge that have to be learned through reading rather than through visual and auditory observations of the environment.

If the lessons designed by the teacher follow a definite plan, if the nature of printed material is presented to the students, and if the adult students are guided and directed to analyse and synthesize information, then comprehension will develop. If adults are taught techniques of rehearsing and practicing newly learned material, then memory for information and procedures for developing memory will be forthcoming. If adults are questioned appropriately and taught the mechanics of answering questions, then they will develop the ultimate skill of learning to ask questions themselves.

REFERENCES

1. Layton, J. R. The Psychology of Learning To Read. New York: Academic Press, 1979.
2. Spache, G. D. *Good Reading For Poor Readers.* Champaign, Illinois: Garrard, 1974.
3. Layton, J. R. A chart for computing the Dale-Chall readability formula above fourth grade level. *Journal of Reading,* 24, December 1980.
4. Bormuth, J. R. "Cloze as a Measure of Readability," in *Reading As An Intellectual Activity.* Proceedings of the International Reading Association, 1963. Newark, Delaware: International Reading Association.
5. McNinch, George, Gary L. Shaffer, James R. Layton. "Language Experience-Reading," in MATERIALS & METHODS in Continuing Education, Chester Klevins, ed., Klevens Publications, Canoga Park, CA, 1978.

Self-Directed Learning

Ralph G. Brockett
Adjunct Instructor of Adult Education,
Syracuse University

Roger Hiemstra
Professor of Adult Education and
Program Leader, Syracuse University

Patrick R. Penland
Professor of Education and Library Science,
University of Pittsburgh

One of the most exciting and important areas of adult education to emerge over the past several years has focused on the topic of "self-directed learning." As defined by Knowles[1], self-directed learning is "a process in which individuals take the initiative, with or without the help of others, in diagnosing their learning needs, formulating learning goals, identifying human and material resources for learning, choosing and implementing appropriate learning strategies and evaluating learning outcomes." Thus, the self-directed or self-planned learning process is one of active participation and performance in the pursuit of change.

While the term self-directed learning has only come into wide usage over the past decade, this approach to learning is firmly rooted in the history of adult education. Until schools began to emerge on a wide scale throughout the world, teaching oneself was the primary way to learn new things. Socrates, Alexander the Great, Caesar, Descartes, Benjamin Franklin, Thoreau, and Thomas Edison are but a few examples of the many prominent self-directed learners throughout history.

Much of the current emphasis on self-directed learning appears to have developed from a foundation laid by Tough's[2] study of adult learning projects. In this research Tough found that nearly 70% of the learning projects undertaken by persons in his sample were planned primarily by the learners themselves, as opposed to a teacher or some other human or nonhuman resource. This awareness of a heavy involvement of "self" has stimulated considerable interest in, research on, and literature about the self-directed phenomenon.

SELF-DIRECTED LEARNING

Research on self-directed learning in adulthood has evolved considerably since the publication of the initial Tough study. Clearly, the major focus of self-directed learning research has been on descriptive studies of the frequency of self-directed learning in different groups of adults. Over the past several years, however, studies have begun to focus increasingly on the relationship between self-directedness and personological variables such as self-concept, curiosity, and creativity.

Learning Projects— Tough laid the foundation for research on learning projects in adulthood by operationally defining key terms and concepts so they could be studied empirically. He examined the "highly deliberate learning efforts" of adults; those learning activities that have been undertaken intentionally where the primary motivation was to produce change. The main focus of the study was on the adult's decision to undertake a learning project and the subsequent planning of that project.

A learning project is defined by Tough as "a series of related episodes, adding up to at least seven hours. In each episode, more than half of the person's total motivation is to gain and retain certain fairly clear knowledge and skill, or to produce some other lasting personal change . . . ." Similarly, an episode is "a period of time devoted to a cluster or sequence of similar or related activities, which are not interrupted much by other activities." Examples of episodes might include reading a newspaper or a chapter of a book, visiting a museum, or attending a class. An episode has a definite beginning and concluding time and the information that has been obtained must be retained for at least two days after the learning activity takes place. This serves to exclude those activities where the learning is intended to serve an immediate purpose, such as assembling a piece of household furniture, and is then quickly forgotten. A learning project, then, is the total of all episodes that a person undertakes in order to gain some specific knowledge or skill.

Tough was very specific in stating that a learning project must encompass a minimum of seven hours. First, this period of time is equivalent to a full working day, which Tough felt to be a considerable investment of time for a single learning project. Second, seven hours was found to work well in interviews with subjects because it eliminated very brief learning activities but not major learning efforts. In addition, "seven hours within a six-month period" was added as a qualification in terms of a **minimum** expenditure of time. In reality, Tough and other researchers have found that the majority of learning projects far exceed this minimum criterion.

There are a number of explanations that may account, at least in part, for much of the popularity of self-planned learning. Some of these include the following:

1. The learner may feel that turning over the responsibility for planning will result in a loss of time.
2. The learner may feel that the planning of the project will be easy and that content for the project will not be hard to locate.
3. The learner may not be certain of the future directions of the project and, thus, may be reluctant to make a commitment to an other-planned activity that may not be in harmony with his or her learning needs at that time.
4. Self-planned learning alleviates the potential difficulty of locating someone or something else to plan the project.

5. Learners who are highly skilled at locating resources and in determining their own learning needs may become frustrated with the greater structure that is inherent in other types of planning.
6. Many learners may take pride in assuming responsibility for the planning of their own learning efforts.

Since 1971, numerous researchers have used the learning projects interview schedule with samples from various segments of the adult population. Penland,[3] for example, looked at a large national sample of adults. Hiemstra[4,5] provided a summary of much of this research.

Self-Directed Learning Readiness — Learning projects research provided the impetus for further study of the self-directed learning concept. While these studies yielded descriptive data demonstrating a strong preference by adult learners for self-direction, it was only possible to speculate about the characteristics that contributed to a student's preference for self-directed learning. A major step in this research direction was the development of the Self-Directed Learning Readiness Scale (SDLRS).[6]

The SDLRS is a 57-item Likert scale designed to determine the extent to which individuals perceive themselves to possess factors associated with self-directedness. Guglielmino reported a reliability coefficient of .87 for the scale. Using factor analysis, he was able to identify eight possible factors related to self-directed learning. These factors include: (1) love of learning, (2) self-concept as an effective, independent learner, (3) tolerance of risk, ambiguity, and complexity in learning, (4) creativity, (5) view of learning as a lifelong, beneficial process, (6) initiative in learning, (7) self-understanding, (8) acceptance of responsibility for one's learning.

Hassan[7] recently reported validation support for the SDLRS instrument. In this study, 77 randomly selected adults participated in learning projects interviews and also were asked to complete the SDLRS. Hassan hypothesized that there would be significant relationships between self-directed readiness, as measured by the SDLRS, and the following: (1) the number of learning projects conducted in the previous twelve (12) months, (2) the type of planner used in projects, (3) the total number of self-fulfillment learning projects, (4) the demographic variables of age, sex, and level of formal education.

It was found that the "SDLRS can discriminate between high and low involvement in learning projects activities," thus indicating high predictive validity for the scale. Further, Hassan found significant relationships between self-directed readiness and the number of self-fulfillment projects as well as level of formal education. However, there was no significant relationship between self-directed readiness and the type of planner used by learners.

Among her conclusions, Hassan stated the following: "Readiness for self-directed learning and formal education have great impact on adult participation in self-directed learning and the adult learning projects activities." This study offers an important link between the learning projects research of the past decade and the SDLRS, which also has demonstrated high correlations in other studies with factors such as creativity, originality, and self-concept.

The SDLRS should prove to be an important tool in attempting to better understand the concept of self-directed learning.

Content Analysis— A third research approach that has contributed to a greater understanding of self-directed learning is the qualitative method of content analysis. Gibbons, et al.[8] analyzed the content of the biographies of twenty (20) individuals "who became expert in any socially accepted field of human activity without formal training past high school or the equivalent" (except for one person who had completed one year of college). Included among these experts were persons from diverse walks of life such as Charlie Chaplin, Harry S. Truman, Walt Disney, Muhammed Ali, Pablo Picasso, Henry Ford, and H.L. Mencken.

As each biography was read, items related to "the subject's nature, life, or times" were recorded. A total of 154 themes emerged from the data. The 10 most prominent of these, as determined by the ratings ascribed by readers, included the following characteristics: (1) primary experience in the area, (2) industriousness, (3) perseverance, (4) self-disciplined study, (5) curiosity, (6) single-minded pursuit, (7) creativity, (8) ingenuity, (9) self-confidence, (10) natural ability.

From this initial study, Gibbons, et al. laid a tentative foundation of principles that might contribute to a theory of self-directed learning. They suggest, in part, that self-education can help individuals assume control for their learning, undertake learning for specific use in the present, promote personal integrity, and develop expertise in an area while remaining open to exploring many fields of activity.

FUTURE DIRECTIONS

Research thus far has exhibited an exciting array of approaches to studying self-directed learning. Descriptive, experimental, and qualitative studies are all needed in the near future. Each will make important contributions to knowledge. Descriptive research is still needed to refine and answer questions about specific sub-groups, learning approaches, and learning resources. Experimental research is needed to examine relationships between the phenomenon and various personological variables.

Qualitative research will contribute to an understanding of the deeper meaning of the phenomenon and, as such, will serve as a tool for the development of theory grounded in the actual learning pursuits. The continued growth of self-directed learning research hopefully will produce a body of knowledge and theory that will exhibit a great deal of breadth as well as depth. The end result needs to be information that will enhance both adult learning and the practice of adult education.

In this regard, for example, further analyses of the literature and practice of adult education are needed. The theory embedded in its present research base can be articulated and developed into research constructs in order to guide investigations of such questions as:

1. How can the self-directed learner be helped to find a way through institutional resources without suffering a loss of control over the development of individual projects?

2. How can community education accommodate the self-directed learner so that the individual can advance outwardly towards an expansive self and a widening interpersonal network?
3. How can institutionally-based professional time be redeployed so that self-directed learners will have access to learning services on a "case-load" basis?

An expansion of empirical inquiry into the dimensions of self-directed learning will enrich the research base of adult education. Since self-instruction is almost by nature interactive, the adult education researcher will be led away from the analysis of limited variable sets towards those multivariate designs which more clearly approximate actual learning conditions. In turn, practitioners too will benefit as the principles of interactivity are applied to the creation of environments within which meaning for the individual learner can be more easily engendered.

One of the most universal criticisms made by many adult education practitioners in regard to research is that the reported results of investigations show little if any relevance to actual conditions in the field. The needs assessment type of investigation offers the adult education practitioner a method which could help to alleviate this predicament. This is especially the case if sections of these multiple surveys of community need could address the widespread phenomenon of self-directed learning behavior among citizens of all ages and interests.

IMPLICATIONS FOR ADULT EDUCATION PRACTICE

What does the current state of the art mean to adult educators who are responsible for developing, administering, and/or implementing programs? It means a great deal! The increasing recognition that self-directed learning is, and has been throughout most of history, a predominant force in terms of adult choices and involvement has implications for learners and teachers alike, as well as for institutions serving adults.

Implications for Learners — In his discussion of andragogy, Knowles[9] outlines four assumptions about adults as learners. These are:
1. Their self-concept moves from one of being a dependent personality toward being a self-directed human being.
2. They accumulate a growing reservoir of experience that becomes an increasingly rich resource for learning.
3. Their readiness to learn becomes oriented increasingly to the developmental tasks of their social roles.
4. Their time perspective changes from one of postponed application of knowledge to immediacy of application, from one of subject-centeredness to one of performance-centeredness.

These assumptions provide a valuable foundation for understanding self-directed learners. The self-directed learner is an active learner. One who is highly self-directed recognizes that learning is too important to turn its planning over to someone else.

Perhaps the most important contribution of self-directed learning research to adult education practice is the formal recognition that most adults are involved in learning. Studies of participation show that a relatively small but highly visible percentage of adults are the primary participants in formal educational activities. By expanding the definition of adult learning to include those activities planned, carried out, and elaborated by individual learners, it becomes clear that nearly all adults are participants at some time or another. Promoting self-directed learning can be an important strategy in reaching learners who are often overlooked in educational programming — older adults, minority group members, and persons residing in institutions, to name a few examples. Through self-directed learning it may be possible to attain the ambitious goal of "serving all adults."

Implications for Teachers — Just as the self-directed learning concept implies a need to redefine what is meant by the "adult learner," so too does it imply a redefinition of who is viewed as an adult educator. Thus, in the broadest sense of the definition, everyone is a teacher because self-directed learning involves some teaching. From a more pragmatic point of view, however, an implication of self-directed learning for adult education is an almost certain expansion of the field. Many persons who may not have considered adult education as their professional role may do so, or at least will be likely to expand their view of this role. A few examples might include librarians, counselors and therapists, clergy, and journalists. More and more people will join the ranks of adult educators, and the field is likely to benefit from the richness of this diversity.

Another implication pertains to skills that the educator will need. As the role of the educator shifts from a primary function of content transmitter to facilitator of learning, he or she will need to develop new attitudes and skills for working with the self-directed learner. It will be increasingly important for the educator to possess the interpersonal relating skills so crucial to the helping professions. Through the development of skills such as empathy, respect, and genuineness or sincerity, the educator should be able to demonstrate a sense of "being with" the learner, to respond to the learner in a way that will help to facilitate further exploration into and greater understanding of the learning task at hand.

Implications for Institutions — The scope and nature of institutions serving adults will be affected greatly by the impact of self-directed learning. This transition has already begun and is reflected in the increasing development of educational brokering services, free universities, and learning exchanges. The role of libraries as a resource for adult learners will be expanded greatly. Social services and health-related agencies will most likely come to consider education a more overt purpose than in the past.

If so, a community-based system of adult education agencies can allow for pre-literacy orientation, resource access, and various program options in addition to adult basic education (ABE). Other individuals may want to

Conceptual Model of a Lifelong Learning Society

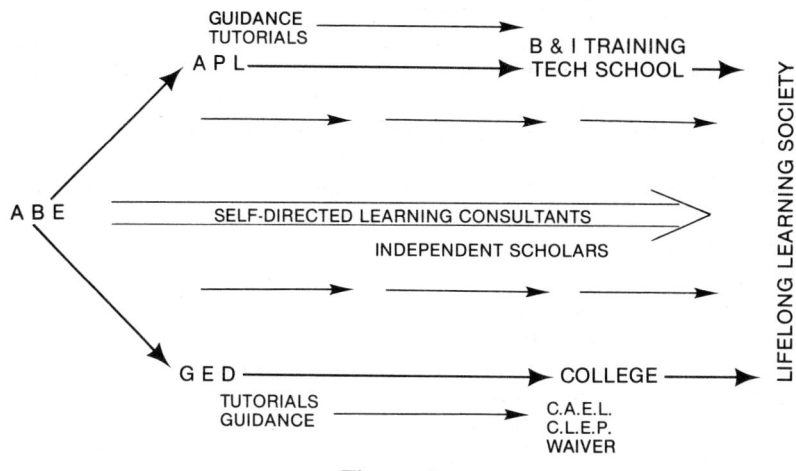

```
                GUIDANCE ─────────────────►
                TUTORIALS
                A P L ─────────────────────► B & I TRAINING
                                             TECH SCHOOL ───►
              ↗   ──────►  ──────►  ──────►
             ↗
    A B E ────── SELF-DIRECTED LEARNING CONSULTANTS ═══►
             ↘          INDEPENDENT SCHOLARS
              ↘  ──────►  ──────►  ──────►
                G E D ─────────────────────► COLLEGE ───►
                TUTORIALS ─────────────────► C.A.E.L.
                GUIDANCE                     C.L.E.P.
                                             WAIVER
```
(vertical label: LIFELONG LEARNING SOCIETY)

Figure 1.

advance through the adult proficiency level (APL) and/or the general educational development (GED) programs. Vocational education may be started in a technical school but on-the-job training is a major investment of business and industry (B & I) in order to achieve worker productivity. (See Figure 1.)

The continuing education "system" in America is fast becoming so networked through the Educational Information Center (EIC) system that entrance requirements and exit (graduation) credentials are becoming meaningless. Thus, the need for continuous supportive resources and expanded learning facilities are the most demanding implications for agencies. More often than not agencies will become a part of the network of widespread involvement in self-planned learning.

The lifelong self-directed learner may want to continue into post secondary education or remain involved as an independent scholar. The general availability of such programs as the Cooperative Advancement of Experiential Learning (CAEL) and the College Level Examination Program (CLEP) has tended to blur the distinction between the wisdom obtained from real life and the knowledge earned in credit courses.

Implications for Communities — The community, and most surely the neighborhood, is the locus for most self-directed learning within the lifelong learning society. It is here that the individual can have an impact upon sociocultural affairs through an interactive network of personal relations. Lifelong learners can increase in responsibility for their own learning and also can share that learning when participating in community oriented projects. The reciprocal effect of this sharing and mutual exploration helps to eliminate competition and promotes cooperation without which the quality of life would deteriorate.

In an effort to increase their visibility many community-based agencies have initiated needs assessment studies. As a result of these surveys, community needs have become better known. Not only may self-directed learning services be included in their program planning efforts but any agency itself may enlarge its mission to include life**long** and life**wide** education for all citizens. If so, **any** citizen (pre-literate or not) should be able to enter the community learning network at any point of personally self-assessed need and be helped toward any other point of self-directed competency attainment.

SUMMARY

The expanding body of research on self-directed learning has done much to increase understanding of the adult learner. By expanding the definition of adult learning to include those activities that are planned, implemented, and evaluated by the individual learner, the field of adult education is likely to experience a transition that will witness changing roles for learners, teachers, and institutions. Ultimately, such a transition should be beneficial since it will promote greater participation in adult learning activities and will ideally expand the breadth and richness of the adult education field.

QUESTIONS AND EXERCISES

1. What are the new roles required of adult educators in working with highly self-directed learners?
2. How will traditional institutions need to change to accommodate the self-directed adult learner?
3. What types of new teaching techniques, learner resources, and methods for evaluating learning are required?
4. Should the adult education profession develop some type of "code of ethics" to protect the learner from those who may wish to "cash" in on the self-directed learning phenomenon? Prepare a code of ethics.
5. Examine your own institution or agency. What changes are required to facilitate the self-directed learner taking advantage of your programs and resources?
6. Examine the report of your last community needs assessment survey. How could self-planned learning behavior have been investigated if it was not included in the study?

REFERENCES

1. Knowles, M. *Self-Directed Learning.* New York: Association Press, 1975.
2. Tough, A. *The Adult's Learning Projects (2nd ed.).* Austin, Texas: Learning Concepts, 1979.
3. Penland, P.R. *Self-Planned Learning in America.* 1978. (ERIC Document Reproduction Service No. ED 152 987.)
4. Hiemstra, R. *Policy Recommendations Related to Self-Directed Adult Learning.* Occasional paper no. 1. 1980. (ERIC Document Reproduction Service No. ED 198 304.)
5. Hiemstra, R. "The Older Adult as Learning Participant." *Contemporary Educational Psychology,* 1980, 5 (Fall).
6. Guglielmino, L.M. *Development of the Self-Directed Learning Readiness Scale.* Unpublished doctoral dissertation, University of Georgia, 1977.
7. Hassan, A.M. *An Investigation of the Learning Projects Among Adults of High and Low Readiness for Self-Direction in Learning.* Unpublished doctoral dissertation, Iowa State University, 1981.
8. Gibbons, M., et al "Toward a Theory of Self-Directed Learning: A Study of Experts Without Formal Training." *Journal of Humanistic Psychology,* 1980, 20.
9. Knowles, M.S. *The Modern Practice of Adult Education (Revised & Updated).* New York: Association Press, 1981.

Participatory Modes

Beverly B. Cassara

*Dean, Graduate School &
Professor of Adult Education
University of the District of Columbia*

While the concept "participatory research" is gaining momentum in adult education on the international scene, especially in the Third World or developing countries, as of now the term, at least, is not widely used or accepted in the United States and some other Western countries. This probably has to do with what might be a confusion over terms. It also has to do with the tradition of research which is seen as only a highly advanced academic endeavor. Would the phrases "participatory action project" or "participatory learning" evoke the same doubts and questions? Probably not; these are related concepts that are gaining in acceptance. In some instances there is only a fine line drawn between and among these terms, at least this appears to be so in practice.

Nevertheless, there is an important concept designated by the term "participatory research" which deserves and is attracting attention. It is a democratic concept and it is more a principle than a method. Many adult educators will recognize that the concept indeed is not entirely new, that it is an idea they may have used in some of their own work perhaps for many years. Hall describes participatory research as a social science "research process . . . based on a system of discussion, investigation and analysis in which the researched are as much a part of the process as the researcher. Theories are neither developed beforehand to be tested nor drawn by the researcher from his or her involvement with reality."[1]

Most authors who write about participatory research see it as an approach to research and not a method — an approach which grows out of the democratic interests of the research and the researched, and out of a belief that people should be the "masters of their own destiny."

The emergence of this concept in its present day context and form is to some extent a natural evolution in educational research in a world that is concerned with self-determination on many levels. With the knowledge explosion and the communication explosion, formerly powerless persons, still even without extensive formal education, are very quickly becoming sophisticated in the ways of this world. They are learning the nature of power and are finding ways to claim it — not always constructively — as the rise of terrorism exemplifies. They are impatient as technology and its salesmen give them daily cause for rising expectations. This is equally true for the powerless minorities in Western countries as it is for large numbers of the population in developing countries. They are tired of waiting for someone to do something for them — things which are seldom efficacious anyway. Treating people as objects in any situation will not enhance their development and will become more and more unacceptable as a way of helping them.

This new sophistication of the powerless became evident in an urban housing project where efforts were being made to expand the city's adult education opportunities to meet the needs of low-income women. The women were friendly enough, but they made it plain from the beginning that they did not want to be studied, did not want to become objects of any more studies that end up in books and that bring no help to them. Some of these women had as little as a fourth grade education, but life had taught them much. They made it very clear that if answers were to be given to the questions, they would be glad to work in the search for answers, but that this should be done only in the context of caring friends who would work with them, respect them, and continue the relationship with them over time. A five-year project which certainly could be labeled "participatory research," was initiated though the term was not in vogue at that time.

Self-Determination — During the 1960's in the United States a new thrust toward self-determination was generated by the Office of Economic Opportunity's Community Action programs which sprang up in urban and rural communities alike, where local groups were supported by government funds to study their own problems and interests and make decisions about improving their own conditions.

The aegis of participatory research was in the air internationally. Largely through United Nations agencies, the World Bank and other such organizations, as well as enlightened governments of new countries who, in their efforts to cast off all vestiges of colonialism, found that decision-making was central to maintaining their newly-gained freedom. People the world over have learned that the best decisions for themselves are made by themselves, even when trial and error may have brought temporary failure.

With this advance in sophistication, self-knowledge and self-confidence on the part of individuals and groups of people, social science research began to make adjustments in the methods of study of cultures and people. Anthropologists had always known you learn about people best by living with them. But, they still performed their studies primarily to gain knowledge to bring back to publish in books. When, and if, they were helpful to those they studied, it was mostly incidental to their first purpose — that of adding to the base of knowledge generally.

One particular newer approach, "The Grounded Theory," which B.G. Glaser and A.L. Strauss published in 1967 was a definite step on the way to the concept of participatory research. Essentially they realized that: (1) many factors influenced any situation, (2) deciding in advance what they should be seeking could obscure reality, (3) all participants in a situation should be studied and should provide information. Results were evaluated by the researchers in the last analysis and while the results were used to expand a base of knowledge which would be of use to administrators, teachers and consultants, there was no specific requirement to get the participants to follow through by deliberating over their own condition and situation and then taking action.

The arrival on the scene of Paulo Freire in Brazil was another significant development. With his deep convictions that some education could be worse than none if it did not help people become aware of the conditions of their own lives and find their own ways to gain control over their own lives, he made an impact that was felt around the world. Not that any number of persons and movements were not espousing similar principles, but it was really due to Freire that the movement took on a name "conscientization" and developed a common focus.

Hall in a recent *Convergence* article wrote how he personally came to the conviction that traditional social science research was not sufficient for today. He stated four shortcomings of the general survey approach: (1) surveys oversimplify through forcing choice and fail to reflect the dynamics of a situation by the presentation of only one moment and through isolating the individual, (2) survey research is inclined to be dominating and oppressive, (3) action is not a concern of the researcher, (4) the principles of adult education are abrogated.

Guidelines for Practitioners — The UNESCO publication *Participatory Research for Adult Education and Literacy: Guidelines for Practitioners*[2] describes participatory research as an integrated three-pronged activity:
1. An approach to social investigation with the full and active participation of the community or workers in the entire research process.
2. A means of taking action for social transformation.
3. An educational process of mobilization.

In this way a new knowledge base was developed. It is a knowledge base which grows out of the natural authentic interests and needs of those concerned. The very fact that such research affects action and education so directly that it can hardly be separated from them, means it is effective research. How often do we wring our hands over the fact that the body of knowledge we have in the books on the shelves so seldomly serves the people researched.

Dr. Matthias Wesseler states:[3]

In view of the growing crises of a culture of alienation, an educational theory of science is needed, which provides a new connection between knowledge and man. Participation is one of the central concepts of this theory. Whilst traditional educational theories start out from a static picture of man and a separation between learning and living, the author projects a new concept of educational science aiming at the education of man in a dialectical process between action and existence, in accordance with the specific cultural and social context. Hence, participation will not mean simple participation in knowledge or action but active participation of the ego in the permanent process of self-realization within the environment.

Given this description one can understand why powerless persons in developing countries would appreciate participatory research; that educational leaders would see it as an effective way of helping people to help themselves.

Unfortunately industrialized countries have not yet realized the extent of the problems that can ensue from the frustrations of the powerless as they endeavor to become masters of their own fate. Even persons without much formal education have wisdom and can constructively participate in studies. The decisions which will alter their lives should grow naturally out of their culture and values.

A New Concept of Research — The question still remains for some as to whether this activity should be called research, given the purist scientific and traditional definition of the term. Speaking to this point in his Jefferson Lecture in the Humanities, Gerold Holton suggested that scientific research is no longer "an isolated esoteric pursuit for a few souls engaged in rapturous contemplation" but rather "an ever more dominant force directing the very course of society."[4]

Participatory research is a new form. In no way does it fit the traditional definition of research. It is a new tool for the enhancement of knowledge and the quality of life.

For the traditional researcher, participatory research misses the boat on several counts:(1) it does not begin with an hypothesis, (2) there is virtually no control for the researcher, (3) it reflects a dynamic situation, so that no one moment reflects reality, (4) conclusions are never final and are viewed differently by the various members affected. Traditionally, researchers have eschewed action, as having no bearing on their work; if their findings warranted change, that was someone else's business — even though no one can deny that in most social science research the activity itself sets up dynamics for change. Participatory research could be seen as undercutting the prestige and status that traditional researchers have enjoyed. Based, as it has been, on intellectual initiative and creativity of thought, and months and years of individual search, traditional research is a distinctly different activity. In so far as that is true, comparisons should be made only for the purpose of understanding the distinctions, and knowing which approach to use in which situation. There will remain a perhaps healthy tension between advocates of the two approaches. One could suggest, as has been done, that the participatory research approach be called by a different name. That would be an avoidance of the issue and not a solution. Why can we not add a new research mode to the established typology?

Is participatory research then really research in the best meaning of the term? There can only be one answer. It is research, with its own approach, methods, participants and purposes. It is research with added features including action, and including politics, both of which have been far removed from traditional research.

From the draft of the guidelines cited in the UNESCO document — "This approach involves the acquisition of more knowledge, more competence and greater self-confidence — in short empowerment — for the otherwise poor and oppressed people. In this sense participatory research demonstrates the general potential of adult education to be emancipatory and liberatory and to promote self-determined, self-reliant development."[2] These words are a very courageous political statement. It reminds us of the wisdom of Paulo Freire who has always realized that the most effective adult education will have political consequences. To even mention political consequences in the context of education has a ring of impurity, subversiveness, and propaganda. Where does this approach leave the educator/researcher? To the extent that the researcher in the participatory mode is true to this philosophy and serves as a facilitator to help people get the facts and analyze their own situation, he/she has promoted a worthy kind of research, education and action. The researcher will not be completely neutral or objective. No researcher ever was, but he/she must make a sincere attempt to be neutral as all the best researchers have always done.

Conference Cases — In the United States a conference on participatory research was held in September of 1979 at New Market, TN which was attended by thirty adult educators from the United States and Canada. To quote from **Second Thoughts:**[5]

> Case studies presented by the participants included "kitchen economics" sessions for Saskatchewan farmers; participant-derived ABE curriculum for Pueblo communities; development of a peoples' occupational health association in the Carolinas; the unionization of GED curriculum for Tennessee textile workers; community self-portraits on video by Latin American immigrant workers in Toronto; popular use of video by community organizations in Rockford, Illinois; resistance by lobster fishermen in Magdalen Islands to a large-scale salt mining project; and strike education and corporate research for the empowerment of coal miners in Appalachia.

An International Forum on Participatory Research was held in Ljubljana, Yugoslavia in April of 1980. Sponsored by the International Council for Adult Education and UNESCO, the conference was attended by fifty adult educators and development specialists from twenty-three countries in Africa, Asia, Latin America, Europe and North America. The purpose of the conference was to ascertain the state of the art, develop guidelines for participatory research and strengthen the movement by bringing together those with experiences to share and those who would learn. Considerable pre-conference planning included an in-depth study of such research in Yugoslavia, and the preparation of case studies from five regions of the world. At the Forum these cases, which addressed "epistemology, methodology, political economy, and dynamics" were studied by the participants to draw up guidelines for using the participatory research approach. The report is available from the International Council for Adult Education.[6]

At the conference, cases from Asia related to farmer-settlers in the Southern Philippines, a women's cooperative in Korea and a women's movement in India were discussed. In Latin America there were cases of rural training in Peru, migrant agricultural laborers in Chile, and community workers in Venezuela. African cases included the role of culture in development in Tanzania, self-awareness of women in the urban slums of Nigeria, and grain storage in Tanzania. In North America two cases were from Canada, one with immigrant workers and one with environment assessment; the U.S. case came from Appalachia and focused on land ownership.

The European cases were from Norway where a trade union problem was faced, from the Netherlands where an open school for women was treated, and in the United Kingdom where the design of materials for slow learners in literacy work was the subject. Several papers were presented on the projects in Yugoslavia.

Two cases are analyzed and compared in an attempt to examine the concept of participatory research. The cultural context as well as the source of initiation of the project, the purposes, the methods and results are described.

The first case concerns the development of a localized women's movement in India. The women in question belong to an oppressed class of landless laborers. They were the victims of a social system of male domination generally and of households where men were often drunk and beat them regularly. The wealthy landowners also took advantage of them sexually in the fields as well as in their huts, and treated them badly otherwise. They were very exploited women. Having heard about women's movements in other places, some of the village women became activists and started a movement for a women's camp, a feature that had previously been only a male aspect of the culture.

After a great deal or organizing activity and many problems, the camp was established and 150 women from a number of villages attended. Untrained in formal discussion and analysis, the women learned how to formulate their ideas and present them orally. When individual women learned the extent of the problems, they decided to start a plan for cooperative action. This plan included breaking the liquor pots in the villages, shaving the heads of men who got drunk, barring bootleggers from the village, and carrying knives to fight off the landowners who would molest them. The result was a new self-consciousness on the part of the women and a confident determination that they should have a say in all village councils.

Research — From this very short description, can we say this is research? Look at it this way. What is research for? If a traditional research project had been undertaken, a person might have gone from dwelling to dwelling asking questions on a survey instrument. if the person were an outsider, would he/she have gotten the full facts? Possibly. As it was, no survey was taken in the formal sense. Yet what was the camp meeting all about? Was it not a survey? Encouraged by each other — the dynamics of the group situation — at the meeting each woman participated in an oral survey of the problems. So it is a definite form of research. Then they checked out all their options. That too is research. Based upon these two stages of research and the education they had all gained from the information gathered in the camp, they decided on some action projects.

In another instance in Canada among Indian women in the northern Kayahna Area Tribal Council, the project did the same things but in a little more sophisticated and formal way. In this case too there were no outside person or persons initiating the project. The Indian people in this area retain many traditional ways and have their own language. They say they have been poor since contact with Europeans, and they do not feel that they get adequate support from the government. They are particularly threatened by multi-national corporations who want to develop their lands.

They say,
> The key to changing this unsatisfactory situation is for government to recognize that the Indian people and communities have a capacity and the desire to provide for their own needs, and must make available the necessary responsibilities and resources so that Indian people are free to develop and provide the services that they themselves choose.[7]

Since the employment and training programs provided have severely neglected women's needs, women themselves got together and made their own survey. Sixty women who had been employed at some point in a four-year period were interviewed about their employment, training and conditions of work and their interests. The results of the survey were carefully charted to show that only 13 had had some form of training. The sixty were asked what kind of training they would like and what kind of work they thought could be developed in their area. The results were studied by the women and decisions were made to set up a day care center, several coffee shops and other projects such as a hairdressing shop and bakery. One problem the women researched quite thoroughly was that of upgrading the processes of human waste disposal. They surveyed the conditions in every household and then looked at the possibilities for improvement, drew charts to show how each house could be improved and then carried out the improvements that were within the capability of the people themselves and applied for aid for further improvement.

Was it research? Absolutely. It was also education and action.

Participatory research is most important among peoples who feel powerless and oppressed. This condition existed in both cases. In neither of these cases was there an outside expert, but there could have been, and indeed the people had previously learned their skills from someone else. In the case of the Indian women, they were asking for consultants and funds but not for anyone to make decisions for them.

These cases exemplify the fact that participatory research is solid research, but research with a difference from the traditional definition, and with the additional components of education and action, all of which are more successful because the people participate in every phase and make their own decisions. At the present time, participatory research is catching on among the poor, the minorities, the oppressed, and the powerless in micro situations.

Some authors are discussing the possibility of extending participatory research to the macro situation. Can participatory research be used effectively when people cannot meet face to face? Perhaps it can, yet no model is available at this time. The organizational aspects of a macro situation might change the nature of participatory research as we know it now.

SUMMARY

Perhaps there is an extensive future for participatory research. One thing seems clear; even if the name gets lost over time, the idea will not. It will continue to grow as the powerless continue to become more sophisticated in the realization that knowledge is power, and that they are equally capable of producing knowledge.

Participatory research adds to the store of the world's knowledge and it also becomes immediately and simultaneously translated into action to improve the quality of life — the one and only reason for developing and increasing the knowledge base.

QUESTIONS

1. How should "research" be defined? Does "participatory research" fit into your definition; if not, why?
2. Do you think that the academic world has been overly possessive about knowledge?
3. What good uses for participatory research can you suggest? Have you already been involved in such research projects under another name perhaps?

REFERENCES

1. Hall, Budd. "Participatory Research: An Approach for Change" in *Convergence* VIII, No. 2, 1975.
2. Draft, *Participatory Research for Adult Education and Literacy: Guidelines for Practitioners.* Toronto, Canada: International Council for Adult Education, 1980.
3. Wesseler, Matthias. *Arbeitsberichte und Materialen.* Witzenhausen, West Germany: Gesamthochschule Kassel, 1980.
4. Ingalls, Zoe. "Where is Science Taking Us? Gerold Halton Maps the Possible Routes." *Chronicle of Higher Education,* May 18, 1980.
5. Jackson, Ted. "Participatory Research" in *Second Thoughts.* Vol. 2, No. 3. Madison, Wisconsin: Madison Campus Ministry, April 1980.
6. *Report on the International Forum on Participatory Research.* Toronto, Canada: International Council on Adult Education and UNESCO, April 1980.
7. Hudson, Grace. "Participatory Research by Indian Women in Northern Ontario Tribal Communities." Vol. XIII, No. 12. Toronto, Canada: International Council for Adult Education, 1980.

Cross Cultural Education

Leonard Nadler

Professor, Adult Education
George Washington University

The term cross-cultural has many meanings and even more implications. It refers to those experiences that one has when going from one culture to another. This is something most of us do, and sometimes we have several different cross-cultural experiences in one day.

There is a need to teach adults about experiencing cross culture, particularly in light of the growing interdependency of the world today. Some of the concepts and material found useful in cross-cultural work both in the United States and in foreign countries, as well as a discussion of cultures and microcultures, and an exploration of some cultural behaviors are of utmost importance to today's adult educators.

CULTURE

There are many different definitions of culture, but the most accepted one is that culture includes:
1. Habits and customs.
2. The way people "develop."
3. The way people cope with living and changing.

To explore "habits and customs" specific and observable behaviors need be noted. Almost all cultural behavior can be observed, particularly by those who are part of that culture. When one hears, "Well, everybody knows," you can almost be certain that what is being referred to is cultural behavior. In truth, only those who are part of that culture "know" what is being referred to. That is one of the functions of culture — to indicate who is part of the cultural group and who is not.

"People develop" culture for it is not something innate or genetic. People may develop cultural norms in a variety of ways, but there is still concern with what people do. One reason people develop cultural norms is to make life more organized, rational, and understandable. If all the people within the same cultural group behave in similar ways, at least some part of life becomes more predictable and the number of new decisions needed to be made each day can be reduced.

Culture is highly changeable. If one endeavors to change a people by prohibiting a particular cultural behavior, or by culturally punishing those who persist in doing it, these same people will develop some new but similar cultural behaviors, if they want to persist in the previous cultural behavior.

In many cases, legal behavior is based on the prevailing cultural norms. That is, a certain kind of behavior becomes highly desirable, and to be sure it does not change, laws are passed. This does not mean that everybody will obey the law (the 55 m.p.h. speed limit) but at least society can easily differentiate between those who are obeying the law and those who are violating it. Once behavior becomes codified in some legal manner, it is no longer cultural behavior. If the law is contrary to accepted cultural behavior, new or different habits and customs will be developed that will circumvent the law, or at least make it less enforceable.

There is another way of attempting to solidify cultural behavior and that is through institutionalization. Look at religion. You may have heard the statement that, "I am for religion, but I am against churches, or synagogues, or mosques." In essence, a person is saying that culturally he wants religion, but he does not agree with those institutions that have formalized it — institutionalized it. When institutions become too rigid, but people still want to practice the particular cultural norm, they develop new and different habits and customs — form a new cultural group.

Exploring the cultural relationship of the domestic and international arena is important to the complete understanding of culture. Many experience a cross-cultural happening yet never leave home. Most countries are made up of various cultural groups of differing race, ethnicity, or religion.

Obviously, when one leaves his/her own country, it is expected that there will be some cross-cultural factors to be dealt with. Every person, when traveling, carries his/her own cultural baggage. Fortunately, perhaps, it cannot be weighed or tagged, nor must it be cleared through customs. Despite this, that baggage is as vital to the traveler as the artifacts and clothing packed into the luggage. You cannot eliminate your own cultural baggage, and there is no reason why you should.

MICRO-CULTURE

There is a tendency, even today, to speak of culture and sub-culture, as if the culture is made up of a group of subcultures. It also implies that the "mainstream" culture is the prevalent and desirable one. In reality, culture, and our world, are made up of numerous micro-cultures.

All of us belong to a variety of micro-cultures — all at the same time. Among them one could list: the company I work for, the people at work I eat with, the religious group to which I belong, my family, the community in which I live, social and political clubs I belong to, and various groups of friends — each a different micro-culture. The list seems almost endless. If drawn as a series of circles, the micro-cultural pattern would show a series of overlapping circles.

The importance of this concept, for adults in a learning situation, is that moving from one micro-cultural group to another requires learning. An adult can do this by trial and error, but an error could cause the adult to be excluded from that micro-cultural group. This was evidenced when programs were designed to help some minority groups enter the work force, and to

Cross Cultural Education

move ahead. Job skills were not enough. It was also important to help those adults learn "how to behave" in those work situations — another way of saying that they had to learn the appropriate micro-cultural behavior for that work situation.

Understanding several micro-cultures is essential for an adult who seeks cultural mobility in any society. When one violates a micro-cultural norm, the group can be very punishing, sometimes unintentionally. Groups do develop some cultural norms just so that they can exclude others, or at least be different from others. This can be a device whereby the group endeavors to protect its own integrity and uniqueness. This is evident in the food practices among many religions. In some, because of their long history, the cultural practice has become legalized by religious fiat. In other religions, it is still a matter of cultural behavior — certain foods are eaten at certain times of the year. When observing food habits and customs of most religions one will find a mixture of the cultural and the legal.

CULTURAL BEHAVIOR

To understand culture, behavior must be observed. It is possible to see and understand culture by observing behavior rather than in seeking to find out what people think. Culture influences how people think, but it is extremely difficult to collect such data. By looking and recording what people do, one can deduce what appears to be appropriate behavior for a particular micro-culture.

Cultural behavior is frequently misunderstood by those who are outside that cultural group. The outsiders tend to think that the group is hiding something, which in turn produces generalizations such as the "inscrutable Oriental," or "Those people keep to their own and don't like outsiders." It may not be a question of liking, but rather one of not understanding the other's cultural behaviors. Caution should be exercised when looking at cultural behavior as many areas of cultural behavior overlap.

LANGUAGE

It has been assumed that if everyone spoke an international language (Esperanto), there would be total global communication. This is highly unlikely, for, according to the sociologists, language is a manifestation of culture. If the cultural behavior does not exist, it is improbable that the language will evolve.

First, let us look at verbal language — spoken and written. Have you ever observed two people in conversation, one whose native tongue is English, and the other who has only a limited knowledge of English? As they begin to have communications difficulty, often the native English speaker will begin speaking louder and louder, as if volume would break the language barrier that exists between them. Obviously, it does not work.

The use of verbal language presents problems. Words can have a variety of meanings that are not immediately discernible. The story is told of three men, none of them having English as his native tongue. The following conversation took place:

Man 1 — "My wife visited our physician today and she writes me that he told her she cannot have another baby."
Man 2 — "Oh yes, I know what you mean. She is impregnable."
Man 1 — "Well, I am not sure that is what it would be called in English. There is another word. It is . . ."
Man 3 — "I know. You mean that your wife is inconceivable."
Man 1 — "That does not sound quite right. Oh yes, I know — she is unbearable."

Obviously, none of these terms would be used by a native English speaker, yet they do make sense for somebody who goes to a dictionary to determine the meaning of words.

Therein lies part of our problem. A dictionary tells you what a word means at the time the dictionary was compiled. Most languages of the world change frequently and continually. It is estimated that English changes about 5-10% a year. That is, each year some of the existing words fall into disuse, a significant percentage of the language are new words which did not exist previously, or at least, were not in common usage.

If you have doubts about this, try an exercise with your class of adults. Ask them to list those words they knew and used in their youth, which they no longer use. Then, ask them to list the words they use now, which did not exist when they were young. After the lists have been analyzed, the instructor and students will be amazed at some of the words on both lists, particularly, if the class contains people who have lived in different parts of the U.S. (a micro-cultural difference based on geography), or are of different ages (a micro-cultural difference based on age cohorts).

Another difference arises when one realizes that certain words reflect the experience of a "people." If we look at the word "snow," many of us will have an image and perhaps even be able to communicate it to others. What of those who live in tropical areas and have never experienced snow? Their language may not have a word for it. Rather, they will speak of "the white things which fall from the sky at certain times, when the weather is colder than we have ever experienced." Culturally, they have nothing in their own habits and customs to deal with that phenomenon. Their language about snow will be sparse, if they consider it at all.

By contrast, it is estimated that the Eskimo language has sixteen (16) different words for snow. In their lives, knowing the exact texture and depth of the snow is a matter of life and death. Their language reflects this need, and they make a variety of cultural adjustments based on what has been communicated among them about the snow.

On a more basic level, the micro-cultural group can sometimes use written language to thwart the efforts of another group. Note this example. The managers (a micro-cultural group) of a manufacturing plant decided to reduce employee smoking. This was due partly to pressures from non-smokers and government inspectors (other micro groups). The workers (a micro group) did not want to give up their smoking privilege. The change was ordered — No smoking on the job. Smoking areas were established away from the job sites, so that smokers had less than ten (10) minutes to smoke and traverse the distance.

Here was a cultural situation (smoking) that was being changed by legal means — using written language to thwart behaviors of a micro group. It was almost inevitable that new cultural behavior would arise. The smokers found a seldom used supply closet, put a fan in the small space allocated for the window, and posted a sign on the door — For Authorized Personnel Only. There was no specification as to who was authorized, but the cultural behavior of the group communicated that the sign meant smokers only. The other micro-cultural groups cited above never did discover the smoking room, as the sign thwarted their efforts in achieving their goals.

Given problems with verbal communication, some people try to resort to the non-verbal or hand signals. There are even those who believe that such signals are universal. Nothing could be further from reality. Actually, there appears to be no universal hand signals. The same signals may exist in different cultures, but can have different meanings.

In Japan a person was on a railway platform getting ready to enter a car. The porter lifted his hand palm down, and seemed to wave this passenger off. A helpful bilingual Japanese explained that the porter was signalling to the waiting passenger to enter the car. Our cultural hand signal for such a message would be to have the palm up and the fingers signifying to come forward — quite different from the signal in Japan.

SPACE

Another cultural behavior is the use of space. One aspect is related to what has been called the territorial imperative. Although most of the research on this has been done with animals, it is possible to observe some similar behavior in humans.

Humans tend to carve up their space in various ways and most of these patterns are related to cultural behavior. Think of the usual classroom. Even if the instructor of adults endeavors to use good androgogical techniques — circles the chairs — that too is an implication of how space is to be used. For one thing, circling the chairs makes a use of space which is far from traditional.

At a recent workshop, where the intent was to eliminate status positions by circling the chairs, the participants entered the room and immediately rearranged the chairs in a fashion which was culturally similar to their norm. Again, there was the traditional classroom seating with the teacher at the head, facing the students.

Furniture occupies space, and tends to divide the space in culturally acceptable patterns. Often the teacher's desk, much like the judge's bench, cannot be approached without prior permission.

In a like fashion, homes are divided into various kinds of living space. Are you still invited into somebody's "living room," even though the only time it is used is when they have guests? There are bathrooms which do not have baths. The family room may more often be called the TV room. (This is an example of the merging of two cultural behaviors — language and space.)

According to our standards, Japanese are underprivileged. They do not have a bedroom, living room, or sitting room, as they have only one room which serves all these purposes. There are cultural, and probably economic, factors related to this. There is also the issue of space, in a country where space is at a premium.

According to Hall's concept of the "space bubble" or proxemics, each of us has an invisible bubble around us or vacant space around us which we need. This space can actually be measured and has a strong cultural base. The North American tends to want about eighteen inches between people in normal conversation. To come closer is to attempt to invade this person's space bubble. Americans, in dealing with Middle Easterners, will find themselves slowly backing up or back-pedaling while their conversation partner slowly but steadily advances into their "space bubble." This may produce feelings of discomfort or annoyance on the part of the Americans.

In the U.S., the cultural behavior related to the "space bubble" can be seen in many ways. At a party, a man and woman (two different micro-cultures) can be conversing. No matter what the content of the conversation, non-verbal communication can procede through the use of space. If the man edges closer towards the woman, he may be making a gesture — he wants to "get to know her better." (Notice the use of euphemisms, understandable only by those who know the cultural implications.) The woman has several non-verbal options to respond to this action through using space. If she backs away slightly, to the culturally accepted eighteen inches, she is "telling" the man that she is not interested in becoming more intimate. If she does not "back off," she is signaling that she might be interested. If he then puts his arm around her, a real invasion of the "space bubble," she must then respond by accepting the advance, or widening the space so the arm cannot remain where he placed it. All this is done almost "automatically," as part of the accepted cultural behavior.

Of course, the scenario played out above has many variations. The locus, or space, would be a factor. A singles bar would have different cultural behaviors than a friend's house. The particular micro-cultural group may accept the closing of the "space bubble" but see no other implications in it. One must study and learn about the culture to be able to interpret the observed behavior.

TIME

People use time differently, depending upon their micro-cultural group. In the U.S., more than ten percent of the work force are on a permanent night shift, and a larger group on rotating shifts. Recently, a large corporation reported that a number of employees were refusing promotions. This was upsetting to the managers of that company. The cultural norm is that people in an industrialized country **should** be seeking promotions.

In that organization, promotion took many forms. One was for people on the night shift to be "promoted" to the day shift so they could work "regular" hours. (Notice, the judgmental language, representing only one of the micro-cultures in the organization.) In interviews, it was determined that the night shift people had reorganized their lives, and those of their families, to be consistent with their jobs. Their use of time was much different from that of the day shift people, and the night shift people felt that they actually enjoyed benefits denied to the day shift.

For example, the night shift people could shop when stores were less crowded, did not have to fight traffic jams, and during the summer had greater access to recreational areas. Moving to the day shift, they reasoned, was not promotion but punishment.

Longitudinal time also has its effects. That is, some people need immediate gratification as contrasted with those who can cope with delayed gratification. The child is brought up on delayed gratification — go to school and learn this now because you will need it in the future. The child who cannot deal with deferred gratification will tend to be a school dropout. Dealing with gratification is learned behavior. Some of it is learned in the classroom, but much more of it is learned from the micro-cultural group to which the child belongs.

It is not uncommon for people to see some cultural behavior and then make a judgment based on their own culture or a misreading of the other culture.

In Venezuela the "siesta" is a two hour lunch period. This confirmed North American beliefs about Latin Americans and their tradition of the siesta. Yet in Caracas the two hour lunch period had nothing to do with the siesta. Rather, there were two other reasons.

It had been traditional for people in this highly family oriented culture to go back to their homes for lunch. Ten years ago, this was no problem as Caracas was much smaller, and there were fewer cars. Today, that is impossible at lunch time, given the distances and the fantastic traffic jams. Therefore, another cultural behavior has evolved — that of eating in one of the downtown restaurants. A part of the previous cultural behavior has been transplanted into this new situation so that the lunch period is still two hours long, which allows for eating and socializing with friends and co-workers.

There is a change coming in the U.S. which can be expected to conflict with some existing cultural behaviors. This is what is generally called "alternative work scheduling" which may be more familiar as flex-time. However, the earlier model of flex-time within a particular day has already been supplemented by flex-days, also known as the four (4) day work week. Also emerging are the flex-week, flex-month, and other variations of the traditional use of time at work. If these innovations are to be successful, adults will have to learn new cultural behaviors related to time.

SEX

Sex provides us with at least two micro-cultural groups. The focus of the "women's liberation" movement is not to eliminate the differences between the sexes, but to recognize the cultural behaviors that may be hindering the freedom of both of these micro-cultural groups. In all cultural behavior there can be a conflict of beliefs and differences of opinion. We find it most often when discussing cultural behavior between the sexes.

In many cultures style or cut of hair is associated with sex-delineated professions and to change one's style or cut of hair signifies a change of or a different profession. In Mediterranean cultures a full head of hair indicates masculinity and virility. However, in this same culture, being a solider is masculine and virile and a crew-cut hair style is acceptable for a soldier.

There is no doubt that cultural behaviors can change. It is not too far in the past when one knew that the female answering the telephone was the secretary, not the boss. Today, it is not possible to make this kind of judgment. The male answering the phone can be the secretary, and have a woman for his boss.

In some countries, the differences in the micro-cultures of the sexes are reflected in language differences. Today, in the U.S., differences in language tend to be a reflection of some other micro-cultural distinction, not that of sex. In most instances, there is little difference between the language of the male and that of the female.

In Japan, even today, there are many words which are exclusively female, and others are used only by males. Some years ago, while visiting Japan, the late Harry Golden remarked on this. He heard some U.S. servicemen using a few Japanese words that were only in the female vocabulary. Of course the soldiers were not aware of this, but Golden remarked that they had probably learned the language at the "tatami level" — in bed.

Cultural behaviors related to sex are changing more rapidly than any other cultural behavior. It is important for the adult learner to identify those behaviors that are culturally induced and to recognize that cultural behavior can change.

INDIVIDUAL AND GROUP

Acceptance and understanding of individual and group behavior is likewise a cultural factor. In the U.S., there appears to be two different cultural groups. Sometimes they almost appear in conflict. On the one hand, we have prided ourselves on individual behavior, on a type of "rugged individualism." Successful people talk about how they made it "on their own" or "pulled themselves up by their own bootstraps."

On the other hand, we have been a nation of group oriented people as evidenced by "barn raising," a group activity to help an individual; or the tremendous amount of volunteering wherein we work in groups to help others. The cultural norms for these behaviors tend to shift depending upon many factors, not the least of which is economics.

Sometimes, we do not recognize similar behavior by people in other cultures. In some Mideastern cultures, family relatives support each other as though they were a "shield" or advocate. Thus solitary or individualistic testing programs often become the basis for shared answers and group effort — commonly called cheating in our culture. When we condemn and punish this behavior, we are directly opposing a learned group cultural behavior.

Industry in the U.S. is looking to Japan to see what lessons we can learn from their economic success. One important element that is overlooked is that in Japan it is culturally inappropriate for any individual to stand out from his group. It is important to be part of a group. When a Japanese works for a company, he is part of that micro-cultural group and that supersedes his identity. This can be observed when one meets a Japanese who works for a large company. On the lapel of his jacket will be a button that is the symbol of his company so that everybody knows the micro-cultural group of which he is a part.

Traditionally, in Japan, when one is introduced one gives the company name first, then his own name. Contrast this to the U.S. where we pride ourselves on our own identity as an individual.

INSTRUCTIONAL STRATEGIES

How does one help adults learn about these cross-cultural behaviors. This can be done by using cognitive and experiential strategies. People learn best by doing. There is little question about the efficacy of experiential instructional strategy, but this does not mean that there is no place for the cognitive and didactic. They should be included in programs on cross-cultural learning. There are reports and similar material that can facilitate the learning process. Many who teach cross-cultural learning have found experiential instructional strategies to be most helpful.

EXPERIENTIAL LEARNING

A direct strategy is the field trip. This can be to some local area where there are residents from another micro-cultural group. Most large cities have areas which have an ethnic tinge such as "Chinatown" or "Little Italy." The teacher of adults should prepare very thoroughly for a field trip of this kind in order to avoid having stereotypes reinforced, and to make sure that the field trip does not become merely a superficial experience of eating and shopping. Adult leaders within most ethnic communities can be called upon as essential resources to make this field trip more meaningful to the adult learner.

Among the more affluent adult learners, foreign study tours can accomplish a great deal, but once again with very careful planning. Study tours for those dealing with adults are available from organizations such as the Adult Education Association and Phi Delta Kappa. Some universities likewise sponsor tours to study cultures of people in different parts of the world.

Given the diverse populations in the U.S., another alternative is to invite "foreign guests" into either the adult classrooms or the students' homes. These would be adults who come from a micro-culture different from most of the students. Time could be spent either in the classroom or in the students' homes where these guests could discuss their micro-cultures, and using the behavioral framework, students could reflect upon these discussions.

There are some numerous sources of foreign guests in almost every community. Some may be contacted through CSERV, an organization hosting International visitors; still others may be contacted through the Experiment in International Living; or from local churches, civic groups, or educational groups. In this way adult students may find it possible to have a "one-to-one" experience with persons from different micro-cultures.

This can thus allow the resourceful adult educator to provide a stimulating and often non-threatening opportunity for adults to expand their cultural horizons. The skillful adult educator handles such experiences carefully so that in the end adults have learned positive things about different people.

SUMMARY

There is no question about the need for cross-cultural learning for adults. Too little has been done with this very vital area. Today, such learning is more important than it has ever been in the past.

Culture contains less mystery than many think. It is possible to observe cultural behavior and to understand it. This does not require an acceptance of it, but understanding can lead to at least recognizing that the differences may not pose a threat to one's own culture, and micro-cultural allegiances.

As and when needed, cultural behavior can change, but first it must be recognized. There is never one best culture for all, but rather an appreciation that if we are to live and thrive, it must be in a cross-cultural world.

REFERENCES

1. Casse, Pierre. *Training for the Cross Cultural Mind: A Handbook for Cross-Cultural Trainers and Consultants.* Washington: Society for Intercultural Education, Training and Research. 1980.
2. Hall, Edward T. *The Hidden Dimension.* Doubleday, 1966.
3. _____. *"The Silent Language.* Fawcett, 1959.
4. Harris, Philip and Robert T. Moran. *Managing Cultural Differences.* Gulf Publishing, 1979.
5. Hoopes, David S. and Paul Ventura (editors). *Intercultural Sourcebook: Cross-Cultural Training Methodologies.* Intercultural Press 1979, Chicago.
6. Imai, Masaaki."16 Ways to Avoid Saying No: An Invitation to Experience Japanese Management from the Inside." Tokyo: *Japan Economic Journal,* 1981.
7. Morris, Desmond, Peter Collett, Peter Marsh and Marie O'Shaughnessy. *Gestures.* Stein and Day, 1979.

Back to Basic Skills

David S. Alexander

Associate Professor, Adult Education
Alaska Pacific University

The adult basic education curriculum has wandered some distance from the spirit of the moonlight schools of Kentucky and the original English programs for the foreign born.[1] Part of this movement can be called progress, but, overall, too much emphasis has been placed on GED preparation and not enough effort has been made to bring reading skills to the forefront. Substantive criticisms of the adult basic education efforts in the United States point up the paradox of selling high school equivalency test training within the confines of a curriculum intended for low level readers.[2]

However, despite the intrusion of the GED preparation format into a literacy skills curriculum, growth has been effected in such content areas as reading, math, writing, employment skills, consumer economics and personal health. Growth has also occured in important service delivery areas such as home based instruction, television programs, teleconference contact, computer programs, programs for the learning disabled, correspondence study, library orientation and community development. Changes in the content and delivery have come about with the curriculum adjustment toward life skills, political-social awareness and vocational training and away from the GED.

Historically, the congressional mandate to develop adult basic education programs should have resulted in government sponsorship of adult literacy instruction. Reading, writing and arithmetic was to be the heart of the curricula for those programs which received federal funding. The programs would have, in the congressional vision, three curriculum tracks — coping (life) skills, computation skills and communication skills.[3]

However, this intent was subverted by the pressing need to count heads as a justification for further funding. Head counts depended on the skills of administrators and teachers in recruiting and retaining adults in classes, and two recruitment problems were perceived. The supposed monotony of a 3R's curriculum for adults held little promise as an off hours pursuit for working men and women. The other major deficit was the lack of reward for completing a curriculum which, even when individualized, seemed nebulous.

The problems of curriculum definition and personal reward were solved by concentrating on preparation for the GED tests. This assured a curriculum which, if still somewhat monotonous, was no longer ambiguous. The reward was a high school equivalency certificate for each person passing the five part test. It was expedient to promote the high school equivalency certificate as the goal toward which students in adult basic education programs would work. The result is that today, in many programs, there is little pretense that beginning reading and math skills are at the core of the curriculum. Many adult basic education programs are straightforward GED preparation centers.

FOUR CHANGES IN CONTENT

Has reliance on the GED test caused a crisis of purpose or simply made the curriculum stagnant? If it is true that most adults who pass the GED reap further economic and social rewards, isn't the certificate a valid goal? It is valid, but the problem stems from conscious and unconscious stress on the certificate as the ultimate criterion for success in adult basic education.

The real problem is that efforts have been limited to looking at alternative criteria toward which the skills-deficient adult can aspire. First of all, more needs to be done to sell basic literacy skills as the tools for carving out a more satisfying place in American society. Secondly, there is evidence in the form of the Adult Performance Level Study and elsewhere that the real needs of adults can be at the core of life skills instruction.[3] Thirdly, certain international efforts, such as Paulo Freire's campaign for conscientization in Brazil, suggest that the political-social aspects of literacy education are motivating forces.[4] Finally, some institutions which offer adult basic education have integrated vocational training into the curriculum. So, there exist life skills, political-social awareness and vocational training as complementary interest areas which may provide the motivation for an adult to learn, or upgrade, reading and math skills. These motives are diverse and, moreover, they are unequal in their import and application. The strength of the adult basic education curriculum lies in this diversity, regardless of current or common practice.

Numerous Approaches to Life Skills — Much has changed in the adult basic education curriculum since the 1973 publication of the Adult Performance Level Survey results. The authors of that study derived a test, applicable in the United States and Canada, which allows the adult basic education instructor to diagnose the student's life skills deficiencies in a systematic manner. Critical observations on the value of this test, some cynical and some sincere, do not lessen its worth as the starting point for a systematic approach to helping adults learn civics, health and job skills. Out of this effort the authors also devised a comprehensive curriculum that focuses on these areas while providing exercises that strengthen math, reading and writing ability. Other approaches to life skills have been described by Adkins and McElreath and are contrasted with the Adult Performance Level Curriculum in *Three Approaches to Life Skills Instruction*.[3] The significant switch from the content of the GED exam including reading in social studies, literature and science to a life skills curriculum including content on occupational knowledge, government and law and consumer economics recalls a more harmonious blend of curricula within adult basic education — those which congressional sponsors foresaw in their vision of communication, computation and coping skills curriculum tracks merging at some points and diverging at others.

The response to the problems inherent in such a switch has been twofold. In one arena, adult educators have worked to have alternative high school diplomas accepted by school districts. Two types of certificates would then be available for the adult to earn. In the other arena, innovative people like Winthrop Adkins have declared the need for a "fifth curriculum" tied closely to the world of work. The notion of the fifth curriculum has its origins in models for adult education that focus on counseling and the handling of the most pressing problems in life. This program represents a radical departure from the GED oriented programs for adults who lack basic skills. And, it represents a bridge to the concept of vocational training for adults. That is, the Adkins Life Skills Program emphasizes the acquisition of those skills that are necessary for vocational training without offering the training itself.

Conscientization as a Motive to Learn Basic Skills — Somewhat on the other side of the spectrum from the pragmatic Adkins program is the socially oriented pedagogy for adults defined and described by Paulo Freire.[4] The focus of this approach to basic skills instruction is the real world in which the adult lives. That real world is defined by the adult student in cooperation with those of his/her neighbors who are working to effect change in their personal lives. In brief, the pedagogy requires the instructor to be a facilitator and, as the Adkins program does, presents the learners with some stimulus (usually visual) that will spark discussion on the ways and means to alter the reality depicted in the stimulus.

The chief difference between a curriculum like Adkins and the pedagogy espoused by Freire is that the former is principally for personal growth and the latter is principally for communal growth. The Adkins program, rooted in the life skills needs of the client, promotes economic change for that person. The Freirean notion of change comes with political-social awareness. The common bond is that each approach emphasizes the participant's ability to do something to change his/her circumstances. Freirean techniques are used in many nations, sometimes in UNESCO sponsored programs and sometimes in government sponsored programs. The content focus of a Freirean program can be political action for radical change or, at the other end, social organization for community development.

One example of the application of Freire's pedagogy is MOBRAL in Brazil. This functional literacy program incorporates into a curriculum of reading and math the motivating force of expansion of the student's social awareness. In the United States, a direct application of methods inspired by Freire's teaching is contained in Jane Evanson's *From Pictures to Passages*.[5] The adult educator who would follow Freire's example, though, must read his works judiciously for he himself denies the existence of a Freirean "method".

Vocational Training: Emphasis on Economic Incentives — While Freire would see vocational training as ancillary to social awareness, a clear link between job training and basic skills acquisition is a motive for many adults to learn reading and math. Whereas a life skills curriculum does not focus on a specific job or category of jobs, vocational training implies student selection of a job or category of jobs for which he/she wishes to qualify. Evidence that ABE students in Alaska wanted vocational training turned up in a 1979 citizens participation planning effort.[3] It was the number two priority after the acquisition of basic math and reading skills. In response to that evidence, one service delivery institution, Kodiak Community College, successfully integrated several vocational courses into the ABE curriculum. Office occupations was offered in conjunction with reading and math instruction in the community college's outreach services to Aleut villages on Kodiak Island. In Kodiak proper, ABE students enrolled in courses developed by adult basic education program personnel and the instructor in such practical areas as navigation, boat building and cabin building.

At the Core of the Curriculum — To return to the heart of the curriculum, changes in the teaching of reading have made this subject much more palatable to adults. Specific methods that motivate adults because of their sound conceptual base are the pictures to passages approach, the Second Step Reading Program and the use of phoneme-grapheme correspondences in teaching beginning reading.

The critical process in the Freirean approach to teaching reading is expanded and modified for either individual or group instruction in *From Pictures to Passages,* This process uses pictures as visual stimuli to aid students in the formation of concepts. From discussion of the pictures comes the identification of the information that forms those concepts in words, phrases, sentences and paragraphs.

Another approach to the teaching of reading was developed by Harry Lewis in 1975 — **The Second Step Reading Program.**[6] Second step concentrates on increasing reading "fluency" by pacing the student's eye movement. The program includes motivational reading materials and requires effective use of the instructor's time while working with groups of three to five students.

Finally, instruction using phoneme-grapheme correspondences is a more creative way to deal with beginning reading than the deductive approach used in traditional phonics.[7] The method is based on the idea that adults can learn letter-sound combinations inductively faster and more effectively than they do when trying to apply the phonics generalizations.

Large Programs Have an Advantage — However, it should be noted that reading and math have enjoyed proper emphasis in the curricula of adult learning centers located in larger communities when those adult programs were conceptually sound in the planning stage. Two examples are the Rochambeau adult school in White Plains, New York and the Mott Adult High School in Flint, Michigan. These and other large programs (500 students per day or more) offer enough variety for an adult to "see" where options in a life skills curriculum may differ from a GED preparation curriculum. The broader range of opportunities in the larger adult schools encourages students to learn or upgrade basic skills prior to the pursuit of a life skills curriculum that will lead to a high school equivalency certificate. In larger communities the concept of adult basic education as a process by which adults may obtain the education they missed or which was denied them is more socially appropriate. In other words, with the adult school offering a range of curricula, the community bias is toward lifelong learning and it reinforces choice based on individual need. This makes it more attractive for men and women to pursue those areas of basic skills development that constitute real need for them.

ALTERNATIVE DELIVERY SYSTEMS

One to One Instruction is Effective — Creativity in curriculum design is not the only secret to promoting basic reading and writing skills, as the two major voluntary literacy organizations will attest. Both Literacy Volunteers of America and the National Affiliation for Literacy Advance (Laubach) make a direct appeal to individual adults to learn to read. Despite the rigid structure of some of their methods and materials, especially Laubach, both groups provide basic literacy skills each year to many adults through volunteer tutors trained by these organizations. It is the method of delivery that is sensible and assures success in these operations. The stress on thorough instruction takes precedence over the number of students involved. Each tutor works individually with the students who are assigned to him/her. As demonstrated by studies done at the pioneering Appalachian Adult Education Center in the early '70's, learning to read through individualized instruction is up to 20% more effective than group instruction when provided in the context of a traditional classroom.[8] When provided in the student's own home, one to one instruction is up to 80% more effective in terms of speed of learning and retention of skills than group instruction in a learning center.

Bringing It All Back Home — Home based instruction is a delivery approach that is successfully used in Vermont. With the help of Literacy Volunteers of America, Vermont's adult basic education personnel gradually switched from traditional learning centers to home tutoring between 1973 and 1977. By 1977, 62% of ABE instruction in Vermont took place in the home.[8] One of the key reasons for the switch was the need to provide adults with some privacy while they received instruction. Unlike the social acceptability bestowed on adult learning activities by centers like Rochambeau, the public acknowledgement of an individual's attendance at a learning center in a rural community can carry with it disapproval or disdain. Rural towns lack the population base to support learning centers like Rochambeau which, by their very size, lend dignity to the idea of adult basic education.

The Potential for Television, Teleconference and Computer Use — Home based and learning center based instruction are both affected by technological advances in the delivery of instruction. Three presentation formats stand out at the moment. Television has already had a tangible impact, teleconferences hold much promise for efficient communication and computers are creating their own revolution in teaching.

Kentucky Educational Television's GED program has assisted in developing several good ITV series including Mississippi Educational Television's **Just Around the Corner** life skills series. These programs are expensive to produce and deliver. Desultory receptions given to such broadcasts as

"Operation Alphabet" in the '60's, the Philadelphia ABE Academy's "Wake-Up" series and the GED preparation series entitled "Your Future Is Now" make commercial companies wary of investment.

Lessons by teleconference, by contrast, require instructor ingenuity, are less expensive, easy to set up and readily available to anyone with a phone. So far, teleconferences have been used chiefly for lecture/discussion presentations but the advantage to phone contact lies in the integration of this communication process with correspondence study, computer study or television study programs.

As they are developed, computer programs will help adults learn basic skills. In reading, and especially in math, there are useful programs for inexpensive systems, like the APPLE, and for sophisticated systems, like PLATO. For people who like the hardware, computers are making adult learning centers enjoyable places to study. For use at home, a computer terminal may soon be less expensive than a television.

A Group Deserving of Mention — One group of students deserving special mention are the learning disabled. Students with handicaps which prevent or distort memory or the acquisition of generalizations and concepts are included in this group. They are mentioned in this section because efforts to serve them spark further interest in newer delivery system. The students and their instructors will benefit from the sophisticated instructional techniques which can be incorporated into both television programs and computer programs. The technology available to those teaching the learning disabled will provide greatly needed diversity in both methods and materials and provide more free time for the most important aspect of the instruction — one to one tutoring. Of course, many adults with learning disabilities will benefit from an emphasis on home based instruction with its attendant comforts.

Some Old Delivery Procedures Return — It is not surprising that interest is being re-kindled in three traditional delivery procedures as well. Correspondence study, library use and community development benefit from technological advances.

More correspondence study programs are being developed for adults because, with a careful mix of television programs broadcast in the home and teleconference contact with the instructor and other students, the verbal and visual stimuli necessary to motivate and direct correspondence study students can be provided. Despite the obvious necessity for a nonreader to have some face to face instruction from a tutor, it would be ignorant to dismiss the potential impact of correspondence study lessons for ABE students. Carefully produced correspondence study lessons provide reliable methods and materials or tutors to use both within and without a "distance education" format.

Since methods and materials for lower level readers are always a concern — that is, there are never enough —, better use of the library is the single most consequential adjustment that can be made to the delivery of adult basic education instruction, especially in medium sized communities where the library may be recognized by many ABE students but not used. Several studies have shown that library centered or library oriented adult basic education programs provide better support and result in greater retention of students. The American Library Assocation (ALA) has consistently maintained a commitment to assist the "adult new reader" since the '60's.[1] Library centered programs — those in which the adult basic education classes actually meet in the library — offer the instructor ready access to a marvelous array of instructional materials. Many ABE teachers talk about multi-media instructional programs thinking of a controlled reader and a few audio tapes, but few places besides libraries have the resources at hand to organize an audio/video/print materials collection.

Another option is the library oriented program where the adult basic education teacher has a close working relationship with the librarian in charge of adult services. For instance, special collections can be established at the library for adult new readers; certain times can be designated during which adult new readers may receive help from staff in the use of library resources; librarians can provide display areas for adult basic education materials. Such support for adults who are learning to read will benefit the entire community. It is a logical extension of the traditional library emphasis on promoting reading in the community. In most communities the development of such programs is long overdue. At a minimum, ABE personnel should count on their local libraries to order and keep up such critical references as the National Multi-Media Center's annotated bibliography of ABE/ESL/GED/Life Skills materials.[3]

Finally, community development may be the touchstone for a combination of educational services to adults. First, the lessons that North Americans can take from the spirit of conscientization are that adults are motivated by an expansion of their own political-social awareness. Second, Americans are a particularly adept people when volunteer help is required to meet a communal goal.

Specifically, it is practical for adult basic education services to be promoted and offered within the context of community development efforts. Community development in the form of issue orientation where a group of citizens set out to solve a social, political or economic problem can be the central purpose for adult and community education in a given locality. With the conservative character of most North American communities, the issues would tend toward resolution of local sanitation problems, housing shortages, health issues, education questions, law enforcement concerns. Instruction in reading, writing, math and life skills can arise from these practical problems that community members band together to face. This approach to adult basic education is ancillary to community organization efforts requires a huge commitment from the facilitators who must allow self-direction on the part of the students who define the issues and serve as leaders in finding solutions.

The two current programs that have a common ground in the concept of community development are community education in the form of community schools and adult education in the form of adult basic education. Some of these programs have a community development orientation, and it would be appropriate for more to evolve.

SUMMARY

Progress has been made in adult basic education programs away from reliance on the GED test and toward a renewed emphasis on basic skills. Four motives for student participation in adult basic education programs are: (1) better materials and methods in reading, writing and arithmetic; (2) practical life skills programs; (3) greater emphasis on the student's political-social awareness; (4) more direct links between vocational training and basic skills acquisition. In addition to changes in content areas such as the 3R's, employment skills, consumer economics and personal health, both new and old delivery systems are helping to change the curriculum. Technological changes make television broadcasts, teleconference contact and computer programs increasingly practical for use by the average instructor. Correspondence study lessons, library orientation and community development can have a significant effect on adult basic education services. Some of the delivery procedures will be further honed in use with special populations, in particular the learning disabled, and most of the procedures will contribute to efficient home based instruction.

QUESTIONS AND EXERCISES

1. Describe an issue which would involve adult basic education students in a community development effort and which would provide a basis for an instructional sequence in the classroom.
2. What aspects of home based instruction make it more effective than learning center based instruction for many students?
3. Choose one of the delivery systems named in the chapter and describe how it might affect instruction in the next ten years. For example, if cable television companies offer instructional programs for adults in reading and math, how will this affect adult basic education programs as we know them today?

REFERENCES

1. Cook, Wanda *Adult Literacy Education in the United States.* Newark, Del.: International Reading Association, 1977.
2. Mezirow, Jack, Darkenwald, Gordon G. and Knox, Alan B. *Last Gamble on Education.* Washington: Adult Education Association, 1975.
3. Alexander, David S. "Three Approaches to Life Skills Instruction." *Method: Alaskan Perspectives.* Volume 4, Number 1, 1982.
4. Freire, Paulo. *Pedagogy of the Oppressed.* New York: Seabury Press, 1970.
5. Evanson, Jane L. *From Pictures to Passages.* Chicago: Contemporary Books, 1978.
6. Lewis, Harry. *The Second Step Reading Program.* Albany, N.Y.: The College of St. Rose Press, 1975.
7. Alexander, David S., Evanson, Jane L. and Sousa, Thomas F. "Using Sound-Symbol Frequencies to Teach Decoding Skills." *Adult Literacy and Basic Education.* Volume 2, Number 4, 1979.
8. Eberle, Anne and Robinson, Sandra. *The Adult Illiterate Speaks Out: Personal Perspectives on Learning to Read and Write.* Washington: National Institute of Education, U.S. Department of Education, 1980.

Adult Learning Patterns

Burton W. Kreitlow

*Professor Emeritus,
Department of Continuing & Vocational
Education, University of Wisconsin, Madison*

It is fun to teach adults. They are the most responsive, critical, concerned, creative, stubborn, challenging, pleasant two-footed animals on this planet. They will help you with anything from room arrangement to doing their own teaching. They will get along without you. They will tell you what they want to learn if you give them a chance. The adult can be reached by mass media, in large groups, in small groups, or as individuals. An adult will learn in any of a hundred patterns a creative teacher can invent. When they want to learn they will bend to suit your moods. When they are not interested in what you have to offer, you will soon know it. They will not all steal away; some will just up and clamber out.

The organization of the setting in which the adult is to learn is the task of the teacher. The teacher may find it necessary to conform to certain broad educational methods established by his agency (public schools, university extension, correspondent schools) but generally the teacher of adults is more subject to the students than to his administration. The broad organizational patterns for adult learning almost always give the teacher the flexibility he needs to teach in any way he likes, or within any pattern that his students like.

A teacher with a student, whether face to face or separated by an international phone line, is a learning situation; either may be an excellent learning pattern. A small group of adults, somewhere between 5 and 40 may be the best pattern of others. Some may do better in a group of 500. While for others, being one of the anonymous number reached by means of the mass media is sufficient for learning. It is within these four broad patterns that adults can be instructed and in which they can learn — individual, small group, large group, and mass education. These four patterns for learning in which the teacher and the adults communicate will be considered here — a masterful teacher uses techniques to fit the pattern, fit the learners, and fit his own abilities.

Individual Learning Patterns — A pattern of individual instruction will be considered inefficient by some people. It particularly will be considered so by those who look at dollar values rather than human values. This is not to say, that all, or even a great deal of teaching should be done on an individual, face-to-face relationship, but there is some content that calls for this particular pattern. The learners in a course in auto mechanics need the special help, and the special touch of an individual specialist in certain kinds of tasks such as getting the car's timing correctly set or trouble-shooting the hydraulic system.

Even more important than the nature of the content are the characteristics of the individual learners. Some learners require individual instruction. During the last two decades one social goal of the American society has been to remove illiteracy. Adult Basic Education Programs which grew in response to this goal used trial and error to find the right pattern for learning. Sometimes the only way to reach illiterates is on the one-to-one relationship. These new learners are found to need the word-by-word, phrase-by-phrase, page-by-page help that a teacher sitting down with them can provide. They also need the encouragement, support, and the security of knowing that someone cares for them individually.

There are a variety of ways of organizing for individual instruction. Some of these are well established and have a long history, as correspondence study, which is not only individualized but is accomplished over great distances without visual contact. The apprenticeship, imported to America from Europe, requires a great deal of teacher and learner standing shoulder to shoulder. Internships in the professional fields have long included a one-to-one relationship. Some of the most complex teaching programs in agriculture from the early days of farm demonstrations through programs of Veterans-on-the-Farm Training to the present programs of computerized farm management demand that the instructor sit with the farmer and pore over rather complex programming problems — all of these have been effective in leading to the most efficient agriculture in the world. Adult education programs in the arts rarely get to the productive stages without the teacher-learner on a one-to-one basis.

For the adult, the pattern of individual instruction tends to develop on a very informal basis. He likes what he feels. Individual instruction often comes as an "ad-lib" to the small group in session or in the halls of a much larger educational pattern. For the regular class the individual instruction may begin at the coffee break and it requires that both the adult who is willing to learn and the instructor make themselves available to each other. Closely related to this is the after class "hang about." They may well begin with the more social and communicative of the learners involved in very informal face-to-face instruction after class. But the adult teacher needs to recognize that the need for such socialization by some may indeed be the clue that cries for individual instruction. The follow-up of group discussion may also be the place where the teacher first recognizes the need to reach out further for certain individuals in the group, who, uncomfortable with their peers, require the security that comes when they talk alone with their teacher. An individual learning pattern may also operate without a teacher, the learner and teacher are one and the same. This is best described by Alan Tough in his work on **Adult Learning Projects.**[4]

Not all instruction should be individual. For that which should be, there are teaching strategies that help. In dealing with individuals, a great deal of openness between teacher and learner is essential. Both must feel free to stop, start, back up, or change direction on the basis of the dialogue. The teacher is the key which encourages the freedom to develop an ordering of educational experiences for the learner. One way would be set goals, plan means, do the job, relook at goals, set new goals, plan means.

A less structured way and one which does work is to "play it by ear." These teachers are often the warm, compassionate co-learners with their student. "Let's do this together" is for some teachers and learners the only way to move to a more efficient learning pattern.

Small Group Learning Patterns — Small group instruction is the standard practice in the field of adult education. This is the learning pattern to which those who participate in adult education programs are accustomed. Getting together in small groups is a characteristic of adults. Their socialization through the early years has led them to expect a variety of educational activities accomplished in the small group. Unfortunately their expectations from elementary and secondary school and even from college is that the small group is a place for a teacher-dominated learning situation. As experienced adults and as participants in the social community, they get "turned off" by this domination even if it was expected. They have grown to a new expectation — that of a participant in their own learning program. Adults appreciate participation in a small group learning pattern because they want to participate in their own curriculum building. They not only want a hand in deciding what is to be taught, they are willing to lend a hand in the actual teaching. In addition to the acceptance of the small group as the expected pattern in which learning occurs, the resources available for adult education programs have been more suitable for small than for large groups or even for individual instruction. It is very easy from the administrative point of view to organize for small group activities.

Because adults tend to accept the small group as a preferred learning pattern and because the resources for small groups are available, it becomes reasonably easy for the teacher of adults to organize for small group activities. It is important in this organization that teachers of adults do not limit themselves to the traditions of the teacher-dominated elementary and secondary school classes. There is content related to certain educational objectives that can well be handled in a teacher-dominated classroom, and the teacher of adults should recognize when the content and the objectives call for this organization. But the teacher should also recognize when the content and the objectives call for a class to be organized as a discussion group or when the objectives and the content call for a seminar, a workshop, or a meeting using special outside resources. A group of twenty adults learning personal typing can perhaps best be taught as a group in a teacher-dominated classroom where the skill of typing is the focus and 60 words per minute the goal. A group of 20 adults studying the modern novel is more interested in a variety of interpretations from their colleagues set against the interpretations from the instructor and other authorities than they are in blindly accepting what the specialists in modern literature say about the novel. Adults are both studying and enjoying; the instructor should spoil neither. Twenty members of a local service club which devotes one meeting a month to an educational program may be willing to accept a twenty minute presentation by an outside speaker, but only if they have an opportunity for a question period and an informal discussion following that presentation.

The adult has far more extensive life experiences that he brings to the classroom than does the child. The adult is anxious to look at immediate outcomes from his learning experiences whether they be related to special content objectives, psycho-motor skills, or new appreciations. Because of this, he is interested in an interchange and a feedback. He is interested in asking his own questions or listening to the questions and the responses raised and answered by his peers.

The adult educator who recognizes the acceptances of learning in the small group as the standard practice in adult education can use a great deal of creativity in dealing with the kinds of programs that may be organized for individual instruction or for large groups. By being creative in these other kinds of programs he can give them the variety that is so often sought by adults and which adds enjoyment to the total learning program.

One of the productive ways of adjusting correspondence study programs is to bring those involved in correspondence study together in groups of 6-10 (as time and travel will allow) to meet occasionally with the instructor or an assistant. This adds the social dimension to a non-social form of individual instruction.

The same principle can be used to adjust large groups to a point where intimate study and exchange is possible. The conference or convention, if planned well, provides a variety of learning patterns. It is a large group meeting which, with proper adjustment and attention given to various objectives, can move from the large general meeting to small group discussions to special interest meetings and to follow-up analyses. The conference planner should take the desire for small group learning patterns into account.

What can you as a teacher do to take full educational advantage of the adult's desire to learn in small groups? First is to recognize that the lecture is not the only effective technique in teaching adults. Yet a lecturer can be the primary catalyst that leads to other techniques that can be used. The effective lecturer who is a connoisseur of special techniques has an unusual advantage in providing the learning situation that leads both to the achievement of objectives and satisfaction with the process. A lecturer who knows how to move from lecture to a brain-storming session, who knows how to organize from lecture to buzz groups, who knows how to move from lecture to the chairing of a panel discussion of participants in the group, who can end the lecture without closure and lead it to inquiry, and the lecturer who can slide from a lecture to role-playing with members of the group is the one who provides the learning experiences for both objective achievement and satisfaction.

In working with small groups, the person in charge, be he teacher, discussion leader, or resource person must be a patient listener. Participation in questioning and in discussion by adult learners can develop if instructors are willing to pause and **listen.** Participation by the learner is the key to the small group. This key cannot be turned if the teacher does all the talking.

Large Group Patterns — The techniques associated with the large group do provide the kind of educational mix that many a volunteer learner is willing to accept. He can become a listener on a take it or leave it basis; he can be anonymous; he can attend in body but not in spirit; he can choose between being at the meetings where large groups are listening to lectures or he can read about the lecture in the conference summary. He may even use his conference time to go shopping or reach other kinds of objectives. Examples of the large group which tend to have acceptance are the teachers' convention, the cooperative extension conference, or the White House Conference on Children and Youth. The voluntary nature of the adult learner means that he can opt to leave the learning experience at any time and return at any time.

It becomes a challenge to educators using the large group as the base for an educational program to make sufficient adjustments in it so that other patterns of learning are possible. Very often the adult educator has no choice whether or not he will operate with a large group or a small group. Many organizations or agencies, through administrative decision, organize large group conferences or meetings for their members or employees. Adult educators are asked to contribute after the planning and are expected to lecture.

Because teaching in the large group tends to be formal and structured, the teacher is either frustrated or challenged by the anonymity of the mass of faces. If challenged one can see the great potential for the use of a variety of techniques to keep such a large audience interested. This challenge can be so great that occasionally the lecturer becomes more of a humorist and a performer than an educator dealing with the reaching of objectives. He may on the other hand be less stimulating because of his frustrations and take the attitude that this group would rather hear the content read than read it for themselves and thus, in a rapid-fire, tightly organized production, lay out bits of content after bits of content, getting through as much as possible in the time allotted.

Working with a large group of four or five hundred adults is not the same as running all the facets of a small group. Yet the responsible adult educator, finding himself in this situation, has an unusual opportunity to use additional resources. This is where specialists can be brought in; where technical equipment and materials can be used to improve the learning environment.

One of the things every adult educator can do if he must work with large groups is to observe successful lecturers who both perform and teach. The adult educator, after these observations must then be willing to enrich the experience of the learners by any means that he can manage. For some it may be by showmanship, for others by distribution of materials related to the content or by the use of visual devices. For still others it is but a willingness to gamble on breaking up large groups into small groups, and by getting the learners themselves to help him. The adult teacher with large groups must be secure enough to try.

Mass Patterns — It is well to recognize that mass instruction does exist and that adults do learn within this pattern. Both private and public agencies and organizations organize to teach this way. Often the organization for instruction that emerges may fit better into the field of mass communication, than it does into education. Very often those who are called upon to take responsibility to organize for learning in a mass situation are not known as teachers, yet they do teach. They teach in the sense that objectives are established, consideration of the needs of the learner is given, material is organized on a plan that will lead the individual learner from what he knows to what he needs to learn, and real efforts are made to determine whether or not individuals are reached by this kind of "teaching." Although educational institutions and organizations are often directly involved in patterns of mass instruction, there is a great deal that occurs through columns in newspapers, via commentators on ratio and television, in contributions of authors whose writing is organized toward certain goals for the readers, by publicists, politicians, union leaders, and a host of others with institutional and organizational objectives to be achieved.

Very often universities, membership groups, government departments and agencies do carefully organize for mass instruction. The professional articles written by scientists and published in widely distributed journals have instruction as their goal. Educational radio and television have been specifically organized in a pattern for mass instruction. Membership groups may develop their organizational journals for publicity purposes yet built into most is a design for education. Mass instruction carries with it the greatest potential for anonymity on the part of the learner.

For the adult educator there is a great potential to develop new means to reach the large numbers of adults who can be contacted by mass communication. To organize so that this contact becomes an educational experience is a challenge. This particular contact can be in a more personalized form. There have been effective examples of personalized mass instruction with some success. Most of these have integrated the concepts of small group meetings with the media of mass communication. The majority of adult educators are not in a situation which require them to get involved in mass instruction yet the great potential of teaching by this means should not be ignored. True, there are very special techniques and skills that are required. For the educator who is accustomed to working with individuals or small groups and who is very close to the product of his teaching, it may be quite difficult to accept the lack of positive feedback on the results of teaching by means of mass communication. There is limited evaluation of mass instruction by other than the simple counting of the number of contacts and surveys of reading, viewing, listening, or subscribing. This limitation should not discourage the educator for recent research has shown that a number of formative evaluation devices can be constructed giving a great deal of feedback data. Specialists in media, whether from the newspaper or tele-communications industry can assist local directors in assessing the effectiveness of instructional programs for mass media. As Cable TV expands and local programming requirements are met, the resourceful continuing educator will find this pattern of instruction viable and rewarding.

SUMMARY

With such a variety of learning patterns for different kinds of adults, the adult educator has a real challenge. Because adults do learn in a variety of patterns there is a chance to adjust instruction to reach adults who approach learning from a variety of stances. The adult educator can learn any of the approaches. Let us recognize however, that effective teaching depends on the teacher's own resources. It is up to the individual to know his own strengths and weaknesses, to concentrate on strengths and to strengthen weaknesses. To be a creative teacher and to adjust to the variety of learning patterns' unique characteristics, each adult educator must be dedicated to his own continued learning.

QUESTIONS AND EXERCISES

Questions	In responding consider:
I. Why is it fun to teach adults?	1. Their: Responsiveness Flexibility Help in planning.
II. What factors should be considered in selecting teacher techniques?	1. Learning pattern in use. 2. Characteristics of the learner. 3. Your own abilities.
III. Under what conditions is individual instruction needed?	1. Objectives of learner, teacher, and institution. 2. Nature of the learning task. 3. Efficiency vs. inefficiency. 4. Alternative patterns available.
IV. Why is learning in small groups the standard practice in adult education?	1. Traditions and expectations. 2. Nature of learner goals. 3. Involvement of adults in planning. 4. Ease of organization. 5. Resources brought to the setting by the learner.
V. What are the advantages of large group learning patterns over reading the same content materials in printed form?	1. Social and emotional factors. 2. Special uses of human and technical resources. 3. Potentials for creative teaching.
VI. By what means can mass patterns of instruction be personalized?	1. Integration with pre or post group patterns. 2. Use of specialists. 3. Feedback.

REFERENCES

1. Grabowski, Stanley M. (ed) *Adult Learning and Instruction.* Syracuse, N.Y.: Clearinghouse on Adult Education and AEA/USA, 1970.
2. Kidd, J.R. *How Adults Can Learn.* New York: Association Press, 1973.
3. Knowles, Malcolm S. *The Modern Practices of Adult Education,* New York: Association Press, 1970.
4. Tough, Alan. *Adults Learning Projects.* Toronto: Ontario Institute of Studies in Education, 1971.

Conceptual Approach to Teaching/Learning

Richard A. Etheridge

*Professor of Adult Education,
Mississippi State University.*

Within the past decade, adult educators have been especially active in developing fresh and imaginative approaches to teaching/learning situations for adult learners. One of the more interesting innovations is the conceptual approach.

The conceptual approach to adult learning encompasses certain fundamental theoretical and conceptual frameworks which undergird both a philosophy of adult education and an understanding of the teaching-learning processes. Fundamental to the purpose of learning is enabling an individual to grow and develop toward adequacy or maturity with concomitant behaviors suitable to himself and his society. Most traditional continuing education programs fail not because the subject matter is uninteresting or unchallenging, but because they fail to take into account the distinctive array of factors inherent in adult psychology and the motivational forces which attract adults to learning. In short, it is necessary to plan experiences in such a manner that learners can readily transfer vicarious portrayals of reality to extensions of their own reality and personal situations.

The concept approach encompasses several distinct dimensions:
1. Concept formation and development.
2. Cognitive mapping.
3. Program development.
4. Individualized strategies for effecting conceptual change.

CONCEPTUAL LEARNING

A concept is a mental image drawn from personal life experiences which enables the individual to understand reality. Thus, the development of concepts is a personal and individual process. These concepts are based on facts and observations, experiences and perceptions of reality, and on mental processes by which abstractions from the real world are generalized to useful and meaningful applications. A concept is composed of meaning and feeling and may or may not be verbalized.

Concepts emerge as mental images or ideas drawn from experiences and give meaning and understanding to such experiences. Thus concepts perform three major functions:

1. Systems for organizing subject matter.
2. Sources for thinking.
3. Predeterminers of behaviors.

As organizing systems, concepts facilitate learning in several ways. Since concepts establish the interrelationships and meanings of phenomenon, knowledge which is organized around concepts is easier to recall than an array of isolated facts or data. In this way, concepts as organizing systems are somewhat economical to the learner in that he may recall only the needed data for any particular coping experience. Non-essential and meaningless data are discarded and unused.

Concepts are formed when one thinks about something he experiences. Once formed, concepts become sources for additional and higher levels of thinking. A concept, then, gives *intention* to thinking and has influence in mentally directeéd behavior.

Some ordering of information is essential for successful operation of mental processes. The process of ordering data which produces concepts into subparts or classes, results in abstractions. Processing which shows relationships among a set of concepts results in generalizations.

Concepts are the ingredients from which decisions and behavior are produced and perform a mediating role between stimuli and response. Therefore, the way to effect desirable changes in an individual's behavior is to help the learner develop clear concepts of the objects, events, people, and other phenomenon in his world of perceptual reality.

Concepts are formed in the mind. Three factors are necessary for concept formation: (1) perceptual reality, (2) experimental reality, (3) reflective thinking.

The first step in concept formation involves sense perception, that is, the discrimination among phenomenon on the basis of immediate experience. Personal experiences with objects, events, or situations occur through the sensory organs. The process by which the senses transmit meaning to the brain is called perception. Perceptual reality is what the learner senses to be fact based on his own personal experience.

The role of experiences in concept formation cannot be overemphasized. The expansion, reorganization or modification of concepts evolves through actual experiences. A variety of real experiences enhances concept expansion, and such experiences tend to be more reliable in effecting concept formation than reading or hearing about the experiences. Thus, the more varied experiences the learner has, the more he is enabled to recognize and understand the qualities, characteristics, uses, and processes involved in the concept and its utility or value.

Reflective thinking about experiences is the means by which progression from perception to conception takes place. Reflective thinking from percepts to concepts has three distinct advantages: (1) less redundant information is required, (2) more irrelevant data can be tolerated without affecting responses, (3) the total information can be integrated over a longer period of time and space separation.

Research indicates that concept formation and expansion are promoted when the educator uses the basic concepts to select behavioral objectives and subject-matter content. Teaching for concept development involves careful attention to the selection of experiences which the learner is able to recognize as those most closely resembling his own personal situation and from which he can transfer meaningfulness, relevance, and purpose.

COGNITIVE MAPPING

Each individual acquires a network of concepts that give meaning and direction to behavior. This network of concepts is called a "cognitive map," a mental layout of directions for behavior. Much like a road map, one's cognitive map enables the individual to determine where he is, where he is going, and what the probable place of arrival will be like, based on his present knowledge and current situation. As new information is acquired or a new goal is sought, the cognitive map is altered or changed. The *process* by which concepts are utilized, developed, and changed is called "cognitive mapping."

The devices applied in the cognitive mapping process by the individual are rational and meaningful. Modifications made in the cognitive map are significantly influenced by the goal sought, the norms held by society, by past experiences, and by one's own personal and unique characteristics.

The adult educator should possess a cognitive map comprised of concepts by which he pursues specific goals designed to effect desirable changes in the behavior of adult learners. The concepts encompassed in the educator's cognitive map are the conceptual tools which he utilizes in attaining these goals.

The Concept of Change — Change is usually thought of as any significant deviation from an established way of life or behavioral pattern. Thus, adult education is a vehicle deliberately used to bring about changes in people's behavior.

The myth that "people naturally resist change" must be vigorously challenged, Indeed, research continuously supports the opposing view — people do *accept* change. People everywhere are constantly accepting changes in their way of doing things, changes in their knowledge about objects and events, and changes in their belief and value systems. Whenever resistance to change is observed, it is usually found that:

1. The proposed changes threaten one's basic security.
2. The proposed changes are not understood.
3. Change is being forced.

Meaningful learning experiences must be provided which take into account the notion that the learner *wants* to change, is earnestly seeking a better way of life, or a new set of concepts which will enable him to more effectively cope with his environment and problematic situations.

The concept of change, then, is the pivotal point of all continuing education curricula. In other words, the entire program development process is directed toward bringing about change in the behavior of learners and the adult educator is thus regarded as a "change agent" because he is the initiator and designer of deliberate and planned change.

The Concept of Need — Our English word *motive* appears to have its origin in the Greek word *orego* — meaning "to reach out" — signifying the mental effort of stretching forth oneself for something, of longing after it, with emphasis upon the object desired. From *orego* is derived the concept of origins which we shall define in behavioral terms as indicating the source(s) from which behavior emerges.

The Greek concept of *orego* embodies three suggestions which should interest the adult educator. A motive which generates behavior includes: (1) an internal state of arousal created by the impingement upon the individual by stimuli, (2) an action response which is a deliberate, purposive, and sustained struggling within the individual in an effort to lower the level of internal arousal, (3) a goal which the individual perceives as being attainable and possessing characteristics capable of lowering or eliminating the internal level of arousal.

Needs represent the central force or catalyst in the motivation to learn. When one is motivated, he is, in fact, "reaching out" to satisfy perceived needs. Recent studies concerning motivational theories tend to support the notion that needs are stimulus factors in motivation. Thus the need to understand and to give meaning to ideas drawn from real experiences in the life of the individual supports the development of concept formation, organization, modification, and application to problem-solving situations.

Need is a gap between what is and what ought to be. People's needs may be identified by determining the actual, the possible, and the desirable. When people recognize that there is a gap between the actual, the possible, and the desirable and place value on attaining the desirable, they become motivated to change. Behavior then becomes directed toward filling the gap between what is and what ought to be.

The Concept of Culture — The concept of culture provides a frame of reference by which the behavior of the learner may be understood in terms of cultural conditioning. Human customs are linked with one another and a change in one's custom, tradition, or way of life consequently affects another's culture. A change in an individual's behavior affects other people in close contact with him. A change in one's behavior thus affects the entire culture to which one belongs.

People everywhere behave in accordance with patterns which they have learned in the process of growing up in society and which make sense to them as a way of life or as an overall design for living. The fact that a long learning experience lies behind every established custom for each individual has several important implications:
1. People practice customs as a part of a pattern of behavior and the continuance of that pattern is in itself a source of feelings of security.
2. These patterns of behavior constitute the social organization or "community" of a people.

3. People do not vary their customary behavior unless they feel some need which existing ways do not satisfy. The response to such a need is to invent or to borrow from someone else a technique, or form, or belief which satisfies that need.

Basically, continuing education programs seek to facilitate the means by which this "borrowing" process may take place. In short, adult educators seek to provide alternatives for the learner in the context of learning experiences whereby he may seek satisfaction for personal needs and realize goal attainment by "borrowing experiences" which the educator provides in a teaching-learning climate.

The Concept of Adult Learning — Learning is change in the behavior patterns of the individual. There are two basic kinds of learning patterns: (1) spontaneous interaction, (2) systematic learning.

The first, spontaneous interaction learning, is essentially caused by a confrontation with one's environment. Generally, this is known as learning from experience. In the course of the individual's life span, things happen that affect changes in knowledge, perception, skills, attitudes. This is spontaneous learning, accidental or incidental, but with no predictable measurable results.

Experience is essential to the maturation process, but it does not provide in and of itself for personal growth and development. Experience can be grossly misinterpreted. It can be dangerously narrow. Experience can have adverse and hindering effects on the learning and growing process. One example is the experience of failure. Many people do not learn from experience per se. There is a basic difference between **experience** and **having an experience!**

The second type of learning is systematic learning. This is a deliberately planned effort to bring about specific, observable, and measurable learning. These changes in knowledge, skills, attitudes and behavior are carefully organized in an effort to cause desired changes in the behavior patterns of the learner with observable and predictable results.

Systematic learning should be the basic learning pattern about which all adult program development activity is focused; thus, some generalizations must be drawn to delineate specific conditions for effecting change in the behavior of the learner. These "conditions" are crucial:

1. The learner is the central figure in the learning process. There is nothing new about this idea to most of us; although it should be pointed out that there are many people who act as though the teacher is the central figure in the learning process.
2. The teacher is part of the learning environment but learning is presumed to be in the hands of the learner. The teacher's role is to help the learner achieve his goals by providing:
    a. A climate or environment conducive to learning.
    b. Alternatives in the problem-solving process.
    c. Relevant and meaningful experiences which satisfy the learner's perceived needs.

All this presupposes a knowledge of, and attitude about, the adult learner which the teacher utilizes in designing and planning learning

experiences to bring about the desired changes in the learner's behavior patterns.
3. The adult educator's concept of adult learning should include the following concepts about the behavior of adults:
   a. **Adults must want to learn.** This is the fundamental factor in an effective adult learning situation. A great deal of effort on the part of the adult educator should be spent on instilling an appreciation for and a recognition of the constant need for upgrading knowledge and skills. The adult educator's primary task is to help the learner perceive a definite need for learning.
   b. **Adults benefit most from active participation in the teaching-learning process.** When real life situations are simulated in the learning experiences, the prospect of success is dramatically increased.
   c. **Adults respond better in an informal atmosphere.**
   d. **Adults progress more rapidly in learning situations that involve dealing with realistic problems.** They expect measurable outcomes from the learning experiences.
   e. **Adults maintain interest better when a variety of methods are used.**
   f. **Adults require reinforcement at each step.** Adult learners neither care to invest effort if they are not confident that they are moving in the right direction, nor want to commit resources such as time, energy, and enthusiasm, only to find that they are misplaced. Reinforcement provides the adult continuous assurance that he is on the right track. Adults want and expect instantaneous feedback.
   g. **Ambiguity has no place in adult education.** Adults respond better when they have a clear understanding of what is expected of them. They are particularly sensitive about miscues and false directions, and they move cautiously until they know that they have a reasonable promise of success.
   h. *Adults should be permitted to practice new skills without threat.*

These four macro concepts: (1) change, (2) need, (3) culture, (4) adult learning should provide a substantial part of the adult educator's cognitive map in his efforts to initiate, plan, develop, implement, and evaluate programs in continuing education aimed at effecting desirable behavioral outcomes in adult learners.

PROGRAM DEVELOPMENT

The question is, "How does the adult educator analyze and synthesize the concepts in his cognitive map in order to effect desirable change in the behavior of the learner?"

The adult educator should have an understanding of behavioral change and how change takes place through learning and that learning is influenced by needs, society, and culture, and that the processes in participatory problem-solving are the channels through which change may be planned within the context of program development.

A problematic situation will serve as an example as to how cognitive mapping may be used as a teaching device. It is assumed that the adult educator — in this case an expert teacher trainer — has been assigned the task of developing an inservice program for new continuing education teachers.

Identifying Needs/Problems

The first dimension or step in this situation is to identify the problem or need. Drawing on the concepts encompassed in the program planner's cognitive map, the actual situation is determined by assembling, analyzing and interpreting information about the new adult education teachers. This may be done by studying their applications for biographical data, interview notations, situational analysis, program reports, or other similar devices.

Various analyses of data would reveal the differences between what is and what ought to be in terms of the new teachers' understanding of adult learning and principles of adult education. The results would probably reveal a substantial need for learning experiences especially designed to close the gap between what is and what ought to be.

Forming Objectives

The second step in planning the training program is to select specific behavioral objectives. The objectives of the training program arise out of the "what ought to be" situation, not the "what is" situation. Although the broad program objective may be stated in terms of the training program goals, these must be further translated into specific behavioral objectives for the learners. These objectives contain three essential elements: (1) the level of the learner, (2) the desired behavioral change expected, (3) the content area within which the behavior is to occur.

An objective is the desired outcome of a learning experience, stated in terms of **observable, measurable** behaviors. Behavioral objectives should be stated using **action** verbs.

Now, if the teacher trainer only wants the new continuing education teachers to be knowledgeable about certain facts and data pertaining to characteristics of adult learners, the behavioral objectives are easily enough developed and stated for the training program. However, the sensitive adult educator will quickly realize that knowledge-getting is the lowest cognitive order of the learning abilities. The teacher trainer may indeed want the new adult education teachers to be able to analyze, synthesize, and evaluate experiences provided during the inservice training program. If this is the case, specific behavioral objectives must be stated which give direction to the organization of these learning experiences. Indeed, the imperative for the teacher trainer is to develop precise and definite behavioral objectives for the learners **before** any attempt is made to implement the inservice training program. In other words, the teacher trainer must know what is **expected** of the learners and this must be expressed in terms of what the learners are expected to do after a particular learning experience. On this all else depends, and the success of the inservice training program will usually be in direct relation to the specificity of the behavioral objectives.

Selecting Learning Experiences — The third step in planning the training program is to select learning experiences which will help the learners attain desired goals. Based on the principles of learning which the teacher trainer has in his cognitive map, the learning experiences can be selected to serve as stimuli which influence the selection of alternatives perceived by the trainees as relevant, meaningful, purposeful, and satisfying personal needs.

The learning experiences should be organized in such a manner that continuity, sequence, and integration of the content areas will occur.

Selecting Methods — The fourth step in planning the program is to select the methods by which the experiences are to be accomplished. Selection of appropriate methods is pivotal in the sense that they must be correlated closely with the experiences the educator has selected to enable the learner to attain the behavior objectives. The selection of particular methods should be determined also by:
1. The character of the subject matter.
2. Available leadership.
3. Available facilities.
4. The character of the learners.

Evaluating Outcomes — The fifth step in planning the training program is to evaluate the outcomes of learning experiences. Evaluation should reflect the behavioral objectives originally stated by the teacher trainer, the content area, the conditions of learning, and the degree of measurable success.

The adult educator needs to have within his cognitive map these concepts which are the tools for analysis in the initiation, execution, and evaluation of an adult education program. The concepts of change, social action, problem solving, needs, society, and culture as well as concepts of adult learning are fundamental components of his cognitive map. There are many more, but these are basic and essential to every sensitive and alert adult educator who veiws his primary role as a professional change agent.

INDIVIDUALIZING TEACHING STRATEGIES

The prime objective of the adult educator is to cause the adult to learn what he needs to know. The problem of integrating these components for the purpose of individualizing instruction is the central concern of all of us in adult education.

Strategies for individualized learning are not new to adult educators. The literature is replete with systems and variations of systems and techniques for individualizing instruction and learning. Educators should cease to be concerned primarily with the technical problems involved in individualizing learning and get to the heart of the issue — the opportunities to individualize instruction provided by these innovations.

The assumptions encompassed in the conceptual approach to individualizing programmed instruction are simple enough; they usually gain in complexity only when certain basic assumptions are neglected.

In devising the strategy for any particular program, several assumptions must be made:
1. The learner's responsibility is to learn and the teacher's responsibility is to make available to the learner what is to be learned, place responsibility for the teaching/learning process squarely where it belongs — in the hands of the learner. The teacher does not cover the course, he uncovers it! The teacher does not need to talk about — or cover — all the behaviors to be changed in the learner. What he *does* need to do is insure that the learner has adequate provisions available in order for a desired behavioral change to take place in a climate of acceptance, reassurance, and reasonable promise of success!
2. The subject matter content must be appropriate to the learner with reference to:
    a. The pace of instruction.
    b. The level of difficulty of the material.
    c. The relevance of the instructional material to reality as perceived by the learner.
    d. The learner's level of need and interest.
    e. The individual learning style of the learner.
3. The size of the group of learners, the composition of the group, and the time allotted to a group should be appropriate to the purposes of the group. Individualized, self-paced, "quantity-quality" monitored learning must be insured.
4. Before truly individualized instruction can become a reality, learning units or packages are needed which will provide for self-paced rather then group-paced or teacher-paced instruction. Learning packages usually include the following eight ingredients for individualizing instruction: (a) concepts, (b) behavioral objectives, (c) multi-dimensional learning materials, (d) diversified learning activities, (e) pre-evaluation, (f) self-evaluation, (g) post-evaluation, (h) quest-problem confrontation, delimitation, research, and resolution.

Integrating these eight curricular elements in the form of learning packages can serve as an important advancement in providing for individualized instruction, especially when so much material is already available from commercial sources. It must be emphasized, however, that all eight of these elements must be included although, commercial packages usually contain about half of these ingredients. The remainder must be developed by the teacher.

This takes a great deal of effort!

It is imperative that the continuing education teacher be loosed from the chains of the immediate, the customary, and the habitual. Indeed, it takes effort to move from the traditional to the revolutionary. What is needed are revolutionary teachers — teachers who are more student-oriented than subject-oriented, more need-oriented than course-oriented, and more person-oriented than program-oriented. This constitutes a radical departure from the traditional role of the teacher.

These efforts can come only when a thorough understanding of the conceptual approach to learning is mastered.

Learning how to learn must somehow overshadow the acquisition of methods, techniques, procedures, skills, and knowledge.

Individualizing instruction is a way of thinking about managing the classroom — it is a strategy, not a method of instruction. It is a way the teacher arranges learners, materials, and equipment so that each individual learner can learn optimally without threat.

SUMMARY

The conceptual approach to adult learning and instruction has as its foundation the application of systematic and appropriate knowledge to human affairs for the purpose of creating intelligent action and change. This change is effected by a conscious, deliberate, and planned effort within the context of continuing education programs to bring into interaction the three central figures of learning — the teacher, the learner, and the content area to be learned. But the heart of the effort is the learner. He is the focal point in any given learning environment. He is the active behaving ingredient in the whole process. His concept of reality and need is basic to instructional planning and strategy. The genesis of any instructional program design is the terminal behavior of the learner!

Adult Instructional Model (AID)

Mary Jane Even

Associate Professor, Adult & Continuing Education
University of Nebraska-Lincoln

There are currently many more instructors working in adult education than there are program planners. These include full-time, part-time, and one-time only instructors who use a variety of titles such as speaker, workshop leader, consultants, resource person; all considering themselves instructors of adults. The settings vary, the topics are numerous and the length of time for the instructional events range from one-half hour to months. The intended outcomes, the goals and purposes are as varied as the occasions, students and their needs. This is the way it is in adult education.

Throughout the long history of adult education instructors have traded problems, remedies, plans, philosophy and theory but not until **now** has a plan been developed which would assist all of the varied instructors in planning and developing instruction for adults.

In fact over the years, instructors of adults have given little, if any attention to the most vital area of concern — instructional development. Too often it has been assumed, and incorrectly, if the program planners plan a program thoroughly enough, the instructor can teach the class effectively based upon the program planners' efforts. This is entirely erroneous. One has only to visit such an instructor's class to understand the lack of techniques, preparation and resultant student boredom. The preparation of instruction requires careful analysis, planning and implementation. Many instructors begin this process of development with a skepticism of the program planners' view. It is only when the instructor is with students can the instructor (not program planner) realize the truth of this healthy skepticism.

In order to maintain a freedom in instructional development a process needs to be available. In this way the right questions are asked beforehand, the correct contingencies organized and the process developed properly.

In the past, instructors of adults have used guides or models for developing instructional designs which originated as program planning models. The models offered by Tyler,[1] Knowles[2] and others, have placed the emphasis on planning rather than the development of instructional designs for the classroom. The eight-step process of Houle[3] or the four-step process by Tyler have been offered to instructors as potential guides, but are second-hand — all are primarily guides to curriculum or program concerns. There are no

Adult Instructional Model (AID)

explicit guides offered to adult instructors to assist them in developing a teaching/learning experience for adult learners. Knowles has suggested techniques and gives some ideas for planning pertinent to adults, especially as they relate to andragogy.

There is a relationship between the program planning process and the instructional design; they are clearly separate in terms of intended outcomes. For an instructor to assume the program planning process can provide him/her with all needed information or that there is little to do prior to walking into the classroom because the program planning process has been carried out may be fatal to instructional effectiveness. Instructors need some guidance, once they have been given their teaching assignment. The program planning model and the instructional design model are two separate and distinct plans about which an instructor needs to be fully cognizant.

The nature of this problem becomes most apparent when an instructor is hired by a program planner or administrator. Given details of the time, space, and dates, the instructor then needs to prepare for the teaching/learning experience. The instructor may be advised by the planner on needs assessment and the topic, and then proceed to plan. At other times the instructor may have been told nothing. Today there are many more instances in which an instructor is hired who is not part of the planning team nor privy to planning needs. Some specific detailed plan needs to be provided to enable instructors to be well prepared to enter the classroom and bring about effective learning experiences for his/her students. In addition, there is a need for a plan which program planners could use with novice instructors to help prepare them to enter the classroom.

After eight years of classroom analysis by at least 1000 students via their development of courses using the model, an instructional development process (AID) was developed. It has been altered through analysis over the years. It is reported by instructors that they are now able to enter their classes with confidence and enjoy classroom effectiveness. The only problem noted presently is that it takes time to prepare. This time is well spent! Some areas of redundance have their purpose — checking different aspects of the same problem enables the instructor to ascertain internal consistency.

The basic education psychology used in this model is the cognitive-field theory where group process and interaction, sharing of experience by students, student involvement in planning, and a general gestalt of an instructional design are considered important. A complete interpretation of this learning theory may be found in *Learning Theories for Teachers* by Morris Bigge.[4]

This model begins when an instructor is hired to teach a course. It provides the instructor with a set of specific questions in five process steps to be answered in sequence **prior** to arriving in the classroom. The outcome of the model is a well-structured adult instructional design whereby decisions are made and concerns are identified for classroom decisions. Thus, the effectiveness of classroom operations will be strengthened.

THE ADULT INSTRUCTIONAL DEVELOPMENT PROCESS: AID

Introduction to the Instructor — As an instructor, you have been hired by an institution, agency, or organization to fill a need for an education offering deemed appropriate because of the purposes and functions of the institution, organization, or agency. Most of the time you are told what the topic area is you are hired to teach. Sometimes you develop this topic area depending on your role and function. In either case, once the topic area has been selected, these processes are appropriate.

It is at this point you gather the pertinent data which will assist you to manage the processes of the instructional experiences. The processes outlined here via questions is a guide to this activity. It is intended that you find out the information asked and write it down in paragraphs under each question.

Process I

1. Organizing course related information, processes, and procedures

    1.a. What are the educational purposes of the organization (institution or agency) which hired you?

    A general description of the educational purposes or functions of the employing organization provides the instructor with the rationale, mission, or purpose of why the educational experience is of value and where it fits in the overall view with other educational efforts.

    1.b. What is the philosophy of the organization regarding teaching and instructional procedures?

    Ascertain if the organizaton has made any specific commitment to the style or mode of instruction for students such as individualized instruction or correspondence study, lecture, or discussion. Seek out the general mood of acceptance and how much latitude you have in carrying out the process.

    1.c. What is the present information regarding your learners? What sources are available? What can you hypothesize?

    Prepare a general statement about the adults you will teach from what the program planner might have told you or you can get from other sources. Ask what other sources are available, see other information such as pre-registration forms and organizations sending adults to class. Add as much data as possible and identify information you will want to ascertain from students in the first class period.

    1.d. What relationship does your course, program, or learning experience have with other programs or courses?

    Specifically, identify the relationship of this course to any other the students may have been given or taken. Can you make any assumptions regarding what the learner's knowledge of the subject may be because of this relationship? Must you follow some framework in regard to amount covered in class?

    1.e. What is the reason you were hired/asked to teach this course, program?

    Clearly identify why you were hired to teach the class. Was it your philosophy on teaching, knowledge of the topic, skills, degrees, experience? What kind

Adult Instructional Model (AID)

of performance has been expected of you? At what level are you to perform? Remember you were chosen for a reason and you need to live up to those commitments.

1.f. How are you going to involve learners or legitimizers in planning the learning experiences?

Begin to identify here the manner in which you will find out what the learners are expecting to learn, the level of their experience and knowledge on the topic, the ways they learn best, and generally legitimize what you think you have prepared to teach is correct for the learners you will have in class.

1.g. What are the apparent organizational needs, the community needs, and individual needs for this course?

Due to the fact that most adult learners have experience or work in various sectors of organizations and community which have needs as well as the individual learner having needs, identify here (as Tyler suggests) the related societal implications which can assist you to work with the students. You will want to demonstrate relevance and practicality of the information you provide via-community, work, or society problems, however, you will need to be well informed about current events and interests. Here is your chance to seek out those examples from many sources.

1.h. What kind of budget requirements are needed for your course? And how much budget has been allocated to you for your course/program?

Before you begin you will want to identify the specific budget for the course so as to be realistic in planning equipment, xeroxing, materials. Who will pay for the handouts? How many are important? Where do you go and to whom for costs? Check on all procedures for financial arrangements.

1.i. What is the title of the course?

State the title and identify what that title means to prospective learners. Sometimes titles mislead students to courses. You may have dropouts if you do not clearly identify in the title the purpose of the course.

1.j. What kind of time limitations are there on the course?

Ascertain the exact timing of the course, the dates, and the length of each session toward planning realistically that which you wish to accomplish or need to accomplish.

1.k. What relationship does this course have to credit, certification, or other standards?

Ascertain if as a result of this course or this course in combination with others some standard, degree, or certification needs to be obtained. If so, you may be committed to dealing with or need to commit yourself to deal with specific information as well as testing procedures. Ask what it is and the expectations others have for you.

1.l. At what level is the course to be taught?

Generally, ascertain if this is a beginning course, intermediate, or higher level. Decide if this means more knowledge or more depth on the topic. Find out the experience people have in working with the knowledge.

1.m. What methods of instruction do you see a need to include at this time? Relate to purpose of course.

By this time, you have formed some initial impressions regarding your course. In general, based upon the purpose of the course, generally review the methods you believe will be used. It is recognized that later you may be more specific and my alter your views.

1.n. What is a representative bibliography or set of resources you will use?

State clearly here your class texts, materials, and other resources you will be using in the class. At this time you will have considered level of readings, finances, and purposes so you can prepare here a list for the organization to order for you (and students if needed).

1.o. What is your tentative outline for your course?

Along with your resources you will probably wish to give the organization a brief overview of the course for their clarification, approval, and you have the basic information in order to do this now. Prepare a general outline of the topics, what topics will be on the days of class and a general comment about the methods you will use. Don't be too specific yet.

1.p. Other resources available to students?

Before moving on, identify here the places, persons, and other resources available to students in the organization which will facilitate learning — library, counseling, service, books.

1.q. Particular concerns for your specific clientele?

If you have identified any particular concerns which your students have for learning or instructing, report them here for future consideration. For example, work problems to be handled in class or resolution of some conflict of students.

Process 2

2. Developing processes for needs assessment and objective formulation.

This section deals with very specific information requiring knowledge related to objective formulation and levels of learning as identified in Bloom's, Krathwohl's, and Simpson's taxonomies of educational objectives[5].

2.a. What are the types of learning and levels of learning to be considered in your program?

Generally state the kinds of learning experiences, the types of learning (knowledge, attitude, or skills), and the level or depth of the learning which is expected you will provide in your course. For example, will it be necessary to have the students evaluate criteria to make judgments on some knowledge or just learn about some piece of knowledge? To use tools or just see a demonstration? To know about process or value it?

2.b. What kinds of educational objectives are appropriate for your program? (Specific or general or both — based on your beliefs about how learning takes place)?

Adult Instructional Model (AID)

Describe how specific your objectives for your class need to be. Will there be tests based upon your objectives? Will the objectives be shared with students? Are they only for your use? The high degree of specificity is needed if used for testing. This will help you determine the amount of work needed. Also ask yourself what kinds of specific objectives are most appropriate to meet your teaching/learning psychology. If very behavioralistic, more specific objectives are a must. If more individualistic, they can be more general. You need to decide.

2.c. What is the appropriate realm of knowledge for your program/course?

Here you clearly analyze the exact nature of the content you will be providing to the students. Clearly identify the framework around which the knowledge you offer is organized.

2.d. How can you specifically narrow the scope of your program/course?

Recognizing that in most all cases instructors offer too much content because of their expertise, identify here how you can narrow the scope of the content without taking out the essentials or making the class too narrow in scope.

2.e. What are the overall and generally appropriate objectives of your program/course?

Cognitive: It is believed that in all teaching/learning situations all three levels of learning identified here are incorporated. Thus, here
Affective: you are asked to prepare the specific objectives you will use in your course based upon the information you prepare in
Psychomotor: answer to the first four questions in Process II area. You may wish to consult some books at this time to clarify objective writing and your philosophy so as to write objectives consistent with your teaching philosophy.[6]

2.f. What specific products or ends does your program require?

Recognizing you now know what end results your course has, it is time to check your objectives to see if the outcomes will be reached via your objectives. Identify how they are to be reached here.

2.g. What further objectives are needed under each of the areas noted above which are needed to provide a complete picture of your program/course?

Since in No. 2.e. above you were asked to provide only general objectives, you are asked to report here any special objectives or needs not identified above. These may relate to a few people in class or special added needs for the students to consider.

2.h. What kinds of process objectives/goals do you need to help you operate efficiently to attain your goals?

Process objectives are those for the instructor to state what he/she will do to support the student learning objectives. For example, to provide an effective climate for learning for adults. State these here.

2.i. How will you assess the students to see what level of knowledge they are coming into your program/course with? (Will differ by program/course and use may be made of more than one kind.)

There are many ways to fill this need. You are asked here to prepare a statement which describes explicitly the form, situation, or event you will use to test whether your perceptions of student needs, your objectives, and goals are correct. It must be done.

2.j. How will you resolve the difference which may result in objectives for course after assessment?

Recognizing all contingencies, what are some changes you can plan to make if needed following the in-class assessment? Identify potential changes in methods, levels of learning, types of things learned, and others.

Process 3

3. Developing the learning experiences and making the instruction plan.

This process step calls for knowledge of adult psychology, group process, learning abilities of adults as well as background on how to instruct adults. References have been given in the bibliography.

3.a. What is the relevance, organization, and meaning of the subject matter for the learner?

One goal sought by instructors of adults is to make the learning meaningful, relevant, and to organize the learning based upon the learning styles of the adults in the class. Examine here how you can demonstrate relevance (refer to Process 1.g.) of subject to the students, how you can get students to relate their own problems to make the subject more meaningful, and how you are going to organize the information to account for different learning styles and modes.

3.b. What are the characteristics of the adult learner we teach? (include motivation, intelligence, readiness to learn)

Examine the potential differences of your students in terms of motivation, age, intelligence, experience, physical activity, readiness to learn, value orientation (refer to Process 1.c.). It is here because of your knowledge of the psychology of adults you could consider those additional aspects which adults bring to any learning experience. These aspects provide you as the instructor more bases for understanding the classroom process and what is happening to the learners in this process. (There are resources on this information given in the references.)

3.c. How do you as an instructor perceive your role in the classroom? (Your method)

Each instructor brings to the classroom a specific philosophy about people and their abilities. What you do in the classroom will reflect this philosophy even if you have no label for it. Describe here your perceptions of yourself as an instructor and your perceptions of your students as learners. (Refer to Process 1.e.)

3.d. What type of teaching-interaction process will you be using in your program/course?

Describe here the manner in which you will be interacting with your students both in class and out of class. As adults view such interaction as a contribution to the meaningfulness of the class, how will you account for it?

3.e. How is the nature of group process going to be dealt with by the instructor?

It is recognized that a group of people learning develop a particular group attitude. Recognition of the nature of group functioning, group behavior via the life cycle of a group, and such, can be a significant part of learning. How will you use it?

3.f. What are the facilities like in which you will be teaching?

Many of the statements you have made thus far imply a certain kind of spatial arrangement of furniture and people. Describe here the manner in which you will arrange the room for learning activities. You may wish to draw a picture of the room.

3.g. What are the external influences brought to bear on the Teacher-Learner experience?

Describe here the influences of administrative, planning, and other policy decisions which need to be accounted for as influences on your teaching. Also describe those problems brought by the learners into your classroom.

3.h. How will you account for learning needs of the adults you teach?

Describe how you will account for learning of adults re these six principles.
1. Learning must be problem-centered.
2. Learning must be experience-centered.
3. Experience must be meaningful to the learner.
4. The learner must be free to look at the experience.
5. The goals must be set and the search organized by the learner.
6. The learner must have feedback about progress toward goals.

3.i. How will you take into account the "Ten Conditions for Effective Learning" in your course outline?

Describe how you will account for Tyler's conditions for learning.[7]
1. The student must have experiences that give him an opportunity to practice the kind of behavior implied by the objective.
2. The learning experiences must be such that the student obtains satisfaction from carrying on the kind of behavior implied by the objective.
3. The motivation of the learner, that is, the impelling force for his own active involvement, is an important condition.
4. Another condition is that the learner finds his previous ways of reacting unsatisfactory, so that he is stimulated to try new ways.
5. The learner should have some guidance in trying to carry on the new behavior he is to learn.
6. The learner should have ample and appropriate materials with which to work.
7. The learner should have time to carry on the behavior, to practice it until it has become part of his repertoire.
8. The learner should have opportunity for a good deal of sequential practice; more repetition is inadequate and quickly becomes ineffective.
9. Another condition is for each learner to set standards for himself that

require him to go beyond his performance but standards that are attainable.
   10. The tenth condition, related to the ninth, is that to continue learning beyond the time when a teacher is available, the learner must have means of judging his performance to be able to tell him how well he is doing; without these means, his standards are of no utility.

3.j. What techniques and devices will you incorporate in your class sessions to demonstrate your methodological views as instructor **and** support the learnings identified in the objectives?

Throughout this section, you have made decisions about how you will instruct, how your students will learn, and what conditions are important for these to take place. Here you are asked to describe the specific techniques and devices (audio-visual materials) you will use in your class which are consistent with your decisions thus far. In addition, you need to refer back to Process 2.a.-j. to check if your methods and techniques are consistent with the objectives and goals you have set for the course.

THE INSTRUCTIONAL PLAN

This step asks you to prepare a specific plan which you will use to present instruction to students. Using information you have made decisions upon early in this development, you can prepare the plan. Some persons use this portion as a report to the program planner or administration. It can also be used as a syllabus for students.

(1) Description of the Course learning activity:
(2) Purposes or goals of the course:
(3) Instructional objectives for the students:
(4) Clientele (students) to be served (target population, participants):
(5) Prerequisite skills and level at which course will be taught:
(6) Content outline including dates, times, and activities (terms, vocabulary, concepts, facts):
(7) References or bibliography for the students:
(8) Resources needed by students, by instructor (materials, equipment, people):
(9) Evaluation procedures (during activity; at conclusion of activity): (refer to Process 5).
(10) Instructors agenda for each class period using the model shown on an 8½ x 11 inch sheet of paper, make three columns and place at the head of each column, these three titles:
  (a) Time Segments
  (b) Activities
       techniques
       objectives-student
       objectives-instructor
       content
  (c) Resources

Adult Instructional Model (AID)

Fill in the chart for time, the activity during the time showing how it relates to an objective, and in the third column place those resources you as an instructor need to use.

Example:

Time Segments Date: Sept. 1	Activities (Techniques, Objectives, Contents)	Resources Needed
7:30-8:30	Instructor: Arrange room, get out materials, set up coffee and name tags. Greet People.	Coffee; name tags; handouts
8:00-8:20	Maintenance: Student objectives: to learn about the content of courses and students	Tables and chair in large U-shape
	Instructor: Provide orientation, description of course content, have each person introduce each other.	
Etc.	Technique: Have persons next to each other introduce each other to class — use class syllabi to help explain course — have students in a circular formation around room at tables	
Account for all time	Etc. . . . Account for all content and objectives.	Etc. . . . account for all resources needed.

Process 4

4. Analyzing the instructional plan and planning for contingencies in carrying out the learning experiences.

   This process asks you to re-examine based upon these questions the plan you outlined. Prepare a statement confirming or justifying your decisions. Be willing to change your mind and redo a portion of the plan if necessary.

   4.a. What evidence is there that a climate conducive for adult learning has been considered and will be carried out?

   Explain what you as an instructor will do to meet the needs of adult learners in your classroom.

   4.b. What evidence is there that possible changes in time and agenda items may occur based on student questions and input?

   Explain how you are going to account for time alterations due to fluid discussions or problems which occur. Adults need to have space in an agenda for discussion. What will your posture be in handling this concern?

   4.c. What evidence is there that flexibility in the learning activities are built into each agenda?

   Describe how you can redistribute topics for discussion, expand or retract time segments, have alloted for time to move into small groups and such.

4.d. Is time used realistically?

Since adults demand the wise use of time in learning, instructors need to be both realistic with time and yet always aware of learner's need for discussion.

4.e. Is there time for opening and closing remarks?

Describe the amount of time provided at beginning and end of class as well as after a break to re-establish the climate.

4.f. Is there time for movement of members to form groups?

Describe the amount of time allotted to movement into groups recognizing it takes at least five minutes for groups of two to three to form and ten minutes for five to six member groups to form.

4.g. Are the resources and activities planned appropriately for the learning objectives? For levels of learning?

Re-examine the activities you have planned in relation to the learning objectives. Remember if it isn't an objective, don't do it, and if it is you must use it.

4.h. What kind of evidence is demonstrated whereby students share in the maintenance of the class?

Describe how you are going to share the maintenance activities with the class and also the planning and teaching aspects of the class.

4.i. Is there involvement of learners in each session?

Describe how you are going to involve the students at least once if not more each class period in planning teaching and/or discussion. Involvement of students is critical.

4.j. What sort of techniques and devices are used to build motivation and interest?

Describe how you are going to build in ways to boost interest, build morale, heighten motivation.

4.k. Is the facility or site being used to advantage?

Describe the room or site used and the manner in which you are going to use it. Draw a picture of some optional ways of arranging the room for large group discussions, small groups, and other activities. Are there other advantages to the use of the room which you could make use of toward making your teaching/learning experience more effective?

Process 5

5. Planning to conduct evaluation during and after the learning experience.

   5.a. What are the ways or means you will use to engage in evaluation during the early stages of the course and during the course? (Formative Evaluation)[8]

   In the formative evaluation what are the essential or prioity concerns to be considered in these processes? Describe how you will account for them during the course:

   Rationale for course:
   Assessment of learners:

Statement of objectives:
Designing the learning activities (method, techniques, devices) carrying out the learning activities:
Evaluation of learning activities:

5.b. What are the means and/or tools to be used to evaluate at the summative and/or final stage of the course?[8]

Here you need to refer back to process 1.k., and Process 2.f.i.j. to reaffirm the position you took or were given for the outcomes of the course. These will guide you in your decision here. Describe your final evaluation or test form recognizing you may need to change it later. What the essential or priority concerns (that is behaviors, attitudes, skills, and processes) are to be assessed? In addition, what are the bases upon which the type of evaluation, (extensiveness, specificity, and method of use) will be based?

5.c. What are the types of inputs (influences, processes or resources) which must be taken into consideration in the examining of the results of the evaluation form process?

Recognizing that the input of students is only one of the inputs in an evaluation process, describe those other persons, groups, or influences which need to have both input and be accounted for in the interpretation when evaluation of your course is made.

5.d. What use will be made of the evaluation results? By the instructor? By the institution, agency, or organization?

In order to make certain that kind of information needed is obtained, you need to ascertain the purpose to which the evaluation results will be used. These uses may mean you add questions or seek comments other than course content. Seek this information from the program planner or administration. Describe how you will account for it.

5.e. How is evaluation of instruction perceived by the institution you work for?

Ascertain how your employing group has dealt with evaluation of courses in the past. Establish your commitment to the form and nature of evaluation used for evaluation of your instruction.

5.f. What type of evaluation report (if any) is to be given to the student?

Ascertain the type and form of evaluation report required by the institution for you to give to the students. Are their grades, personal reviews of papers, projects? Are there student conferences? Describe how you can meet these commitments.

5.g. What type of overall report needs to be made to the institution?

Ascertain what kind of closing report you are going to have to present to the employing institution. Will the nature of this report influence any other methods or procedures planned earlier.

5.h. How will **you** judge **your** effectiveness as an instructor?

Personally, you will want to make some decisions about your effectiveness as an instructor toward your own growth and development. Several references in the adult education literature (including Klevins and Knowles in the bibliography) give examples of instructor evaluation models. You could select one or develop your own.

SUMMARY

A completed report delineating answers, forms, and materials sought in these questions is an instructor's guide with which to begin any learning experience with much confidence. It is a time-consuming process but will provide freedom for the instructor to facilitate learning rather than be caught up in day-to-day organizational concerns. Experience with this set of processes has proven to be most valuable.

QUESTIONS & EXERCISES

1. State the pros and cons of using the Adult Instructional Development (AID) model.
2. Name some of the resource persons you would utilize in developing an AID.

REFERENCES

1. Tyler, Ralph, *Basic Principles of Curriculum and Instruction*, Chicago: University of Chicago, 1971.
2. Knowles, Malcolm, *Modern Practice of Adult Education*, New York: Assoc. Press, 1961.
3. Houle, Cyril, *The Designs of Education*, San Francisco: Jossey-Bass, 1972.
4. Bigge, Morris, *Learning Theories for Teachers*, New York: Harper-Rowe, 1976.
5. Bloom, Benjamin (Ed), *Taxonomy of Educational Objectives: Cognitive Domain*, New York: McKay, 1956.
   Krathwohl, David, et. al. *Taxonomy of Educational Objectives: Affective Domain*, New York: McKay, 1967.
   Simpson, Elizabeth, "The Classification of Objectives," *Psychomotor Domain*, Research Project No. OES-35-104, Urbana, Il: Univ. Ill., 1966.
6. Mager, Robert, *Preparing Instructional Objectives*, Palo Alto: Fearon Pub., 1962.
   Popham, James, *The Evaluation Guidebook*, Los Angeles, Instructional Objectives Exchange, 1972.
7. Tyler, Ralph W. "New Dimensions in Curriculum Development," *Phi Delta Kappan*, Vol. XLVIII, No. 1, Sept. 1966.
8. Anderson, Scarvia B.; Samuel, Bill; and Murphy, Richard T. and Associates, *Encyclopedia of Educational Evaluation*, San Francisco: Jossey-Bass, 1975.

(These references support completion of Process III)

Stanford, Gene and Albert E. Roark, *Human Interaction in Education*, Boston: Allyn and Bacon, Inc., 1975.
Klevins, Chester, *MATERIALS & METHODS in Continuing Education*, Canoga Park, CA: Klevens Pub., 1976.
Knox, Allan, *Adult Development and Learning*, New York: Jossey-Bass, 1976.
Bischof, E., *Adult Psychology*, New York: Harper Row, 1976, ed.
Tough, Allen, *The Adults' Learning Projects*, Toronto, Ontario: Institute for Studies in Education, 1973.
Knowles, Malcolm, *The Adult Learner: A Neglected Species*, Houston, TX: Gulf Pub., 1973.

Holistic Learning

Carroll D. Brown
Department of Education
Austin Peay State University

Patricia Terrell
Department of Elementary Education
East Carolina University

James R. Layton
School of Education & Psychology
Southwest Missouri State University

For the past decade both American educators and the American people have been told that the abilities of American students to perform basic mathematics and language arts skills are deteriorating and that an educational crisis exists. The persons issuing the cries of doom, often with educators among their groups, usually gain their information from various media reports containing nationally-collected achievement tests results. The solution of a large majority of the advocacy groups for this problem of declining test scores is for American educators to return to teaching the basics.[1]

A closer examination of back-to-the-basics advocacy groups will reveal that many persons are using the same terms, but do not agree on the definition of **back-to-the-basics.** For some non-educational persons, the term means teaching only the 3R's in the public schools; to others, it implies removing objectionable books from the libraries and classrooms; and for some, removing frills from the curriculum such as sex education and modern dance. To some educational personnel, back-to-the-basics means a monitoring system whereby basic skills competency test (criterion referenced) results are used to guide and direct educators in improving the teaching of basic skills, theoretically improving students' skills. Other educators differ with both groups and maintain that empirical evidence is availabale to support the designs, procedures, and techniques presently employed in the schools and also that dwindling test scores do not truly reflect students' lack of ability. According to members of this group, the social aspects of American life, the diversity in the student population, and other variables are at the root of the problem — not lack of ability per se.

There are students in secondary school and colleges who have the intellectual skills to perform the tasks called upon but are sorely lacking in basic skills. Some students may withdraw from high school only to return years later to obtain the essential skills necessary to pass the GED (for self-improvement), or to help their own children as they struggle through school.

And too, many of these students may complete the minimum requirements for high school graduation. These adult students, along with GED certificate holders may enter college (especially colleges with open-door policies) with only a few, if any, vital skills needed to complete a desired course of study.

Adult basic education teachers and remedial or basic skills teachers will find valuable information in this chapter. It is usually their task to identify weaknesses in students' abilities, to plan an effective basic skills program, and at the same time, to provide these students with techniques to pass other courses even though these learners may have limited abilities. This group of teachers has one of the most difficult tasks in education today . . . their responsibilities transcend the usual definition of **teaching**.

The following are major premises:
1. Students enter ABE and college or university basic skills classes each year with weaknesses in basic skills development. In addition to diagnosing and remediating these skills, teachers also must evaluate other variables that may interfere with learning.
2. A basic skills program is incomplete if it is designed to allow teachers to remediate basic skills and does not contain provisions for students to learn to apply those skills in subject matter courses, or to apply them to daily living problems.
3. It is a serious error to assume that ABE or basic skills teachers (adult educators) are the only teachers with the responsibility of assuring students that they will show an upward gain in achievement and be successful; every administrator and teacher who is involved with any facet of students' education, must share equally in planning programs, procedures, and techniques to aid all students to succeed.

All adult education must be viewed as an adventure in caring for the total needs of an adult human being — to develop holistic rather than patchwork models.

A VIEW OF HOLISTIC EDUCATION
The Student — Adult educators who teach in remedial-type or developmental settings must be aware that students entering their classes have had limited success in school. There are specific reasons why some students did not learn well in high school and there is a strong possibility that these students still possess some of those traits, whether they are cognizant of them or not. Adult educators must be aware of these behaviors or characteristics and aid students in overcoming them.

When students enter adult classes, the teacher should evaluate the students' present abilities by using some type of test. From these screening measures, grade equivalent or percentile norms are obtained and teachers can specify the arithmetic, reading, spelling, language, cognitive, and possibly composition performance levels of the students. An astute observer may ask the question: "If the student has learned **this** much and can do **these** things, then why has **more** not been learned?" It is an appropriate question; in reality, the test scores described above reveal nothing related to the reasons the student

learned or **did not learn.** The test scores may be interpreted to mean only two things:
1. At this point in the student's life, a certain amount of information and skills have been learned.
2. If the student has learned a given amount, then under specific conditions, more can be learned.

Certainly, the use of initial screening devices and subsequently employed diagnostic instruments are both very necessary types of measures. However, those steps only partially complete the analysis of the students' behaviors that will be needed to design an instructional program for them (holistic educational model). Stauffer, Abrams, and Pikulski[2] specified that a host of variables are specifically related to problems that children encounter in learning. If those problems persist to adulthood, then the student may still not be able to learn. The adult educator must look for the following behaviors or personality traits.

Impluse Control Checklist
1. Inability to keep a balanced reaction to internal or external stimuli not related to the learning task.
2. Inability to postpone gratification of internal instinctual tension that is unsatisfied.
3. Sublimation problems that surface as immature, inappropriate behaviors when compared to the students' social background and behaviors of their peer group.
4. Students must discover if they are accepted, wanted, or loved by using reality testing to determine consequences of specific behaviors.
5. Inability to synthesize information.
6. Inability to analyze information.
7. Inability to integrate information.

Defense Mechanism Checklist
1. Repression characteristics, or an apparent unconscious mechanism in which the students reject any thoughts or tasks having painful and disagreeable contents.
2. Isolation characteristics, or students who withdraw from group participation as a result of personality difficulties (poor academic performance based on items in these checklists).
3. Reaction formation, or the development of desirable or acceptable behaviors or acceptable behaviors or traits to conceal undesirable ones (being able to do many things well except academic tasks).

Reaction-To-Learning Tasks Checklist
1. Type and/or degree of stimulation that is required to interest the student in a particular learning task.
2. Amount of tension (if any) that appears to be generated by the student when a learning task is presented or during the learning task.

Major implications that may be drawn from the foregoing information is that adult students may not attend to the printed matter to be learned for a sufficient length of time to store it in their short-term memory banks. Additionally, the students may not be given, nor know how to provide, practice and rehearsal exercises to transfer the data to long-term or secondary memory stores. Adult educators can be instrumental in guiding students to develop these skills.

Not only does the student need to develop behavior patterns which will aid in learning, but content needs to be so structured that it will develop a maximum in know-how to provide practice, drill, and review.

THE BASIC SKILLS PROGRAM
Spelling — The **Wide Range Achievement Test** commonly referred to as the WRAT will yield spelling norms for an individual or a group of students. However, for teachers wishing to perform an indepth evaluation of students' weaknesses in spelling, Spache[3] has developed a spelling errors test for that sole purpose. By administering the specific words on the test and categorizing the errors made, the teacher can identify as many as thirteen possible types of errors. Another excellent test that teachers in adult centers may find valuable is the **California Phonics Survey** which can also provide valuable clues to spelling problems. Spache's test will yield information relative to the following types of errors:
1. Omissions — silent letters, sounded letters, doubled letters.
2. Additions — doubling letters, single letters.
3. Transpositions or reversals — letters in incorrect order.
4. Phonetic substitutions — vowels, consonants, syllables, words.
5. Nonphonetic substitutions — vowels, consonants.
6. Unrecognizable or incomplete spellings.

Whatever error patterns are identified by the adult educator, the problem of teaching a student to spell and how to learn to learn to spell, still is not solved. When severe problems in spelling are encountered, the best course of action is to employ the techniques of Fernald that are described in her classic book **Remedial Techniques in School Subjects.** However, to use Fernald's techniques requires a high level of student motivation and perserverance.

The following steps have been effective with many ABE and college students.

Step 1. Teach that learning to spell is both a visual and auditory task, but that certain words and word parts may require one, the other, or both.

Step 2. Demonstrate word units that can be identified by sounds (mainly certain consonants as a rule or units such as, re-, de-).

Step 3. Demonstrate the troublesome vowels and common patterns that must be learned by sight (-er, -ir, -ur; -ee-, -ea-, -ei-, -ie-; -est, -ist; -c = k,s).

Step 4. Teach students to look at the word they are to spell, say it in syllables, and try to visualize the word with their eyes closed.

Step 5. Direct the student to count the number of syllables in the word, and draw a line for each of the syllables (redirect - re · di ·rect (3) - ___ ___ ___).
Step 6. Then, without looking back at the word, the students should attempt to spell only the portion of the word that they can hear and parts they can visualize; afterward they should look back at the word and copy the missing portions.
Step 7. When the students have the word committed to short-term memory, they should write the word at least ten (possibly twenty-five) times every twenty-four hours until it has transferred from the short-term to the long-term memory. As the student writes the word, each letter in each syllable should be pronounced aloud as the letter is formed (do not separate or name the letters, r-e-d-i-r-e-c-t, but synthesize, re · di · rect, smoothly).

NOTE: By writing the word, looking at it, and pronouncing it aloud, all of the students' mental faculties are attending to the word; there is little opportunity for other stimuli to interfere.

Subject matter teachers must assume the responsibility of stressing spelling in their classes, but must also be lenient in grading spelling. Those teachers should also provide the students with spelling clues or techniques. But ultimately, rather than identify 100 or 500 words that all adult students should know how to spell, subject matter teachers, adult basic education teachers, and students should cooperate to devise lists of words needed in school and in daily living.

Composition — By implementing a holistic model into adult basic education problems, teachers can assure themselves that each student is receiving a well-balanced program of basic skills, subject matter or content area skills, and life survivial skills. By doing this, teachers can assure students that upon withdrawal or upon graduation they will have developed minimum competencies in vital educational areas. The ability to compose grammatically correct, logically sequenced, comprehensible sentences, paragraphs, and compositions is one of those vital skills areas.

The study of finite state or traditional grammar has been required in secondary schools, ABE classes, and colleges and universities. Students are also tested on their abilities to identify subjects and predicates, specify parts of speech, and recognize correct and erroneous punctuation. As long as institutions maintain such requirements and as long as state basic education tests, the GED, and other tests employ such measures as indicators of language proficiency, then adult educators must teach those skills.

Diederich[4] produced an excellent guide for teachers to use in evaluating students' growth in composition. According to Diederich, five variables should be used to evaluate composition: **ideas, organization,** wording, flavor, and mechanics (usage, punctuation, spelling, and hand-writing). However, ideas and organization were each rated twice as important as each of the sub-areas of mechanics. Every adult educator should consult his book for extended reading.

O'Hare[5] presented empirical evidence to support the idea that providing students with sentence combining exercises will improve their writing skills regardless of their knowledge of English grammar. O'Hare also showed that sentence combining would exploit the students' linguistic competencies already possessed. Students who participated in O'Hare's study experienced approximately twenty times normal growth in composition ability. In a more recent study, Tagtmeyer demonstrated that sentence combining not only improved remedial students' composition writing abilities, but improved their reading comprehension as well.

Sentence combining exercises appear to fit well into the theories of transformational grammarians. Briefly, a kernal string can be separated into parts or deep structure. **Deep structure** connotes all of the experiential knowledge that a person would need to read a simple sentence such as: **The child is father of the man.** Certainly, those words cannot be assigned literal meanings in that syntactical pattern. Rewritten the sentence would read: **The man is the father of the child.**

In finite state grammer (traditional), sentences are studied or analyzed in a left to right sequence. Transformational grammer is sometimes taught in the same fashion — from the whole to the part. Sentence combining exercises reverse that; students are presented with several, short, single concept sentences, and are requested to combine them into one sentence.

Example:

| Kent will mow the lawn. | | Kent will do two chores. |
| Kent will trim the hedges. | | Kent will do them on Saturday. |

| Kent will mow the lawn and trim the hedges on Saturday. | or | Kent's chores on Saturday will be to mow the lawn and trim the hedges. |

In addition to providing students with sentences to combine, Horst and Rosenberger[6] recommended a second phase which consists of a set of useful words for combining ideas. They specified nine categories with many more combining words than listed here. Their lists include words for: (1) additional ideas (and, moreover, also, furthermore), (2) contrasting ideas (but, however, yet, instead), (3) causes and results (so, therefore, since), (4) time (earlier, later, then, now), (5) giving specific information (in fact, indeed), (6) choices (either, neither, or), (7) conditions (if, unless), (8) purposes (to, for, so that), (9) place (where, wherever). Add punctuation marks (; : — , ( )) as useful tools in teaching sentence combining.

Example:

Derek played in the football game.
Derek kicked three field goals.
Derek was convinced he could have kicked more field goals.

Combine to show contrasts: use the word, **nevertheless.**

Derek kicked three field goals in the game; nevertheless, he was convinced that he could have kicked more.

In addition to sentence combining, Horst and Rosenberger expanded their recommendations to include sentence combining that would result in a paragraph containing a main idea and supporting details. The first set of short, clear, simple sentences contain the main idea. The next few sets of sentences can be combined for supporting or sequential details; and, the final set of sentences can be integrated to form a summary sentence or a transitional sentence which leads to the next paragraph.

Many innovative psycholinguistically-based abilities can be stimulated. The following types of riddles can be developed.

Example:

Mary had a baby sheep.
The baby lamb was small.

The baby sheep had hair (fleece).
The baby sheep's hair was white.
The sheep's hair looked like snow.

Mary went many places.
The baby sheep went everywhere with Mary.
The baby sheep made sure it was always with Mary.

In order to involve content or subject matter teachers in sentence combining exercises, basic skills teachers should demonstrate the techniques so as to convince all other teachers that sentence combining exercises can serve as practice and reinforcement activities for information that is to be learned.

Example:

Abraham Lincoln is a famous American citizen.
Abraham Lincoln was a famous president.
Abraham Lincoln is given credit for freeing the slaves.
Abraham Lincoln was assassinated.

Abraham Lincoln is a famous American president who is given credit for freeing the slaves; unfortunately, he was assassinated.

If several other groups or clusters of single concept sentences were written about Lincoln, the students could combine the clusters into sentences and the sentences into paragraphs.

Taking Notes — Two of the major demands required of adult education students is that they listen carefully and take notes. Using those notes and other sources, students study for examinations and demonstrate proficiency. For many students, the system works; for others it does not work.

There are several excellent study techniques that students can use to study textbooks independently. There are also several excellent notetaking/study techniques that are very useful. Adult educators often teach those techniques to ABE students; however, a problem arises when the subject matter teachers do not teach in a manner commensurate with the study techniques learned by the students. The result is that students reject the notetaking and study techniques.

Until basic skills teachers and subject matter teachers learn to cooperate and devise holistic approaches to education, many students will continue to do inferior work; when all along, they could be learning subject matter as required by the teachers and at the same time developing independent learning skills that will be useful throughout their lives.

Pauk[7] contended that students should **make notes,** not **take notes.** According to Pauk, students should reserve a two inch column on each page of their notebooks to use after lectures to summarize the most important aspects of the lecture. Those summary statements would be condensed in the form of key concept words that the students would use for review purposes and to study for examinations. Pauk also stated that during study and review periods, students should rehearse or practice aloud, not silently. He also pointed out that the use of tape recordings and short-hand are not effective study methods.

Students need to learn that there is no **one** method of making notes. The reasons for any **one** method not being effective are many. However, the most glaring difference is that the various subjects are different in nature; therefore, the notemaking demands are **different.** If students learn a variety of notemaking methods and techniques to apply those methods to various subjects, then they should be able to use their notes much more effectively. The study of biology involves the structure and functions of things (Describe the structure and functions of flagella.) and the relationships among those things. The study of sociology involves a concern for the applications of certain principles or theories of human behavior to explain the values found in a given culture. Since there are some basic differences in subjects, notemaking methods should reflect those differences.

Notetaking from Written Material[7] — Whenever students read printed material, they should take notes. Since it is impossible to remember each major point and equally difficult to scan through the text to find such points, students should learn how to make notes of important facts or concepts. Writing notes also tends to enhance the memory. Care should be exercised in ensuring that students learn that notetaking from written material is **not** recopying the material verbatim. Notetaking may take the form of: (1) underlining, (2) outlining in the book, (3) outline, (4) study guide, (5) mapping.

Although students prefer underlining because it is faster, it is not always feasible. If the book does not belong to you or if it is written in a particularly difficult style, some form of notetaking may be necessary.

Some suggestions for improving your notetaking ability are:
1. Begin taking notes after you know what the materials or topic is about. Begin writing **after** reading, not while reading.
2. Do not plan to rewrite notes. This is time consuming and inefficient.
3. Take notes in your own words (except for technical terms) rather than copying them from the book.
4. Develop a systematic way to take notes.
   a. word, phrase, or sentence outline.
   b. summary.
   c. be concise.
5. Develop a type of shorthand appropriate for each subject and yourself.
6. Practice relating subordinate ideas to main ideas by way of indenting, numbering, and underlining.

Listening — Notetaking during lectures is a vital skill for survival in many classes. Much of the information and concepts for which students are responsible is dispensed verbally in class. Since it is impossible to accurately remember much of what is heard, it becomes necessary to record or make a record for future reference. Even with the advent of compact and inexpensive audio-recorders, notetaking still remains the best method of recording because of the ease and speed of locating and reviewing the material.

The skills of notetaking from a lecture are similar to notetaking from written material: (1) main points are the goal, (2) organization should be visible, (3) key words and phrases rather than sentences should be recorded, (4) use your own words rather than the speakers.

Researchers have found that college students spend about half of their waking hours in the act of listening, but unfortunately remember only about twenty-five (25) percent of what they hear. What interferes with good listening? It would be wise for students to check their listening habits. In fact, before taking notes many students will need to be sure they have good listening habits. These might possibly be four of the major factors which affect listening: (1) lack of motivation, (2) negative affective response, (3) improper interpretation, (4) lack of notetaking ability. Completing the following activities will help students develop a better ability to listen:

Inventory of Listening Habits

		Yes	No
1.	I often think a subject is uninteresting.		
2.	The speaker's way of talking often bothers me.		
3.	I often get excited by something a speaker says.		
4.	I listen mostly for facts.		
5.	I always try to take notes in outline form.		
6.	I pretend to listen even when I am not.		
7.	I tolerate distractions.		
8.	I avoid listening to difficult material even on television.		
9.	The speaker's choice of words often turns me off.		
10.	I find myself daydreaming when I should be listening.		

Listening is different from reading in that "re-listening" is impossible. There are no italics or bold print to point out the key ideas. Students must learn to know each teacher's techniques for emphasizing vital concepts. Some commonly used techniques are: (1) a change in voice pitch, (2) a reduction in the rate of speech speed, (3) a pause, (4) repetition, (5) use of key phrases such as "now I will list . . .," "there are several problems . . .," "in the first place . . .," "on the other hand . . . ."
The following suggestions will also aid the listening notemaker:
1. First, date and title the lecture. If a title is not given, make one at the end of the talk.
2. Apply the listening method by tuning in and establishing questions to be answered during listening.
3. Take notes in your own words. Do not be concerned about spelling. Develop a method of shorthand. Leave a two inch margin on the left side of the page.
4. At the end of the lecture write a brief summary.[8]
5. Before memory dims, edit the notes. Fill in phrases that add clarity; correct spelling or abbreviations that may be difficult to recognize when the notes are cold. Most importantly, build in organization by underlining, numbering, or writing in the margins.

Pauk[8] urges all educators to guide and direct students in study skill development, but not as an end in itself. The process should lead to developing **independent studiers** and that leads ultimately to the **independent learners**.

Reading — In aiding reading skills development, a holistic approach requiring a great amount of information can provide a framework for adult education instructors to use in teaching reading. It is important for adult educators to be knowledgeable of adult learners' experiential backgrounds, memory abilities, learning styles, and other information that will allow them to provide for individual needs of adult learners. Additionally, adult educators must evaluate materials for inclusion into the basic skills classes as well as subject matter classes. In some instances materials may have to be constructed by the adult educators. Developing a holistic curriculum is no easy task.

Once teachers are assured that materials are appropriately matched to their students' reading abilities, then they should begin to teach the students to use the following four reading rates:
1. Slow, careful reading — a technique that is employed when the material being read has to be remembered or mentally manipulated (reorganized, analyzed).
2. Faster, normal rate of reading — a technique that is employed when answers to specific questions are being sought, to appreciate diction or literary style, or to remember material for oral reports.
3. Skimming — a rapid reading technique used for locating details and main

ideas, to gain implicit or explicit information for making inferences, or for review purposes.
4. Quick or rapid reading (scanning) — skipping or jumping over information quickly to locate specific information such as names and dates. Rapid reading is also used to gain a quick impression of the materials or for review purposes.

Students who can employ those skills and combine them with notetaking and study skills will notice a rapid improvement in the quality of their work. However, adult basic educators should not teach these skills in isolation. Subject matter teachers must provide situations for their use and share the responsibility of guiding students in using the techniques.

Another area of reading skill development that must be shared by basic skills teachers and subject matter (content area) teachers is that of matching specific types of reading skills, notetaking skills, listening skills, and study skills with specific content areas within the total curriculum. There are specific, specialized vocabularies that can be matched to each content area. Science materials should be read more slowly than short stories, especially when directions are to be followed. Layton[1] reviewed and outlined all that information and it should be highly useful to adult educators. His book also contains other reading lesson plans that would be valuable to ABE teachers.

SUMMARY

As the reader may have surmised, the foundation or substructure of the holistic model is a **total language program.** Even mathematics and science courses are language-based — it is the problems students have in reasoning, rather than computation, which frustrate them. But, until basic skills teachers and content area teachers cooperate, few problems will be solved.

Basic skills teachers should be called upon to conduct inservice workshops for subject matter teachers. The content of those workshops would contain practical information related to:
1. Characteristics of adult learners, especially learning style and memory abilities.
2. Reading skills, techniques, and readability.
3. Composition writing and speaking techniques, including spelling.
4. Notetaking and listening skills.
5. Methods of pre-and post evaluation and matching evaluation procedures with study procedures.

Basic skills students at universities and colleges and many ABE students already possess the ability to call words and react to what they read at the literal level. However, if students are to become independent learners, they must be able to react to study materials critically and analytically. The curriculum should also provide help in areas that create anxieties for students. Thus a holistic curriculum should consider areas that will help students reach **that** critical level of understanding and **that** will ensure independent, self-motivated, critical reading.

QUESTIONS

1. Briefly discuss four (4) major differences between holistic learning and traditional learning.
2. As an adult educator, you have discovered that some of your students are unable to analyze information. What would you do to help these students?
3. Why should every teacher be a teacher of basic skills?

REFERENCES

1. Layton, J. R. *The Psychology of Learning to Read*. New York: Academic Press, 1979.
2. Stauffer, R. G., Abrams, J. S., and Pikulski, J. J. Diagnosis, Correction, and Prevention of Reading Disabilities. New York: Harper and Row, 1978.
3. Spache, G. D. Diagnosing and Correcting Reading Disabilities. Boston: Allyn and Bacon, 1976.
4. Diederich, P.B. *Measuring Growth in English*. Urbana, Illinois: National Council of Teachers of English, 1974.
5. O'Hare, F. "Sentence Combining: *Improving Student Writing Without Formal Grammar Instruction.*" Urbana, Illinois: National Council of Teachers of English, 1973.
6. Horst, W. A. and Rosenberger, D. A. *Sentence Combining*. Sacramento, California: McDougal, Littell, 1981.
7. Pauk, W. Notetaking: The Great Cue Column. *Reading World*. 1979.
8. Pauk, W. The Super-Glue of Study Skills. *Reading World*. 1980.

Learning Feedback — Effective Teaching

Gerald D. Bailey

Professor of Education
Kansas State University

Robert E. Scott

Professor of Education
Kansas State University

Conscientious and effective adult educators always desire valid learner feedback. The use of learner feedback can be a primary method for improving classroom instruction.[1] Unfortunately, few adult educators (teacher, facilitator and instructor) have been taught how to gather and use learner feedback efficiently and effectively.

Adult educators need help in designing and creating feedback instruments. The actual creation of learner feedback instruments is not as awesome as it might initially appear. Creating learner feedback tools requires common sense and knowledge of basic rules as they relate to improvement of instruction.

Obviously, a prerequisite in student feedback practices is recognizing the importance of systematic and effective instruction.[2] Prior to any work with learner feedback instruments, the teacher needs to identify the different sources of feedback which could be used when engaging in instructional improvement: (1) learner, (2) self, (3) peers and (4) administrator or supervisor.

All of the feedback sources for improvement of instruction should be carefully considered. No single source can or should be used exclusively by the teacher when engaging in improvement of instruction activities. Information gathered from learners can be compared with other information from peers, supervisors or administrators and even self. The value of several sources of feedback is that information can be compared and contrasted to determine congruity or incongruity of opinions.[3]

Pros & Cons — "Learner feedback" describes the process of collecting information for the purpose of instructional improvement. Various authorities have focused principally on the gathering of learner feedback as a method for teacher evaluation, however, teachers can also use learner feedback for improving instruction. Hence, it is very important for the teacher to weigh potential strengths and weaknesses of a feedback system before selecting or creating this kind of instrument. The advantages and disadvantages of learner feedback include the following:

Advantages

1. The solicitation of learner opinion represents a potentially large sample or measure of information. Most other sources of information concerning the teacher or course lie in the hands of one or two people.

2. Learner opinion is based on direct observation. Other sources of information concerning the teacher or course do not have access to the teacher on a regular basis.

3. The solicitation of learner feedback can be accomplished quickly and frequently as compared to other sources of information.

4. Collection of learner feedback allows the teacher additional information which may not be provided by other sources. The collection of learner feedback frees the teacher from dependence on the administrator or supervisor in the process of instructional improvement.

Disadvantages

1. Whether learners will reveal their honest opinions is subject to question. Since the teacher may represent an authority figure, the learner may be reluctant to reveal candid opinions.

2. Teachers often do not know what to do with the feedback information once it is obtained. Without training in learner feedback analysis, the process of gathering learner feedback becomes an end in itself.

3. Assuming that teachers can acquire valuable information from learner feedback practices, will the teacher change instructional techniques to meet learner approval? If this is the case, teachers may either directly or indirectly make changes based on considerations other than improved instructional techniques.

The balance between the positive and negative attributes of learner feedback practices is not always easily recognized. Many of the advantages and disadvantages are based on the degree of knowledge and training that the adult teacher has had in learner feedback practices.

COMMERCIALLY-PREPARED VS SELF-MADE INSTRUMENTS

The teacher who makes a decision to use learner feedback will need to consider two types of learner feedback instruments: commercially-prepared and self-made. Commercially-prepared instruments are those tools created by professionals in the field of learner feedback or teacher evaluation. Self-made learner feedback instruments are those tools created by adult educators for exclusive use in their own classroom. Classroom educators need to note the differences between commercially-prepared and self-made learner feedback instruments. The following **advantages** and **disadvantages** should be kept in mind when viewing commercially-prepared learner feedback forms:

Advantages

1. Commercially-prepared learner feedback instruments are usually prepared by experts in the area of evaluation. As a result, many have been field-tested and validated. The teacher can place con-

Disadvantages

1. Often commercially-prepared instruments are complicated. The learners who complete the forms cannot understand the questions; the teacher then finds the completed answers difficult to interpret.

Advantages (cont.)

siderable confidence in the information provided by the author and publisher.

2. The information from commercially-prepared learner feedback instruments usually yields information that lends itself to varied in-depth analysis by the teacher.

3. Commercially-prepared forms are usually comprehensive; they look at many different aspects of classroom instruction.

4. Commercially-prepared forms usually contain a series of directions on how to administer the form as well as how to analyze the information submitted by the learner.

Disadvantages (cont.)

2. Commercially-prepared learner feedback instruments tend to provide general information. The collected information lacks substance which would allow the classroom educator to identify specifically "What and how" to improve.

3. Commercially-prepared learner feedback instruments which are used by many teachers in the same school can lead to learner boredom since the learner is required to complete the form several times for different teachers.

The adult educator who is systematically engaging in instructional improvement activities will immediately recognize the limited availability of commercially-prepared learner feedback instruments. The dearth of commercially-prepared instruments can be easily documented by referring to Borich and Madden.[4]

Observations about the current state of commercially-prepared learner feedback instruments include the following:

1. They have been designed for the purpose of evaluation rather than improvement of instruction.
2. They have been designed for use at college or university level of instruction.
3. They have been well researched at the level for which they were designed — higher education.

In light of these revelations about commercially-prepared learner feedback instruments, the adult educator needs to be extremely cautious about premature conclusions concerning the availability and value of commercially-prepared learner feedback instruments for their level of instruction.

Self-made learner feedback, on the other hand, are those instruments created by the adult educator who wants to use them for a personalized self-improvement program. Experiments with self-made learner feedback seem to suggest that these instruments have equal or greater value than commercially-prepared learner feedback instruments.[5] Self-made learner feedback forms are becoming more acceptable to learner feedback practices, but have some limitations:

Advantages

1. Self-made learner feedback instruments allow the teacher to ask questions which are personally significant to respective situations.

Disadvantages

1. The creation of self-made learner feedback instruments is time consuming and requires considerable effort.

Advantages (cont.)

2. Self-made learner feedback instruments can be very creative in design. These instruments have the potential to capture information which is impossible or difficult to obtain in commercially-prepared forms.

3. The time and patience required to create a a self-made learner feedback instrument fosters a personal commitment to the regular use of the instrument.

Disadvantages (cont.)

2. Usually self-made learner feedback instruments are not field-tested. Measures of reliability and validity seldom have been calculated by the creator.

3. The bias and prejudice of the teacher/creator becomes apparent in self-made learner feedback forms. Thus, the instrument only provides that information which the creator deems important.

4. The design of self-made learner feedback instruments are often simplistic. As a consequence, the instruments do not lend themselves to in-depth analysis by the teacher.

Weighing the benefits and shortcomings between commercially-prepared and self-made learner feedback instruments is subject to endless debate. Many adult teachers have found use of both types of instruments to have been valuable.

Evaluation vs Improvement of Instruction — Adult educators should be aware of a pitfall that can present itself when using learner feedback instruments. Since, historically, these instruments have been used for evaluation purposes. Even those used for improvement of instruction may be interpreted to give value judgements as to the worth of the teacher. Unfortunately, evaluation tends to polarize around high student evaluation being equated with good instruction. Thus learner feedback becomes another judgmental opinion of teacher worth.

On the other hand, the use and creation of learner feedback instruments does not always need to be aimed toward evaluation of teachers; rather, learner feedback instruments can be designed by the teacher to engage in systematic instructional improvement. Viewed in this manner, learner feedback activities become a series of activities separated from the total teacher evaluation process. The teacher can periodically ask learners to **provide information** which informs the teacher about certain instructor qualities or class conditions without requiring a rating **or an evaluation** of teacher or class qualities.

CREATING SELF-MADE LEARNER FEEDBACK INSTRUMENTS

What Should Be Asked? — There are four major question areas to consider when creating self-made learner feedback instruments. These include questions about (1) teacher behavior, (2) course qualities, (3) learner behavior, (4) learning environment qualities (see Figure 1). The value in distinguishing between and among these four question areas is that the teacher can compare and contrast a variety of information gained from learners.

SPECIFIC AREAS OF INTEREST IN OBTAINING SELF-MADE LEARNER FEEDBACK FORMS

Teacher Behavior segments: Teacher Methods and Strategies; Verbal Cues; Nonverbal Cues; Planning Skills; Individual and Personal Cues.

Course Qualities segments: Subject Matter Content; Assignments; Evaluation and test Construction; Text or Readings; Course Organization.

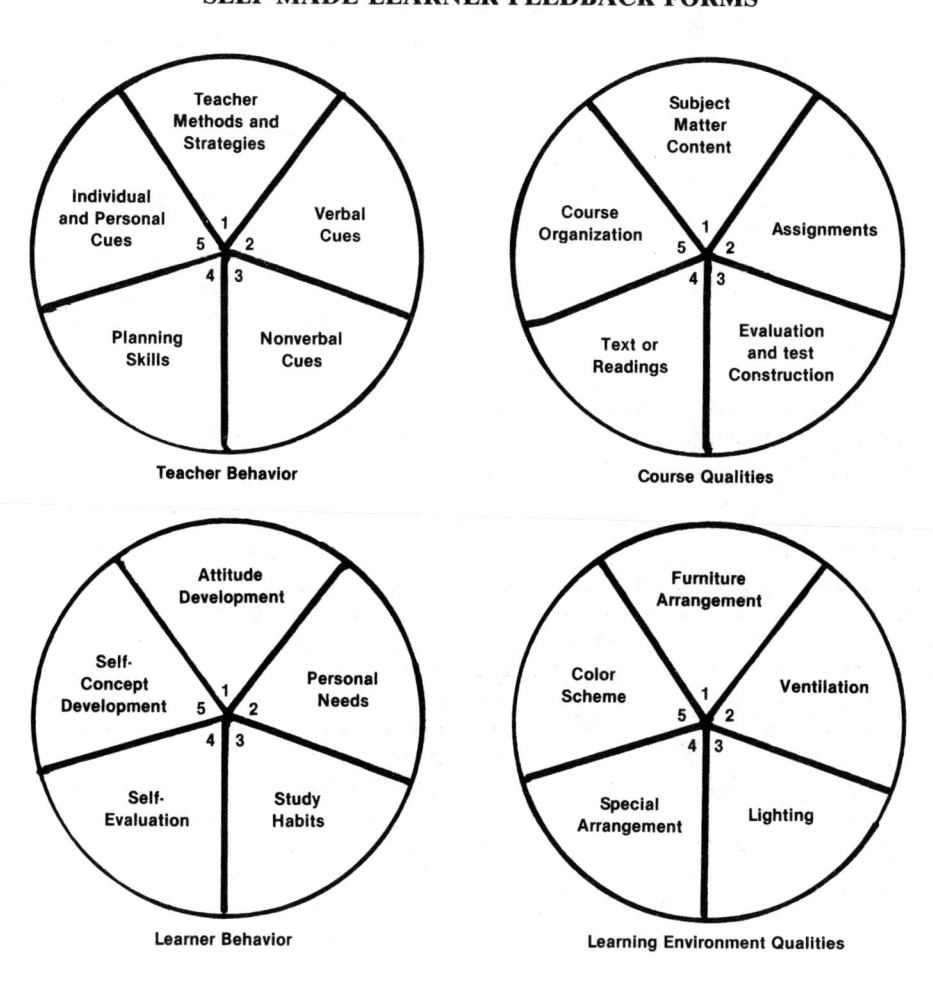

Learner Behavior segments: Attitude Development; Personal Needs; Study Habits; Self-Evaluation; Self-Concept Development.

Learning Environment Qualities segments: Furniture Arrangement; Ventilation; Lighting; Special Arrangement; Color Scheme.

Figure 1

Framing questions around four major question areas allows the teacher to gather comprehensive information concerning improvement of instruction. The different segments of information can be compared and contrasted to ascertain consistency and inconsistency between and among responses of learners. Many learner feedback rating systems (evaluation forms) only ask questions concerning the teacher; teacher behavior is central to most self-made instruments since it is the teacher seeking the information.

Teacher Behavior — Teacher behavior can be broken down into five specific components: (1) teacher methods and strategies, (2) verbal cues, (3) nonverbal cues, (4) planning skills, (5) individual and personal cues. The following represent sample questions drawn from the five components found in teacher behavior:

Illustrative Questions for Teacher Methods and Strategies

Directions: Code your answers by selecting the most appropriate answer.

    sa = strongly agree   a = agree   d = disagree   sd = strongly disagree

Teacher Methods and Strategies

Lecture   sa a d sd   1. The lectures for this course were exciting and relevant.

Small Group Discussion
    sa a d sd   2. The small group instruction exercise gave me the opportunity to express my personal feelings.

Illustrative Questions for Verbal Cues

Directions: Answer the following questions using the following number code.

    1. much less than other teachers   4. more than most teachers
    2. less than most teachers   5. much more than other teachers
    3. about average

Verbal Cues

Asking Questions 1 2 3 4 5   1. The teacher used questions which made me think (higher thought level questions).

Criticizing   1 2 3 4 5   2. The teacher's criticism of learner behavior or answers could seldom be characterized as a personal attack on that individual.

Illustrative Questions for Nonverbal Cues

Directions: True/False. if the statement is True, then circle the T; if the statement is False, then circle the F. Select the response which most accurately reflects your opinion.

Nonverbal Cues

Mannerisms   T F   1. My teacher has a number of distracting mannerisms such as tapping pencil, scratching nose, hitching pants.

Energy Level   T F   2. My teacher's energy level influences my attitude toward the subject (excitement or enthusiasm).

Illustrative Questions for Planning Skills

Directions: Circle the answer which most correctly identifies your opinion using the following codes.

    sa = strongly agree   a = agree   d = disagree   sd = strongly disagree

Planning Skills

Lesson Plans   sa a d sd   1. The teacher's lessons show careful thought and planning.

Planning Time   sa a s sd   2. The teacher seldom runs out of time when covering the subject during the teaching period.

Illustrative Questions for Individual and Personal Cues

Directions: Complete or fill-in-the-blank with the most appropriate answer which describes your personal feelings. Your current opinion represents the correct answer.

Individual and Personal Cues

Friendliness   1. When my teacher greets me, he/she usually acts _____.

Rapport   2. In this class, learners feel _____ about the teacher.

Course Qualities — The second major areas to be considered when constructing learning feedback stems includes questions about the course. They include: (1) subject matter content, (2) assignments, (3) evaluation and test construction, (4) text or readings (5) course organization.

Illustrative Questions for Subject Matter Content

Directions: Circle the answer which most correctly identifies your opinion.

sa = strongly agree   a = agree   d = disagree   sd = strongly disagree

Subject Matter Content
Topic Inclusion or Exclusion
          sa a d sd   1. The concepts on electricity should be kept in the course.
Interest   sa a d sd   2. The topics on car safety were motivating and interesting.

Illustrative Questions for Assignments

Directions: These are multiple choice questions. Select the correct response which represents your opinion.

Assignments
Length   1. The amount of time required to complete the assignments in this class are usually:
                              A. about right   B. too long   C. too short
Time Consumption   2. The number of assignments given in this class are usually:
                              A. about right   B. too long   C. too short

Illustrative Questions for Evaluation and Test Construction

Directions: Use the following codes to determine your opinion concerning the question being asked.

sa = strongly agree   a = agree   d = disagree   sd = strongly disagree

Evaluation and Test Construction
Learning   sa a d sd   1. The tests in this class help me learn as well as test my knowledge of the material.
Higher Level Thinking
          sa a d sd   2. Test questions used in this course permit me to think (analyze) as opposed to merely recalling specific facts or details.

Illustrative Questions for Text and Readings

Directions: Circle T (True) if you agree with the item or circle F (False) if you disagree with the item. Your current feeling represents the most appropriate answer.

Text or Readings
Stimulation   T F   1. The text motivates me to investigate additional information concerning the topic.
Organization   T F   2. The text is well organized for the learner to follow.

Illustrative Questions for Course Organization

Directions: Please place the word(s) in the blank which best represents your opinion related to the statement.

Course Organization
Importance   1. The topics or concepts which are most important in this course include:
                (a) _____ (b) _____ (c) _____
Inclusion   2. Additional topics which should be included in this course are:
                (a) _____ (b) _____ (c) _____

Learner Behavior — The third major area found in the self-made feedback form concerns the learner. This area is often overlooked in learner feedback instruments. The questions related to learner behavior can include: (1) attitude development, (2) personal needs, (3) study habits, (4) self-evaluation (5) self-concept development.

Illustrative Questions for Attitude Development

Directions: Draw a circle around the T if you believe the statement to be True and draw a circle around the F if you believe the statement to be False. Your current opinion is the correct answer.

Attitude Development
Attitude Variation Toward Course
    T F   1. My personal feelings toward this course change regularly.
Attitude Variation Toward Teacher
    T F   2. My attitude about the teacher has generally been positive this semester.

Illustrative Questions for Personal Needs

Directions: Circle the response which best represents your feeling using the following code.
    sa = strongly agree   a = agree   d = disagree   sd = strongly disagree

Personal Needs
Freedom of Speech
    sa a d sd   1. I am not afraid to state my opinions when called upon in this class.
Teacher-Student Relationship
    sa a d sd   2. The teacher is aware of how to get me involved in class discussion without embarrassing me.

Illustrative Questions for Study Habits

Directions: Select the opinion which best represents your opinion. Use the following statements to indicate your feeling.
    sa = strongly agree   a = agree   d = disagree   sd = strongly disagree

Study Habits
Daily Preparation
    sa a d sd   1. I make a conscientious effort to be prepared for this class.
Test Preparation
    sa a d sd   2. I study before tests in an effort to do my best work.

Illustrative Questions for Self-Evaluation

Directions: Select the response that best represents your current opinion. There is only one correct response.
    sa = strongly agree   a = agree   d = disagree   sd = strongly disagree

Self Evaluation
Seeking Help
    sa a d sd   1. I seek help from the teacher when I am confused or lost.
Personal Reflection
    sa a d sd   2. I periodically examine my own strengths and weaknesses to do a better job in this class.

Illustrative Questions for Self-Concept Development

Directions: True/False. If the statement is True, then circle the T; if the statement is False, then circle F. The correct response is your personal opinion.

Self-Concept Development
Personal Self-Worth
    T F   1. I have positive feelings about myself most of the time.
Success   T F   2. I am usually successful when I attempt different assignments in this class.

Learning Environment Qualities — The fourth major area of concern in learner feedback includes questions which relate to the learning environment. The learning environment plays an important part in the success of classroom interaction. Those qualities that a teacher may wish to consider include: (1) furniture arrangement, (2) ventilation, (3) lighting, (4) spatial arrangement (5) color scheme.

Illustrative Questions for Furniture Arrangement

Directions: Select the response which best represents your current opinion. Use the following code.

    sa = strongly agree   a = agree   d = disagree   sd = strongly disagree

Furniture Arrangement

Variety   sa a d sd   1. The teacher changes the arrangement of the desks on a regular basis.

Methodology
            sa a d sd   2. The chair and desk arrangement is often changed according to how the teacher is teaching the lesson (e.g., small group circles, lecture rows).

Illustrative Questions for Ventilation

Directions: Please place the words in the blank which best represents your opinion related to the statement.

Ventilation

Air Circulation   1. When I come into the room, the movement of the air appears to be _____

Coolness vs Warmth   2. The room's temperature is often _____.

Illustrative Questions for Lighting

Directions: If the statement is more True than False, circle the T; if the statement is more False than True, circle the F.

Lighting

Work Conditions T F   1. The lighting in the room seems adequate for studying or reading.
Relaxation   T F   2. The lights do not affect me when I am trying to relax.

Illustrative Questions for Spatial Arrangement

Directions: Select the response which best represents your current opinion. There is only one correct response.

    sa = strongly agree   a = agree   d = disagree   sd = strongly disagree

Spatial Arrangement

Personal Space sa a d sd   1. I often feel "closed in" by others in this class.
Accessibility   sa a d sd   2. If I need something from the laboratory area, it is easy to obtain.

Illustrative Questions for Color Scheme

Directions: True/False. If the statement is True, then circle T; if the statement is False, then circle F to indicate your opinion.

Color Scheme

Attitude   T F   1. The color of this room seldom has any effect on my attitude toward this class.
Temperature T F   2. The color of the walls makes me feel warm and comfortable.

The four areas of focus: (1) teacher behavior, (2) course qualities, (3) learner behavior, (4) learning environment qualities are all equally important. However, the teacher must decide which kind of stems will provide the most desirable information in each of the four areas. In the past most learner feedback forms have concentrated heavily on teacher stems. The purpose of emphasizing the four major question areas is to show that a balance of questions may reveal a more total picture of why and how learner opinions are formulated. Hence, the teacher has more information to engage in improvement of instruction activities.

STEM FORMAT

There are many options in the actual selection of the response stems or questions. The selection or creation of stems for learner feedback is similar to the creation of a good test. The creator must remember that learner feedback items created for improvement of instruction may be considerably different than learner feedback items created for teacher evaluation or teacher rating scales.

Thus, the selection or creation of the learner feedback stem must be carefully considered. The following principles must be kept in mind when selecting the stems.

The teacher has to have a commitment to:
1. Improvement of instruction as opposed to evaluation or rating of teacher.
2. Gathering information concerning the total teaching/learning act (teacher, course, learner and physical environment).
3. Creation of questions which elicit honest and candid learner answers.
4. Creation of questions which elicit maximum information allowing the teacher to analyze the teaching/learning act.
5. Creation of questions which lead to subsequent analysis as opposed to questions that are an end in themselves.

The types of stem formats include: (1) continuum response, (2) short answer or fill-in-the-blank, (3) essay, (4) multiple choice (5) true/false. The following examples illustrate the five major stem formats:

Illustrative Questions for Continuum Stems

Directions: Select the response that best represents your current opinion.
    sa = strongly agree   a = agree   d = disagree   sd = strongly disagree
    sa a d sd   1. My teacher dresses appropriately.
    sa a d sd   2. My teacher does *not* have distracting mannerisms.

Illustrative Questions for Short Answer or Fill-In-The-Blank Stems

Directions: Place the term or phrase in the blank that best represents your opinion. The correct answer is one that describes your current opinion.
1. My teacher reinforces learners by _____.
2. When I come into the class, the teacher is usually _____.

Illustrative Questions for Essay Stems

Directions: The following essay questions are designed for you to provide an extensive response concerning this teacher and course. React to the question in complete and concise sentences.

1. Describe the most valuable concepts in this course. Explain why you think they were valuable.
2. In your own words, describe what you like most about your instructor. Be specific.

Illustrative Questions for Multiple Choice Stems

Directions: Select the most appropriate answer that represents your opinion.

___ 1. The teacher's introductions for each teaching period were:
    A. Motivating and informative   C. Uninformative
    B. Informative   D. Boring and uninformative

___ 2. The course structure was
    A. Highly organized B. Organized C. Disorganized D. Highly disorganized.

Illustrative Questions for True/False Stems

Directions: Place a + for the items which are True and a 0 for the items which are False.

___ 1. The teacher provides adequate explanations when returning examinations.
___ 2. The assignments are often difficult.

Stem Format Selection — Decisions about which format to select are always difficult. Ultimately, the answer lies in the mind of the teacher. The teacher should remember the following:

1. Maximum information is needed to engage in improvement of instruction. Thus, stems must provide maximum information.
2. Accuracy of information is always desirable.
3. Information must be solicited which is most suitable for your personal use.

If the teacher were using self-made learner feedback form as an evaluation device, the continuum stems would be preferable to other formats. This type of stem would allow tests of statistical reliability and validity. However, teachers using learner feedback for improvement of instruction can rely more heavily on other stem formats depending on the kind of information needed.

Learner Risk — Under ideal conditions, there should not be any risk to the learner who participates in learner feedback exercises. As a consequence, the teacher needs to take special precautions. One of the major ways to deal with the learner risk factor is to provide a comprehensive orientation to the use and purpose of learner feedback. If adequate explanation is provided, then the learner should not develop unnecessary fears about learner feedback. Explanation should include a careful discussion on:

1. Why the feedback information will be requested.
2. How the feedback information will be collected.
3. How often the feedback information will be collected.
4. How the feedback information will be used by the teacher and school.

Teachers should strongly consider guaranteeing learner anonymity. This guarantee establishes some degree of assurance that the teacher will not be biased toward the learner in future classroom contacts.

Teacher rewards and/or retaliation associated with learner feedback will soon diminish the learner's zeal to participate in learner feedback and there is no place for reward or punitive exercises in instructional improvement efforts. **Teachers should strive to prevent specific respondent identification.**[6] The following concepts will need to be considered in this approach to total anonymity:

1. **Handwriting.** If any kind of handwritten feedback is required, will the teacher be able to intentionally or inadvertently identify the learner by name?

2. **Timing of Feedback.** When will the information be examined? If the data is being used prior to the course termination, the teacher will need to insure that this information will not be used in determining grades for learner performance in the class.

3. **Stem Creation.** Will certain questions inadvertently identify the learner by a personal response?

Considerable energy needs to be expended prior to the administration of learner feedback. These precautions are necessary so that the learner will be honest and candid in response.

PHASES IN SELF-MADE LEARNER FEEDBACK FORM CREATION

The decision to use learner feedback as a source of information for instructional improvement is a sound strategy. Learner feedback can be used as valuable information in the quest for improved classroom instruction.

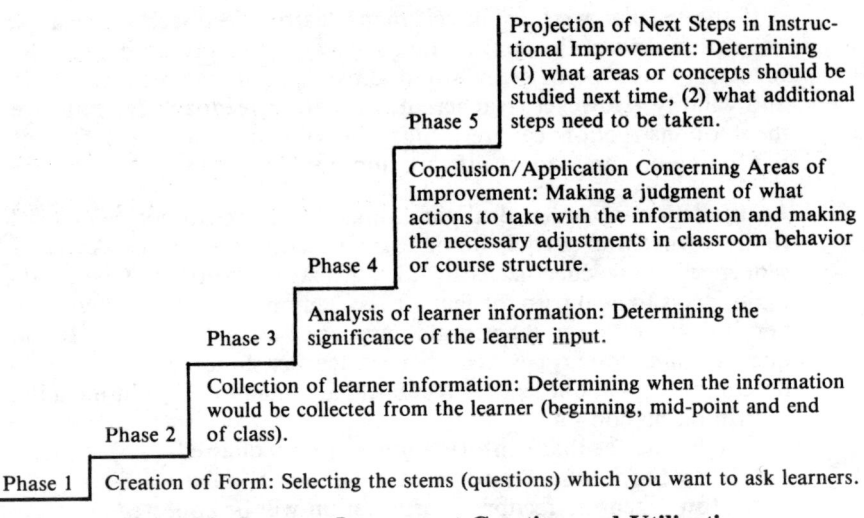

Phase 5 — Projection of Next Steps in Instructional Improvement: Determining (1) what areas or concepts should be studied next time, (2) what additional steps need to be taken.

Phase 4 — Conclusion/Application Concerning Areas of Improvement: Making a judgment of what actions to take with the information and making the necessary adjustments in classroom behavior or course structure.

Phase 3 — Analysis of learner information: Determining the significance of the learner input.

Phase 2 — Collection of learner information: Determining when the information would be collected from the learner (beginning, mid-point and end of class).

Phase 1 — Creation of Form: Selecting the stems (questions) which you want to ask learners.

Phases in Learner Instrument Creation and Utilization

Figure 2

However, many people do not plan beyond the actual collection of learner-feedback. The creation and use of learner feedback instruments must be seen as a series of continuous phases: (1) creation, (2) collection, (3) analysis, (4) conclusion/application, (5) projection (see Figure 2).

The importance of Figure 2 is to illustrate that creation and collection of learner feedback are preliminary steps in utilizing learner feedback. The analysis and conclusions drawn from the information from the learners are equally important. The projection step (Phase 5) suggests that the process of making instructional modification does not stop there. There is a specific period of time when the teacher needs to plan or project the next activities dealing with the use of learner feedback.

SUMMARY

Adult educators who are truly interested in improving their instructional behavior should capitalize on the wealth of information inherent in the learner. Obviously, entering the realm of learner feedback is neither easy nor always painless. Common sense, a commitment to instruction and creativity constitute the very essence of learner feedback. Those adult educators seeking decisive, effective methods in instructional improvement will find learner feedback fruitful and exciting.

REFERENCES

1. Etheridge, Richard A. "Conceptual Approach to Teaching/Learning." In *Materials and Methods in Adult Education.* Ed. Chester Klevins. Canoga Park, CA: Klevins Publications, Inc., 1976.
2. Bailey, Gerald D. "Improving Classroom Instruction: Is There a Better Model?" National Association for Secondary School Principals *Bulletin,* 62, No. 414 (January 1978).
3. Peterson, Richard E., et. al, ed. *Lifelong Learning in America.* San Francisco: Jossey-Bass Publishers, 1979.
4. Borich, Gary D., and Susan K. Madden. *Evaluating Classroom Instruction: A Sourcebook of Instruments.* Reading, Mass.: Addison-Wesley Publishing Company, 1977.
5. Bailey, Gerald D. "Improving Classroom Instructions with Student Feedback." *Educational Technology.* 17, No. 10 (October 1978).
6. Dutton, Donnie and Don F. Seaman. "Self-Evaluation." In *Materials and Methods in Adult Education.* Ed. Chester Klevins. Canoga Park, CA: Klevins Publications, Inc., 1976.
7. Bailey, Gerald D. and Robert E. Scott. "How to Use Trainee Feedback to Improve Trainer Behavior." *Training Magazine,* 16, No. 4 (April 1979).

Teaching — Learning Through Discussion

Huey B. Long

Professor of Adult Education, Director of Graduate Studies,
College of Education, University of Georgia

Few teaching-learning techniques have generated more comment and diverse opinions than the discussion technique. Strong proponents usually will support the use of discussion over most other techniques most of the time; in contrast, avid opponents usually will denigrate the discussion technique. Moderates concerning the use of the discussion technique tend to be characterized as individuals who recognize that discussion is an appropriate and valuable technique that should be, like all other teaching-learning techniques, rationally selected.

Discussion has a number of purposes. Through discussion we engage in social interchange about a variety of topics such as the weather, politics and religion. Discussion is also frequently used to solve problems, gather information, and make decisions. It is possible that learning frequently occurs through discussion regardless of the purpose for which the discussion takes place. However, we are concerned here with the kind of discussion activity that is specifically designed to achieve predetermined learning objectives.

Group discussion as a teaching-learning activity has occasionally fallen into ill-repute for a number of reasons. In some instances the kind of information shared has been of such questionable value as to result in group discussion being labeled a "pooling of ignorance." On other occasions the lack of structure has resulted in the conversation ranging sufficiently broad and wide as to have little relationship to any specific learning need. A third criticism concerns the lack of participation by individual group members; the group has either abdicated its responsibility or the leader has usurped the group's prerogatives. In such cases, the discussion usually concludes on a rather flat note with few participants benefitting from what promised to be a provocative, interesting and helpful experience.

A fourth criticism of the discussion technique that is equally applicable to other teaching-learning techniques concerns the assumed universality of the technique. Some instructors and learners tend to become mono-technique oriented (they prefer **one** teaching-learning technique under **all** circumstances). Adherents to the mono-technique school fail to recognize learning objectives differ among learners and the teaching-learning techniques may very from one setting to another.

The discussion technique would appear to have great appeal and appropriate application to a wide range of adult education settings. If Bligh[1] and Flavell[2] are correct in their observations that suggest much of adult education is more concerned with the development of patterns of thought, attitudes and motivation than with the acquisition of information, then the discussion technique should be widely used in adult education. Even this assumption, however, does not suggest that discussion is an appropriate technique for every learning setting.

Definition — The discussion technique is defined here as a procedure designed to generate purposeful, rational conversation and deliberation about a pre-determined topic of mutual interest among more than two individuals, under the guidance of a trained participant called a leader. To qualify as an educational technique the conversation must have an educational or learning objective.

The above definition serves to distinguish between the educational discussion technique and the problem solving discussion technique frequently used by committees and community development workers where a group consensus is sought. The discussion technique employed in an educational framework does not necessarily require a **group** report or a **group** consensus; educational goals may be met even though individuals continue to hold to different views.

The educational group discussion technique has several desirable outcomes that commend it as a useful teaching-learning technique when appropriately used. Three favorable results of group discussion are as follows:
1. Group discussion encourages the learner to organize his/her thoughts on a particular issue.
2. Organization and expression of an idea or concept moves the idea or concept from the intuitive realm to the explicit.
3. Explicit expression contributes to the opportunity to analyze and test ideas and opinions.

The potential value of the educational discussion is further enhanced when one accepts the three educational outcomes identified by William Kilpatrick decades ago. Kilpatrick identified three kinds of learning outcomes: (1) primary learning, (2) associate learning, (3) attendant learning. The primary learning outcomes are the ones identified through the statement of learning objectives. These learning goals are specifically determined and sought through a learning activity (to find out about a specific item of interest or to train oneself to acquire a particular skill or knowledge). The second kind of learning Kilpatrick defined as associate learning. This kind of learning is associated with the primary learning as a related outcome (When a student sets out to learn a foreign language additional interests may be stimulated). These interests may include customs, art, architecture and/or history, to name a few. Finally, attendant learnings are defined as the acquisition of general attitudes, dispositions, and standards of reference that are related to the development of personality. In some instances, attendant learnings may be of greater importance than the primary learnings that originally provided the impetus for the learning activity.

Lasker[4] noted that attendant learnings are not only unplanned but also are often unrecognized by those responsible for the direction of the learning experience. He suggested that attendant learning takes place in a discussion group when the participants lose the combativeness with which, at the beginning, they attacked controversial issues, as they come to recognize, in those whom they originally had thought to be their antagonists, many traits with which they could sympathize, and many objectives they mutually shared.

Elements — The elements of a successful group discussion include: (1) a trained/experienced leader, (2) learning goals, (3) a provocative topic, (4) a group of individuals willing and able to rationally and deliberately share their knowledge and attitudes concerning a selected topic in a disciplined manner. Each of the elements is necessary and no single element is sufficient to achieve success; they all interact. The interaction of the above elements results in a productive discussion while the absence of any one of the elements will significantly affect the benefits of the discussion.

THE PROCESS
Discussion Leader — The good discussion seldom develops without effort and study. The discussion leader draws heavily upon science and art. He appreciates the scientific data on group dynamics and is able to skillfully apply that understanding in a variety of settings with diverse groups. It is not, however, impossible for the novice to pick up good ideas from observation and participation in group discussion, both as a leader and a participant.

The leader is skillful in helping frame provocative questions or in presenting stimulus at appropriate times to keep the discussion from becoming mired in confusion, inattention, or complexity. The leader is skilled in: (1) keeping the discussion disciplined and pointed toward an appropriate target, (2) contributing to a supportive warm climate that eschews personal criticism, (3) being sensitive to the needs of various members of the group. The good leader is tactful in preventing domination of the discussion by one or two individuals and is able to fade into the group except as when needed to provide leadership.

Two of the most frequent questions raised by novice discussion leaders concern two kinds of individuals on polar extremes: (1) "How do I keep one person from dominating the discussion?" (2) "How do I get full participation?" Both kinds of individuals, the domineering and the retiring types, present a challenge. Several techniques for reducing the dominance of one individual are available. One procedure is to appoint that person as an observer with specific duties, such as plotting an interaction chart or an assignment that will require a brief summary at the end of the session. Another procedure is to firmly, but tactfully, remind that person that he is a member of a group and that ethically there must be consideration shown to other members of the group so that they may express **their** opinions. Sometimes the retiring, quiet and non-aggressive member of a discussion group must be encouraged to share. Such encouragement may be direct or indirect where the non-participating members are directly addressed or carefully assigned to a small sub-group that **requires** interaction at that level before involvement with the larger group.

Learning Goals — Not all learning goals can be achieved through the educational discussion process. Some goals such as learning to repair a small internal combustion engine, how to write a legible hand, how to perform some difficult motor skill or how to perform specific procedures to solve some technical mathematics or chemistry problem are not necessarily achieved through discussion. This process is clearly not equally relevant to all courses of study. In the usual computer language course, designed to give students certain fundamental operational skills, there would be little use for the discussion technique.

On the other hand, there is reason to believe that learning of attitudes, values, beliefs and related concepts that constitute a large part of adult learning and which influence behavior may be effectively learned through discussion that aims to help students gain an understanding of important and basic concepts.

Bergevin[5] has identified seven purposes for which the discussion technique is appropriate. They are as follow:
1. To encourage people to become aware of and learn about problems of their neighborhood, community, institution or organization.
2. To enable the participant to express his/her opinions in a group.
3. To learn about topics of mutual interest.
4. To develop a nucleus of persons for intelligent leadership in a neighborhood institution or organization.
5. To learn about relationships necessary to mature living.
6. To identify, explore or solve a problem.
7. To decide on a plan of action.

Group discussion is likely to have the greatest educational benefit when members of the group are: (1) perplexed to some degree by a particular question, situation or event; (2) aware that the issue may have more than one answer; (3) willing to join with others in a search for the **best** way of resolving the issue.

Discussion Participants — In a discussion some individuals have been attracted to participate in the educational activity through an institutional affiliation that strongly encourages or requires the individual to attend. In other situations the individual's participation is completely voluntary, but the broad topic area has already been structured around a particular curriculum. Finally, in the least structured situation the participants voluntarily come together to discuss a topic that they select and agree upon. Continuing Education is concerned with the first two kinds of conditions where the broad topic or content area is a given, such as in a non-credit course on energy, a unit of instruction in a history course, or practical politics.

Discussion Topic — The locus of responsibility for establishing the question for discussion will be determined by the degree of structure desired. In some situations where discussion of a broad topic may continue over several sessions the discussion may evolve from a condition of high leader direction to a condition of limited leadership direction. In another situation the series of discussion topics may evolve democratically around some central concern of the group. A third condition concerns a multiple topic series where a new book, problem, issue or some other question is to be discussed at each meeting.

The concern here is with the group discussion that reflects, at least in the beginning, high structure where the discussion leader (teacher) and the group are working within a curriculum framework that specifies the discussion topic from a moderate to high degree of specificity. In such situations the discussion leader with or without an advisory committee is responsible for initiating the discussion. At a later point in time other members of the group may evolve as discussion leaders, but such a development is dependent upon the success of the first and subsequent discussion sessions.

Selection and initiation of the discussion topic should be influenced by one of the basic principles of adult education — adults are interested in immediate application of new learning. This principle suggests that the discussion topic should have immediate use and is best initiated by relating the topic to a timely or current item of relevance to the group. For example, suppose that the class or group is engaged in a study unit based on the family and family relations. The age, concerns and developmental tasks, as suggested by Havighurst, may indicate several topics that might be of salient interest to the group. If the participants are approximately 30 years of age they may have great interest in the biological and mental development of their children, how to relate to grandparents, and similar issues related to the tasks of new parents. If they are above 40 years of age they may be interested in topics related to setting their children free, establishing new relationships with independent children, and tasks the parents face in establishing a new relationship with each other in a home no longer populated with small children as well as with concerns of relating to aging parents. Note this topic is concerned with a perplexing situation; it may have more than one answer and there may be several solutions.

Discussion may be initiated by several different techniques. The leader or prospective leader is reminded, however, that the discussion should have an objective; there is a purpose to the discussion, and it should be initiated and structured so as to contribute to the achievement of the objective. Let us return to the example presented above where the group is involved in a study of family relations and the mean age of individuals in the group is 45-50. Most of the group members have children between 19-24 and many of the parents in the group have experienced some conflict with their children over life styles, values, life goals and parent-child relations. The stated objective of the discussion on this topic is to help parents identify the sources of conflict, assess the nature of the conflict and formulate some possible course of action that may reduce the conflict and improve relationships.

The discussion may be initiated by any of the following procedures:
1. The leader or a member of the group may state the objectives of the discussion in this manner:
    "As parents most of us probably have experienced some conflict with our children over life styles, values, goals and relationships. Because of these conflicts, we are naturally interested in improving our understandings concerning these differences of opinion. It is possible that this goal may be achieved to some degree if we can identify the sources of the conflict, assess the nature of the conflict and try to determine selected courses of action. With some flexibility we should be able to examine these three dimensions of the conflict situation in the next two hours by devoting the first 30 minutes to identifying the conflict areas, the next 45 minutes to analyzing the conflicts identified to determine the true nature of the conflicts and finally devote the last 45 minutes to considering some possible courses of action open to us.
    Thus, during the next few minutes we will use a brainstorming session to form a list of some conflict areas. Remember, in a brainstorming session we are merely to list items, not discuss the merits of the suggestions or to critize them. Who has an item with which to start the list? How about you . . .?"
2. Other procedures could be identical to the above procedure through the end of the first paragraph. The second paragraph would differ as shown below:
    A. "Here is a picture illustrating a family activity. What are they doing? What are they discussing?"
    B. "Projected on the screen is a newspaper story about life styles in a large American city. How does this story reflect our concerns and experiences in this community?"
3. Another procedure is to use a dramatic presentation or skit. Three individuals could be requested to read from a prepared script and play the roles of father, mother and child. Before the skit is performed the group members should be advised to look for certain things and after the script these observations become the basis of the discussion.
4. Prior to the meeting, or at the beginning, the group is given a short paper on the topic to read. Instructions to the group members are for them to: (a) note statements with which they agree, (b) observe statements with which they disagree, (c) list statements that need elaboration, (d) cite statements that reflect local or current conditions.
5. A simple procedure requires the group leader to formulate a general question and merely ask in a very direct manner for an answer, then to redirect the question, "What kind of conflicts characterize parent-child relationships when the child is about 18-25 years of age and is living at home? George? Sara?"
6. Finally, when there is time and if the discussion is based on advanced reading the group members can be encouraged to prepare a discussion outline that will guide the discussion.

The Groups — Groups frequently need a little encouragement, coaching or related instruction before they become effective problem solving or educational discussion groups. Failure to understand group discussion characteristics by individual participants frequently places a heavier than normal responsibility on the group leader who must continually devise alternate strategies to encourage disciplined group participation. Some common difficulties include: (1) talking only to the discussion leader, (2) responding only when directly questioned, (3) rambling comments on unrelated topics, (4) failure to **listen** to the comments of others, (5) withdrawal, (6) dominating the discussion.

It is profitable when working with a new group to agree on some ground rules for the discussion that is to follow. These ground rules relate to the role of the leader. The leader's role is to see that the discussion is initiated and proceeds according to the objectives set for the discussion. This role sometimes requires the leader to ask questions, reformulate statements, summarize, prevent serious arguments, reduce dominance of the discussion by one or two individuals, bring all group members into the discussion, and keep the discussion on track. At the same time the leader has to be alert to keep from becoming the dominant discussant; he must be willing to allow some silence. It is not necessary that the leader respond to every question or play the expert too frequently; the leader must be careful about expressing his own values when reformulating statements of others.

In turn the group members should accept and abide by some guidelines that emphasize their roles. They have a responsibility to:
1. Listen to the comments of others.
2. Keep their comments in context and related to the discussion goals.
3. Be sensitive to how much they as well as others, are talking.
4. Try to make sure that everyone has an opportunity to participate.
5. Test their own comments and be aware of the authority of their comments (based on authoritative sources).
6. Test the comments of others, while refraining from personal attacks (courteousness, even in disagreement).
7. Share responsibility for advance preparation whenever opportunity is provided.

SUMMARY

Teaching and learning may be enhanced through the use of an educational discussion. This kind of discussion is usually more structured than other kinds of discussion techniques and is developed around a set of predetermined learning objectives. The educational discussion does not necessarily seek group consensus of outcomes. Individuals may continue to hold to different opinions while significant learning objectives may have occurred as primary learnings, associate learning, and attendant learning.

Educational discussion has a variety of characteristics that commend it to use as an educational technique. There are, however, some conditions and uses for which it is better suited than others.

Four elements are necessary for a productive educational discussion. They are: (1) a trained/experienced leader, (2) learning goals, (3) a provocative topic that is perplexing, may have more than one answer or solution, (4) a group that is willing and able to rationally and deliberately share their knowledge and attitudes in a disciplined manner.

REFERENCES

1. Bligh, Donald M. "Are Teaching Innovations in Post-Secondary Education Irrelevant?", in Michael J. A. Howe (Ed.), *Adult Learning: Psychological Research and Applications.* London: John Wiley and Sons, Ltd., 1977.
2. Flavell, John H. "Cognitive Changes in Adulthood," in L. R. Goulet and P. B. Baltes (Eds.), *Life-Span Developmental Psychology.* New York: MacMillan Company, 1970.
3. Kilpatrick, William H., cited by Bruno Lasker. *Democracy Through Discussion.* New York: H. W. Wilson, Company, 1949.
4. Lasker, Bruno. *Democracy Through Discussion.* New York: H. W. Wilson, Company, 1949.
5. Bergevin, Paul, Morris, Dwight, and Smith, Robert M. *Adult Education Procedures.* New York: Seaburg Press, 1963, (paperback edition, 1966).

Preferential Styles — Cognitive Mapping

Linda H. Lewis

Assistant Professor, Adult Education
University of Connecticut

In the past, educators have focused on the development of newer and better materials and methods such as computer-assisted instruction, programmed texts, and modular scheduling. Although very useful, these strategies have not proved helpful to **all** students. What happens to have been overlooked in the thrust toward innovative programming has been one critical variable — how an individual learns best.

An Alternate Approach — "Learning style" refers to an individual's consistent way of responding to stimuli in the context of learning.[1] It deals neither with one's level of academic achievement nor ability. Rather, it refers to an individual's characteristic way of perceiving, thinking, problem-solving, and remembering. Are you a listener or a reader? Do you work more effectively alone, through peer interaction in a group, or in a highly structured setting? Do you prefer to reason by making comparisons and seeing differences or by discerning relationships and similarities?

PREFERENTIAL STYLES

Cognitive mapping, the assessing of an individual's educational cognitive style, is being used in a variety of settings to discover how students prefer to learn and seek meaning. Within cognitive mapping are several identifiable learning styles:
1. Auditory
2. Visual
3. Kinesthetic-tactile

Adult educators now have at their disposal a fundamental new approach to organizing and designing appropriate learning opportunities for adult students.

For those who are interested in assisting high-risk students, preferential style programming can play an important role. It is a holistic approach which focuses on individual needs and is concerned with "who" the student really is. Preferential style methodology honors all ways of reasoning. No value judgments are made, either by students or teachers, and no one style is seen as best. Rather, the motto is, "I like your style, and his style and her style." Each individual is special and unique.

Philosophically, teachers of adults should have no difficulty deciding if the concept of educational cognitive style is applicable in their classrooms. Adult educators have been trained as facilitators and catalysts who arrange conditions and materials, motivate students, and reinforce understanding so that learning can take place. It is the role of the teacher to facilitate the transmission of knowledge. By utilizing information about students' preferred learning styles, teachers have an opportunity to enhance the individual's learning potential by building upon the student's strengths, while simultaneously developing skills in identified areas of weakness. This personalized approach to education not only assists teachers of adults in increasing the learning potential of students, but leads to improving retention and success ratios in the classroom. Research studies have revealed that in learning situations where preferential learning style concepts and methods have been implemented, increases in grades,[2] in attendance, and in self-concept[3] have been noted.

Differential Profiles — The manner in which information is most effectively and efficiently absorbed differs greatly from individual to individual. Each person has clearly dominant learning styles, or major learning preferences, along with minor and less preferred styles. Additionally, different groups of individuals appear to display distinctive patterns. For example, adult basic education students, as contrasted with university students, tend to be much more restricted in both the number and variety of ways in which they function best. These students may also exhibit a greater number of negative preferences, or negligible styles, which pinpoint situations, structures, and environments in which they are uncomfortable or do not work well. In relationship to the classroom, this suggests that some students may experience difficulty learning the material as they are more limited in the manner and variety of ways in which they can best process and assimilate information.

When reviewing the preferential profiles of university students, it is not surprising to find that they have the ability to shift from one learning style to another. It is, in part, this facility to adapt to different educational requirements that has contributed to their success within the educational system. On the other hand, special-needs populations, the culturally unique, the disadvantaged, and the adult basic education students represent a distinctive number of individuals who oftentimes did not "make it" in the traditional system because they could not adapt to fit the mold in which education was being marketed. Consequently, these individuals often dropped out of programs or were screened out.

Assessing Preferential Style — There are two ways to determine an individual's learning style — assessment through either observation or instrumentation.[4] Those who favor an observational approach suggest that formal and informal diagnosis through group feedback or sensitive observation in the classroom will yield information as to how to personalize the curriculum.

For example, by noting who sniffs the freshly dittoed handouts that are being disseminated in the classroom, a keen observer can identify those who have a sensitivity to smell. This information can be useful in structuring class activities. Asking students to bring in a flower that "smells like peace" can provide the basis for a productive discussion which centers in the affective domain. Such a strategy serves to capitalize on the preferences some individuals have for taking information in through their senses. It serves not only to motivate such students, but it helps to make the experience and lesson more meaningful.

Instructors can develop a sensitivity to the signposts which signal specific learning preferences. Figure 1 outlines some of the ways to identify specific learning styles and to utlize the information in developing appropriate instructional methods in the classroom.

IDENTIFYING STYLES — AUDITORY LEARNER
Observations
1. Often a "talker" — seldom is quiet. Tells jokes, tall tales, is full of excuses why something is not done.
2. Often has rather poor handwriting, drawing and other art work. Has trouble reproducing seen figures, letters — has poor visual memory.
3. Remembers spoken words or ideas quite well. May answer better when questions are read to him/her than when they read them themselves.
4. Likes musical and rhythmic activities and records.
5. Sometimes memorizes easily; often knows all the words to songs.
6. Quite often is physically awkward.
7. Appears to be brighter than his/her group-recorded I.Q. score.
8. Often has a poor perception of space and may get lost in unfamiliar surroundings.
9. Often has poor perception of time and space and often does not keep track of time easily.
10. Often has mixed laterality (left handed — right footed).
11. Often reverses p-q, b-d, n-v, when writing.

Teaching Methods — Auditory
1. Teach them to talk through the steps in a task or activity.
2. Encourage them to spell out loud so they can hear the letters.
3. Say the syllables out loud when attacking words. Point to written words.
4. Encourage them to think out loud, and listen to what they are saying.
5. Encourage oral reporting.
6. Name (say) the punctuation marks when learning to read orally, for awareness.

Teaching Adjustments — Auditory
1. Take out as much noise as possible.
2. Find a quiet place for the student to work.
3. Very soft music background may be used, but definitely not bouncy music.
4. As a teacher, do not talk too much so as to distract the learner.
5. Use as few words as possible.
6. If you repeat, use the same words.
7. Speak directly to the individual.
8. Make use of ear phones and tape recorders to help cut out

Figure 1

Preferential Styles — Cognitive Mapping

Teaching Methods — Auditory
7. Utilize tape-recorded instruction for information and/or examination.
8. Use lots of audio equipment in the learning process.
9. Pair the individual with a visual learner.

Teaching Adjustments — Auditory
distractions of other noises.

IDENTIFYING STYLES — VISUAL LEARNERS
Observations:
1. Often do better when you show them rather than tell them. May have difficulty getting directions orally.
2. Have the tendency to watch your face intently when they are read or spoken to.
3. Like to look at books and pictures; often enjoy working with puzzles.
4. They like things orderly and neat. They often dress in an attractive manner.
5. They can generally find things that are lost, and seldom misplace their own things.
6. They often can recall where they saw something some time ago.
7. They notice details. They are good proof readers; see typing errors, notice if your slip is showing.
8. They can find pages and/or places in a book quite easily.
9. They often draw reasonably well — at least with good balance and symmetry.
10. May use minimal words when responding to questions; may rarely talk in class.
11. May often have auditory problems such as difficulty remembering the alphabet unless starting from the beginning. May reproduce sounds and syllables in odd ways while exhibiting speech difficulty. May have trouble hearing other languages and producing unfamiliar sounds.

Teaching Methods — Visual
1. Give visual directions and demonstrations as often as possible.
2. Use flash cards and wall visuals. Use "look-say" whole word visual discrimination clues in teaching reading or foreign language.
3. Use plenty of maps, graphs and charts using legend symbols.
4. Use color coding systems and and Cuisenaire rods, abacus and other highly visual aids.
5. Teach diacritical marks as pronunciation aids, and employ visual symbols for sounds.
6. Use mirror practice in speech training, and use rulers and and number-lines to develop their

Teaching Adjustments — Visual
1. Take out visual distractions whenever possible.
2. Leave a frame of blank wall space around visual displays.
3. Put a heavy line around worksheet items to help students attend to one item at a time.
4. Give the student a marker to highlight items of importance.
5. Allow the student to point if necessary.
6. Have the student work in a cleared area.
7. Allow the individual to work on one sheet at a time rather than handing the student several papers at once.
8. Try not to stand in front of a

Figure 1

Teaching Methods — Visual
concepts of numbers and number skills.

Teaching Adjustments — Visual
cluttered background when teaching.
9. Give one step of an assignment at a time.

IDENTIFYING SKILLS — KINESTHETIC-TACTILE LEARNER
Observations:
1. Is often quite literally a "mover" and considered hyperactive.
2. Appears to want to feel and touch everything. Rubs hands over objects; "can't keep hands to him/her self."
3. Is usually quite well coordinated.
4. Enjoys doing things with his/her hands. Likes to take things apart. Likes to put things together.
5. May truly enjoy writing things down.
6. Utilizes concrete objects as learning aids, especially those that can be manipulated easily.
7. Learns best by doing and exploring the environment.
8. Often has difficulty with numbers, letters, counting, sequencing and alphabetizing. Has difficulty establishing one-to-one relationships in number values and difficulty learning abstract symbols.
9. Could be labeled an "underachiever."

Teaching Methods — Tactile
1. Use movement exploration. Use a ruler or other device as a number line to learn to count, add, subtract.
2. Have them tap numbers, syllables and tempo.
3. Use learning aids such as sandpaper for tracing and felt markers for reinforcement.
4. Use all the concrete, manipulative devices possible in the teaching/learning mode.
5. Employ role playing where possible.
6. Let them "assist" you in creating learning aids.

Teaching Adjustments — Tactile
1. Use pictures to help establish associations whether in area of words, numbers, or meanings.
2. Attach verbal labels whenever possible.
3. Use visual-auditory, tactile, kinesthetic methods for teaching writing.
4. Allow for planned times for movement and breaks and reorganization of classroom space.

Figure 1

Preferential Inventories — An alternate group of educators is committed to individual diagnosis and evaluation through instrumentation. By means of various discriminators, an individual's cognitive style is ascertained by means of a self-assessment inventory.

There are instruments available for determining educational cognitive style. Discriminators identify and categorize somewhat different items which, when combined, yield a personal profile. While it is not feasible to outline all of the various assessment tools and their discriminators, in an effort to provide a more detailed view, Figure 2 delineates the twenty-seven (27) preferential categories inventoried in just one — the Modified Hill. This cognitive mapping instrument, first developed by Joseph E. Hill of Oakland Community College, can be utilized in a variety of educational environments and requires a minimum expenditure of time to administer.[5] It is currently in use in a number of community colleges committed to the concept of preferential learning style.[6]

ELEMENTS OF COGNITIVE STYLE

1. **Auditory Linguistic** — tendency to acquire meaning through hearing spoken words.
2. **Auditory Quantitative** — tendency to find meaning in terms of numerical symbols, relationships, and measurements that are spoken.
3. **Visual Linguistic** — tendency to find meaning from words you see.
4. **Visual Quantitative** — tendency to acquire meaning in terms of numerical symbols, relationships, and measurements.
5. **Auditory** — tendency to perceive meaning through hearing sound other than spoken words.
6. **Olfactory** — tendency to perceive meaning through smell.
7. **Savory** — tendency to perceive meaning through taste.
8. **Tactile** — tendency to perceive meaning through touch and temperature.
9. **Visual** — tendency to perceive meaning through sight of things other than the written word — pictures, graphs.
10. **Proprioceptive** — ability to synthesize a number of parts into a performance demanding monitoring of a complex task involving controlled musculature — small, large and fine.
11. **Empathetic** — sensitivity to the feelings of others; ability to put oneself in another person's place and see things from his/her point of view.
12. **Esthetic** — tendency to derive meaning through the enjoyment of the beauty of an object or an idea.
13. **Ethic** — commitment to a set of values, a group of principles, obligations and/or duties.
14. **Histrionic** — ability to exhibit a deliberate behavior, or play a role to produce some particular effect on other persons.
15. **Kinesics** — ability to understand and to communicate by non-linguistic functions such as facial expressions and motions of the body — smiles, gestures.
16. **Kinesthetic** — ability to perform motor skills, or effect muscular coordination according to a recommended, or acceptable form.
17. **Proxemics** — ability to judge the physical and social distance acceptable between oneself and another person.
18. **Synnoetics** — personal knowledge of oneself.
19. **Transactional** — ability to maintain a positive communicative interaction which significantly influences the goals of the persons involved in that interaction. Both sides profit from this interaction.

Figure 2

20. **Temporal** — ability to respond or behave according to time expectations imposed on an activity by those associated with that activity.
21. **Associates** — shows the influence on the meaning of symbols derived from the peer group or those with whom the student associates. It is frequently evidenced by an individual who understands that which is under consideration, but explains or discusses with his/her associates.
22. **Family** — stems from the influence of the group of persons an individual considers to be his/her family. The student possessing a strong sense of family relies heavily upon authority figures.
23. **Individuality** — manifest in a student's ability to move freely in a variety of roles and normative situations with particular emphasis on self-directed or self-confident independent behavior.
24. **Difference** — this pattern suggests a tendency to reason in terms of one to one contrasts or comparisons of selected characteristics or measurements.
25. **Magnitude** — a form of categorical reasoning. Persons who need to define things in order to understand them reflect this modality.
26. **Relationships** — this modality indicates the tendency to synthesize a number of dimensions or incidents into a unified meaning, or through analysis of a situation to discover its component parts.
27. **Deductive** — indicates deductive reasoning of the form of logical proof used in geometry or that employed in syllogistic reasoning.

Figure 2

CARE TECHNIQUE

Making a determination of one's preferential learning style, either by formal or informal assessments, does not mean tracking students. The concept does not suggest that it is the instructional goal to teach only to one's preferred mode. On the contrary, the idea is to capitalize on the educational conditions under which a student is most likely to learn, as well as to assist students in identified areas of weakness or non-preference. In an effort to provide a guideline for maximizing learning potential, the CARE strategy was devised. In working with students, teachers should:

1. **Capitalize** — put to advantage an individual's cognitive strengths.
2. **Accommodate** — reduce the task demands on an individual in her or his non-preferred learning style.
3. **Remediate** — equip students with the skills necessary to become more successful in their non-characteristic modes.
4. **Evaluate** — continuously reassess student performance to determine the effectiveness and appropriateness of current instructional methods.

By assessing and inventorying strengths and identifying deficiencies, teachers can plan strategies to enhance the teacher-learner transaction and thereby teach the necessary skills. For example,[7] suppose the majority of students in one class take in information through the written word. It behooves the instructor to insure that a textbook, handouts, visuals, a supplemental reading list, and bibliography are available to students. Despite whatever additional classroom strategies are employed, such as lectures, films, tapes, or field trips, students who need to see the information are insured the opportunity to learn and reinforce in the way that is most meaningful and workable for them.

Employing Preferential Style — It is important to remember that a preferential approach to learning does not mean that the teacher must revamp an entire curriculum. Rather, it means that a variety of techniques must be utilized and a whole array of learning opportunities offered. If a classroom assignment requires that students research and report on a newspaper story, why not facilitate learning and enhance motivation by allowing them to choose from a number of options in accomplishing the task (working independently, in dyads, or in small groups). The same assignment can be modified in numerous ways to make the process enjoyable and meaningful for the learner while still ensuring the completion of the task.

Conversely, if a class in leadership is organized for students to work in small groups for the entire term, does it mean that those who do not function well in a collective environment should be given an alternate option? It is up to the instructor to determine the instructional objective and decide if the goal of the course is to give students experience in group dynamics and process, or if such a format was chosen merely for ease and facility. Often, information about learning style is used intentionally to broaden a student's educational horizons by requiring individuals to work in a non-characteristic manner. By mismatching an individual's learning preference with the performance requirements for a class, the instructional goal is to expand the student's skills through exposure to non-preferred activities and experiences. If, in the case of the leadership class, the instructor chooses to require everyone to work in groups, it is incumbent upon that same instructor to offer support and special assistance to those who are clearly operating in a non-characteristic mode to help them attain the skills and self-confidence necessary to achieve and succeed.

Personalizing classroom experiences is not a monumental task. Often, it is simply a matter of rethinking a traditional approach. Also, reanalyzing the use of preferred style can be beneficial to both teacher and student. Another way is to use non-traditional methods within the learner style. A good way to do this is to personalize classroom experiences. For example, a student, who displayed a strong auditory preference, said it was necessary to be absent for a few days. It was suggested that an audio tape be made of the sessions to be missed. It would be much more meaningful for the student to "listen" to what went on in class than to try to interpret someone else's written notes. Although the initial reaction was astonishment over such an idea, the final evaluation was, "Why haven't I ever thought of that before?"

This illustrates a second important point: students must take responsibility for designing new ways to enhance their own learning. By understanding their own preferential profiles and cognitive styles, students can begin to improve their study habits and skills by selectively choosing the settings and materials that are most appropriate for maximizing their potential. Instructors can assist in the process, but students ultimately assume the responsibility. Adaptability and flexibility are watchwords for both students and teachers as each begins to work on developing unique approaches and alternative strategies which enhance individual learning.

Multiple Uses — Information about an individual's educational cognitive style and preferential approach to learning is being utilized in a variety of ways. It serves as:
1. A basis for helping students plan their own educational programs and develop life-long learning habits.
2. A means by which classroom teachers can modify the learning environment to provide a variety of learning activities consistent with individual needs.
3. A basis for re-examining delivery systems to determine if the learning environment is biased.
4. A basis for career counseling and vocational guidance.
5. An alternative method for re-examining staffing patterns and designing management teams to ensure a variety of perspectives and a broad representation of individual strengths and styles.
6. A basis for the development of teacher-student learning contracts which specify the methodology appropriate for the achievement of goals and objectives.
7. As a means of celebrating individual differences and honoring diversity in adult education classrooms.

SUMMARY

Preferential learning style, or cognitive mapping, is not an educational panacea. It should be used carefully and tentatively as a professional tool to assist in personalizing and revitalizing instruction. Educators can learn to transpose learning style information into instructional improvement plans and successfully modify their own teaching styles through pre-service and inservice training.[7]

Adult educators have an opportunity to further refine the science of andragogy by translating preferential style information into more effective classroom strategies that will enhance the process of lifelong learning and maximize the learning potential of adult students.

Although the previous educational emphasis has been on teaching "content" in a singular, step-by-step, logical, rational manner, the emerging paradigm suggests that the emphasis is on the "context" of learning. Students are learning how to learn, and how to process information in ways which are most meaningful to them. The confluence of analytical, linear, left-brained, rational strategies with holistic, intuitive, right-brained strategies, has resulted in a whole-brained approach to education. The goal is to design programs to fit learners instead of fitting learners into standardized programs.

QUESTIONS AND EXERCISES

1. As a classroom teacher, you are faced with the option of implementing a preferential style approach to learning in your classroom. Cite the reasons for supporting or opposing such an idea.
2. Once an individual's educational cognitive style has been determined, how should this information be utilized by both the teacher and the student?
3. Describe at least two methods or techniques that can be developed for working with auditory learners? With visual learners?
4. What can you do to modify your own teaching style and leraning environment to "personalize" the curriculum?

REFERENCES

1. Witkin, Herman A. et al, "Field Dependent and Independent Cognitive Styles and Their Educational Implications," Educational Testing Service, *Review of Educational Research*, Winter, Vol. 47, No. 1, 1977.
2. Witkin, Herman, "Cognitive Style in Academic Performance and in Teacher Student Relations," in *Individuality in Learning*, San Francisco, Jossey-Bass, 1976.
3. Terrell, William R., "Anxiety Level Modification by Cognitive Mapping," *Community and Junior College Quarterly*, October/December, 1976.
4. Dunn, Rita, Kenneth Dunn, Gary Price, "Learning Styles: Research vs. Opinion," *Phi Delta Kappan*, May, 1981.
5. Hill, J.E., and Nunnery, D.N. *The Educational Sciences*, Bloomfield Hills, Michigan, Oakland Community College Press, 1976, Revised.
6. Keyser, John S., "Cognitive Style Mapping at Mt. Hood Community College," *Community College Review*, Volume 8, 1980-81.
7. Doebler, L.K. and Eicke, F.J., "Effects of Teacher Awareness of the Educational Implications of Field-Dependent/Field-Independent Cognitive Style on Selected Classrom Variables," *Journal of Educational Psychology*, Vol. 71, No. 2, 1979.

Use Volunteers Successfully

Jonathan McKallip

Director of Field Services
Literacy Volunteers of America, Inc.

Volunteer: One who enters into or offers himself for any service of his own free will without expectation of remuneration.

Alexis de Tocqueville, in his book *Democracy in America,* wrote:
In no country in the world has the principle of association been more successfully used or applied to a greater multitude of objects than in America ... There is no end which the human will despairs of attaining through the combined power of individuals united in a society.

Thus it is in this country — volunteers crucial to an evolving and functioning democracy. Today's volunteers are indeed on the front line of social progress, continuing to shape tomorrow. But this shaping emanates from a rich volunteer heritage.

In the 18th century and earlier, the typical American volunteer was not known as a "volunteer," and by today's standards, did not act like a volunteer. He or she — frequently he and she together — were simply helpful neighbors, as the typical American family farmer. They were members of a closely knit face-to-face community centered around a small village or town.

In 1866, a post Civil War literacy campaign was launched to educate Blacks in the South. During this drive, it seems, only 1,300 literacy volunteers taught approximately 90,000 students in some 1,000 southern schools. Within three years, literacy work grew. By 1869, there were nearly ten thousand teachers addressing this task. And even with the repercussions of slavery during this era, it seems that only half the tutors were white. The rest were northern and southern Blacks.

Ellis and Noyes,[1] in their book *By the People,* mention the growth of the Moonlight School in North Carolina, which emphasized education for mill workers. In 1915, North Carolina had eighty-two evening schools with 1,600 illiterate students enrolled. By the next year there were seven to eight hundred classes with an enrollment of nearly ten thousand.

Volunteerism is a significant, valuable and exciting field. Like other institutions, change came slowly. In this time of rapid change, however, a long view can provide a perspective and a sense of direction which will help us keep those institutions which are important to us.

In order to do this, there must be effective management of volunteer programs. To discuss the essential functions of a successful volunteer program, apply them to an imaginary ABE program. There are over 300 students in this rural program and only five teachers. Funds are scarce, and the only way

Use Volunteers Successfully 279

to meet the needs of many of the students is to use volunteers to augment the work of the teachers.

THE VOLUNTEER PROGRAM

Planning/Coordinating — The Director of Adult Education, with the permission of the Superintendent of Schools, and the endorsement of the Adult Education Advisory Committee, has the responsibility for answering the following questions:
1. How many volunteers can we use?
2. What services will they provide?
3. What kind of training can we give them?
4. How many students will they reach?
5. Who will supervise them?
6. How much will the program cost?

He decides to spend some of his scarce funds to hire a Coordinator of Volunteers to organize the program. Together they make a decision to use volunteers to supplement the work of the teachers — teaching the lowest level students on a one-to-one basis. They plan a yearly calendar beginning in the fall, marking off dates for public relations activities, pre-service and inservice training sessions, recognition events, reports.

They also set goals for the year expressing them in terms of the number of volunteers to be recruited and trained, the number of workshops to be held to train, and the projected number of students to be taught. In order for these goals to be met each of the functions must work together. They draw up job descriptions for each volunteer job, noting the requirements for the job, the training provided, to whom the volunteer is responsible, and the time commitment required. Each volunteer will be given a copy of these standards, thus diminishing the chances of misunderstandings.

Recruiting — The Coordinator of Volunteers decides to seek the help of a public relations consultant (a volunteer, of course) to carry out the public relations campaign. This campaign, they decide, must be constant and ongoing. The ABE name and program must be kept before the public. Special newspaper stories, radio spots, and posters will be used to recruit volunteers. Flyers will be put in bags at the local grocery store, and each church in town will be asked to put an announcement in their weekly bulletin. These activities will be repeated throughout the year.

Training — Volunteer programs often succeed or fail depending on the extent to which they provide training for volunteers. The Coordinator of Volunteers decides to follow the model for successful programming, and uses three steps:
1. Orientation.
2. Pre-service training.
3. Inservice training.

Orientation will be held two to three weeks prior to the first pre-service training session. At this session, potential volunteers will be given an overview of the program, exactly what is expected of them, and an appointment to sign up for the workshop. Often people decide this is not what they thought it was going to be; often they get so excited they recruit other friends to join. An orientation session removes many of the problems that can occur in volunteer programming because volunteers are made aware that they are going to be treated professionally.

Prior to this orientation, a session has been held to acquaint the ABE staff with the fact that volunteers are necessary to the effective delivery of services in their area. The staff is also invited to the volunteer orientation, so they begin to perceive the volunteer as a partner in the education of adults.

Pre-service training sessions need to be designed to help volunteers do their job better. Since the volunteers will be teaching students on a one-to-one basis, they need an orientation to adult students — something of their background and life styles; techniques for teaching basic reading and writing, oral communication, and/or computation skills. Sessions will be held over a two-week period on Tuesday and Thursday evenings, and take approximately twelve hours. The Coordinator uses ABE teachers as workshop leaders, utilizing their talents in an effective manner. The outline of the training session is drawn up to include not only teaching techniques but also an orientation to the ABE Center: its facilities, its policies and procedures, and the relationship of the volunteer component to the rest of the programs.

Inservice training has already been scheduled for ABE teachers periodically throughout the year. All volunteers will be invited to participate in these sessions, but the Coordinator realizes it is also important to have special sessions for the volunteers, too. After all, some of their needs and concerns are different from those of the ABE teachers. So an inservice session is planned for six weeks after the volunteers begin teaching in order to get them together and let them discuss successes, problems, areas of concern. Another one will be planned for the Spring.

Matching — There are numerous tasks a volunteer can perform in the total operation of a literacy program — tutor, recruiter, matcher, public relations consultant, supervisor, workshop assistant and/or leader.

When matching volunteers with the job and the student(s) they are best suited for, the Coordinator takes into account numerous factors. Included are: skills, training, times available, geographical location, and personality traits. These are some of the same factors that are looked at from the student's point of view also. One way to insure volunteer satisfaction, is good job placement, and the Coordinator understands the necessity for matching carefully. However, poor matches are sometimes made, but are not irrevocable. Changes can be made and satisfaction guaranteed.

Supporting Roles — The Coordinator of Volunteers realizes that ongoing support of the volunteer is vital to a successful volunteer program. This support comes in many forms, but two of the most important are supervision and communication. Each volunteer is assigned to an ABE teacher — their first-line supervisor. That teacher will help them plan; answer questions when problems arise; encourage them when things seem rough. That teacher will also be the volunteer's friend, making him/her feel a part of the program.

Communication is also an important support function and manifests itself in three ways: newsletters, meetings, and accessibility of leadership. Newsletters for the volunteers are vital for many reasons: to let them know when inservice training sessions will be held; new teaching techniques; new student books in the area of adult education; new volunteers' names and addresses (everyone likes to see his/her name in print); announcement of other local, regional, state or national conferences which would be helpful to the volunteer. Meetings for the sake of meetings are useless, and no one likes to attend them! Therefore, the Coordinator decided early on that meetings will be held only when they are necessary, and that they will have a very specific purpose, with that purpose made known to the participants.

Accessibility of leadership is one aspect many volunteer coordinators forget. That accessibility to the leadership is very important to the volunteers. They need to know who the Coordinator of Volunteers is; who the Adult Education Director and Superintendent of Schools are — and that they can be approached with ideas and suggestions which will be listened to. Time is therefore made for the leaders to speak at each training session, to have them indicate their respect for the volunteers' commitment and contribution to the program.

Record Keeping/Accountability — At some point, the Superintendent and Advisory Committee is going to ask: "Is this volunteer program working?" In order to begin documenting this, the Coordinator designs forms which keep pertinent volunteer information: name, address, phone number, workshop(s) date(s), assigned student, areas taught, special talents, inservices attended and dates, other relevant information. From time to time questionnaires will be designed to gather specific information; workshop and inservice evaluation forms show reactions to specific topics and indicate need for additional work. Student information is already kept on prescribed forms by the adult education administration. Volunteers should be encouraged to add their comments to these records.

Evaluation — At the beginning of the program year, certain goals were established. At the end of the year, it is time to see if those goals have been met. To avoid one common pitfall of volunteer programming, the Coordinator decides to do a written evaluation of the program. This evaluation includes an objective look at each of the goals and how well they were met, as well as recommendations for changes that will improve the program next year. This is also the time to establish goals for the next year, and a tentative calendar. In effect, the evaluation function is the end process, but also the beginning of the planning process for the coming year.

Recognition — Payment for volunteer services comes in numerous guises. But the biggest payment is in **recognition.** There must be ongoing informal recognition — a pat on the back by the ABE teacher; a "how are things going?" from the Director of Adult Education. But there must also be public formal recognition. The Coordinator decides that in the spring there will be a Recognition Banquet, perhaps with the meals being donated by local merchants. Included in the program will be words of welcome by the Superintendent of Schools; recognition of the number of hours volunteers have served, with special recognition for those who have served over 100 hours during the past year; and an entertainment program. This is another way to create public awareness of the program for there will be publicity before and after.

Budgeting/Financing — Volunteer programming is not without costs. But the cost is far less for the services rendered than it would be if full-time teachers were hired. Some of the costs include volunteer tutor materials, in-service materials, administrative costs (supplies, postage, reproduction), public relations, recognition events. These are, for the most part, "up-front" costs. The Coordinator of Volunteers also realizes the value of in-kind services — meals donated by local merchants; cost of printing of posters; value of time donated by volunteer tutors, public relations consultant, in-service leaders, tutor designed materials. But all of these should be included as the total cost of a volunteer program is compiled. What do we get as income (real or in-kind)? What are the costs (real or in-kind)?

SUMMARY

A volunteer program in adult education can be a great addition to the delivery of services in these times of deep budget cuts. There are a number of things that must be kept in mind before embarking on a volunteer program.
1. To be successful, a volunteer program must have the active, visible support of the administration and staff. All must be willing to work together for the ultimate benefit of our adult students.
2. The essential functions — planning/coordinating, recruiting, training, matching, supporting, record keeping/accountability, evaluating, recognition, budgeting/financing — must mesh together in order for a program to be successful. If one function is weak, the whole program will exhibit signs of weakness.
3. The benefits of community support are enormous. As people become actively involved with a program, they feel a sense of ownership. When a program budget is in the process of being cut, these actively involved volunteers will fight for the program.

Recognition that volunteer programs are not without cost will finally permeate. Recognition will also come that expenditures for volunteer programs purchase what money cannot buy — citizen awareness, citizen concern, and the neighborly knowhow . . . No force is great enough to stop the concern of the citizen for his fellow man.[2]

REFERENCES

1. Ellis, Susan J. and Katherine H. Noyes. *By the People: A History of Americans as Volunteers.* Philadelphia: ENERGIZE, 1978.
2. Nathan, Cynthia. "The Volunteers of the Seventies." *Vocational Guidance Quarterly,* June 1971. p. 42.
3. Ilsley, Paul J., and John A. Niemi. *Recruiting and Training Volunteers.* New York: McGraw-Hill Book Company, 1981.
4. Loeser, Herta. *Women, Work and Volunteering.* Boston: Beacon Press, 1974.
5. Naylor, Harriet H. *Volunteer Today — Finding, Training and Working with Them.* Dryden, New York: Dryden Associations, 1973.
6. Schindler-Rainman, Eva, and Ronald Lippitt. *The Volunteer Community.* Washington, D.C.: NTL Learning Resources, Inc. 1971.
7. Wilson, Marlene. *The Effective Management of Volunteer Programs.* Boulder, Colorado: Volunteer Management Associates, 1976.

Keep Your ADA

Gordon G. Darkenwald

*Associate Professor & Director of the Center for
Adult Development, Rutgers, State University of New Jersey*

Because adults are usually voluntary learners, recruitment and retention of participants are major concerns of both researchers and practitioners. Retention and recruitment are closely linked. Some of the factors that promote or deter participation likewise affect retention or dropout rates. More to the point is the obvious futility of recruiting adults for educational programs only to have them leave shortly after enrolling.

Why do adults drop out? What can be done about it? Drawing on the thin base of theory and research currently extant, some responses are evident. First, however, it is important to consider what the terms "dropout" and "dropout problem" mean.

Defining the Problem — Although the concept of dropout seems like a straightforward one, in reality it is not. One can look at the issue from a teaching or administrative perspective, or from the vantage point of learning and of the learner. Emphasis on the learner's intentions is important. Therefore, the following definition will be employed: "Dropouts are persons who, having enrolled in an adult education course or other learning activity, and having completed at least one class or comparable activity, cease attendance before having satisfied their objectives for participation."[1]

This definition highlights the voluntary nature of adult education and the primacy of learning over teaching. It also acknowledges the reality of "positive dropouts," that is, persons who cease attendance when their particular learning objectives have been achieved. Consider, for example, a course in filmmaking. One person may enroll to learn scripting techniques and another to acquire skill in using 16 mm. cameras. Both, after gaining the knowledge they want, may stop attending the course. Are they really dropouts? They might have to be counted as such for administrative purposes, but conceptually such "positive terminations" are different from negative ones. The problem lies with the latter, the true dropouts. There are also, of course, "no shows" and chronic absentees. They too pose difficulties, especially the irregular attenders who, in many cases, end up as dropouts.

Put simply, adults drop out from educational activities because they see little benefit in persisting, because they find it difficult to maintain attendance, or for both reasons. From the learner's point of view, dropping out is not the problem but the solution. The question, then, is what is the cause of the problems? Often the problem lies with the educational program itself: (1) poor planning, (2) poor management, (3) poor teaching. To the extent that this is the case, adult educators must be concerned, for we are inflicting harm on both our students and ourselves. The most obvious harm to students is that they fail to gain the knowledge or skills they want or need. In addition, some may suffer the effects of diminished self-esteem if they blame themselves for having in some way failed. Even more serious is the possibility that a very negative experience may transform a dropout into a permanent non-participant. The adult education program and its staff pay a price too. Dissatisfied dropouts communicate their negative feelings about the program to others, creating a host of potentially serious problems. Budgets and jobs may not always be jeopardized, but professional self-esteem generally is.

Understanding the Dropout Phenomenon — Nearly twenty years ago, Verner and Davis reviewed some 30 dropout studies and concluded in effect that there was nothing to conclude.[2] In the last two decades many more studies have been conducted, some using sophisticated research methods. What is lacking are conceptualizations, models, or theories — frameworks to guide fact collecting, to give form and meaning to data, to help us understand what we know or think we know.

If the facts — the research findings — fail to speak for themselves, one approach to the problem is to begin with the theories or conceptual frameworks and then examine the facts to see if or how they fit the explanatory scaffolding. Although attempts at theorizing are not well developed in this area, even a crude theory can be useful in helping us organize our thinking.

Theoretical Perspectives — Two of the more sophisticated efforts to explain why adults persist in or drop out from educational activities are: (1) Boshier's congruence model[3], (2) Rubenson's[4] expectancy-valence schema.

The concept of congruence is used by Boshier in several ways. Intraself congruence is the equivalent of healthy psychological adjustment, and is manifest in growth-oriented or self-actualizing persons. Its flip side, intraself incongruence, is characterized by "deficiency-motivated," other-directed, or neurotic behavior. Boshier asserts this is more prevalent among lower than middle or upper class adults. The model predicts that intraself incongruence leads to self/other incongruence (between self and other students, and self and teacher) and that self/other incongruence, in combination with certain unspecified social, psychological, and subenvironmental (classroom) factors, leads to dropout. Although Boshier has not demonstrated a connection between intraself and self-other incongruence, he has reported evidence that measures of self-ideal self, self-other student, and self-teacher incongruence are associated with dropout behavior.[3] Thus, adults who feel "different" or uncomfortable in a particular educational setting are likely to drop out. It seems almost certain that such persons, had they expected to feel incongruent or out-of-place, would never have participated to begin with. Apparently, then, incongruence often stems from discrepancies between one's expectations of what a learning situation will be like and one's actual experience of it.

Expectancy-Valence — Interestingly, the concept of "expectation" is at the heart of expectancy-valence theory. The theory, simple put, asserts that learners will persist if they perceive a specific course or other learning activity as satisfying an important need (positive valence) **and** if they expect to be able to maintain attendance or otherwise successfully cope with the demands of the activity in question (positive expectancy). If expectancy and valence are both highly positive, then one would predict persistence. If both are low, or one has a value of zero, then dropout would be predicted.[4] The basic features of the model are shown in Figure 1.

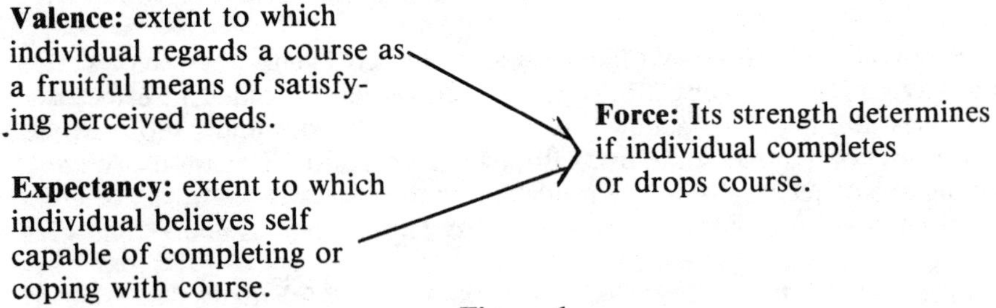

Valence: extent to which individual regards a course as a fruitful means of satisfying perceived needs.

Expectancy: extent to which individual believes self capable of completing or coping with course.

Force: Its strength determines if individual completes or drops course.

Figure 1

A virtue of this model is its recognition of the importance of barriers (both internal and external to the individual) in accounting for dropout. The benefits to be gained from a course may be highly valued, but if an adult experiences or anticipates difficulties with learning or regular attendance (examples of expectancy factors), then persistence becomes doubtful.

At least three general propositions can be deduced from the congruence and expectancy-valence theories:
1. Adults whose personal dispositions or abilities tend to be incompatible with the interpersonal or task orientations of an instructional situation are likely to drop out.
2. When an adult perceives that his or her expectations of gaining specific benefits from participation are unlikely to be realized, he or she will probably drop out.
3. When barriers to participation or other costs are perceived as greater than the anticipated benefits, the probable outcome is discontinuance of attendance.

RESEARCH FINDINGS
Incongruence/Lack of Fit — Research shows that dropouts, compared with persisters, are not likely to be well-educated, white, and middle class.[5] Age is also a factor. Dropouts from vocational training and adult basic education are considerably more likely to be in their teens or early twenties rather than mature, "settled down" adults. On the other hand, if one examines dropout

rates among adults 60 years of age and older, the relationship is reversed. The "old-old" (75 and over) are more likely than the "young-old" (55-75) to drop out.[5] Clearly, the former face considerable greater obstacles to maintaining participation. Research by Zahn, however, suggests that where ability is relevant to performance or success in adult education, it is likely to be linked to persistence.[6] These findings support the notion that dropout is related to a "lack of fit" or incongruence between personal characteristics or needs and the characteristics or demands of the typical classroom environment.

Frustrated Expectations — Not surprisingly, adults who feel they are not gaining the benefits from participation that they expected are very likely to become dropouts. In fact, satisfaction, measured as the expected versus actual helpfulness of a course in meetings one's objectives for participation, is ever more potent than educational level in predicting dropout. When expected benefits are relatively clear or concrete, the perception that they might not be obtained is especially likely to promote attrition. For example, Lewis et al.[7] studied participants in a human resources training program who expected that the training would help them find satisfying employment. When it became clear that the training would not be likely to lead to good jobs, they dropped out. Clearly, frustrated expectations are a major contributor to the dropout problem.

Excessive Costs — When the costs of continued participation are perceived to outweigh the anticipated benefits, adult students will usually drop out. The term "cost" refers to any negatively perceived concomitant of participation — inconvenience, anxiety, frustration, boredom. Costs arise from the nature of the teaching-learning transaction itself (difficulty of learning), program context factors (availability of support services), and external situational factors such as illness, childcare problems, and overtime work. The research suggests that all three categories of costs, often in combination, affect persistence. Boshier indicates that adult students who feel "psychological distance" or incongruence between themselves and their teachers or other aspects of the learning situation are likely to become dropouts. On the other hand, Darkenwald suggests that teacher sensitivity to the needs and life experiences of undereducated, minority group adults is closely linked to lower dropout rates. Other research indicates that, on the programmatic level, courses that meet over many weeks or months have higher dropout rates than short courses.[5] Such findings as these have important practical implications. How a program is designed and administered and the teaching-learning process are factors that administrators and teachers can in part control.

PREVENTING DROPOUT

Success in recruiting students is achieved through effective program planning and promotion; success in retaining students is due to the effective and sensitive management of the teaching-learning transaction.

Administrative Considerations — Poorly planned and promoted programs set the stage for student frustration and attrition. The most serious and widespread defect in program planning is insufficient attention to needs assessment, leading to programs or courses that fail to provide what learners want and expect. As a rule of thumb, the greater the input (however obtained) from the target population of learners, the better the needs assessment. Other problems in planning relate to the appropriateness, utility, or convenience of format and methods, facilities, support services, and scheduling. For adults, conserving time and "blocking" it in convenient ways are especially important considerations in designing and scheduling learning activities.

With regard to promotion, two principles should be kept in mind to minimize the dropout problem: (1) promotional messages should not promise more than the course or program can deliver, (2) communicate accurately, clearly, and in sufficient detail what the prospective student can expect to learn, how the course will be taught, and how the learning may be used for needs satisfaction. Care must also be taken to convey clearly any experience or skills that may be prerequisite to success in a particular learning experience. Adherence to these principles will minimize the gap between the learner's expectations and his or her perception of the actual learning experience, thereby reducing incongruence and attrition.

Teaching-Learning Considerations — To retain adult students, the teacher or group facilitator must make every effort to create congruence between the students' expectations of the teaching-learning process and their actual experience with it. On a general level, most adults expect the following:

1. To actualy learn what they want to learn.
2. To be able to apply their learning in the real world.
3. To be capable of coping with the teaching-learning process.
4. To be treated like adults in an open and relaxed learning environment.
5. To be given a measure of responsibility or allowed some self-direction in their learning.
6. To have whatever relevant experience they or others possess acknowledged and utilized in the learning process.
7. To receive timely feedback on their performance, including assistance and encouragement from the teacher/facilitator.

First Class Meeting — The first meeting of a class or group is particularly important for promoting student retention. Most teachers are aware that the first session can "set the tone" for what follows. More to the point, it creates initial impressions (that is, expectations) that, if negative, can be difficult to alter. The initial meeting is also critical because it is the appropriate time for the teacher and students to discuss and "negotiate" their expectations concerning the objectives and procedures of the learning process. The teacher has the opportunity to make adjustments in his/her initial plans to accommodate the needs, interests, and capabilities of the learners — to undertake an informal needs assessment. Teacher and student expectations of objectives and the learning process are often at odds, leading to incongruence from the student's perspective and thus dissatisfaction and attrition.

Therefore, it is important to create an informal, adult-like atmosphere to set people at ease and reinforce positive expectations. Informal seating arrangements, refreshments, self-introductions, and ice-breaking exercises are some of the techniques for accomplishing this. The teacher or facilitator should conduct an informal needs assessment, tailoring techniques for doing so to the size, purpose, and composition of the class or learning group. As a rule, information from students should be elicited first (their problems, concerns, interests, goals). With this information at hand, the teacher/facilitator can then discuss and adjust or negotiate his or her expectations with those of the group.

Teacher's Role — Following the first class session, preventing dropouts is mainly a matter of being a sensitive, flexible, and capable facilitator of learning. Involving adults actively in their own learning, drawing on their experience, encouraging increasing self-directedness, and addressing individual needs and differences in learning style are especially important. So, too, is sensitivity to the fact that many adults are full of anxiety and self-doubt when returning, after many years, to the role of student. They require ongoing positive feedback, assistance, and encouragement.

Very often in adult education it is necessary for the teacher to assume the role of counselor. Many adults, particularly those who are less advantaged, are overwhelmed by personal problems that can interfere with learning or continued attendance. Teachers can help by making referrals (to health or social service agencies), by providing information and advice, or simply by being a sympathetic listener. Finally, the teacher of adults must be alert to signs of trouble that can lead to dropping out. Irregular attendance is the most obvious. Less self-evident are symptoms of frustration or stress, including inattentiveness, apathy, irritability, withdrawal, and negativism. Two successive absences are reason enough to follow-up and show concern, either informally through other students or by phone or by mail. As for symptoms of frustration or stress, once the teacher recognizes them he or she can often deduce the cause and perhaps do something about it. If the cause cannot easily be determined, a sensitively worded question or two can often uncover it. The counselor role may not be a familiar or welcome one for many teachers, but to prevent student dropout it is often necessary to assume it.

SUMMARY

Dropouts are students who cease attendance without having satisfied their objectives for participation. Dropping out is a solution to problems that often stem from poor planning, administration, or teaching. Discrepancies between students' expectations of a learning activity and the activity as they actually experience it promote dissatisfaction and attrition.

Adult educators can minimize the gap between expectations and reality by communicating accurately what students can expect to gain from a course, the methods of learning to be employed, and any prerequisite experience or skills. At the classroom level, it is important that teachers adjust their initial plans and expectations so that they are congruent with those of the group. This can be accomplished by soliciting information from students at the first class session concerning their needs, interests and general expectations. This needs assessment should be repeated at regular intervals throughout the duration of the course. Finally, teachers must often be willing to play the role of counselor. They need to be alert to signs of frustration or stress, and take action to identify and resolve problems that interfere with learning or continued attendance.

REFERENCES

1. Darkenwald, G. *Retaining Adult Students.* Columbus: ERIC Cleainghouse on Adult, Career, & Vocational Education, Ohio State University, 1981.
2. Verner, C. and Davis, G. "Completion and Dropouts: A Review of Research." *Adult Education* 14 (Spring, 1964).
3. Boshier, R. "Educational Participation and Dropout: A Theoretical Model." *Adult Education* 23 (Summer, 1973).
4. Rubenson, K. and Hoghielm, R. *The Teaching Process and Study Dropouts in Adult Education.* Stockholm: Stockholm Institute of Education, 1978.
5. Anderson, R. and Darkenwald, G. *Participation and Persistence in American Adult Education.* New York: College Board, 1979.
6. Zahn, J. "Dropout and Academic Ability in University Extension Classes." *Adult Education* 15 (Fall, 1964).
7. Lewis, M. et al. "Recruiting, Placing, and Retaining the Hard to Employ." University Park: Institute for Research on Human Resources, Pennsylvania State University, 1971.
8. Darkenwald, G. "Some Effects of the 'Obvious Variable': Teacher's Race and Holding Power with Black Adult Students." *Sociology of Education* 48 (Fall, 1975).

Helping Adults Get /Hold Jobs

Harlan L. Polsky

*President, Human Discoveries, Inc.
Instructor, California
State University, Los Angeles*

Edgar M. Easley

*Dean, Continuing Education
City University Los Angeles*

People have always entered adult classes for a variety of practical reasons. With millions unemployed and other millions in fear of unemployment, chances are that more adults than ever are looking for ways to get a job or hold on to the one they have. As an adult educator, you can help them. Whether or not you have developed a course, "How to Get a Job," you can provide practical, workable strategies helping your students get/hold a job. There is little mystery in getting a job; there is a rational set of strategies to put the student where the job opening is and let the student put "his best foot forward." Adults should, in so far as possible, be aware of the real world of work and how employment offices operate. Stating it otherwise, the student needs to be aware of the technical/social systems that make for compatibility with his/her unique set of skills.

JOB GETTING STRATEGIES
Step 1. COMPLETING APPLICATIONS — The first step in getting a job is to complete an application. Sample application blanks can be obtained from local employers or offices of the Employment Development Department (EDD) — this assures that applications are relevant to local needs and demands. Secure a supply of job applications and prepare activity kits for **each** student. How to make a packet:
   1. Obtain manilla envelopes or folders.
   2. Glue a sample application, properly completed, to the front of the folder.
   3. Place a blank application in the folder.
   4. Write a series of directions on the back of the folder for the student to follow relating to properly filling out the job application.

Resumes should be inserted in the folder before the unit is finished and mock interviews can be role-played from the completed applications. Primarily the student must be able to complete the application to the standard of 100% accuracy with all pertinent data filled-in. Keep in mind that a well prepared application raises the applicants self-esteem and helps ensure that the interview will have a positive conclusion — **being hired.**

Step 2. TEACH THE PACKET — The student should be taught the following:
1. Read all the directions **before** filling in any blanks.
2. Use the completed application on the cover as a model.
3. Check application after it is completed; have another student check it; have the instructor check it.

Step 3. CHOOSING WHERE TO APPLY — Students need to know that some companies are better suited to their needs than others. How do they judge where to apply? This involves looking at both sides of the employer-employee relationship — the technical/social system of the employer and self-assessment of the job-seeker. Several ways may be used in judging the technical/social systems of a company:
1. Visit the company. Check the location for transportation traveling time.
2. If possible, speak with employees. Are they satisfied?
3. Ask questions of the Employment Development office. Is there a high turnover? Why?
4. What kinds of goods and/or services are produced?

It is fruitless to seek employment in a company where the student's needs and desires are not compatible with the organization. It will be a short-lived employment.

Step 4. REVIEW THE APPLICATION — Before assuming that a completed application is an understood application, go over it with your students. Do they understand the terminology? What are "dependents"? How specific must one be in listing "physical handicaps"? It is important to have students check the accuracy of dates, names, and addresses. Are the dates jumbled so that a person worked at two places at the same time? Will the tracer letter return due to an insufficient or incorrect address? Remember, the application often **precedes** the applicant's going through the door of the employment counselor. Are qualifications met — "Graduated high school" is not the same as "Left in the 12th grade." Also, ask your student to assess the companies in terms of his/her capabilities:
1. Will the company require independence of judgment and decision making?
2. Is there a merit system for recognition of outstanding performance?
3. Is the company one that has innovative and rapidly changing procedures?

4. Is job performance rated often and rigorously?
5. Is personal contact with supervisors encouraged or is it managed by bulletin and memo?
6. Does senior management become personally interested in day-to-day operations?
7. Do fellow-workers tend to divide into neighborhood, racial, or social cliques?

All of these are important questions (some may not be answered) and can also lead to that inevitable time when the applicant is asked, "Do you have any questions?"

Step 5. JOB PARAMETERS — It is well enough to want a job, but it is better to know some of the ramifications of seeking a job. They are twofold: (1) personal dimensions, (2) career and vocational dimensions. From a personal viewpoint some areas of employment bear heavily on personal life. Is the student "bondable"? Bonding can lead to an exhaustive review of prior employment and personal life.

Some students should be made aware of this. In the same light an honest discussion of arrests should be undertaken — never in the specific; always in the general. Equally as important is the impact of social security information on some students who may be in social service programs. Will employment lead to being "cut-off"? What is the cost of the "trade-off"? Some companies encourage relatives to bring in prospective employees; others discourage it. What is the effect of Cousin Charles having told the student about a job opening?

What does the application say about you as a person? Is it neat, accurate, complete? Are lines scratched out; handwriting illegible? Is printing done when called for? The other side of the larger area of job seeking is related to whether the prospective line of work is one in which there is substantial demand. Obtain assistance from your local EDD office on job trends and openings. Incidentally, this provides an excellent opportunity for the teacher to provide career education training.

Step 6. ROLE-PLAY — THE INTERVIEW — A job interview is a traumatic experience for many; you can build confidence through a relaxed series of role-playing exercises involving you and the students (instructor/employer — student/applicant, student/employer — instructor/applicant, student/employer — student applicant which allows for developing ease and familiarity. Before the role-play begins discuss what each party wants from the interview. The employer **wants** a good employee; the applicant **wants** a good job. It may be wise to have the initial role-play built around the completed applications. This also reinforces the belief that a properly completed application aids the interview. Make sure that the role-play asks for references, past experience, work schedules, hours available. Do not allow personal or privacy invasion questions to be asked, nor tolerated. Care must be taken to give each student practice in speaking.

Possibly, a tape recorder would be the best device for building awareness of diction, the inevitable "UH's" and the lack of response to direct questions. Some successful teachers of interviewing also relate the skills to:
1. Written summaries of the interview.
2. Telephone follow-up. Thanking the interviewer for the interview is not only courtesy — it keeps you in mind.
3. Repeat the interview with a foreman or supervisor on more technical aspects of the job.

A written summary of an interview is one of the best self-teaching devices a student can use in perfecting interview techniques. This leads to the next and inevitable step — preparing a resume.

Step 7. PREPARING A RESUME — Writing a resume is a major challenge for many students. Often they have great personal charm and good verbal skills, but the resume may be woefully inadequate. There are some important facts to know about resumes:
1. Each resume gets about a 45 second review.
2. Usually three out of five are given closer inspection.
3. Approximately one out of 150 applicants for each position is chosen for an interview.

Earlier, mention was made of self-assessment. Just as it is an important part of preparing for an interview, it is also an important preparation for writing a resume. Some steps for self-assessment are:
1. Develop a short but thorough autobiography.
2. Chronologically list education and jobs.
3. List professional goals or job interests.
4. List and rank significant achievements.
5. List some personal highlights (travel, trophies).
6. Hobbies and leisure activities.

A word should be said about style and format (see Figure 1). Always have the resume typed. If it is not possible to have it typed, a business letter is preferable. This applies even if it is a blue-collar skilled job. Have the students go back to their packets and pull pertinent information needed in the resume. They will be surprised to know that different companies emphasize different aspects of an applicant's background. It is well to emphasize:
1. Use plain English. If a sample of literary work is desirable, it should be attached.
2. Practice writing the resume several times. They usually improve with repetition.
3. Use the resume writing as a language lesson. Let the students find synonyms for often-used words, thus avoiding dullness.
4. Encourage each student to think of his/her own unique capabilities. Before moving to the next step, review the resume for completeness and accuracy. Does it contain: vital statistics, employment goals, education and training, work experience?

SAMPLE CHRONOLOGICAL RESUME

Sara Jones
1111 Wilderness View Drive
Los Angeles, California 90000
(213) 555-1010 — Hone
(714) 555-1111 — Office

Marital Status — Single
Age — 23

CAREER OBJECTIVE
Writer in the public relations department of a large manufacturing firm.

EDUCATION
June, 1980 — Bachelor of Science Degree in Communication Arts — California Polytechnic University, Pomona

RELATED COLLEGE ACTIVITIES/EXPERIENCE

September, 1979 To June, 1980 — Publicity Chairperson for Cal Poly Pomona Concert Choir. Responsibilities included coordinating mailings, designing posters, and issuing press releases.

September, 1978 To June, 1980 — Staff writer for the Cal Poly Pomona student newspaper. I wrote articles and sold advertising.

January, 1977 To June, 1980 — Cal Poly Pomona chapter of the Public Relations Student Society of America. I was the Vice-President and planned competitions, seminars and social functions.

June, 1979 To September, 1979 — Jones & Associates, Inc. — Montclair, California I served an internship as a writer, creating public relations and advertising material.

WORK EXPERIENCE

March, 1979 To Present — First Intercity Bank — Pomona, California I am responsible for marketing banking services and processing customer transactions. I also coordinate the bank's payroll bond program.

June, 1978 To March, 1979 — Pomona Parks & Recreation Department — I was the Music Director for the public relations program.

References are available upon request.

Figure 1

Step 8. THE INTERVIEW — The students is ready for the big day — the interview. Are you sure? His/her personal behavior is now to be reviewed by the prospective employer. A poor presentation can undo all the good work of a completed application or of an excellent resume. Here is a list of items to note for that day:

1. Does the student have the appearance of really wanting the job — bright, alert?

The teacher you can help by having a file of pictures of people in various occupations. Let your students see how workers are dressed and evaluate the appropriateness of each. In looking at Figure 2 have the students review certain important aspects of the "Do's and Don't's."
3. Does the student's manner project a sincere, forthright attitude? Watch for shifting eyes, timid seating, slouching.
4. Is his/her rate of speech too slow or too fast? This is an art that requires practice to get "just the right pace."
5. Is the interview relaxed due to being on time and mentally prepared? Are there signs of "fidgeting"?
6. Has the student thought of questions to ask the interviewer?

INTERVIEW DO'S

DO Practice interviewing techniques with family and/or friends.
DO Be well groomed and dress appropriately for every interview.
DO Arrive early for any and all interview appointments.
DO Smile and be friendly with the interviewer and other staff.
DO Shake hands firmly with the interviewer — this goes for ladies, too.
DO Speak clearly and concisely at all times.
DO Be aware of body language during the interview.
DO Clearly identify specific job and/or career goals.
DO Ask questions about the firm and the position for which you are applying.
DO Listen carefully to questions and instructions.
DO Be prepared to discuss compensation and benefits.
DO Introduce pertinent information as necessary during the interview.
DO Ask for the job — if you really want it.
DO Follow-up with a "thank-you" letter within one day after the interview.

INTERVIEW DON'TS

DON'T Appear overly anxious — to get hired or to get a paycheck.
DON'T Smoke, chew gum or eat mints during the interview.
DON'T Be critical when discussing former employers.
DON'T Talk about things which are unrelated to the interview.
DON'T Try to dominate the interview.
DON'T Forget that every interview is a two-way street.
DON'T Be falsely modest when discussing your education, abilities, & experience.
DON'T Be overly confident, either.
DON'T Be afraid to ask for the job, if you really want it.

Figure 2

Step 9. **DEVELOP JOB-GETTING MIND-SET** — One of the most important things students may need in getting a job is mind-set. Think about employment — think about many kinds of jobs. Make a survey of fifty (50) jobs available within a mile radius of the students' home or the adult education center. Look at the richness and breadth of employment. It is said that often jobs are like rocks at your feet — waiting to be turned over. Discuss jobs in other areas especially if unemployment is high locally. Have some frank discussions of the pros and cons of commuting or relocating. Assist your students in deliberation over rumors of good jobs 1,000 miles away. Be positive about the need for family security, combating loneliness, "tide-over" funds. You have a responsibility to assist students in learning how to make decisions. If they decide to relocate, assist them in securing information so as to make the move in the best way.

Another essential factor in job mind-set is thinking "like the boss." Discuss why employers demand punctuality. Develop the concept that productivity provides a paycheck. A popular news columnist recently reported that many of today's youth do not relate productivity to Friday's paycheck — being physically present merits a paycheck. Adults cannot afford this mind-set — they need to get and hold a job. Practice and emphasize reasons why following directions are important. Students should be made aware that rules infractions often violate safety regulations and may have serious consequences. A good spelling and vocabulary lesson might be to use a list of employer "attribute" words such as **dedication, conserving, preparation, malingering** and then discuss the concepts of these terms.

Step 10. **REWARD AND CLOSURE** — When a student has gone on a successful interview, let him/her share it with the class. If they were employed, let them tell what it was that brought success. It may be well to have a question and answer period. After all, they can teach this lesson better than you.

For some students a written summary can be given. Let them give you a paragraph or two for subsequent students to read. After all, nothing validates your teaching like an employed student.

Sample Student Report — I am _____. I am now a truck driver. True, I knew how to drive a truck, but I didn't know much about getting a job. In this class I learned how to look for a place that needed truck drivers and how to prepare myself for an interview. I practiced interviewing and when I went on an interview the first time I didn't get hired. I practiced some more and on the second try I got the job. I'm happy I practiced learning how to get a job.

SUMMARY

There is almost no mystery to getting and holding a job. These are skills that can be taught. When students are aware of the real world of work, they can begin to approach job-hunting in a systematic fashion. Classroom learning can provide this system. The technical/social system of each company that a student should consider can be the basis for considerable discussion before wasting time filling out applications at every open door. Have your students ask themselves if it is a place where they would like to work.

Then engage in role-play until they are comfortable with interviews and be sure they know the local job-hunting resources. Above all, teach students:
1. Have a mind-set to want a job, want **this** job.
2. Stay on the point and answer questions directly, honestly, and forthrightly.
3. Use good standard English.
4. Tell the employer you want the job.
5. Avoid discussion of troubles with past employers.
6. Know what is expected of you — hours, days, extra assignment pay, benefits.

With this in mind, send your students off to happy job seeking.

Use Non-Paid Professionals

Golda Bockbrader

*Director of Special Volunteer 310
Project for Adult Basic Education
State Department of Education
Lincoln, Nebraska*

Leonard R. Hill

*Chief, Adult and Community Education
State Department of Education
Lincoln, Nebraska*

Shirley Heymann

*Coordinator Adult Basic Education Division
Phoenix Union High School System*

Volunteers, also known as non-paid professionals, are capable of becoming a viable force in the adult education field. As tax dollars are declining, administrators are looking for ways to maintain the levels of their programs with reduced funds. Many progressive administrators are utilizing volunteers as they realize a person does not have to be paid to provide quality education. VOLUNTEERS CAN BENEFIT THE PROGRAM.

The volunteer of today is a precious commodity and resource. No longer is the volunteer visualized as "the little old lady in tennis shoes" who delivers flowers or magazines in hospitals. Today the volunteer serves in many capacities and has a wealth of knowledge and energy to share.

Volunteers are people who know they have but one life to live and endeavor to make the world a better place than they found it while they are here. The challenge for administrators is to entice these volunteers to serve in their program.

Volunteers can serve in many and various capacities. An administrator needs to be prepared to identify them for the services they can perform. In designing a program to fit your specific needs, remember this fact — YOU CAN'T BUY WHAT A VOLUNTEER GIVES!

With the working hours and strains of one's profession today, people are looking for an outlet to relieve their tensions. The volunteer assignment, therefore, has to be one that is worthwhile and rewarding. It cannot be "busy" work as the volunteers have to feel that they are needed and are making a real contribution. People are realizing the need to volunteer but will be most selective in how and where they give their time. The volunteers have the personal need to achieve while on assignment or they will not meet or attain the goals they set when deciding to volunteer. As with all of us, they need to feel good about themselves and what they are doing.

SETTING UP A PROGRAM

Before designing the program one needs to consider the problems as well as the strengths of utilizing volunteers. Problems might be:

1. **Staff acceptance versus rejection.** Many professional people feel threatened by volunteers entering their profession. Without adequate preparation and acceptance a professional can ruin a volunteer program as fast as it is developed. There are many ways to obtain acceptance but perhaps one of the most effective is to have the professional prepare a "dream list."

   This could be accomplished by asking the adult educators to objectively review the necessary tasks they perform in class and what needs to be done for the students who are attending and who are not attending. After listing all of the tasks associated with the program, the professionals should place an asterisk(*) before the items they feel a volunteer could perform so they could use the volunteer's experience and training to better advantage. A double asterisk (**) should be placed by the students who could benefit from individual volunteer tutoring.

   On a separate sheet, the adult educator should prepare a dream list which would consist of things they would like to do in class or see the agency do, but are not being done now. The reasons may be lack of time, skills or other resources. After compiling the list, conduct the following test:

   a. Are volunteers capable of performing the tasks?
   b. Could volunteers be trained to perform the tasks?
   c. Is the adult educator comfortable delegating the asterisk and dream list items to volunteers?
   d. Will the agency hire paid staff for these tasks?

   After the adult educator has identified how volunteers could benefit the program, volunteers should be recruited and assigned by the adult educator to perform the tasks. Of course, it is anticipated the majority of tasks will be individual tutoring, counseling or follow-up.

   In following the format, the adult educator should not feel threatened by the volunteer entering an established class. Cooperation is an essential element in the growth of feeling non-threatened. A sense of camaraderie, when developed, will be built around both professional and volunteer understanding that they share a common goal — providing service to the students. Open communication and ready accessibility, as well as an openness to change, are factors decisive in creating a cooperative spirit.

2. **Administrative problems can be numerous** — yet pre-planning will overcome most of them. Some of the pre-planning tasks of the administrator are:
   a. Orientation — No matter how qualified the volunteer is, they need and must be acquainted with the theories and procedures in the program and/or classroom. A typical twelve hour orientation might consist of seven (7) hours of theory and procedures and five (5) hours devoted to cultural and language differences of the anticipated students.
   b. Record keeping — There are some necessary forms associated with volunteers. Examples are a data form, contract form, time sheet to be used for tax purposes, recognition, and evaluation.
   c. Recruitment efforts — Using volunteers is not confined to the education field and the competition is keen. You are going to have to expend time to entice the volunteer to your agency. This means developing brochures, handouts, preparing news releases, making presentations to civic and church organizations, keeping the program constantly before the public. Volunteers do not just appear. Here is an example of a successful flyer distributed to churches, community clubs, shopping malls, schools, other adult education students, volunteer agencies, selected industries, radio and TV stations and local newspapers.

LEARNING ENGLISH AT HOME
IS THE FIRST BIG STEP TOWARD PERMANENT SELF-RELIANCE FOR THE INDOCHINESE REFUGEE NEW TO THE VALLEY.

Have you been thinking you'd like to do SOMETHING to help the Indochinese Refugees but don't know just what or how? Would you like to acquire a skill, learn about Indochinese cultures and help people in the process? The Volunteers for Refugee Self-Sufficiency Program (V-FoRSS) is now training volunteers to teach English-as-a-Second Language to Vietnamese, Cambodian and Laotian refugees who are resettling in the Phoenix area. If you would like to learn how to help these people learn English, and are able to give four (4) hours a week of your time for three (3) months, please call V-FoRSS and add your name to the growing list of volunteers who would like to receive this training and be of help. KNOWLEDGE OF A FOREIGN LANGUAGE OR PREVIOUS TEACHING EXPERIENCE ARE NOT REQUIREMENTS; SENSITIVITY TOWARD AND TOLERANCE OF CULTURAL DIFFERENCES ARE.
For more information, call _____ and ask for _____

Figure 1.

   d. Writing and keeping assignment descriptions current and ethical — A Volunteer will be quickly "turned off" if it is not clear what exactly is expected of him. Assignment descriptions should contain: assignment title such as tutor, teacher aide, hours of assignment, supervisor's name, location of assignment, approximate length of assignment including beginning and ending dates, skills required, training required, goals and objectives of assignment, overall description of the expectations of the volunteer. Also, volunteers may feel more comfortable with a description of the students' responsibilities to the volunteer.

e. Interviewing — This is a must to enable the coordinator to assess the volunteer's skills and match those skills to program needs. It is at the interview that a number of things can be discovered and it is here that the ultimate judgement must be made as to whether the volunteer will be beneficial to the program.

f. Recognition — This should never be overlooked. This is a top priority item in a good program. A lack of recognition may give the volunteer a feeling that he/she is not performing a useful service.

g. Communication — Allow time for the volunteers to discuss their concerns about what is occurring in the classroom and provide input of how possibly things may be done differently. In many cases the director's only source of information regarding some aspects of instruction are the volunteers.

h. Inconsistency of time given — Even the most dedicated volunteer will encounter situations which will cause them to be absent from their assignment. This has to be accepted and allowed in scheduling.

i. Turnover requires training — About the time you think you have a solid program, you will encounter volunteers who have to leave for a variety of reasons — loss of babysitter, accepting a paid job, illness in the family.

j. Student or client rejection — There are some students who are reluctant to accept the volunteer. The ground rules must be clearly established beforehand and carried through in a consistent manner. However students should not be allowed to choose volunteers in a thoughtless manner.

k. Flexibility in utilization of volunteers — The staff has to be flexible in utilizing volunteers. Some thought has to be expended to use the volunteers in a productive manner. Should their students fail to come to class, rather than sending the volunteer home, substitute other meaningful tasks for them to accomplish.

STRENGTHS

1. **Student benefits** — The students greatly benefit from volunteers in the classroom by receiving more individual attention. This can result in progressing at a more rapid rate or thereby encouraging them to attend more regularly. A contagion quickly develops in a structured program — the volunteers feel good about themselves — the students acquire

improved self esteem and the teacher can take pride in what is occurring in the classroom.
2. **Staff/teacher benefits** — The staff or teacher benefits by having more time to devote to other duties and other students, thereby allowing for more planning time.
3. **Community benefits** — As the community becomes involved in the program, the program becomes more effective. If funding cuts are huge, it certainly helps to have the community knowledgeable about the program and to have letters written to those who can affect the cuts.
4. **Students feel a greater responsibility to attend** — After all if a volunteer is willing to give of their time to assist, the student feels a greater commitment to be present — to be helped.
5. **Program growth** — As volunteers accept responsibility to help your program, your need for tax dollars can decrease as well as your abilities to provide additional services increases.
6. Other strengths — Volunteers benefit your program in many ways outside the classroom: in areas of legislative issues, clerical, public relations, babysitting, artwork, advisory boards, cooperative efforts committees, student recruitment.

When it is truly recognized that strengths outweigh the problems, then develop and implement a good volunteer program.

SETTING UP A PROGRAM

The success of a volunteer program, once it is endorsed and accepted by the administrator, will depend on the selection of the volunteer coordinator (paid or unpaid). Qualifications specify good organizational skills and ability to deal with people. In reviewing the responsibilities of the coordinator one does not have to question why organizational skills carries a top priority. Taking into consideration that the coordinator may not have prior experience in the area of education, the first criteria is a thorough orientation of your philosophy and program. The coordinator is the liaison between your program and the community.

TITLE: Adult Education Volunteer Coordinator
QUALIFICATIONS: Previous experience as a volunteer or volunteer coordinator.
Good organizational skills
Enjoy working with people
JOB RESPONSIBILITIES:
1. Volunteers:
   a) Recruitment of volunteers
   b) Orientation of volunteers
   c) Train volunteers — develop training sessions and materials for initial and inservice training sessions
   d) Placement of volunteers
   e) Maintain follow-up of volunteers
   f) Evaluation of volunteers

g) Provide recognition of volunteers
   h) Establish recordkeeping system for volunteers
   i) Coordinate with local education inservice training.
2. Clients:
   a) Identify areas where prospective clients are located
   b) Recruitment of clients
   c) Referral of clients to the program which best suits their needs
3. Community Resources:
   a) Identify community resources interested in this project
   b) Recruitment of persons from various sectors such as business, education, and libraries to assist in this project
   c) Identify ways these community resources can assist with this project e.g. establish an advisory committee, enlist support for specific purposes
   d) Maintain a community support system
   e) Identify learning sites
4. Referral Agencies:
   a) Identify referral agencies
   b) Establish a written procedure for referrals
   c) Maintain a good working relationship with the referral agencies
5. Promotion:
   a) Presentation to community organizations
   b) Develop promotional literature
   c) Work with local media for public information, recruitment, and awareness purposes

Be certain you have obtained staff acceptance of volunteers. Time and money will be wasted as well as a loss of volunteers if one has not thoroughly accomplished this task.

Develop an advisory committee to work directly with your coordinator. Select key people from the community. Representatives from various organizations and individuals such as librarians, former students, American Association of University Women, retired teachers, coordinators of other community volunteer programs. Select, if possible, those who "know how to get things done." The purpose of this advisory committee is to set goals and objectives for the growth of the volunteer program and to assist the coordinator in reaching these goals. When necessary make sure your advisory committee works closely with the advisory committee of the parent (funding) organization.

Recruitment — The primary rule is: "Do not overlook anyone." Do not decide for anyone that they will or will not volunteer. Ask them. Let them make the decision.

Recruiting volunteers should not begin until a complete file of assignment descriptions has been written. It is important that when someone asks for help they can explain what they want done. You are involving the volunteer in a professional field and should be professional in knowing what is wanted in the line of service. This will enable them to make an honest commitment. Many methods of recruitment are available to an ambitious coordinator who is prepared to use them.

One of the most successful is a satisfied volunteer recruiting volunteers. An enthusiastic volunteer can convey a feeling of need for more help in a program in a way that makes people want to say, "yes."

"Word of mouth" from a student telling a neighbor about the great volunteers helping in the classroom, spreads the word. Or, someone hears a volunteer telling of his/her experience and again the word spreads.

Use the news media in presenting human interest stories about the students and volunteers and what is happening. Get the public interested in the human side of your program instead of quoting statistics. Make use of public service time available through radio and television stations. Use volunteer artists to design coordinated posters and brochures (keep them simple — do not overwhelm people with detailed printed material). Let your students know you are looking for volunteers as they have contacts in many areas of the community. One danger in students' recruiting volunteers is that often they are not aware of the criteria for volunteers. Unless the criteria is explained thoroughly, students may recruit a large number of persons who may not or could not be used as volunteers.

Letters to the ministerial association will secure both students and volunteers. Organizations will not generate as many volunteers but should be included for program presentations. Members of these organizations have spouses and acquaintances who might be sent your way. Establish contacts in organizations and secure membership lists if available. Turn on the enthusiasm and do some telephone calling.

Do not sign up the volunteers over the phone. Instead, invite them to visit your program so you can explain it in person.

Be flexible in the amount of time you ask them to commit. Some volunteers will help every week while others are willing to serve as a substitute. Know how to utilize the time they have available and take advantage of any and all time.

Look for every available sign board or electronic sign and get your catchy message about needing volunteers in front of the public. Learn why the volunteers who are serving have volunteered. From this determine if there is a recruitment tool you haven't utilized.

Placing — Before assigning the volunteers, have them fill out a data form which can be used as a basis for the initial interview. Follow the interview with a tour of the learning site, observing their reaction to students, teacher and classroom setting. This gives an opportunity to alleviate their fears and answer questions. Remember that not every volunteer belongs in the classroom. You can still use their expertise. If volunteers have a preference of assignment, try to assign them in that area or explain why it is not possible at the time. Do not let them start with a false conception of their placement. It is wise to have a **Volunteer's Manual** in which the various roles of the volunteer are spelled out. Before placement let them review these roles and allow them, whenever possible, to choose the placement they wish.

Terminating — This is a term that creates concern used in conjunction with a volunteer. But the time has come to take such steps if volunteers are being used in a professional manner. Termination is never an easy task but it is one that must be done eventually if wrong placement has occurred.

If termination is necessary, it must be accomplished in a tactful way. Suggest other assignments the volunteer could perform in your program or if the problem warrants termination, suggest other agencies as an alternative. **Terminate but do not alienate.** Evaluation of the volunteer's performance will assist in this task. If you have faithfully evaluated and discussed the volunteer's performance, you are not going to have as difficult a task as it otherwise could be.

Promoting & Rewarding — To coordinate a successful volunteer program, recognition must be provided for your volunteers. There are as many ways as there are volunteers to provide recognition. It is up to the coordinator to implement those which meet the needs of the volunteer and the budget of the program.

Some examples of recognition are listed:

1. Promote a volunteer to another assignment as progress in their present assignment is made. Example: A volunteer who excels in tutoring could be utilized to orient new volunteers or could be used as a recruitment presenter.
2. A recognition ceremony, no matter how elegant or how simple, should be held at least on an annual basis.
3. A certificate of appreciation says "Thank You" in a professional way and can be used for the volunteer's portfolio.
4. Individual recognition on a daily basis using terms such as, "We missed you last week when you were absent," "How was your vacation?" "Thanks, you are a great help." "Susie is certainly advancing with your help."
5. Birthday cards (if budget allows) or a personal letter of appreciation on the volunteer's service anniversary date will let the volunteer know he/she is not taken for granted.
6. Letters of reference for work credit will be appreciated by the volunteer who finds it necessary to seek paid employment.
7. Often students wish to give recognition to their volunteer tutors. These expressions of gratitude, simple as they may be, often mean more to the volunteer than all of the certificates in the world.
8. A subtle, but effective form of recognition, is for the administrator to visit the instructional scenes many times. The volunteer knows that you are interested and appreciates your interest when you drop in and show your personal concern.

SUMMARY

Volunteers will bring new life to a program that has been in existence for years. The secret to success in benefiting from volunteers is to remember that professional people need to accept the fact that volunteers of today are also professional, with the difference being they are unpaid and have chosen who they want to serve. **Take advantage of the volunteer's expertise but do not take advantage of the volunteer.** Do not ask the volunteer to do what you would not be willing to do.

When you have a good volunteer do not "wear" them out. Make the experience an enjoyable venture. Be prepared to stand up and fight for the needs and rights of the volunteers you represent.

REFERENCES

1. Naylor, Harriet H. *Volunteers Today: Finding, Training and Working With Them.* New York: Association Press, 1973.
2. Scheier, Ivan H. *Winning With Staff, A New Look at Staff Support for Volunteers.* Boulder, CO: National Information Center on Volunteerism, 1978.
3. Wilson, Marlene. *The Effective Management of Volunteer Programs.* Volunteer Management Associates, Boulder, CO, 1976.

Career Planning — Job Getting Skills

Richard S. Deems
*Assistant Professor, Adult Education,
Iowa State University; Consultant, Career Development*

John Hartwig
*Consultant, Adult Education, Iowa State Department of Public
Instruction; author of articles on Adult Counseling*

Life/Career planning and Job Getting Skills are based on the process of life/work planning developed by John C. Crystal in the late 1940's. Crystal reported 86% of those who used the process found ideal jobs in a reasonable amount of time.[1] Deems found 50% of those persons taking part in career planning workshops in a three state area had changed jobs, and 92.1% reported the process had helped them make decisions about their futures, whether they did or did not change jobs.[2] In a recent study, Deems concluded that using Holland's "My Vocational Situation" Inventory pre-post measure, program participants: (1) made significant changes in the areas of occupational choice, (2) identified factors involved in career decision making, (3) developed strategies involved in finding a chosen job.[3] These skills were observed as a result of participation in career planning workshops.

Total life planning is the goal of the career counseling program.[4] The basic philosophical foundations of this program closely follow the precepts described in the conceptual model. It takes into consideration that people change, and introduces a process that can be used repeatedly in one's life.

Consideration of a person's life style is an integral part of this program in which personal values and life goals are identified and articulated. The whole person's life, or life space, is explored: temperament or personality strengths, barriers, external considerations, and short/long range goals and objectives come into focus during the program. It is a program that focuses on total life planning in a way that assists in interfacing all aspects of life.

As Figure 1 illustrates, an "Ideal Job" is the result of interfacing one's total self. The skills one most enjoys using is a significant part of this interfacing process to determine an ideal job. Significant variables such as values, preferred working environments, and life-goals are taken into consideration. External variables such as health needs, family considerations, consequences of previous decisions, and financial needs also interface. Finally, temperament or personality is considered when defining an "ideal job."

IDEAL JOB MODEL

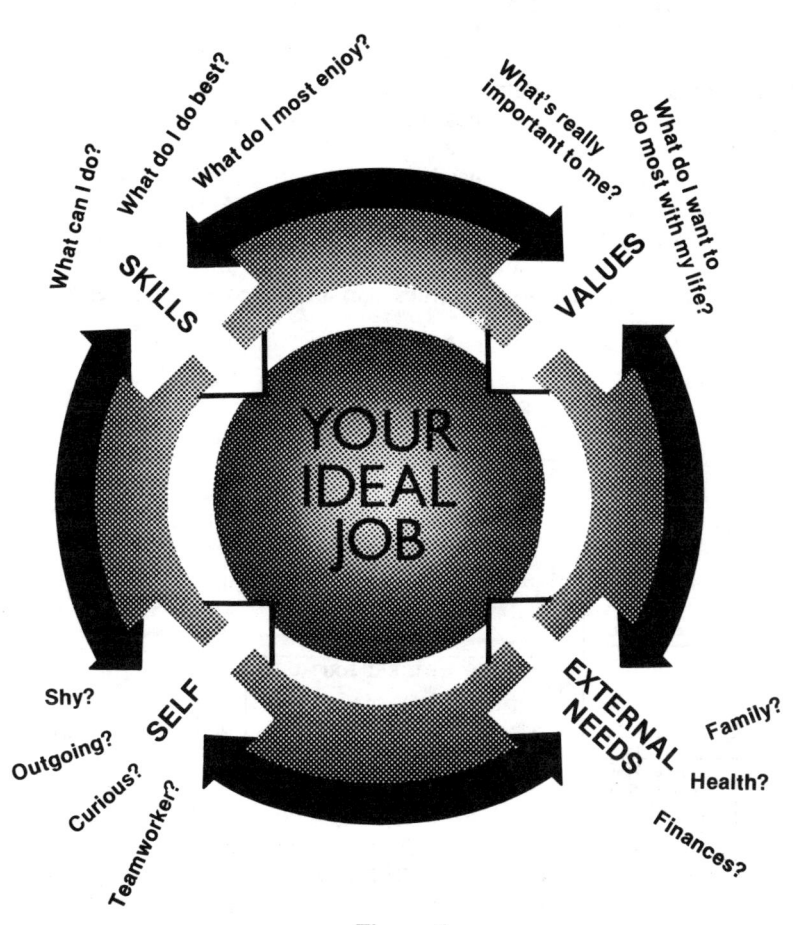

Figure 1

The career counseling program postulates three main questions: (1) WHAT do I want to do? (ideal job tasks) (2) WHERE do I want to do it? (ideal job purposes) (3) HOW can I find it? (Ideal job description).

IDEAL JOB TASKS

The first question, "What do I want to do?" relates to skills and skill identification as a major component in identifying ideal job tasks. Using either the autobiographical approach[1] or the matrix approach,[5] persons were able to identify several hundred functional, transferable skills. Either process makes use of life experiences with transferable skills identified through a process of analyzing life events.

Though this process may take longer than utilizing standardized interest inventories, experience has shown it is far more beneficial: (1) it identifies more skills than other kinds of instruments, (2) it is more personal, since skills are identified through a personal life history — this approach tends to have more power and meaning, (3) it helps relate skills to specific life events. In a hiring interview, one can easily and quickly discuss transferable skills in relation to specific times those skills have been used.

Figure 2 is a Planning Chart used within the program which illustrates the many dimensions considered in the ideal job. As noted, not only transferable skills but skills a person most enjoys using (prioritized skills) are considered. The prioritized skills are usually the most highly refined skills. Once these prioritized skills are identified, values and preferred environments can be brought into focus.

PLANNING CHART

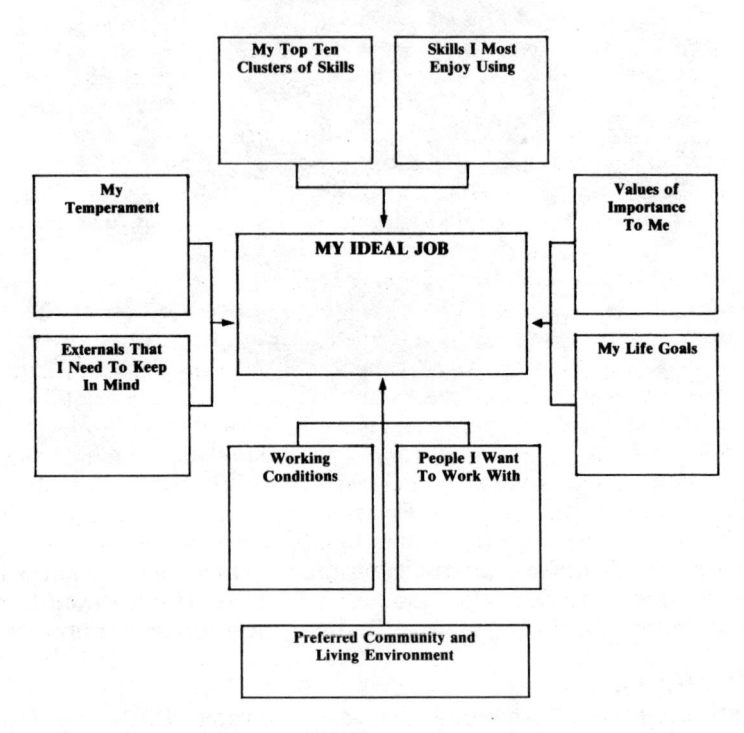

```
         My Top Ten          Skills I Most
       Clusters of Skills    Enjoy Using

   My                                        Values of
Temperament                                  Importance
                    MY IDEAL JOB                To Me

 Externals That                              My Life Goals
 I Need To Keep
    In Mind

            Working         People I Want
           Conditions       To Work With

              Preferred Community and
                Living Environment
```

Figure 2

One's temperament or personality strengths are identified and become part of the interfacing process. This process insures that temperament and personality strengths become essential ingredients of the ideal job. For example, a shy person should not consider being a salesperson, or one who likes to work as part of a team effort would not enjoy working in relative isolation. By identifying primary temperament characteristics, the process facilitates designing an ideal job that is suited to the individual.

Identifying values and life goals is important. The purposes for which skills are used can be an essential part of job satisfaction or dissatisfaction. If one's job is not an extension or compatible with one's life goals and objectives, that job will often be viewed as unimportant. The result is job dissatisfaction.

IDEAL JOB PURPOSES

The second question, "Where do I want to do it?" focuses on values and goals. These are the first major components of ideal job purposes.

"The main purpose of adult counseling is to help adults identify those behavioral changes that are personally significant."[4] Similarly, the main purpose of values clarification and goal-setting, within this process, is to assist adults interface their personal values and life goals into their ideal job. Thus, their job becomes an extension of what is important to them.

The process assists in identification, establishment and attainment of life goals. The steps needed to reach each objective are formulated resulting in a detailed plan-of-action. If a given objective is to be obtained, the following steps must be considered: (1) develop an appropriate plan of action, (2) identify proper sequence of life experiences, (3) predetermine time parameters, (4) implement the plan of action.

The kind of environment in which one lives and works is the second major component of ideal job purposes. The process assists identification of: (1) working conditions liked or disliked, (2) kinds of people with whom one **wants** to work, (3) kinds of people with whom one does **not want** to work, (4) what ideal community-living arrangements would be. Crystal refers to this concept as "The Principles of Exclusion." The concept stresses becoming thoroughly familiar with the factors one likes or dislikes, the result of which is to exclude possible job opportunities with distasteful conditions and focus energies on obtaining the kind of job which will be satisfying and rewarding.

External variables, with this model, refer to those factors primarily outside one's control, but which still need to be considered when designing an ideal job. For example, health is a consideration for persons who can not function well in cold weather, or persons with allergies would not choose to live in certain parts of the country. Salary one wants to make (or needs to make) may also be considered, since previous decisions often determine the income a person needs to pay bills. Family commitments must be thought of as an external variable. If a commitment has been made to care for elderly parents, then a new job several hundred miles away is not realistic unless your parents can also move. Commitments to "significant others" may be involved, so consideration of a job in some other location is not realistic.

The third major component of ideal job purposes is the "tradeoff" concept. This concept needs to be emphasized when dealing with external variables. The tradeoff concept is referred to when one gives up something in order to obtain something else of equal or greater value. For example, one may tradeoff living in the beauty of the north woods in order not to suffer from a cold and damp climate. On the other hand a sacrifice may be made by not moving to another city for a job in order to continue living with a significant-other person. The main point to remember about tradeoffs is options are chosen which most closely identify the life forces considered relevant to the situation. No one forces anyone to make a tradeoff.

Thus, the three major components comprising the process of discovering ideal job purposes are: (1) identification of life values and goals, (2) type of working and living environment, (3) the tradeoff concept.

IDEAL JOB DESCRIPTION

The third queston "How can I find it?" identifies the process and components of developing the ideal job description. The planning chart, Figure 2, outlines the process by which the ideal job description is identified. When the planning chart is transferred to a large sheet of paper, and the information for each component duplicated, one is ready to let creativity work. Time is needed to think about the various components and how they interact with each other.

In writing the ideal job description, Figure 3, one of two approaches may be considered: (1) a person can write a detailed description of the ideal job, (2) if it is easier to think in want-ad terms, write that ideal want-ad as if it had one's own name on it.

Here are two examples:

"I am looking for a line position as Director of a team which designs, pilot-tests, refines, and conducts training programs which help adults become increasingly self-directed. Must be able to use my skills in innovative program design, supervising, motivating, and conducting training events. Located in Minneapolis. Salary to be $x. Some international travel involved. Time also provided for writing and consulting. Flex-time work schedule."

"Help Wanted — Energetic innovative program designer needed to direct a team of co-workers to design, test, and conduct programs which help adults become self-directed. Must have highly refined skills in program design, working with a team, and conducting training programs. Located in Minneapolis, with some international travel. Time provided for consulting and writing. Work schedule for team can be flexible. Salary range of $x-$x."

In either form, the ideal job description must focus on the following: (1) skills used, (2) tasks performed, (3) responsibilities assumed, (4) level of position, (5) salary range, (6) what purposes/goals/ends. The more detailed the ideal job description, the easier it will be to locate or create.

At this point, note — no job title has been used. The ideal job description must first be written before a title is assigned. The reasons are: (1) job titles

Career Planning — Job Getting Skills

SUMMARY — LIFE/CAREER PLANNING

**—1—
COMPLETE PLANNING CHART**

SKILL IDENTIFICATION
SKILL PRIORITIZING
VALUES
LIFE GOALS
PEOPLE ENVIRONMENTS
WORKING CONDITIONS
COMMUNITY AND LIVING CONDITIONS
EXTERNALS
TEMPERAMENT

**—2—
IDEAL JOB DESCRIPTION(s)**

DESCRIPTION OF IDEAL JOB(S) FOCUSING ON:
. SKILLS USED
. TASKS PERFORMED
. RESPONSIBILITIES ASSUMED

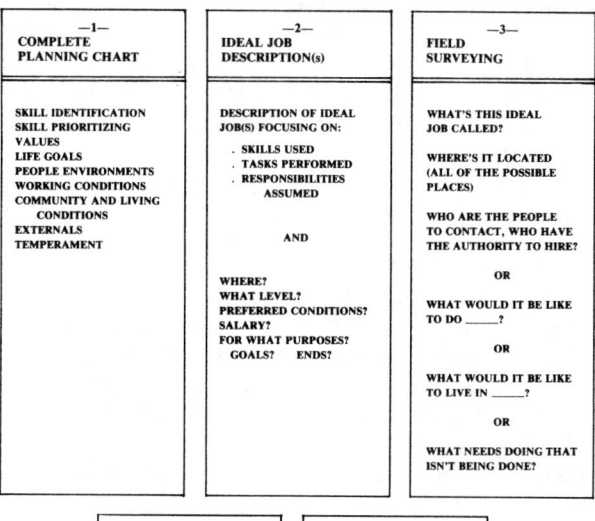

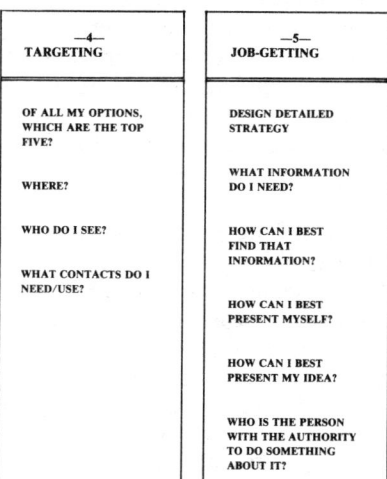

AND

WHERE?
WHAT LEVEL?
PREFERRED CONDITIONS?
SALARY?
FOR WHAT PURPOSES?
GOALS?   ENDS?

**—3—
FIELD SURVEYING**

WHAT'S THIS IDEAL JOB CALLED?

WHERE'S IT LOCATED (ALL OF THE POSSIBLE PLACES)?

WHO ARE THE PEOPLE TO CONTACT, WHO HAVE THE AUTHORITY TO HIRE?

OR

WHAT WOULD IT BE LIKE TO DO _____?

OR

WHAT WOULD IT BE LIKE TO LIVE IN _____?

OR

WHAT NEEDS DOING THAT ISN'T BEING DONE?

**—4—
TARGETING**

OF ALL MY OPTIONS, WHICH ARE THE TOP FIVE?

WHERE?

WHO DO I SEE?

WHAT CONTACTS DO I NEED/USE?

**—5—
JOB-GETTING**

DESIGN DETAILED STRATEGY

WHAT INFORMATION DO I NEED?

HOW CAN I BEST FIND THAT INFORMATION?

HOW CAN I BEST PRESENT MYSELF?

HOW CAN I BEST PRESENT MY IDEA?

WHO IS THE PERSON WITH THE AUTHORITY TO DO SOMETHING ABOUT IT?

Figure 3

change from company to company and from city to city for the same type of work, (2) the same job title may describe two totally different kinds of tasks (and skills needed to complete those tasks) because the jobs are located in two different organizations, (3) a job may be created.

After an ideal job description has been written, there is a need for further exploration to determine if this is the ideal job. Field surveying is a process of discovering information so informed decisions can be made. It enables exploration of job characteristics without actually taking such a job.

The process includes discovering someone doing job tasks similar to the ideal job description. A careful introduction, with an emphasis on discussing job tasks usually results in a positive field survey. In discussing job tasks, Crystal and Bolles suggest three major questions: (1) How did you get into this? (2) What do you like best? (3) What do you like least? If one wishes to continue exploring this job, an additional question may be asked: Who else do you know who does this?

By asking questions and actively listening, valid perceptions can be obtained whether that kind of work is desirable.

JOB GETTING SKILLS PROCESS

In 1979 a meeting was held with John Crystal, Richard Deems, Virginia Dennehey, Roger Hiemstra, and David Tiedeman, to provide input for a career counseling program for undereducated adults. David Tiedeman felt the emphasis of the program should be on "job getting" skills as opposed to "job seeking" and/or "job hunting skills." Thus the term, "Job-Getting" was originated.

The term changes just one word, but that one word change has a very potent effect on the client. In this model, the emphasis is on "getting." Job getting can only occur after completion of the life career planning model. Job getting strategies essentially exist to **obtain** a job as opposed to **looking** for a job.

The "ideal job" results from interfacing various dimensions of: (1) learned skills, (2) values, (3) goals, (4) preferred environments, (5) external variables, (6) temperament. An ideal job is a function of life stage, life style, life space and total life planning.

Eight Step Process — The strategies for developing successful job getting skills involve eight basic steps:
 1. One has to understand some basic job getting facts:
  — Approximately 20-30% of the available jobs are listed; such as in want-ads or through employment agencies. This fact, first reported by Bolles,[6] has been validated by other studies.[7]
  — Employers use want-ads or employment agencies only if they cannot fill the position through friends or other employees.
  — A job is an unmet need — it follows, them, that if one wants a job, an awareness must exist of what the unmet needs are.
  — The use of resumes is a device to screen people out.
  — The basic decision to hire is typically made within the first five minutes of the interview.

By understanding these job getting facts, and designing a strategy that considers the implication of these facts, job-hunting can turn into job-getting.

 2. One needs to discover companies which hire people doing work similar to one's ideal job description. Using contacts and networks, identification of companies should be made. Once identified, field surveying can continue to determine what it would be like to work for organization A, company B, or agency C.

3. "Targeting" is the term used for the third step in job-getting. Targeting refers to narrowing of options to the most promising companies. The targeted companies are the ones which receive most attention.

4. Discovering who has hiring authority to meet the unmet needs of one's ideal job is the fourth step. This person is the object of the final job-getting strategy.

5. Researching the company to find out as much as possible about job functions and real needs. Since a job is an unmet need, the research effort should focus on those unmet needs. A job can be created by asking, "What needs doing that is not being done that I would like to do?" Creating a job takes additional time and effort, but the payoff is often greater than only looking at existing positions. Whether one is attempting to design a job specific to individual needs or responding to a known position, the process is still the same: discover as much as possible about the company.

6. Thinking through the process of addressing unmet needs is next. Take the information gathered, and begin to formulate a plan. This plan focuses on two options: (1) how to meet those unmet needs (create a job), (2) approach the tasks and responsibilities of the vacant position (applying for a known vacancy). For example, if a company were hiring and three people were finalists and only one applicant had thought about how to begin the job — whom would the company most likely hire?" It is that simple.

7. Deciding the best way to present one's self during the job interview. Research of the company (step five) should provide clues to this final phase. Information gathered about the person with the authority to hire is also important. The main thing to remember is to tailor one's presentation to the needs, the organization, and the person who can do something about it.

8. Following through with the job getting plan. Too many plans are shelved at the last minute, because carry through is not implemented. The only way to turn job-hunting into job-getting is to be pro-active.

SUMMARY

Life Career Planning and Job Getting Skills is a synthesis of an academic discipline and a practical series of behavioral procedures.

A combination of life stage, life style, life space, and total life planning orientation is a series of learnings based upon philosophical and psychological principles. They assist adults in identifying significant behavioral changes, in developing an awareness of options for changing behaviors, in achieving personal satisfactions, and in developing a sense of how different life roles make life more fulfilling.

The other orientations is that of the practical counselor — helping adults get a job. Thus it may be used in many different situations since the end result is helping an individual get a job that matches that individual's total life planning concept. It can be readily seen that a concept is the foundation for a practical procedure. This practical procedure utilizes the following strategies: (1) basic understanding of job getting facts, (2) location of work environments which have similar characteristics of ideal job description, (3) targeting of potential work environments, (4) identification of key personnel within the organization who have authority to hire,(5) researching the organization's structure to determine job needs, (6) planning a strategy to meet the job needs, (7) planning an effective job interview presentation, (8) final follow-through on the planning and implementation phases.

REFERENCES

1. Crystal, John C. and Bolles, Richard N. *WHERE DO I GO FROM HERE WITH MY LIFE?* San Francisco: Ten Speed Press, 1976.
2. Deems, Richard S. "Mid-Career Planning Workshops," in *PROGRAMMING FOR ADULTS FACING MIDLIFE CHANGE,* Alan Knox, editor, San Francisco: Jossey-Bass, 1979.
3. Deems, Richard S. "Job Getting Skills — Final Report", ABE Special Demonstration Project, Des Moines: Iowa Department of Public Instruction, mimeographed, 1981.
4. Hartwig, John "Counseling: A Systems Development" *MATERIALS & METHODS in Continuing Education,* Chester Klevins, Ed., Canoga Park, CA 1976.
5. Bolles, Richard N. *WHAT COLOR IS YOUR PARACHUTE?* San Francisco: Ten Speed Press, revised annually since 1975.
6. Bolles, Richard N. *THE QUICK JOB HUNTING MAP — ADVANCED VERSION.* Berkley: Ten Speed Press, 1975 Edition.
7. Deems, Richard S. and Hinman, Dorothy. "Determining the Local Job Market," *JOURNAL OF ADULT EDUCATION,* December, 1980.

Decision Making Techniques

Sally Brew

Counselor, Education Faculty
San Jose State University

Decisions! Decisions! Daily our lives are bombarded by decisions to be made. From the moment we rise in the morning until we go to bed at night, we must make decisions. Think of the decisions you have already made today. What to wear? Should I eat a second piece of toast? Should I scold my son for not doing his homework? Should I quit my job?

How do we make all these decisions? How can we become better decision makers? Decision making is a **skill** that can be learned, can be taught and can be practiced.

To begin, write down briefly the decisions you have made today. Now, evaluate whether these are important decisions for you. What does make one decision more important than another? You might reflect that one decision is considered more important than another if:
1. The decision has long range consequences.
2. The consequences of the decision are unchangeable.
3. The decision affects other people.

Thus, whether to eat a second piece of toast at breakfast is not as important as the decision of whether or not to have a baby, which clearly has an unchangeable outcome. The decision on what to wear today, for most people, on most days, would not be considered important. However, if you had a job interview today, the decision could become important.

STRATEGIES

For many decisions we do not go through a great lengthy process to make the decision. We simplify much of our decision making by routines in our lives. Thus, we choose the same seat in a class. We eat the same breakfast every morning. We choose the same toothpaste every day.

However, if we carefully examine our decision making, we may find that we use a range of decision making strategies which are determined by the decision we are making. We could think of choosing a decision strategy like choosing a club from a bag of golf clubs. We could say that we have a possible bag full of decision strategies at our disposal. We choose the strategy for a decision depending on the type of decision we are making.

Think back over your life and reflect on the decision you have made at major transition points of your life. Transition points are similar for most adults: choosing educational institutions, choosing jobs, making moves, getting married, becoming divorced, having children, entering retirement. What

strategies did you use at transition points in your life? Some strategies are:
1. Choosing intuitively or by what feels right.
2. Choosing to delay or put off a decision until the decision is made for you.
3. Choosing to be compliant or to go along with someone else's decision.
4. Choosing to do what your parents or your spouse would want you to do.
5. Choosing impulsively or leaping into a decision.
6. Choosing rationally or through careful planning.
7. Choosing to do that which makes you first or best.
8. Choosing to do what your family wants you to do.

Thus, we have a choice of strategies. Sometimes we may choose the intuitive strategy or we may use the strategy that is best for one's family. The choice of strategy to be used depends on the situation.

The Rational Strategy — The strategy that most of us would want to choose for important decisions is the rational strategy. The rational strategy takes time to learn and to practice in order to become a skillful decision maker. To begin with, examine the four basic information requirements needed to make a good decision:
1) What are the possible **alternatives?**
2) What are the possible **outcomes?**
3) What is the **desirability** of these outcomes?
4) What is the **probability** of these outcomes?

DECISION TREE
XYZ MODEL OF DECISION-MAKING

Alternatives (3)	Outcomes (5)	Desirability (Rate of Outcomes—5 as high, 1 as low)	Probability of Outcome	Product	Sum
X	X_1 X_2 X_3				
Y	Y_1 Y_2 Y_3				
Z	Z_1 Z_2 Z_3				

Instructions: Choose your decision. Pick 3 alternatives and write them in the space provided (XYZ). Pick 5 possible outcomes for each alternative. Evaluate under colums 3, 4 & 5. Find the products for each outcome. Add the products for each alternative. The alternative with the highest sum is the most rational decision.

Figure 1

Decision Making Techniques

In order to be a skillful decision maker, a decision "tree" should be used to summarize the information. An outline of a decision tree using the four information requirements is given in Figure 1. Suppose you have three alternatives for your decision: x, y, z. You may have some dissatisfaction with your current job. Your decision concerns what to do about your job dissatisfaction. Three alternatives to your decision of relieving your job dissatisfaciton may be:
1. x = make change to another company and do same job.
2. y = seek another position within current place of employment.
3. z = make no change.

Actually, there are more alternatives to this decision, but for simplicity purposes, only three alternatives (x, y, z) will be used in this example.

Alternatives
x = make change to another company
y = make change within company
z = make no change

The next step in the rational decision making process is to examine the possible outcomes for each alternative. The outcomes can be generated by using Figure 2 in terms of gains and losses to self and others.

	GAINS	LOSSES
SELF		
OTHERS		

Figure 2

In a job decision, possible outcomes to be evaluated are: (1) money, (2) advancement, (3) security, (4) relationships, (5) challenge, (6) location, (7) training, (8) stress, (9) self-approval, (10) family impact.

The next information requirements for a rational decision are to determine the desirability and probability of each outcome. Therefore, if an increased income is an important outcome to consider in a job decision, then you need to ascertain the desirability and probability of earning more money in the event of a job change.

Desirability is really values-clarification. What do you want most in a job? Right now, make your own list of the outcomes which are most important to you in making a career decision. The ten outcomes listed above are suggestions of what may be of importance to you.

To determine the probability of each outcome occurring in an alternative is a tricky, subjective task. Yet, in decision making, estimating the probability of an outcome occurring is often overlooked. For instance, you desire to earn more money in a job change, but what really is the probability of your earning more money — 25%, 50%, 75%? To determine the probability of an outcome occurring, one needs to gather information from all possible sources such as friends, library, career centers, and fellow workers.

After the four information requirements are known, the information should be put into a decision tree (Figure 1).

An effective means to use this model is to take the five most desirable outcomes from Figure 2. State each outcome as a positive outcome. Give the number 5 to the most desirable outcome, 4 to the next desirable, and so on for each alternative.

Then multiply the desirability number by the probability of the outcome occurring. The products for each alternative need to be totalled. The best alternative, using this rational method, is that alternative which has the highest probability of the most desirable outcome occurring. Decision making theorists call that alternative — the alternative with the highest expected value. Obviously, the alternative with the highest sum is the best choice and follows the theory that the choice with the highest expected value is best.

The steps for a rational decision using the decision tree are:

Step 1. Determine alternatives for the decision. Put them into the decision tree as x, y, z.

Step 2. Determine the outcome for the alternatives using Figure 2 for gains and losses to self and others.

Step 3. Determine five of the most desirable outcomes for the decision.

Step 4. Put those five outcomes ranked in order from 5-1 (5 = most desirable) for each alternative on the decision tree.

Step 5. Determine the probability in approximate percents for each outcome and put it on the decision tree.

Step 6. Multiply the desirability by the probability of each outcome.

Step 7. Sum the products for each alternative.

The alternative with the highest number is your best choice using this method. However, do note how a change in your desirability or probability rating will alter the results. For examples of how to apply these steps in decision making refer to examples 1 and 2.

Fate Control — At this point you might feel there is too much work involved in a rational decision making process. You might decide just to rely on the intuitive strategy or the delaying strategy. However, these two strategies allow fate to control the outcome. You have become a reactive decision maker. In order to have a greater control over one's life, one needs to become a proactive decision maker. A proactive decision maker exercises as much control as possible over his/her fate and this creatively generates alternatives to

Decision Making Techniques

follow. A good exercise is to examine a recent decision you have made and reflect on how much you controlled the "fate" or outcome of the decision. Could you have exercised more control of the outcome in that decision?

EXAMPLE 1
Mrs. H's Decision

Alternatives (3)	Outcomes (6)	Desirability	Rating high to low	Probability (%) Guessed from available info.	Product	Sum
X Stay home but become more active in volunteer work and social life.	X_1 At home she suffered from depression and emotional outbursts periodically. She was fed up with social life and had no interest in volunteer work. Staying home would mean perpetuation and worsening of symptoms.		1	60%	1x.6 = .6	
	X_2 Plenty of time to spend with children and husband but no further psychological growth. Might become overly dependent on husband and children emotionally and psychologically.		4	40%	4x.4 = 1.6	2.2
Y Find a job and a babysitter for children.	Y_1 Might become overworked, irritable with family, dissatisfied with babysitter, dissatisfied with conditions at home and inability to keep up with demands for time and attention.		3	40%	3x.4 = 1.2	
	Y_2 More money for material things. Opportunity for further growth by contact with professionals and others outside the home. More stimulating life.		5	60%	5x.6 = 3.0	4.2
Z Return to school and improve her education and ability to earn and procure work more interesting and challenging to her.	Z_1 She could still take good care of children and husband and keep up work at home as well as attend university. The study would be stimulating and invigorating and the contact with teachers and students would promote rapid growth and change. Her self-image, which was becoming rapidly negative, could become more positive and she could win the respect of family and others by success in school.		6 6	95% 95%	6x.95 = 5.7 6x.95 = 5.7	
	Z_2 She could estrange herself from her family by becoming ego-inflated from her advanced education. She could become so interested in her studies that her home and family could be neglected.		2	5%	2x.5 = .50	6.7

Mrs. H., housewife, with 3 children, became very restless and dissatisfied with life when her youngest child started school. She needed some outside activity that would stimulate her mind. She had three alternatives: X, Y, and Z. Which is best?

SUMMARY
In order to become an effective decision maker, one must:
1. Recognize the variety of strategies one can use to make a decision.
2. Utilize the four basic information requirements for making a good decision: alternatives, outcomes, desirability, probability of outcomes in a decision tree.
3. Learn to control as much as possible one's fate.

We may encounter pitfalls in our decision making, however by becoming more aware of the process of decision making and practicing the skills of a good decision maker, we can gain a greater control over our lives — a goal desired by those who wish to live a meaningful, successful and productive life.

> "Destiny is not a matter of chance, it is a matter of choice; it is not a thing to be waited for; it is a thing to be achieved."
>
> William Jennings Bryant

EXAMPLE 2

Sgt. McCartney's Decision

Alternatives	Outcomes	Probability	Desirability (5 = high, 1 = low)	Products	Sum
Stay in Forces at present rank (accept transfer in April 1982)	Higher pay	Low 20%	Good 5	1.	
	Work satisfaction	Very low 10%	Good 4	.4	
	Job security	Very high 90%	Good 3	2.7	
	Temporary separations	High 75%	Bad 2	1.5	
	Frequent moves	Very high 100%	Bad 1	1.	6.6
Apply for Warrant Officer school and get out if rejected	Higher pay	High 75%	Good 5	3.75	
	Work satisfaction	Medium 50%	Good 4	2.	
	Job security	Very high 90%	Good 3	2.7	
	Temporary separations	High 75%	Bad 2	1.5	
	Frequent moves	Very high 100%	Bad 1	1.	10.95
Get out of Forces and try Civilian Electronic Industry	Higher pay	Very High 90%	Good 5	4.5	
	Work satisfaction	High 80%	Good 4	3.2	
	Job security	Medium 50%	Good 3	1.5	
	Temporary separations	Low 25%	Bad 2	.5	
	Frequent moves	Very low 10%	Bad 1	.1	9.8

NOTE: Final decision was to get out of the Forces for a civilian job.

As one can tell from the example an individual may decide not to take the alternative with the highest sum. One may utilize a different strategy in the final decision and resort to, "I'll take Z because Z feels right."

	GAINS	LOSSES
TO SELF	Higher salary Enjoy work Self approval Take a risk Job security Less moves	Lower salary Not enjoy work Self disapproval No risk, very conservative Loss of job security More moves
TO OTHERS	Less family separations Higher salary Fewer moves Better family relations	More family separations Lower salary More moves Worse family relations

REFERENCE

H.B. Gelatt, *Teaching Personalized Decision Making*, a module developed by students and faculty at San Jose State University.

Be A Better Teacher

McKinley C. Martin

President, Coahoma Junior College

Adult and continuing education has a diversity of instructional formats available to all teachers. Equally diverse are the students attending adult classes. Each student comes with a specific thought in mind.

The learner (student) is definitely motivated; he/she is there for a purpose — to obtain a certificate, to acquire a skill or special knowledge in order to obtain a job, self-development, cultural and leisure time instruction, or for the opportunity to talk with other adults.

The instructor must be aware of these collective needs and meet each need individually through group and/or individual interaction.

Adult education instructors must examine the methods they use to communicate with students. Such an examination will reveal that the mere dispensing of information is not always the most satisfactory mode of communication. The interest and attention of even the most avid learner is apt to wane when he is continuously subjected to nothing but a barrage of facts. It is, therefore, the responsibility of the instructor to create a "learning experience," instead of being no more than an instrument in a learning situation. Once this responsibility is realized and acted upon by the instructor, he/she will find that as the class becomes a more profitable enterprise for the students, his/her own worth as an instructor will increase.

As the adult education instructor becomes aware of the many and various media and techniques available to him for the creation of a "learning experience," he/she will also begin to see his/her role as that of learner as well as teacher. Recognizing the need to adapt to technological advances and to become familiar with new methods, the instructor will no longer think solely in terms of convenience (having every member of the class perform the same task — reading Chapter 7, or making bookshelves). He/she must become concerned about questions such as, "Why is this skill important?" and "Of what use will it be to the student after he has left the class?".

First Class Meeting — When the class meets for the first time, the instructor must be cheerful, confident, and welcoming. The atmosphere of the classroom must be warm and open so as to build the students' confidence and desire to remain and also to return. A few simple rules:
1. Learn the students' names.
2. Be sure they know your name as well.
3. A short explanation of the objectives (purposes) of the class, with positive in-put from the students.

4. Have each student make at least one or more statements during the first session.
5. Any other activities to reduce the students' tensions of being "in school."

Successful Teaching — The key to successful teaching is good planning. There is no substitute for it! One of the most effective ways of improving your teacher-student relationship is to know what you are doing, when you are supposed to do it, and especially, why you are doing it. Adult students are so different in their experience, background and behavior that overplanning is important to assure adequate planning. Be sure that you have involved your adult students in all of this planning. This is a simplified, but quite adequate, daily lesson plan (Figure 1).

SAMPLE DAILY PLAN

Subject _____ Period _____ Date _____

1. Why am I going to teach this session? (learning goals)
2. What do I expect students to learn in this session?
3. How am I going to teach this session? (class procedure)
   ____ Teacher/pupil discussion
   ____ Demonstration
   ____ Interaction by students
   ____ Lecture
   ____ Group work
   ____ Audio visuals
   ____ Debate/panel discussion
   ____ Quiz or test
   ____ Reports
   ____ Role playing
   ____ Other
4. What materials am I going to use? (books, visuals, paper)
5. What is the next sessions assignment?
6. How could today's session have been improved?

Figure 1

HOW LESSON PLANS HELP YOU TEACH — A good lesson plan helps you in many ways.
1. A good lesson plan gives you confidence while teaching.
2. It helps you think through the lesson before it is taught. Learning difficulties can be anticipated and decisions made on ways to overcome them.
3. It describes how facilities, equipment, instructional aids, time and content are organized for attainment of course objectives.
4. It helps you stay on a schedule, and insures that the procedures selected can actually be implemented with the time and facilities available.

5. It insures that all essential information is included.
6. A lesson plan insures that there is good sequence and that proper emphasis is given to the various lesson parts, including those requiring student activity.
7. It inserts questions and key discussion points as needed.

The best lesson plans are of no value unless they work for you and your students. Above all they must be designed to help you present instruction effectively and in an organized fashion. The following questions, when answered, will help you adapt a lesson plan to the specific needs of your students:
1. Are the objectives specific? Do they state the outcome of the instruction in terms of student skills and understanding?
2. When you introduce the lesson plan do you tell your students what will be covered in the lesson?
3. Does the introduction describe how the class will be conducted?
4. Does the introduction suggest to the students how they will use the material or the skills acquired from the lesson?
5. Is the time spent on various parts of the lesson consistent with the importance of those parts?
6. Are there sufficient questions for checking student understanding or key points of the lesson?
7. Are training aids scheduled at the right time for maximum effectiveness?
8. When a film is used, does the lesson plan provide for an introduction to the film? Does it also provide for follow-up?
9. Does the lesson plan provide for maximum student participation and drill without sacrificing other important phases of the lesson?
10. Have you provided for repetition and emphasis of important points?
11. Have you planned a simple evaluation to check if your teaching was successful?

Some successful teaching techniques are:
1. **Group Discussion** This can be used to develop critical thinking, explore ideas, organize thoughts.

Have students ask questions and when possible have another student answer these questions. If necessary, the instructor may ask questions to start the discussion. The instructor must: involve all students, be positive, use group evaluation.
2. **Demonstrations** Most skill classes require teacher demonstrations and student participation in practicing the skill. Some tips that will make demonstrations more effective are:
   a. First demonstrate the skill and describe what you are doing.
   b. Perform the same demonstration while a student tells the class what you are doing.
   c. Have all students perform the skill under your supervision.
   d. Go over the main points more than once for emphasis.
3. **Use of Media** Overhead projectors are very effective particularly for

diagrams and explaining dynamic processes. Maps and drawings can be projected so that all students can see them while explanations are being given.

Tape cassettes can be individualized so that each student can practice or drill that portion of the lesson most important to him/her. It also allows for repetitive drill while the instructor is engaged in working with another group.

Films and filmstrips can provide a structured lesson on materials not readily available as well as provide enrichment and extension. In all cases a follow-up should include an evaluation of the media presentation.

4. **Student or Community Expertise** Often students or community persons can provide interactive experiences worthwhile to other students. Descriptions of uncommon experiences, other cultures, or other countries can build empathetic understandings. Use of external and internal resource persons add tremendously to students' acceptance of concepts that they are unfamiliar with or things that threaten the students belief system.

5. **Tests** Tests and evaluations can be used as teaching devices. Students may review no-fault quizzes and learn from a review of the correct answers. In addition there is another whole arena of teaching test-taking.

Most adults have looked upon tests as unpleasant and fear evaluations as a subjective statement of their worth. However, if they are taught that test-taking is a skill, they may soon develop quite a skill in that area. Tips for students before taking any test:

Students' chances for success are better if given typed copies of these tips to study.

   a. **Read all the questions before you start** answering any one of them.
   b. **Read the test instructions carefully.** If there are any questions you are told you must answer, do them first. It is better to tackle them immediately, so you won't come on them too late, after you have run out of time.
   c. **Find out how the test will be scored.** If the instructions do not tell you, ask the teacher. Some questions may give higher marks than others, so of course you will want to answer them first, and to figure out how much time to give them.
   d. After you have found out which are the highest-scoring questions, **answer the easiest of them first.** This helps you get as many points as possible as fast as possible. It may also give you clues to answering the tougher questions.
   e. **Try to avoid careless errors** that may lower your score even though you know the subject matter well. For example, if you read the test instructions quickly and superficially, you may not notice that you are only required to answer three out of four questions in a certain section. If you answer all four you are wasting valuable time you may urgently need to finish another section. It may even be a good idea to underscore such important parts of your instruction sheet, and refer to them from time to time as you move through the test.
   f. The final step is one of the most important, but it's amazing how few people take it. After finishing the test, instead of breathing a big sigh of

relief and turning it in — **read it carefully from beginning to end** with one purpose in mind: to find any errors or slips of the pen that could cost you points. For example, you may have inadvertently put an X in the wrong square, marked choice B instead of D by mistake, or miswritten a date that you knew perfectly well.

6. **Individualized Instruction** Individualized instruction or small group instruction allows students to begin at the place of learning difficulty. Since most adults have had varied educational and experiential backgrounds, few of them are at the same learning place at the same time. Paraprofessionals or tutors are invaluable in assisting in individualized instruction, either one-on-one or in small groups.

7. **Role Play** Role play and simulated experiences often help students learn in different modalities. A few of the benefits of role play and simulation are:
   a. Students can observe concepts in action.
   b. It motivates students to attempt to place learnings in action.
   c. It emphasizes sequential behaviors.
   d. It allows for group feedback.

Cardinal rules for teachers of adults:
1. Greet your students by name.
2. Treat them like adults — which they really are.
3. Before dismissal, review what they have learned. Be sure each student is aware that he/she has learned something new this session.
4. Leave them with a cheery note and a smile.

SUMMARY

Good teachers of adults plan by developing lesson plans. They use differing techniques as students and materials dictate. Good teaching approaches students on a level that they can understand. Though not everyone can define all the qualities of a good adult education teacher, the ones who are successful are highly motivated, constantly seeking new ways to teach, and strive to improve their instructional repertoire. It is important that teachers work to meet the needs of the students instead of the students being guided to meet the needs of the teachers and the agency or institution.

REFERENCES

Techniques. NAPCAE, Washington, D.C.
MATERIAL & METHODS in Continuing Education. Klevins, C. ed. Canoga Park, CA: Klevens Publications, 1978.
The Heart of Instruction. Ohio Dept. of Education, Division of Vocational Education.

Identify & Teach the Non-Literate

Ahnal M. Criego de Gammarra

Instructor, Education Department,
California State University at Los Angeles

America has always been the land of opportunity and waves of immigrants have come to its shores drawn by the "lamp beside the golden door." Most of these early immigrants came from Western and Eastern Europe and though they may not have been proficient in English were from countries whose tongues were similar and which had a strong, rich literary tradition. In the 1970's and 1980's new waves of immigrants have come to this land of opportunity, yet many of them are from lands in which the language is totally different from English and many are even illiterate in their own tongue. Among recent arrivals are several groups; some who cannot read or write at all and often speak their native language incorrectly, some who do not speak English and have marked deficiencies in language and other basic skills, still others are functionally illiterate in terms of American standards, though they may have functioned adequately in their native land.

Adult students of English as a Second Language (ESL) need a lot more than simple instruction in English speaking, reading and writing, As adults, they have a wide variety of specialized needs and expectations when they enter a class — they require lots of individual attention. Some come to class wanting training in only one of the four skill areas, some need basic survival English, others need help for citizenship courses, and some expect specialized language training as preparation for college or university work.[1]

TEACHING OUR CULTURE AND HOW TO COPE IN IT — To many ESL students, learning the proper behavioral patterns is as important as learning verbal proficiency in English. They must know the proper procedures for riding buses, renting apartments, banking, using community services, and similar activities. They need to be made aware of subtle behavioral traits (that vary from one culture to another), such as:

1. Spatial relationships — what distances between one person and another are tolerable in various social situations.
2. Temporal relationships — what latitude may be employed in the measurement of time, especially in the business world.
3. Male/female relationships — what behaviors are expected of men and women in our culture.

4. What Americans value and defend — property, democracy, freedom, privacy.

The teacher of ESL can play an important part in showing students that accepting another's culture is not to deny or belittle one's own . . . that one can prefer his or her own culture without making value judgments about others. All cultures are relevant and valuable. It is in the sharing of the different cultures that the educational and social growth of students is enhanced.[2]

SOME DO'S FOR TEACHING ESL

1. Present just one or two new structures a day, and give plenty of opportunity for oral practice.
2. Review often, and review related material before you present something new.
3. Test often. Devise aural discrimination, oral comprehension, and speaking tests.
4. Teach the four skills in their natural order: listening, speaking, reading, writing.
5. Use materials that have been written with the ESL student in mind, so that distracting vocabulary and assumed cultural background do not interfere. Remember that survival vocabulary is of the highest immediate interest to the student.
6. Teach students who have a different writing system to **read both** English print and script. You may teach them to **write** only in print, since it is easier to master.
7. Be careful about pointing to or touching students. We do need to teach them American customs, but do not risk offending them before they understand our ways. Be careful not to draw hasty conclusions about their behavior.
8. Emphasize the student's being understood, without demanding perfect pronunciation.

The recent immigration from non-Anglo Saxon areas of the world has presented adult education, and especially ESL, with the problem of teaching those below functional literacy. When the non-literate populations were small, it was easier to work with them; but now this population has grown so that teachers are crying for help. Teachers have usually recognized this population immediatley without having been given any assessment or placement direction from the administration. These students do not fit into the typical instructional patterns of the ESL class, nor do many possess the typical physical and/or mental attributes of most ESL students.

When the teacher knows nothing of that student's language or background (including the culture) and in some cases even which part of his name is the first, middle, or last — that teacher has a distinct problem.

Since teachers have been left on their own, they began separating literate from non-literate students, hoping to reach the non-literate before he/she dropped out of the program.

Eventually program directors recognized the teachers' plight and began developing separate classes for illiterates. A few publishers attempted to develop special "literacy materials." However, this problem is not being addressed directly. Why? The answer is found in a complex triangle shaped by: (1) low expectations (These students will not be doctors, lawyers, or professional persons.), (2) unusual language problems (compounded by the fact that some had no written language experiences), (3) lack of funds to develop specialized materials, to train specialized teachers, and to provide specialized social and health services.

Identifying the Non-Literate — Before setting up a classroom or curriculum for the non-literate, it is essential to identify the problems and characteristics of these special groups:
1. A **pre-literate** is a person unable to read and write and who comes from a culture without literacy tradition.
2. An **illiterate** is a person who is unable to read and write and who comes from a literate culture.
3. A **semi-literate** is a person poorly-schooled in his/her native language and who comes from a literate culture.
4. A **literate non-English reader** is literate in his/her own language but has trouble with the English language. This person should be placed in a regular English class.
5. A **functionally illiterate** is any person who cannot read or write in English at the sixth (6th) grade level. Functional literacy was the subject of the "Right to Read" program whose major emphasis was the development of survival skills necessary for full participation in American society.

CHARACTERISTICS OF NON-LITERATES

The non-literate has not been the subject of the intensive study given to the ESL student. Though the non-literate is a heterogeneous group, there are several characteristics which present learning difficulties. Some of these problems arise from the differing nature of teaching non-Romance and Germanic languages from languages using characters and unusual phonetics. Still another difficulty arises out of the purposes of education in that in the American culture, education promotes heterogeneity while in some non-literate cultures education promotes homogeneity. Still other difficulties arise from the students' unfamiliarity with American teaching methods (question-answer dialogue). Yet, still another difficulty often arises from cognitive and motor differences in the students.

Motor development — Many non-literate learners have difficulty with sensory-motor or perceptual-motor learning. These students may even walk with an awkward gait, and even after several demonstrations, may have difficulty holding a pencil correctly. They may have trouble opening and closing doors or sharpening pencils. This motor problem occasions trouble forming letters or completing the simplest handwriting tasks. If the root of the trouble is because of non-familiarity with the tasks, with practice they will learn and their other abilities will fall in line. However if their coordination or motor development is such that it is undeveloped even as an adult, the prognosis for their learning is poor.

The motor development viewpoint suggests that the study of human movement is inseparable from the study of learning because: — As humans move, they learn. To understand the dynamics of learning, often involves an understanding of movement and motor development. Motor activity thus becomes the foundation for much learning and those who possess limited motor development present still another task to the classroom teacher.

Hyperkinesis or hyperactivity — The hyperkinetic adult often exhibits the same characteristics as hyperkinetic children. They are in constant motion, are unable to concentrate on learning tasks, cannot sit still in their seats and are constantly touching things and bumping into furniture. You need to give them situations in which to channel their energies.

Perceptual Abilities — Perception seems to be a learned skill. This implies that the teaching process can have a direct impact on the student's perceptual development. Non-literate learners may have difficulty with visual or auditory perception, both of which lead to reading failures. A reading difficulty may reflect a deficit in the perceptual area. Watch how they sign their names — is it on the line or in some other space?

Memory — A non-literate youngster needs 76 times more repetition and 30 hours more of instruction to learn a single concept than does an educated child. Memory pertains to sensations and data already received and perceived The ability to receive, store, and retrieve previously experienced sensations and perceptions is called memory, imagery, or recall. Adults with memory problems seem to forget information shortly after it is learned — sometimes within the same hour. They cannot remember oral vocabulary, written words, or computation facts. Non-literate learners frequently have difficulty recalling how things looked or sounded.

Memory of past experiences must be retained and compared in order to organize and interpret experiences. Otherwise, each experience is unique with no connection to previous experience and past learning. Memory refers to the recall of nonverbal as well as verbal experiences, to visual as well as to spoken language. Memory problems can be related to a specific perceptual modality, such as visual memory or auditory memory. There are other categories of memory that can be differentiated, such as rote memory, immediate or short-term memory, sequential or serial memory, and long-term memory.

Language — Language and memory go hand in hand. Students with language difficulties may have trouble remembering words or putting words together to make sentences. Current research reveals that many students who have difficulty reading, suffer from underlying language problems. In many cases, it is the language problem rather than the reading problem that needs remediation.

Cognitive Skills — Many low-level learners have difficulty with cognitive skills — that is the ability to conceptualize, use abstractions, and to think creatively and critically. Even filling in blanks (cloze tests) becomes difficult for them.

Attention — Some poor readers have attention problems. That is, they have short attention spans and are easily distracted. They are unable to concentrate on a task for an extended period of time. These problems require specific teaching techniques and may be related to hyperkinesis.

Maturational, Emotional, and Social Characteristics — Many non-literate learners show a slowness in maturation. They still think many times as a child. Their emotional characteristics or their personality development has not followed a normal patten. Many of them do not feel their self-worth. Their environment and their lack of education and their constant maneuvering to cover it up keeps them from receiving normal satisfaction from achievement.

Although it is more common in children than in adults, many non-literate students will show a definite lack of social skills. This is due to lack of exposure and experience. A deficit in social skills appears to be a lack of sensitivity to people and a poor perception of social situations. This apparent lack of politeness skills seems to be due to not knowing how to obtain permission to get what they want (Please, May I . . .). Also, they have difficulty knowing how to channel anger (the limits of verbal confrontation and acting out). These are skills that need to be taught.

CURRICULUM CONTENT

Since some illiterates may not understand the concept of a sentence or even English phonetic sounds, they may need to learn fundamental phonetic language building blocks. Possibly their native language (Arabic, Chinese, or?) does not contain the letters that we use to represent sounds — even some Americans have difficulties with some sounds like pr, tr, and kr. In addition, some pre-literates have learned fragmented language patterns that read right to left or vertically. One excellent device to counter this is to introduce pictures and drawing that move from left to right.

Another device that works well is to relate whole words to phoneme parts. This may be difficult in the beginning, however, as the students advance they can utilize the concept of whole and parts to learn comprehension and other cognitive skills. Another area of curriculum development is providing words in conceptual and contextual phrases. Few realize that when the illiterate learns a word or a phrase, they learn it for life. Each new meaning is like learning a new word all over again.

A list of curriculum concerns might include:
1. Teach writing and printing. (Watch to see if the writing is on the line.)
2. Make sure the tasks are simple enough to be completed in one session.
3. Practice listening, speaking, reading, and writing.

Figure 1 is a simplified daily lesson plan for working with preliterate and literate students. Volunteers or peer teaching assistants should be worked into the program schedule whenever possible to assist both the teacher and the students. Since the adult attention span of this group is limited, try to direct lessons in twenty minute segments.

DAILY LESSON PLAN

Teacher
Whole Group
Oral Activity

Preliterate
Teacher directed specific
skills lesson.

Literate
Written assignment
Tape lesson, groups
listening or recording,
or lang. masters

Teacher
Whole Group
Oral and/or written activity

Preliterate
Reading Skills Development;
simple written follow-up to
oral exercises.

Teacher
Literate
Check Assignment
Specific Skills Lesson

BREAK

Teacher
Whole Group
Oral Activities

Teacher

Preliterate
Paired peer teaching

Literate
Paired peer teaching

Teacher
Whole group
Closing Oral Activity

Figure 1

SUMMARY

Non-literate adults may not be able to read or write and come from a culture without a literacy tradition, or they may come from a culture with a literacy tradition and may have never learned to read or write, or they may have had inadequate schooling in their native language. They may exhibit characteristics of slow learners, yet may not be learning disabled.

The pace of instruction must be geared to overcoming motor, perceptual, language, cognitive, and social handicaps. With understanding, patience, and love they will learn to read.

It may be well to remember that a simple thing like holding a pencil may be difficult to one who has never used a pencil before. Remember how difficult it was when you first used chopsticks?

Build your students confidence and let them know when they are showing improvement.

REFERENCES

1. *Study Guide for Teaching English to Speakers of Other Languages*, Department of Adult Education, Montgomery County (Md.) Public Schools.
2. *Techniques* NAPCAE, Washington, D.C. Feb. 1981.
3. "Do's" and "Don'ts", Maryland Association for Publicly Supported Continuing Education (MAPSCE).

Evaluate: Student, Staff, Program

Robert A. Fellenz
Associate Professor, Interdisciplinary Education,
Texas A&M

Gary J. Conti
Assistant Professor, Interdisciplinary Education,
Texas A&M

Don F. Seaman
Professor, Interdisciplinary Education
Texas A&M

One of the most misunderstood concepts in education is evaluation. Although teachers, administrators, and board members use the word and almost every program design refers to it, evaluation is often considered a foreboding process which intimidates subordinates in the name of accountability. Yet, evaluation does not have to be threatening. When it is conducted as a comprehensive process involving both formative and summative stages within a trusting environment, evaluation can be a constructive educational tool.

Comprehensive evaluation applies to all parts of the adult education program. While summative evaluation consists of final judgments at the culmination of an activity, formative evaluation involves on-going feedback to influence the future direction of the activity. These forms of evaluation are complementary, and both are necessary for the effective evaluation of students, staff, and programs.

STUDENT EVALUATION

A recent Texas study indicated that the teacher competency considered most important to student growth was the teacher's ability to relate well to the adult student. The concern, patience, and kindness of the teacher were repeatedly pointed to as the dominant factors influencing student learning and growth. The helpful teacher was the one who made students begin to believe in their worth, whose acceptance made it possible for the students to accept others, and whose encouragement made them determined to succeed.

But also very important were the teacher traits of the assessment of learner needs and the evaluation of learning activities. Apparently one of the reasons these two factors were valued so highly by the adult learners was that they saw them as essential to the whole process of being treated as adults. For these learners, being treated as an adult meant that "the teachers found out what we needed before they decided what to teach us." Thus, need assessment and evaluative feedback emerged as two teacher behaviors essential to the whole process of treating adult learners as adults. Not to be asked about needs or wants or not to be given feedback about progress was equated with being treated like a child.

Provide Student Feedback — It would seem that once we begin to think of education in terms of a learner-centered enterprise, three reasons for the teacher to provide evaluative feedback to the learner immediately become apparent. First is the centrality of evaluation to the very act of learning. New knowledge, new values, and new skills cannot be accepted until they have been validated by some kind of test or standard. Before new insights and skills are made a relatively permanent part of the repertory of the adult learner, they must be compared to past experience, to effectiveness in practice, or to feedback from some important "other" such as the teacher. While this need for evaluation of the new exists at all ages, it is particularly critical for adult learners. Accustomed to taking charge of their own lives, adult learners expect to weigh the feedback and to juggle the options before buying into the new. Thus, the development of good channels of feedback become vital in the design of learning activities.

Moreover, it has almost become legendary among experienced teachers of adults to plan to give new students opportunities to immediately experience success. In addition to reassuring the individual, it introduces the whole process of clarification of objectives and opens the path to continuous evaluation of progress toward goals. These are two of the most essential tasks that can be performed by any learning facilitator who is truly interested in helping the adult student maintain a desire to learn. For unless feedback is constant, reassuring the student that he/she can learn and is learning, the student will soon give this time to other activities.

Adults are very goal directed in their motivation for beginning learning activities. They want their learning to have a purpose and an immediate usefulness. They are quite impatient with teacher or course requirements that have little apparent relationship to their goals. All these factors help explain why they relate well to the teacher who keeps track of how well they are doing and shares this knowledge with them.

A third characteristic of the adult learner that seems to relate in a special manner to teacher/student evaluation is the self-directed nature of most adult learning. Most adult learning is self-initiated and self-directed; educators are increasingly becoming aware that even in formal learning activities, the adult retains much of this sense of self-direction. Thus, those working with adult learners are much wiser in providing feedback that makes it easier for the learners to make adjustments or to redirect their learning activities than to try to do this for them. It is quite evident that the teacher who is providing channels of feedback that enable adult learners: (1) to evaluate the new, (2) to reassess their goals and progress toward them, (3) to re-direct their learning efforts has indeed established a learner-centered environment.

Formative Student Evaluation — Up to this point formative approaches to the teacher's evaluation of the learner have been considered. For the most part, such approaches are the most appropriate for they are aimed at improving the learning experience while it is on-going. In the classroom, formative evaluation can be viewed as the "organizing and carrying out the learning and teaching process in a manner that is maximally adaptive to the characteristic of the learners."[1] Diagnosis, placement, and monitoring are steps in this definition of formative evaluation.

Diagnosing refers to discovering the ways in which a particular student learns best. Adults differ in their preferred learning styles. Some like to read; others prefer to hear and talk about issues; others need to see it to grasp it. Small groups are the best learning situation for some while others learn best by themselves or in a one-on-one situation. Much is being written about cognitive styles and the influence upon learning of such elements as field dependence vs. field independence or global vs. analytical styles. Would it help adults to know some of these things about their own learning style? It seems logical that the more we know about some activity the better we should be able to carry out that activity. Thus, feedback from the teacher about more productive approaches to learning could improve the learning transaction. Teachers have found such diagnostic feedback especially beneficial when dealing with psychological barriers to learning and change. Hostile attitudes, touchy self-concepts, or prejudicial biases can certainly be impediments to learning, but impediments that sometimes can be weakened or removed by the very realization of the barrier's existence. Feedback from the teacher might accomplish what the adult could never do on his own.

Proper placement is perhaps the greatest challenge for most teachers of adults. Start adults at too low a level, and they soon quit because they are wasting their time. Start them at too high a level, and they give up in frustration. Organize a group learning activity where there are a dozen adult learners entering at different levels of readiness, and you multiply the problem a dozen times. Apart from complete individualization of learning plans or multiple developmental sequences, there is no way of eliminating the problem of varied entry levels; however, evaluative feedback can assist mature students. Comparing specific learning goals and objectives with competencies they already possess allows adult learners additional control over their learning efforts. This not only eliminates needless frustration on the learner's part but also might even lead to a greater appreciation of the role of the teacher.

The monitoring process should not be equated with tests or grades. The grading of assignments or tests for the purpose of entering information into records may be useful in the evaluation of instructional materials, methods, or personnel, but the monitoring process that is beneficial to the learners is the feedback concerning their individual progress provided by the teacher. The final goal of the learning activity is often the only goal of which the learners are conscious. Making them conscious of intermediate goals and of progress toward them can be very motivating. The fact that adults are hungry for such information can be seen from the popularity of all the "Know Yourself" and "Test Yourself" gimmicks and devices sold today. The unpopularity or downright fear of educational tests is often due to the way they are or have been administered and graded. The anonymity stressed by the popular press approaches to self testing should give teachers a clue. After all, is it necessary even for the teacher to know the results of a test if its major purpose is to enable the adult learner to monitor progress?

Summative Student Evaluation — Although summative approaches to the evaluation of the learner are less frequently used by teachers of adults, there are occasions when they could be of value. Summative evaluation deals with "assessing and recording what the learners have accomplished."[1] This definition involves crediting, certifying, and selecting functions that serve as beneficial forms of summative learner evaluation. For example, adults who have gone through a learning activity frequently want to have their efforts recognizes. Here the teacher's role becomes one of crediting academic efforts. It may surprise us to see how much value some adults will give to a certificate that indicates that they have earned so many CEU's or credits. When viewed as a symbol that reinforces their sense of accomplishment, it is readily understood. Lifelong learners are those who recognize past learning successes and the benefits of these activities. Much the same can be said of certifying which also implies recognition, but in addition, more strongly connotes the identification of this individual as someone competent in a certain skill or knowledge area. This type of summative evaluation is needed by adult students not only for the psychological boost it supplies but also for employment purposes. Teachers can provide this formally through cooperation with certifying agencies and through less formal means such as letters of recommendation or conversations with potential employers. Selecting, a third type of summative evaluation of the learner, relates to the process of picking out those who have done very well or of making comparisons among learners on the quality of their performance. Grading is a version of this type of evaluation.

Although celebrations are seldom thought of as part of the evaluation process, they could have a distinct role in learner evaluation. To celebrate means to recognize the goodness or worth of a person or occasion and to do so publicly with joy. Thus, a celebration could fulfill both certifying and crediting functions. Its power lies in that it can do it with joy — with an emotional impact of some intensity. As such, it can be in itself a learning experience which intensifies the lessons already absorbed and which instills an impulse for lifelong learning. Celebrations in the learning environment can be as simple as a spontaneous coffee break or as elaborate as a well-planned dinner and presentation. They can be woven into lectures or set up as special events. They are times when we say, "It is good to be a learner!"

As mentioned above, a group of adults were interviewed in Texas regarding the teacher traits that contributed to their personal growth and development. They indicated that the traits that they felt most influenced their own growth were the teacher's establishment of rapport, assessment of needs, and provision of evaluative feedback. Perhaps they were not really listing characteristics of good instruction as much as they were describing the **good teacher**. True evaluation of the learner would be a most difficult process for the person who did not understand the needs and interests of the learner. It would be even less likely to occur in situations where little rapport had been established between the teacher and learner. But it certainly should occur frequently in learning experiences directed by adult educators who are concerned about people and their learning needs.

STAFF EVALUATION

Effective staff evaluation results from communication and the cultivation of interpersonal skills. Because of past abuses and limited uses, evaluation often carries negative connotations when it is associated with program personnel. For a majority of those teaching in the field, adult education is a secondary occupation. Many of these teachers bring experiences to the program which link evaluation to a yearly assessment of job performance. This makes evaluation an economic issue and threatens to reduce greatly its purpose and applicability. Similarly, many have experienced evaluations which were biased towards the "a priori" goals of the evaluator and which did not accurately reflect the teacher's interpretation either of the task or of his/her performance. Because of the potential of these negative experiences, the continuing education administrator should take special care to design and carry out responsive evaluations and to communicate the purpose and process of responsive evaluation to the staff.

Responsive Staff Evaluation — Evaluation should be a continuous interactive process which is responsive to the issues and concerns of those involved.[2] In such a situation, the evaluator's role is not that of a disinterested outsider collecting information for the purpose of making a final decision concerning future employment of a staff member. Instead, evaluators are facilitators who are responsible for maintaining a communication network for uncovering, sharing, and reformulating information which can be used to help achieve individual staff and institutional goals.

When evaluation is conducted in this manner, it can be productive and non-threatening. It can be used to make both a formative and summative evaluation of the merit and worth of each staff member. These assessments may be achieved by means of continuous informal evaluations throughout the academic year and by formal performance appraisal interviews scheduled at regular interviews.

While program administrators are charged with the task of staff evaluation, their primary function is to serve as supervisors. As such, they are helping agents to assist staff members in providing quality instruction. Through numerous, daily contacts they have the opportunity to interact with staff members and to provide feedback concerning teaching techniques, classroom organization and management, relationships with students and peers, and compliance with institutional regulations. Equally as important, this dialogue provides staff members with an opportunity to share their ideas and perceptions related to these items. This interaction can allow mutual understanding, can foster input from each concerning evaluation criteria, and can permit the clarification of acceptable performance standards. It can also provide opportunities for discussing current practices so that undesirable behaviors can be eliminated or so that misunderstood behaviors can be clarified.

On-going communication and feedback with each staff member concerning performance permits formative merit and formative worth evaluation. The purpose of formative merit evaluation is to provide information related to the staff member's competencies, skills, and aptitudes for functioning in the adult education setting. Formative worth evaluation, on the other hand, provides staff members with information relating their performance to the needs of the local program and clients.

Feedback and Staff Evaluation — In order to maintain open communication, the administrator must develop and use skills in giving feedback. Giving feedback is the verbal and nonverbal processes through which an individual lets others know his/her perceptions and feelings about their behavior.[3] Feedback provides the administrator with the opportunity to reinforce desirable behavior, relate staff behavior to intentions, and identify areas of concerns. Meaningful feedback, however, requires an atmosphere of trust and concern. In such an environment, formative evaluation information can be provided to staff members by feedback which:

1. Is direct in describing the actual observed behavior rather than placing a value on it.
2. Is specific rather than general.
3. Is directed at behavior which can be changed.
4. Is given shortly after the event.
5. Allows the staff member a choice concerning change.[3]

Formative feedback is intended to be helpful and to clarify the perceptions of both the administrator and the staff member concerning behavior in relationship to goals. This clarification should focus on both institutional and individual goals. The administrator is responsible for implementing institutional goals, but, are staff aware of these goals? Equally important, what are their interpretations of the mission and goals of the organization? Likewise, what individual goals does the administrator have for the program, and how do these relate to the personal goals of the various staff members? In uncovering and discussing these, the administrator should provide feedback related both to the staff member's intrinsic merit as a teacher of adults and to that member's contributions to the program. After this information exchange, the responsibility for change rests with the staff member, and the consequences of the actions taken by the staff member are discussion topics for the summative evaluation.

Conducting Effective Summative Staff Evaluation — Informal formative staff evaluation should be capped with formal summative evaluation addressing the elements of individual merit and worth. This can be most easily accomplished by a performance appraisal interview. This technique is a direct interview between the staff member and the supervisor in which skills and abilities are discussed, in which activities are encouraged by exploring existing incentives and barriers, and in which role perceptions are clarified. Although direct interviews have been used in the past as a management tool, effective performance appraisal interviews differ in focus, purpose, emphasis, goals, and follow-up activities from the traditional employee-employer job appraisal review.

Effective performance appraisals follow a definite pattern. First, a majority of the interview content focuses on the future. Past experiences and the staff member's reaction to formative evaluation are analyzed to provide insights for improving the future. Second, the interview's purpose is to solve problems rather than to fix blame. The typical question posed in the interview is "What is the problem?" This contrasts sharply with the ineffective approach of "Who is at fault?" The first approach allows the supervisor to probe and uncover the staff member's opinions concerning ways of avoiding or solving problems. Third, the emphasis is on observable behavior. While ineffective interviews tend to deal with unalterable traits and force the staff member into a defensive position, effective appraisals use actual samples of the employee's behavior, and those involved discuss these behaviors in an adult-to-adult manner. Fourth, in this goal oriented process, specific changes are discussed. In order to increase the staff member's psychological ownership, new performance targets are mutually developed. Finally, follow-up is an integral part of the process. Since new performance goals and deadlines have just been agreed upon, the concluding activity for the interview should be the scheduling of the next formal appraisal conference.

Effective performance appraisals can serve as the vehicle for summative evaluations of both merit and worth. The summative merit review should focus on the innate qualities possessed by the staff member for the job. Does this staff member have the skills, aptitudes, knowledges, and attitudes necessary to work with adults in the continuing education setting? If not, what can be done to acquire these needed abilities? Merit also includes effort. Is the staff member exerting a sufficient effort to perform adequately, and what factors may be inhibiting individual effort?

The summative worth review, on the other hand, should focus on the value of the staff member to the local program. Does the staff member have an accurate perception of his/her role in the program? Does he/she perform the assigned tasks well and thereby contribute to the overall goals of the organization? The answers to summative evaluation questions such as these can serve as indicators for staff development activities, for needed intrinsic and extrinsic rewards, and for continued employment and promotion decisions.

The evaluation of staff, thus, involves both a formative and summative examination of individual elements of merit and worth. Continuous formative evaluation is achieved through the exercise of good communication and interpersonal skills in daily contacts as the supervisor functions as a helping agent for staff members. Regular appraisal interviews can be scheduled with staff members to provide a formal vehicle for summary evaluations. Like the feedback of informal formative evaluation, these interviews can constructively address both merit and worth when they are conducted effectively.

PROGRAM EVALUATION

The importance of evaluating educational programs seems to have increased greatly during the past few years. However, before ensuing in such discussion, two concepts which needs to be defined are assessment and evaluation. Assessment consists of the gathering of information, such as, facts, data, and perceptions, which can be used to determine if an objective or goal has been reached. For example, if the stated goal was to reach 500 participants with an educational program and if 475 were actually reached, the data to indicate this is derived from assessment. The describing of the results or of "what happened" is assessment.

Evaluation, on the other hand, occurs when some value judgment is made in regard to what happened in a program. An examination of the term itself indicates the root word "value." In evaluating the above assessment data, the question must be asked, "Was 475 out of 500 a 'good' or acceptable number to reach even though the goal was not achieved?" Someone must make that value judgment. Once it has been made, evaluation has been achieved. Thus, program evaluation is "the process of judging the worth or value of a program. This judgment is formed by comparing evidence as to what the program is with criteria as to what the program ought to be."[4] It centers around the notion of value judgments. "Intimately associated with evaluation is the need to gather or make judgments about educational programs. Evaluation is determining value or merit . . ."[5]

Evaluating Programs — The reasons for conducting program evaluation are many and varied. Although individuals may disagree on the relative importance of the reasons, there seems to be general disagreement that program evaluation is justified in order:

1. **To determine how well the program objectives are being achieved.** Did the participants acquire the knowledge or skills they were expected to acquire? Do they feel they will be able to utilize the information? If all of the objectives are not being reached, is the program still worthwhile?

2. **To make decisions related to program improvement and future operation.** Will the program either continue or be cancelled? Was enrollment sufficient to sustain the costs? Did the participants or staff feel the program was worthwhile? What kinds of changes would improve the program if continued or offered again at a later time?

3. **To meet the requirements of the program sponsor.** Funding agencies have, fortunately, increased the attention and emphasis placed upon program evaluation in recent years. However, does the evaluation output produce the

kind(s) of data desired? How can the desires of the sponsor and the program administrator be made congruent?

4. **To provide a feeling of worth or accomplishment to the program staff.** Everyone needs positive feedback, and evidence that an educational program is really helping the participants can be a source of great pride for the staff. How does the staff feel about the program? Are the feelings being expressed openly or hidden?

5. **To describe what happened so that other educators can determine if they wish to duplicate the program.** Disseminated results of success or failure can provide others with data for effective decision-making. Are the conditions so similar that the same results would probably be achieved? Were the results from another program the kind which would enable our organization to move toward its objectives?

6. **To become or remain accountable.** There are many audiences to which a program must be accountable: participants, staff, agency administration, or even the general public. What information would best fulfill accountability needs? Can needed information be obtained efficiently?

7. **To provide learning experiences for anyone interested in the program.** The data from assessment and evaluation activities can be a learning resource for the staff, participants, and those who read the evaluation report. New information, insights, and generalizations can be gained from evaluation data. What is being learned from this program? How can the results be made available for others who may be interested? [6] [7] [8] [9]

Although several reasons for conducting program evaluation pervade in the literature, Grotelueschen[5] indicates that:

> Whatever its specific rationale, the basic goal of an evaluation is to determine the worth of what is being evaluated. This point has both theoretical and practical significance: theoretically, it distinguishes program evaluation from other forms of inquiry such as educational research; practically, any information on program merit contributes to the evaluation process, aiding an administrator deliberating between alternatives.

When to Evaluate Programs — As with student and staff evaluation, program evaluation involves both formative and summative evaluation. During one period of time in the evaluation of educational programming, the emphasis was on evaluating the end result or product. Results were compared to expectations, and at that point decisions were made.

More recently, a trend has evolved for a broader and more comprehensive approach to program evaluation. The current focus is on on-going evaluation that begins at the time the program is initiated and continues until the program has been completed. Advantages of this formative evaluation include:

1. If the program is not making expected progress, that lack of progress can be detected before the program has gone too far. Then, proper changes can be made to improve the effectiveness of the program.

2. If necessary, a decision can be made to terminate a program before excessive wastes in time, energy, and resources are incurred.

2. Unrealistic expectations from one or several audiences can be determined in time to clarify and communicate what can actually be expected from the program. This avoids possible disappointment and anger at the conclusion of a program.

Any phase of the program can be evaluated at almost any time. For example, value judgments can be made in regard to program objectives, organizational structure, methods of teaching, personnel performance, or expenditures. The current popularity of formative program evaluation is due largely to the increased program efficiency made possible by continuous evaluation. In this process, effective programmers are constantly evaluating their program in order to detect any area where a change could substantially improve the results.

Evaluation Techniques — The first step in evaluating is to determine the standards or criteria which can be judged in relation to the program objectives. Without those, there is no basis for comparing what happened with what "should have" happened. To produce an accurate evaluation, these must collectively reflect and consolidate the criteria for success of the adult learners, teachers, and programmer. Once the criteria have been determinted, they need to be clearly communicated to everyone involved in the program.

After establishing criteria, the next procedure is to begin collecting evidence to assess the degree of progress. A variety of tools is available for the programmer to utilize in this endeavor. Such tools may include survey instruments, rating scales, observation reports, historical data, standardized tests, and similar devices. **The important consideration is to use the tool which is best suited for the information needed.** For example, if the programmer needs to know if the participants' behavior has actually changed as a result of an educational program, a mailed questionnarie may not produce that kind of information. Actual observations or interviews with either students or employers are likely to be more appropriate.

Questions to consider in selecting the techniques and/or materials to utilize in the evaluation process include:

1. Will the evaluation tools enable me to acquire the kind of information I really need?
2. Are the instruments we need readily available or will we have to construct our own questionnaires, rating scales, or other devices?
3. What will be the costs for developing or purchasing the needed evaluation tools?
4. How much data are needed?
5. To whom and how soon should the data be disseminated?

The evaluation can utilize a mixture of techniques, and in a complex program, this is quite often the best strategy. The staff must be careful in the selection and use of collected materials and must guard against accumulating data just because it is convenient to do so. The purpose(s) and goal(s) of any evaluation activity should be cleay identified and agreed upon by the staff and the evaluator(s) if the two groups are not the same individuals. Then, participants are not hasseled by too many evaluation activities, and no "surprises" are incurred during the evaluation process.

Once assessment of what has occurred has finally been completed, the value judgments must be made. This is usually done by the individual most responsible for the program. This is the most sensitive aspect of the entire evaluation process because those who now must make the judgments are often the individuals who have invested the most time and effort in the program. As Boyle[10] cautions:

Judgments are made by people who are dependent upon them. Judgments are influenced by the past experiences and beliefs of the individuals making them. They may be reliable, valid, and objective, or highly biased, depending upon how well the individual is able to control her or his own mental activity and screen out biasing factors.

As indicated previously, determining the value of how well a program is progressing is an important phase of evaluation. Continuation of the curricular offerings and the funding support is dependent upon these judgments. In addition, the jobs of staff members and the reputation of the program and director may be affected by these judgments. Therefore, the summary of the evidence and the conclusions which follow are the important culminating factors in the evaluation process. Only when such judgments are made is program evaluation complete.

SUMMARY

Comprehensive evaluation can be a constructive process for improving student learning, staff performance, and program efficiency. Effective evaluation involves both formative and summative evaluation. Formative evaluation is rooted in continuous feedback to clarify and improve the interpersonal relations among those in the program. Summative evaluation involves using a wide range of data to make final judgments after the formative process. Successful evaluation requires an environment which fosters trust and mutual respect. Finally, good evaluation is constantly focused on developing strategies to improve the future.

REFERENCES

1. Skager, R. *Lifelong Education and Evaluation Practice.* New York: UNESCO Institute for Educ. '78.
2. Guba, E.G., & Lincoln, Y.S. *Effective Evaluation.* San Francisco: Jossey-Bass Inc., 1981.
3. Hanson, P.G. "Giving Feedback: an Interpersonal Skill." In J.E. Jones & J.W. Pfeiffer (Eds.), *The 1975 Annual Handbook for Group Facilitators.* La Jolla, CA: University Associates, Inc., 1975.
4. Steele, S. "Program Evaluation — a Broader Definition." *Journal of Extension,* 1970, *8* (No. 2).
5. Grotelueschen, A.D. "Program Evaluation." In A.B. Knox (Ed.), *Developing, Administering, and Evaluating Adult Education.* San Francisco: Jossey-Bass Inc., 1980.
6. Knowles, M.S. *The Modern Practice of Adult Education.* New York: Association Press, 1973.
7. Knox, A.B. (Ed.) *Developing, Administering, and Evaluating Adult Education.* San Francisco: Jossey-Bass Inc., 1980.
8. Lauffer, A. *The Practice of Continuing Education in the Human Services.* New York: McGraw Hill Book Co., 1977.
9. Lenz, E. *Creating and Marketing Programs in Continuing Education.* New York: McGraw Hill '80.
10. Boyle, P.G. *Planning Better Programs.* New York: McGraw Hill Book Co., 1981.

Self-Assessment

Mark H. Rossman

Associate Professor
Higher & Adult Education
Arizona State University, Tempe

It would be almost impossible for any adult educator to master all of the eighty (80) models of teaching promulgated by Joyce and Weil.[1] Each is clearly grounded in a rationale or theory and is sufficiently developed to be of practical value when used in the appropriate context.

Implicit however, is the assumption that regardless of the model used, the instructor utilizes one or more teaching skills to facilitate adult learning. Little has been done to substantiate this assumption, particularly as it relates to the identification of the necessary skills for teaching adults. The *Catalogue of Adult Education Projects* for the Fiscal Year 1978, identified 116 staff development projects funded under sections 306 and 309 of the Adult Education Act of 1966. Relatively few of the projects were designed to identify the specific skills needed to teach adults. Other attempts to discover projects specifically designed to identify skills for teaching adults have usually been confined to instructors at the college or university levels.

It would seem logical that prior to improving one's own teaching skills, knowledge of the skills for teaching adults is required. It cannot simply be assumed that skills for teaching youth and children are the same skills needed for teaching adults. Once the necessary skills are known, the next step is to assess which skills are essential in one's own teaching situation. Clearly, the skill of responding to questions would be more important to a facilitator of a small group meeting for one hour, twice a week than it would be for an instructor teaching a course primarily consisting of lectures. Only after assessing one's own skills in relation to the given teaching situation, can a meaningful program for self-improvement be undertaken.

A useful program in this regard was the Clinic to Improve Teaching established at the University of Massachusetts from 1971-1976. This program provided for teaching improvement based on the individual needs of faculty participants. This process, totally voluntary in nature, identified specific instructional strengths and problem areas. Through a combination of methods and techniques, the faculty member decided which skill or skills needed to be improved. A teaching improvement plan was designed, consultation was provided and the plan was implemented. Continual assistance was available until such time as the instructor was satisfied that improvement was obtained. A key development of the project was the identification, development and elaboration of twenty skills for teaching adults.

Self-Assessment

The twenty skills for teaching adults and the subsequently developed SKILLS FOR TEACHING ADULTS SELF-ASSESSMENT INVENTORY (STASAI) provide useful ways of critically assessing one's own adult teaching skills. The STASAI is particularly beneficial to the novice adult educator. The Clinic[2] also has determined that this list is *not* useful in comparing the work of one instructor with another as there is no way to provide for the effect of individual variables such as the entering behavior, knowledge and motivation of the students; the intellectual climate of the institution; the nature of student rewards; the learning styles of the individual adults; the subject matter itself; physical characteristics of the classroom. All these variables interact in such a way as to affect the quality of education provided and have been demonstrated to render this list virtually useless when used to compare one instructor against another.

Now, read and complete the SKILLS FOR TEACHING ADULTS SELF-ASSESSMENT INVENTORY (STASAI). It is important to consider this scale in relation to your own teaching situation, only.

SKILLS FOR TEACHING ADULTS SELF-ASSESSMENT INVENTORY (STASAI)

INSTRUCTIONS: THE SKILLS FOR TEACHING ADULTS SELF-ASSESSMENT INVENTORY (STASAI) is designed to help you determine your individual strengths and problem areas. The rating scale that follows should be used to assess both the skills that are relevant to you in your own teaching situation as well as your present level of development as it relates to each skill:

0	1	2	3	4	5
Absent	Low (awareness)	Deficient (uses rarely)	Moderate (conceptual understanding)	Proficient (uses often)	High (expert)

On the scale following the description of each skill, place an "R" above the appropriate number to indicate the "Required" level of the skill for you in your own adult teaching situation. Next, place a "P" above the appropriate number to indicate your "Present" level of development of the skill. For example, you may feel that skill number 7, RESPONDING TO QUESTIONS, is very important to you in your teaching situation and that you are not very accomplished in the development of this skill. Your responses would be recorded as follows:

EXAMPLE Remember — "R" is the required level of skill
"P" is your present level of skill

7. **RESPONDING TO QUESTIONS** The instructor's skill in answering questions clearly and concisely.

```
         P              R
   ─────────────────────────
     0   1   2   3   4   5
```

Those skills which you feel are strongly required (those you rated 4 or 5) and the development of which you rated absent or low (0 or 1) might indicate skills you wish to improve upon. Use the STASAI in this way to help you to determine those skills you want to improve upon.

---

1. **ESTABLISHING A LEARNING SET** Skill in creating in students a readiness to begin a given learning activity.

```
   ─────────────────────────
     0   1   2   3   4   5
```

2. **LOGICAL ORGANIZATION** Skill in arranging and presenting content and learning activities so that students understand the relationships among the various topics, ideas, activities, etc. to be covered.
3. **PACING** Skill in introducing new topics or activities at an appropriate rate and in spending enough, but not too much, time developing these topics or activities.
4. **ELABORATION** Skill in clarifying or developing an idea or topic.
5. **EXPRESSION** Skill in using verbal (voice tone, inflection, pitch, emphasis) and nonverbal (facial expressions, gestures, body movements) techniques to increase the power and meaning of the communication.
6. **ASKING QUESTIONS** Skill in using various questioning techniques at appropriate times and for a variety of instructional purposes.
7. **RESPONDING TO QUESTIONS** Skill in answering questions clearly and concisely.
8. **STUDENT PARTICIPATION** Skill in facilitating student participation in class discussions.
9. **CLOSURE** Skill in integrating the major points of a lesson or unit of instruction, establishing a link between the familiar and the new thereby providing the student with a feeling of accomplishment.

Self-Assessment 349

10. **EVALUATION** Skills in specifying the criteria for evaluation, in designing valid and reliable evaluation procedures and in providing adequate evaluative information regarding student progress.

---

0   1   2   3   4   5

11. **LEVEL OF CHALLENGE** Skill in selecting appropriate course objectives, content, and activities which challenge students but which are not too difficult for the students to master.
12. **VARIETY** Skills in selecting and using various teaching methods, techniques and materials effectively and appropriately.
13. **CREATIVITY** Skill in combining methods and materials in new and unusual ways.
14. **MANAGEMENT** Skills in performing the organizational and administrative tasks in providing learning experiences for students.
15. **FLEXIBILITY/INDIVIDUALIZATION** Skill in dealing with differing interests and abilities among students and in responding constructively to student suggestions, criticisms and comments regarding teaching strategies.
16. **INTERPERSONAL RELATIONS** Skills in relating to students in ways which promote mutual respect and rapport.
17. **LEARNING ENVIRONMENT** Skill in creating and maintaining an atmosphere conducive to student involvement and learning.
18. **ENTHUSIASM** Abilities to conduct and direct learning activities in a dynamic manner and to stimulate interest and excitement in course content and activities.
19. **PERSPECTIVE** Skill in establishing a frame of reference for concepts, issues, ideas and expanding that frame of reference to include an increasingly wider variety of viewpoints, implications and relationships.
20. **VALUE CONTEXT** Abilities: (a) to identify explicitly his or her own values and to clarify the implications of those values in the selection and interpretation of subject matter, (b) to explore other values and their implications as they relate to the subject matter, (c) to help students clarify their values and recognize the implications of those values for their professional and personal conduct.

STRENGTHEN YOUR SKILLS

Having completed this self-evaluation, you should have some idea of those skills you might wish to improve. Each of the following sections contains a description and elaboration of the appropriate skill, and provides practical advice and suggestions for strengthening competence as it relates to the skill.

1. **ESTABLISHING A LEARNING SET** Skills in planning and implementing specific pre-instructional strategies designed to clarify, explain, or arouse interest in subsequent learning activities. It also refers to the skill of

the instructor in creating a readiness to learn the material or lesson that has been planned.

These pre-instructional strategies are more likely to be successful when they are related to experience or prior knowledge of the adult learner. It is quite useful, therefore, for the instructor to be knowledgeable of the background of the students prior to designing the strategies.

There are several types of pre-instructional strategies that are useful in focusing student interest and attention on the material to be learned. It may be something as simple as saying, "I would like to begin by directing your attention to the material on page 222 where it says . . .," or it may be something more elaborate.

The following strategies are likely to increase both learning and motivation:

(1) **Pre-test or diagnostic device** A set of questions, an essay or some other type of diagnostic instrument designed to determine what the student already knows. It can also serve as a way of focusing attention on the material that is to follow. It is also effective when students perceive that the purpose of the instrument is diagnostic rather than evaluative. Results should always be shared with the adult learner.

(2) **Specific learning objectives** A learning objective is a statement of intended outcomes expressed in terms of student behavior. When used as pre-instructional strategies, they are particularly helpful as they provide not only an overview of subsequent material, but they also serve to alert the adult learner that instruction is about to begin.

(3) **Provide overviews** An overview or summary of what is to be done is used to emphasize the main points by condensing, simplifying or repeating key ideas in a brief and precise manner. Overviews may take the form of: a preview of topics to be covered, an outline of a lecture or film, a list of steps required to complete a task, a worksheet focusing on key material, key questions, lists of terms, unfamiliar words or phrases, a course syllabus.

(4) **Selecting advance organizers** As a pre-instructional strategy linking new and unfamiliar material to the knowledge and experience already possessed by the learner, advance organizers may take the form of the following:
    a. arousing controversy — stimulation of interest by the introduction of the topic as being controversial,
    b. using surprise tactics — use of an incomplete report leading to an inaccurate conclusion may be an example,
    c. using analogy — linking instructional goals with student experience,
    d. use of the media — current events may provide an effective transition to the material to be covered.

2. LOGICAL ORGANIZATION Arranging and presenting course material and learning activities so that the relationship among the various topics and activities are clear.

In designing a logical organization framework, several suggestions are offered:

(1) Select course objectives and learning resources that are appropriate to the learning needs for the tasks.

(2) Courses should be reviewed by colleagues and/or students so that the sequences are apparent.

(3) Discuss the revised course and/or material with the students at the outset of the learning experience.

Throughout the presentation of the new material, the instructor should provide continual reference to the framework or outline. There should be a clear signal when a transition is being made from one part to another, thus helping students to see where they are in relation to the plan. Often a particular framework may assist one student to understand material but does not facilitate integration or understanding for others. The task of the facilitator may more appropriately be to assist the students to find their own framework in which to fit the variety of materials and experiences.

3. PACING   The rate at which new ideas and activities are introduced or the amount of time spent on a particular topic or task.

Decisions about pacing need to be made during the initial planning of the learning experiences. *When* a topic is introduced and *how much* time should be spent on it should be considered when planning the unit.

Effective performance of this skill demands an ability to change the pace or flow when appropriate. If a "teachable moment" has been created, the effective instructor will need to adjust the time spent on subsequent material in order to fully capitalize on the needs of the moment.

While it is impossible for the instructor in a classroom situation to respond to the pacing needs of each student, there are several indicators that suggest when pacing may need to be adjusted:

(1) **Non-verbal behavior**   A bored or disinterested class may suggest that the pacing is too slow; similarly, signs of frustration or confusion may indicate that the pacing has been too fast.

(2) **Poor results on tests or quizzes**   This might suggest that the rate at which the instructor has been going is too fast. The successful instructor must be sensitive to the needs of the student and must be able to change the rate or level of instruction in order to best facilitate the learning needs of the class.

4. ELABORATION   Skills in clarifying an idea or topic. Elaboration takes the form of illustrative examples, documentation, analogies, comparisons or any of a myriad of means to expand upon a point, idea, or concept. The teacher must be particularly concerned with the way in which the material is organized and of the educational experiences of the students.

Several methods of elaboration have proven to be effective:

(1) **Comparison**   Clarification by comparison of the new information to a set criteria or standard.

(2) **Use of relevant terminology**   Explanation using vocabulary, examples or illustrations that are familiar to the student.

(3) **Visual Aids**   Use of charts, graphs, slides, pictures, transparencies for further elaboration.

(4) **Contrast**   Elaboration is enhanced by the use of opposing elements or arguments.

5. **EXPRESSION** Skills using verbal and non-verbal techniques to increase the power and meaning of communication. The use of humor, body language, voice modulation, good diction, articulation and gestures are all ways to increase expressiveness. In order to increase proficiency in this skill, the following might be helpful: (1) enroll in a speech or drama course, (2) visit classes of effective instructors.

6. **ASKING QUESTIONS** Ability to use different types of questions for different instructional purposes. The quality of the questioning technique is.in the *focus* rather than the quantity of questions asked.

In order to ask good questions, several points should be kept in mind:

(1) **Questions should reflect a definite purpose** They need to reveal a direct relationship to the objectives of the material being presented.

(2) **Questions should be concise** Questions should be well thought out as this increases the likelihood that they will be meaningful to the students.

(3) **Questions should require thoughtful responses** Questions requiring thought strengthen problem solving skills and assist students to develop higher cognitive level skills.

(4) **Address the questions to the class first before asking a specific person to respond** This allows all class members to formulate a tentative answer while also serving to keep their attention.

(5) **Allow sufficient response time** Allow time for phrasing an answer before asking the question again or rephrasing the question.

(6) **Evenly distribute questions to all class members** By distributing questions evenly, all students, rather than just those who volunteer, will know that they are expected to respond and will be waiting for such an opportunity.

(7) **Accept all answers** This does not mean that all answers are praised or allowed to remain uncorrected, for incorrect responses need to be corrected, but the skillful instructor will tactfully respond to the incorrect point rather than to belittle the student who offered the incorrect response.

(8) **Avoid teacher dominance** Encourage students to respond to one another. This helps to break the more usual pattern of the instructor asking one question followed by a student response, followed by another question, discussion and student response.

Instructors who have given consideration to the types of questions to be asked, have planned the questions, and are skillful in the way in which they ask those questions are more likely to produce students who have higher cognitive functioning skills.

7. **RESPONDING TO QUESTIONS** Skill at answering questions clearly and concisely in ways that promote understanding and further participation.

Within an adult learning environment, it is quite important that an atmosphere be created whereby the student feels comfortable and free to ask questions without the fear of embarrassment. Effective answering requires careful listening.

Suggestions that may aid in responding to questions clearly and concisely:

(1) **Focus on what has been said rather than on the speaker** This allows the instructor to respond to the point rather than to the particular student thereby more effectively involving all students.

(2) **Focus on the exploration of alternatives rather than on answers and solutions.** This encourages students to provide creative answers as well as recognizes different cognitive learning styles of individuals.

(3) **Focus responses on the amount of information the questioner needs rather than on the amount of information the instructor would like to give.** This is difficult to assess but can be developed over time.

(4) **Redirecting** The redirecting of the question to another student. This technique, used judiciously, can increase student participation while encouraging student interaction.

(5) **Probing** The instructor pursues the implication of a particular question or clarifies the original question with another question to the same student thus helping the student to clarify and answer the question individually.

(6) **Postponing** Questions relating to the interests of only a few students may best be served by having the question postponed to another time. In such instances, the instructor may suggest that those students consult after class. Postponement of a question may also be appropriate if time is a serious consideration or if the issue being raised will be covered at a later date.

8. STUDENT PARTICIPATION Promoting participation in classroom activities and guiding that participation in fruitful directions.

The amount and type of student participation will vary depending on the subject matter, method of presentation, size of class. However, regardless of the context, student participation will be increased if the amount and type of participation desired by the instructor is known, has been discussed, and accepted by all.

These response patterns will also increase student participation:

(1) **Simple acknowledgement** Recognition, either verbal or non-verbal, that the student contribution has been heard. It does not convey any evaluative judgement. Examples are, "Yes. Thank you."

(2) **Praise** Essentially a positive statement about all or part of the student comment. Examples might be, "Yes, that's correct," "That's right!" or "I'm not sure I agree with all you have just said but the part about its implications is quite thought provoking."

(3) **Restatement** Repetition, modification, clarification or similar expansion of a student contribution — recognizes an idea and emphasizes its importance.

(4) **Redirecting** Often the student may better respond when the question is rephrased or follows another student's reply.

(5) **Probing** Searching for deeper meaning can often assist students to develop higher cognitive faculties.

The adult educator who wishes to increase participation in discussions will find the literature in group dynamics invaluable. This is strongly recommended as a tool for improving classroom discussions. Examples are buzz groups, debates, reaction panels, role playing and brainstorming.

9. CLOSURE Bringing together the major points of a discussion or lecture at the end of a topic or class.

Closure has two main functions. One is the identification of relationships among topics previously presented and those currently under discussion. The second involves summarizing major points and reviewing relationships among them. Primarily, it is a summary by the instructor or the facilitation of a group summary discussion.

Some successful closure techniques are:

(1) **Application in new problem settings** Restating the concepts and materials taught in new time frames assist in summarizing key concepts. Often a skillful instructor will present the material as a solution to a different problem and thus can indicate transfer of learning.

(2) **Emphasis and planned repetition of major points during a summary** Prior to the summary the instructor has identified essential material.

(3) **No-fault quizzes** This is a non-graded, diagnostic series of questions designed to promote discussion regarding the points under discussion. This device frequently signifies the instructor's intent to move on to another topic and may encourage questions indicating that more elaboration is needed.

(4) **Asking for student recall of major points** A very direct form of closure is asking students to recall or summarize the material under discussion. Avoid eliciting a mere "parroting back" of what has been presented. Closure activities help the adult educator to organize the material so that it is seen as being logical and sequential. Furthermore, they assist students to identify relationships among topics and understand how the topics fit in with the larger unit and also serve to alert the students that the end of the presentation is near and it is time to raise questions.

10. EVALUATION Specifying the criteria for evaluation in designing valid and reliable evaluation procedures and in providing adequate evaluative information to the students refers both to what is commonly referred to as the "measurement" process (the design, construction, administration and scoring of tests) and the "evaluation" process (the interpreting or assigning of values to test scores). The effective adult educator must be familiar with both aspects.

(1) **Criteria for evaluation** Evaluation should serve to provide: information regarding progress to the adult learner, the student with some idea of what additional material is needed to be learned, information which is useful in assessing student learning.

(2) **Designing evaluative instruments:** The key to designing effective evaluative instruments is to have clearly stated and understood learning objectives. Once the instructional objectives are clear, however, a second key is to be able to write correct evaluation questions. Several suggestions follow: strive for verbal clarity, state the questions as concisely as possible, write the question in such a way that the correct answer is not obvious, avoid negatively worded questions as they tend to be confusing.

(3) **Grading student learning** Students' evaluation should be for the purposes of providing constructive feedback to students regarding their progress. When possible, it is suggested that grading be avoided as it seemingly does little more than add unnecessary pressure to the adult learner. When

grading is necessary, the following suggestions might reduce some pressure: be sure that the basis for grades are clearly understood by all concerned, grade performance periodically throughout the learning experience, discuss the grades and their results as soon as the grades are available, be willing to admit instructor error.

Evaluation is one of the most complex of the skills for teaching adults and is a highly emotional subject.

11. **LEVEL OF CHALLENGE** Selecting course objectives, content and activities that challenge students' abilities but that are not too difficult for students to master. When considering the appropriate level of challenge, the instructor must be aware of the varying needs of the students in the class as well as the content to be covered. Experience with the subject matter and the students provide a good indicator regarding the level of challenge. There are also several strategies for testing and adjusting the level of challenge:

(1) **Clarify expectations** Telling the students what is expected of them will increase student learning.

(2) **Pretest** Given for the purpose of determining an appropriate level of challenge, pretest should be designed to answer two basic types of questions: to determine if the students have the necessary learning skills relative to the material to be presented; to determine the knowledge already obtained through life experience or other means. With this type of information readily available, the instructor will be better able to adjust the level to provide an appropriate challenge for the students.

(3) **Conduct periodic checks** Ask specific content oriented questions periodically throughout a lecture. Ask for specific questions from students regarding the material just presented. Provide no-fault quizzes — a nongraded quiz designed to provide information to the instructor regarding whether or not alterations are needed. Check for non-verbal clues which indicate confusion, frustration, boredom or other signs that the material is either too easy or too difficult.

12. **VARIETY** Knowing when to use various teaching methods, materials and techniques and can vary the use of these in response to student and content needs.

The Clinic to Improve Teaching presents a useful summary model:
(1) Specify the goal of instruction.
(2) Generate possible teaching methods and materials for achieving this goal.
(3) Consider the importance of student learning styles, teacher methods previously used, teacher interest, environmental restrictions.

13. **CREATIVITY** Combining or restructuring existing methods and/or materials into new and creative ideas. The primary focus of this skill is to produce insight for the student.

Much traditional instructional practice has concentrated on the building block approach which develops vertical thinking or analytical problem solving. While this is essential to the acquisition of knowledge, skills in creative or lateral thinking are similarly important and often lacking in traditional teaching. Instructional methodology incorporating the characteristics of lateral thinking encourage and foster the development of insights and creativity by the adult student.

The following processes may be utilized by the instructor concerned with developing creativity:

(1) **Generation of alternatives** Seeking different ways of looking at a problem rather than on arriving at a solution.

(2) **Challenging Assumptions** Each student response is probed with another "why" question which is directed toward some aspect of the previous statement or response. The intent is to create discomfort with any explanation as no automatic response is accepted, no matter how obvious it may appear.

(3) **Reversals** The learners are asked to look at a situation in new ways. For example, the instructor might ask, "What would happen if we started at the end of the book and read the last chapter first? Is this possible?" or "What would happen if teachers were paid based on the number of adults enrolling in their course?"

(4) **Brainstorming** A problem is presented and all participants offer possible solutions. All responses are accepted and written down. No judgments are made regarding each response. The written comments are classified as immediately useful, worth further exploration, new approaches to the problem.

14. MANAGEMENT Performing the routing administrative tasks in a classroom that allow instruction to proceed smoothly and efficiently. The teacher must be able to sustain more than one activity simultaneously, to maintain continuity without confusion, keep the group alert, hold the interests of the learners, generate enthusiasm and be able to provide variety in work assignments and classroom activities.

To be successful at this skill, the instructor must plan in advance, identify needed resources, determine how they fit into the instructional sequence, and have them available (on hand).

15. FLEXIBILITY/INDIVIDUALIZATION Skills in dealing with differing interests and abilities among students and in responding constructively to student suggestions, criticisms and comments regarding teaching strategies. An adult classroom often contains learners with widely varying abilities, interest levels or experiences. There are several ways of individualizing the learning experience:

(2) **Use learning contracts** In *Self-Directed Learning,* Malcolm Knowles[4] fully describes this approach to individualizing adult learning. Essentially, it involves the negotiation of learning objectives, methods for accomplishing the objectives, and evidence between the learner and the facilitator that the objectives have been accomplished.

(2) **"Modularize" the instructional unit** It is highly effective when the information to be conveyed can be set forth in "yes-no," or multiple choice answers. Students can work independently, at their own rate of learning, and on specific materials to be learned. These models are well typified in computer assisted instruction and in programmed learning labs.

16. INTERPERSONAL RELATIONS   Relating to students in ways that promote mutual respect and rapport. A positive classroom atmosphere is one of the more critical variables influencing classroom achievement.

Developing interpersonal relations also means the creation of a collaborative rather than a competitive classroom. There are several ways in which this might be done:
(1) Learn student names.
(2) Use recognition and praise.
(3) Allow instructional options for those who can demonstrate prior knowledge.
(4) Encourage alternative views to be expressed.
(5) Take advantage of "teachable moments."
(6) Encourage alternative evaluation devices — oral assessments, projects, self-assessments.

Openly discuss all aspects of the teaching/learning transaction.

17. LEARNING ENVIRONMENT   Create and maintain an atmosphere conducive to student involvement and learning.

When discussing the learning environment, at least three aspects need to be considered. They are the intellectual, social and physical characteristics. The intellectual aspects of the learning environment include the course content, study and evaluation procedures and intellectual interaction between student and instructor. Social aspects include family pressures, peer interaction, the need for acceptance and the presence or absence of threat in the classroom. Physical aspects include the lighting, temperature, size and type of furniture and other considerations relating to the personal safety and comfort of the adult learners.

In order to create a learning environment which fosters active learning, the instructor should be aware of the following:
(1) Provide for a variety of learning experiences.
(2) Mutual respect between the instructor and the learner.
(3) Provide interactions between the instructor and the learner both in and out of the classroom.

There are a number of considerations that overlap with other teaching skills when attempting to establish a positive learning environment. It is suggested that if the reader is concerned with the development of a positive environment, the sections relating to CREATIVITY, VARIETY, INTERPERSONAL RELATIONSHIPS, STUDENT PARTICIPATION, LEVEL OF CHALLENGE and PERSPECTIVE be reviewed as they provide additional suggestions for the development of this skill.

18. ENTHUSIASM   Abilities to conduct and direct learning activities in a dynamic manner and to stimulate interest and excitement in course content and activities.

Enthusiasm can be conveyed in a variety of behaviors. The following "highly expressive" behaviors and attitudes were found to be associated with increases in student achievement and satisfaction with instruction. The instructor:

(1) Stresses important material due to concern for student understanding.
(2) Feels responsible for whether or not the students understand the material.
(3) Feels that part of teaching is keeping student attention.
(4) Is interested in the subject.
(5) Uses humor.
(6) Wishes to stimulate thinking regardless of student goals.

19. **PERSPECTIVE** Establishing a frame of reference for concepts and ideas and expanding that frame of reference to include an increasingly wider variety of viewpoints, implications and relationships. By creating a proper perspective, the adult educator places the subject in a context that is meaningful to the student.

The establishment of a perspective that coincides with the interests and prior learning of the student will not only aid comprehension but will also add to the retention and transfer of learning.

When considering a subject to be taught, the instructor must consider its relevancy to the learner. The following factors might be considered:
(1) The interests and motivations of the learners.
(2) The educational backgrounds of the participants.
(3) The demographics of the class (age, socio, economic levels, race).
(4) The political, social and cultural mores of the group.

20. **VALUE CONTEXT** Utilities to identify explicitly his or her own values and to clarify the implications of those values and their implications as they relate to the subject matter, to help students clarify their values and recognize the implications of those values for their professional and personal conduct.

Value context refers to the inclusion of opportunities for students to make decisions about value laden issues within the subject matter of a course. The instructor should provide a classroom atmosphere wherein students can judge, argue, give opinions, compare, contrast, debate, accept and reject issues in relation to their own value system. The instructor concerned with providing a value context sees an honest exploration of values combined with a discussion of the subject as constituting education in the fullest sense. Some suggestions are:
(1) Ask questions that call for comparison.
(2) Ask questions that call for contrast.
(3) Ask questions calling for a statement of opinion.
(4) Role play. The players might take a role that is the opposite of their own.
(5) Provide sentence fragments demanding evaluative completion positions. "I feel abortions should be available on demand because . . ."

Knowledge needs to be put in a value context in order to encourage the development of commitment and subsequent action. In today's world of increasing complexity, it becomes all the more important that the instructor view this skill and its improvement as being beneficial not only on a personal level but on a professional level as well.

SUMMARY

It is important to realize that while the twenty skills have been treated as being discrete, in reality they are not. Each must be viewed in relation to those other skills which obviously interrelate. It would be inadvisable, for example, to only concentrate on PERSPECTIVE without considering how this skill relates to ESTABLISHING A LEARNING SET, LOGICAL ORGANIZATION, LEARNING ENVIRONMENT, and VALUE CONTEXT. These skills provide a collection of building blocks that can be assembled and reassembled in numerous ways. The nature of the subject matter itself, the entire educational environment, the style of the instructor, the mastery of the subject matter by the instructor are all important and help to determine the importance of specific skills. The aim of the Clinic is to assist instructors to self assess their own strengths and areas of need and provide information and references so that instructional behaviors most appropriate for themselves and the adult learners may be developed.

REFERENCES

1. Joyce, B. & Weil, M. *Models of Teaching (2nd Ed.).* Englewood Cliffs, New Jersey: Prentice-Hall, Inc., 1979.
2. Clinic to Improve University Teaching. *Working Definitions of Some Technical Skills of Teaching.* Amherst, Massachusetts: University of Massachusetts, 1977.
3. Knowles, M.S. *The Modern Practice of Adult Education (2nd Ed.).* New York: Association Press, 1980.
4. _____. *Self-directed Learning: A Guide for Teachers and Students.* New York: Association Press, 1975.
5. Learner, M. *Values in Education.* Bloomington, Indiana: Phi Delta Kappa Educational Foundation, 1976.
6. Davis, J.L. *Strategies for College Teaching.* New York: Fearon Publishing, 1976.

Information Retrieval Systems

John A. Niemi

*Professor, Graduat Studies
in Adult-Continuing Education
Northern Illinois University*

Susan Imel

*Assistant Director,
ERIC Clearinghouse on Adult,
Career, and Vocational Education
Ohio State University*

Intelligent adult learners constantly search for new ways to solve problems, whether pursuing activities in formal or informal settings. Adult learners are those who undertake purposeful activities ". . . with the intention of increasing their knowledge, developing and updating their skills, and modifying their attitudes throughout their lifetimes. This may happen in formal settings such as schools, or in less formal settings . . ."[1] Information retrieval systems — with special emphasis on the Educational Resources Information Center (ERIC) — is one of the multiple resources available in the learning society. The concept "adult learner" will be used in a broad sense to include all persons interested in adult education — administrators, counselors, researchers, students, and teachers.

It is axiomatic that in order for adult learners to respond creatively to everyday challenges and to anticipate new ones, they must keep abreast of developments. It was not difficult to do so before the knowledge explosion generated a vast array of materials that grows daily at a rapid rate. Adult learners, like other learners, were book-oriented and accustomed to seeking help from institutional resources. Libraries offered guides in the form of standard reference works such as **Education Index, Encyclopedia of Educational Research, The Readers' Guide to Periodical Literature,** and **Dissertation Abstracts International.** Professional organizations like the Adult Education Association of the U.S.A. (AEA) and the National Association for Public Continuing and Adult Education (NAPCAE) stood ready to help, as did faculties and colleges of education. (AEA and NAPCAE have recently been merged into the American Association for Adult and Continuing

Education.) These resources are still indispensable. However, the overwhelming mass of knowledge that now confronts anyone wishing to investigate a particular problem in education has demanded a new approach to research.

"Information retrieval systems," or "databases," are terms commonly applied to systems that have sprung up in the attempt to make information more readily available to seekers of knowledge. The functions of information retrieval systems may vary; but most evaluate, abstract, and index documents relating to topics within specific areas. Although a number of information retrieval systems are useful to adult learners, the Educational Resources Information Center (ERIC) is considered to be the primary system for education due to both its purpose and its history of service to the field. The ERIC system is described in detail below, following some general information about information retrieval systems.

Information Retrieval Systems — What and How — Usually when people speak of retrieving information, they are referring to retrieval of documents that have been stored in a database. When stored, the documents have generally been indexed or classified using a vocabulary control device to facilitate their retrieval. Vocabulary control devices may consist of a thesaurus, a list of subject headings or a specialized subject classification scheme. This vocabulary control is used to retrieve information from a database.[2]

From the large number of existing databases, individuals seeking information must select those that best serve their needs. There are a number of resources available that can be used in selecting the appropriate database. The most comprehensive reference is **Encyclopedia of Information Systems and Services, Fourth Edition.**[3] Available at most libraries, it provides a guide to information storage and retrieval services, database producers and publishers, online vendors, computer service companies, computerized retrieval systems, libraries, government agencies, networks and consortia, information centers, data banks, clearinghouses, research centers, associations and consultants. Because it has a subject index, it is easy to use. Of particular interest to adult learners is a publication titled **Databases and Clearinghouses: Information Resources for Education.**[4] It lists one page summaries of more than fifty databases and over forty clearinghouses, and provides explanations of how to interpret database and clearinghouse information sheets. Other database reference sources exist, similar to the two mentioned here; information about them may be obtained through libraries and other resource centers.

Online information retrieval systems also ease the database selection problem by making available, on a national basis, a large number of databases through a single source. Online services available through private organizations known as "vendors" provide access to more than 150 databases containing bibliographic and/or document related data covering virtually every field. They include millions of references to journal articles, technical reports, patents, books, conference papers, annual reports, trade publications, newspaper and magazine articles, Congressional proceedings, government documents, theses and dissertations, abstracts and bibliographies and more.[5] These records are accessed through the vendor's (or source's) computer with searching provided by telephone hook-up to the user's computer terminal, usually located in a library or other resource center. Three information retrieval systems (or vendors) currently offer most of the databases useful to educators: BRS, available through Bibliographic Retrieval Service; DIALOG, available through Lockheed Information Systems; and ORBIT, available through System Development Corporation, SDC Search Service.[4] Searching of these online retrieval systems is usually performed by trained personnel, called searchers, who are familiar with the characteristics of the systems. Searchers can help decide which databases will be most useful to access in locating desired information.

When seeking information, adult learners may turn to a number of information retrieval systems using the processes and resources described above. However, because it has been designed specifically for the field of education, ERIC is the system used most often in searches for educational materials.

WHAT IS ERIC?

Educational Resources Information Center (ERIC) is a nationwide information system that has existed since 1966 and is currently supported by the National Institute of Education. Designed to put the results of educational research and development in the hands of researchers, practitioners, and other adult learners, ERIC consists of a central unit in Washington, D.C. and sixteen clearinghouses located throughout the country, each focusing on a specific field of education.[6]

Individual clearinghouses are responsible for acquiring, selecting, abstracting, and indexing materials in their assigned scope areas, while the central unit maintains the database and prepares the monthly journal of abstracts, **Resources in Education** (RIE), using material submitted by the clearinghouses. A second monthly index, **Current Index to Journals in Education** (CIJE), is prepared for the ERIC system by a commercial publisher. To date, more than 215,000 documents have been abstracted and announced in RIE and annotations of more than 250,000 journal articles have appeared in CIJE. Together these entries form the ERIC database that can be used to locate information.

In addition to building databases, the clearinghouses also develop printed materials for their assigned scope areas and respond to questions of requests for information. The ERIC Clearinghouse on Adult, Career, and Vocational Education (ERIC/ACVE), located since 1976 at the National Center for Research in Vocational Education, The Ohio State University, has major responsibilities for servicing the field of adult and continuing education. Its scope is as follows:

1. The formal and informal education of adults, related to all adult-life roles and stages of the adult life-cycle. All levels of education are

included from basic literacy training through professional skill upgrading.
2. Vocational and technical education, including new and emerging vocational and technical fields for a wide spectrum of high school, postsecondary, adult, and vocational rehabilitation populations.
3. Career education, formal and informal, from preschool to adult, encompassing career development materials related to attitudes, aptitudes, interests, values, decision making, self understanding, and occupational information.

ERIC/ACVE collects materials from adult educators throughout the country for consideration for inclusion in the ERIC database. It also creates and prints fact sheets, "minibibs," and major publications on topics of interest to adult and continuing educators.

Three other clearinghouses also serve scope areas that are concerned with adults and their needs. These are the ERIC Clearinghouse on Counseling and Personnel Services, the ERIC Clearinghouse on Higher Education, and the ERIC Clearinghouse for Junior Colleges. For persons wishing to contact ERIC/ACVE or any of the other three clearinghouses with specific questions or a request to be placed on their mailing list, their addresses appear at the end of this article.

ERIC places at the disposal of adult learners, including those in decision-making positions in the field, the accumulated experience and wisdom of others who have faced similar problems. The system holds great promise for them because it utilizes the capabilities of print, microfiche, and the computer. As adult learners become acquainted with ERIC and proficient in using it, they will become increasingly independent and more sophisticated in their pursuit of learning. ERIC offers an option that can be used alone or can augment and assist familiar options such as classroom learning, correspondence study, help from a tutor, programmed texts, and the conventional use of libraries.

ERIC REFERENCE TOOLS — In order to locate information in the ERIC database, it is important to become familiar with the monthly indexes **Resources in Education** (RIE) and **Current Index to Journals in Education** (CIJE), as well as with the **Thesaurus of ERIC Descriptors.**

The **Thesaurus of ERIC Descriptors** is a controlled vocabulary of educational terms called "descriptors." Descriptors are used to index and enter documents and journal articles into the ERIC system and to assist users in retrieving information from it. With the help of the Thesaurus, all materials processed by ERIC can be identified by manual searches of the printed indexes of RIE and CIJE or by computer searches of the ERIC tapes.

Resources in Education (RIE) is a monthly publication of abstracts of the nearly 1,200 documents that pass the ERIC selection criteria at the clearinghouses each month. Recently completed research reports, curriculum and teaching guides, instructional materials, descriptions and evaluations of exemplary programs, and other documents of educational significance are examples of the types of adult and continuing education materials that are announced in RIE. An attempt is made to secure "fugitive" materials for the ERIC database, those that might not be seen by or widely available to adult learners if not announced in RIE. Documents that appear in RIE are indexed by subject, author, institutional source, and publication type. Most of the documents are available on microfiche or in print form for a small charge.

Current Index to Journals in Education (CIJE), another monthly publication, contains annotations of articles from more than 700 major education-related journals. In addition to a main entry section listing the annotations, CIJE is indexed by subject, author, and journal title. Because of copyright laws, the articles are not available on microfiche through ERIC, but CIJE directs users to reprint sources.

Two additional reference tools are directories giving information about ERIC collections and services. More than 700 libraries throughout the country house ERIC collections, with copies of RIE and CIJE and microfiche of more than 160,000 of the documents announced in RIE. The **Directory of ERIC Microfiche Collections** contains a listing of organizations with sizable ERIC microfiche collections organized alphabetically by state and by cities within each state. The Directory of ERIC Search Services lists and describes briefly more than 500 organizations currently providing computerized searches of the ERIC database. It, too, is organized alphabetically by state and city, and includes search cost information. Single copies of these directories may be obtained free of charge by writing or calling the ERIC Processing and Reference Facility, ORI, Inc., Information Systems Division, 4833 Rugby Avenue, Suite 303, Bethesda, Maryland 20814; (301) 656-9873.

SEARCHING ERIC

Define the Subject — When preparing to do a search of the ERIC database, either by hand or computer, it is important to determine exactly what information is desired. The subject that is to be the focus of an ERIC search must be defined as precisely as possible if the search is to be truly productive. The first step, "Define the Subject," is useful when a person is interested in a broad subject like "adult learning," but it is somewhat vague (perhaps because of insufficient knowledge) about the specific information sought. On the other hand, individuals who know exactly what they want from an ERIC search can move directly to step 2, "Identify the Concepts."

1. Think about the subject. Ponder its nature and scope, the important concepts involved, its relation to other subjects or fields. Try to formulate questions or statements (including hypotheses) you wish to pursue. Write down all the ideas you can think of, even if, at this preliminary stage, they seem broad, tentative, overlapping, or even clumsy.
2. Talk about the subject and your statements or questions with colleagues, friends, university professors, librarians, searchers, especially persons who have an interest in or knowledge of the subject. Such conversations will often help you to clarify your thinking, give you new insights, or

suggest new avenues of inquiry. The staff of ERIC/ACVE are always more than willing to help you.
3. At this stage, you should refine your questions or statements to make them as precise as possible; they should state exactly what you want to know. Be alert to vague language, ambiguities, or irrelevant ideas that may have crept in. Addressing yourself to such questions as these might assist you:

>In which area of adult education am I interested?
>What information is already known and/or available?
>Should I set a time limit on the information sought, such as last year, the previous seven years?
>How will the resulting information be applied in administrative decision making, in the classroom, for my own professional growth?

Identify the Concepts — Analyze the subject by breaking it down into its major concepts, or factors. Find the descriptors in the ERIC Thesaurus that best fit with those concepts. If, for example, your topic is "Adult Learning Disabilities," it contains two concepts: (1) adults, (2) learning disabilities. Some appropriate descriptors that might be selected for each of these concepts are:

Concept: **Adults**
(1) adults
(2) adult basic education
(3) adult students
(4) adult education

Concept: **Learning Disabilities**
(1) learning disabilities
(2) remedial reading
(3) learning problems
(4) educational diagnosis

An example of a Thesaurus descriptor entry appears as Figure 1, which shows the descriptor "adult education."[7] Each descriptor entry contains the following information; (1) the date the descriptor came into use in the ERIC system, (2) the number of times each descriptor has been used to index materials for CIJE and RIE, (3) a scope note (SN) defining how the term is used in ERIC, (4) what other terms the descriptor is used for (UF) or instead of, (5) broader terms (BT) and related terms (RT) that represent other ERIC descriptors to be considered in conducting the search.

For the descriptor Adult Education, the following information is available. It came into use as a descriptor in July, 1966, and has been used in indexing 3,601 journal articles in CIJE and 5,752 documents in RIE. The scope note (SN) is "providing or coordinating purposeful learning activities for adults." It is used for (UF) or instead of the terms **Adult Education Programs** and **Further Education.** (In other words, neither of these terms is used as a descriptor in ERIC; so information relating to these concepts is indexed with the descriptor Adult Education.) Eight narrower terms (NT), one broader term (BT), and twenty-five related terms (RT) are listed. Depending upon the objectives of the search, some of these terms may need to be considered for use in conducting it.

ADULT EDUCATION Jul 1966
           CIJE: 3,601   RIE: 5,752   GC: 340

SN	Providing or coordinating purpose-ful learning activities for adults	RT	Adult Students
			Community Education
UF	Adult Education Programs (1966 1980) #		Continuing Education Centers
			Continuing Education Units
	Further Education		Correctional Education
NT	Adult Basic Education		Educational Gerontology
	Adult Vocational Education		Extension Education
	Continuing Education		High School Equivalency Programs
	Labor Education		Lifelong Learning
	Migrant Adult Education		Noncredit Courses
	Parent Education		Nonschool Educational Programs
	Public School Adult Education		Post Secondary Education
	Veterans Education		Professional Continuing Education
BT	Education		Professional Education
RT	Adult Development		Refresher Courses
	Adult Dropouts		Retraining
	Adult Learning		Special Degree Programs
	Adult Programs		Training Allowances
	Adult Reading Programs		Womens Education
	Adults		

Figure 1. Entry for descriptor *Adult Education* from *Thesaurus of ERIC Descriptors*.

In conducting either a manual search or a computer search, the initial steps are identical. You first identify the subject, analyze it according to concepts, and then consult the **Thesaurus** for relevant descriptors.

Manual Search — Locating information in ERIC by using the printed indexes, CIJE and RIE, constitutes a manual or hand search. In a manual search, you select one of the descriptors you have identified to begin your search. With the example "Adult Learning Disabilities," the descriptor **Learning Disabilities** is the best place to start. Look up "learning disabilities" in the subject indexes of both RIE and CIJE and select those entries that seem most relevant. (RIE uses ED numbers to list entries and CIJE uses EJ numbers to list journal entries.) Once you have found ED or EJ numbers, you can look up the abstract or annotation in the main entry section of the index to determine if you wish to acquire the entire document or article. If you cannot tell from the abstract or annotation, you may need to consult the document or article itself before deciding on its usefulness. Repeat this process with all descriptors to identify relevant information. Figure 2 depicts the process of a manual search.

Computer Search — Searching the ERIC database by computer is faster and more efficient than searching it manually, provided you have selected the proper descriptors. All the descriptors you select can be entered at once at the

MANUAL SEARCH PROCEDURE

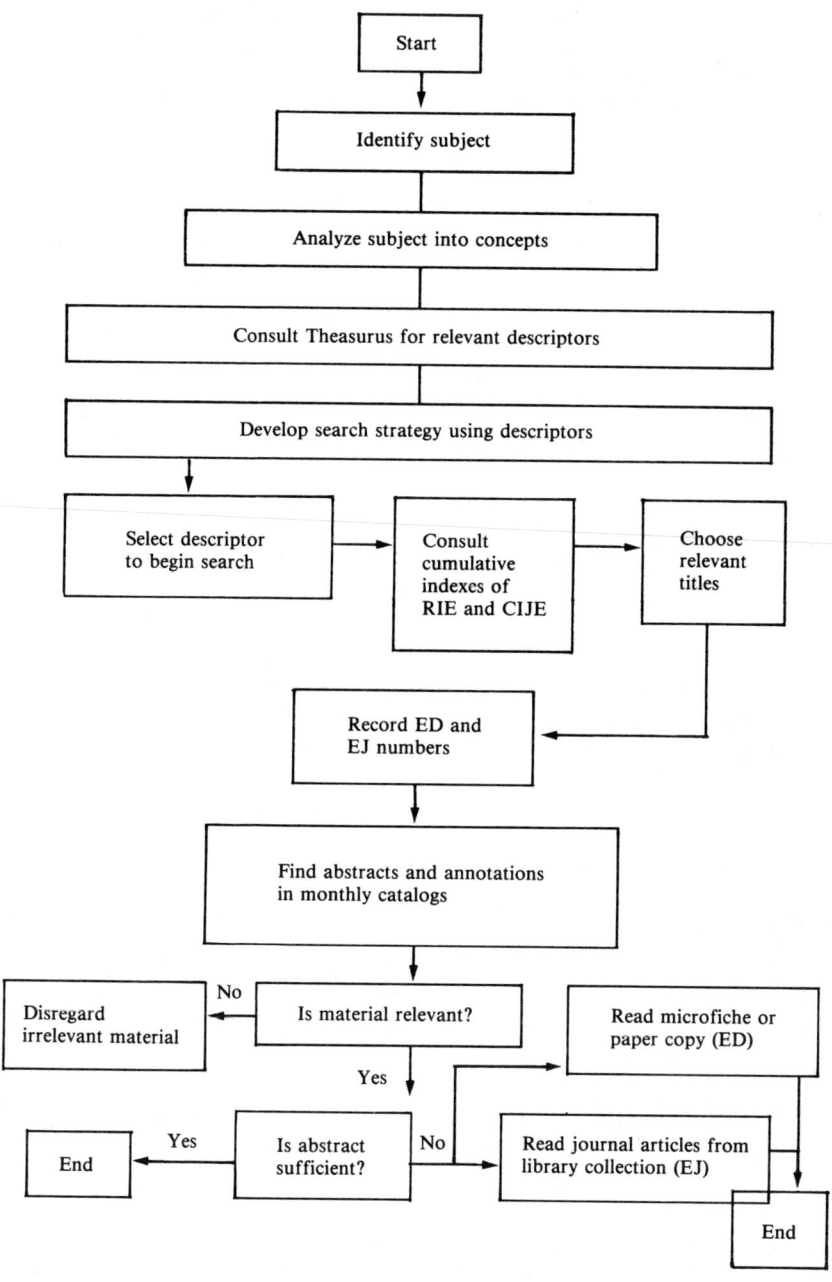

Figure 2.

COMPUTER SEARCH PROCEDURE

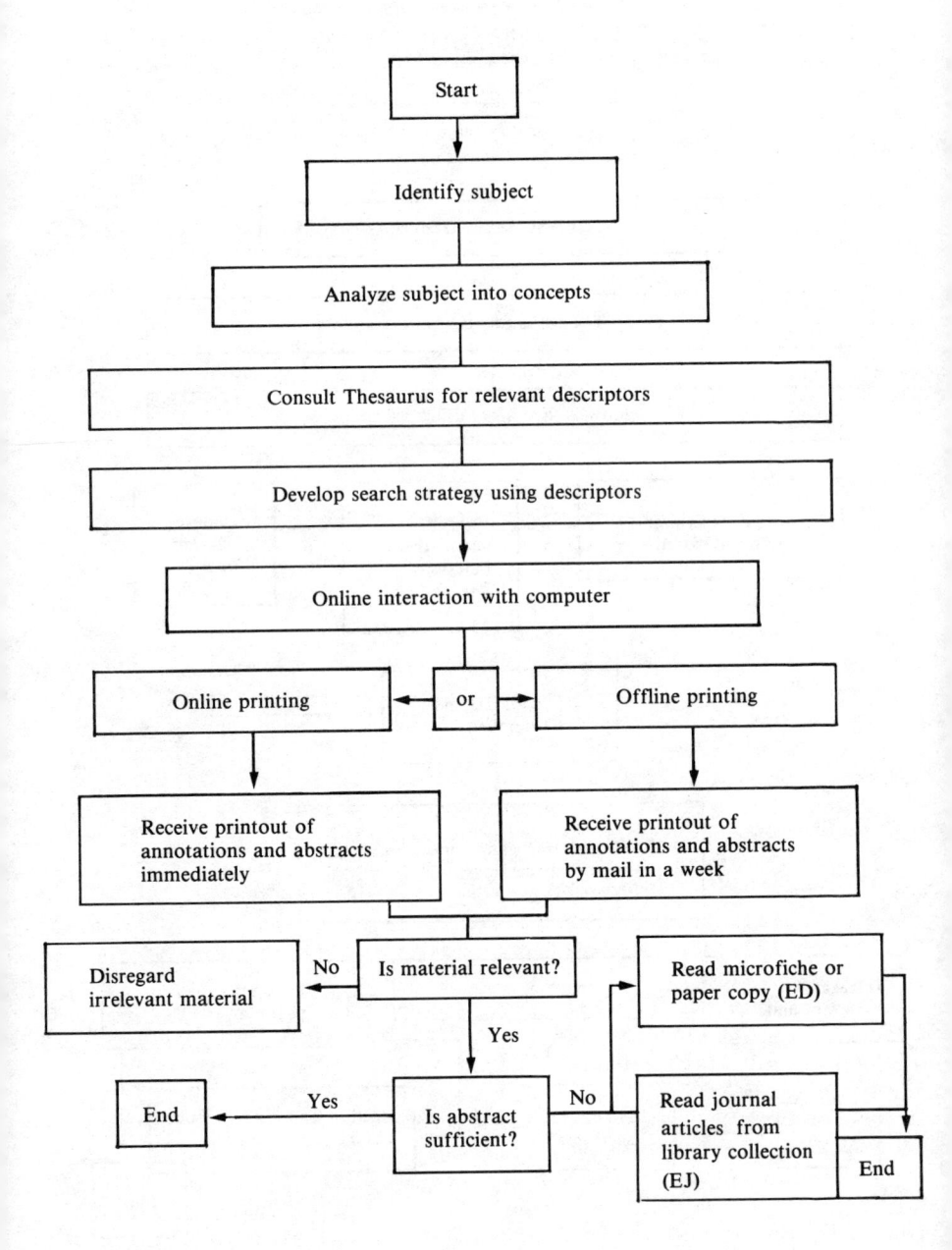

Figure 3.

terminal. Through a crossing technique based on Boolean logic principles, a search is performed of the entire database in seconds. The unique feature of online computer searching is that the user gives input to the computer in the form of descriptors and receives immediate feedback. If the computer reports a large amount of available material, it may be that the subject is too broad, and the user will normally respond by making the necessary adjustments. Conversely, if insufficient material exists, it may be that the subject is too narrowly defined, or perhaps there is a paucity of research in that area. Generally a trained searcher will conduct the search for you, but you should be present if possible, to respond to clues received when the online search is being conducted. The searcher may also help you plan your search strategy, that is, determine what descriptors you should use to retrieve the desired information. You can also get help with search strategies from the ERIC Clearinghouses listed at the conclusion of this chapter.

When you have done a computer search, the full abstracts or annotations can be printed online and become available immediately, or offline, and become available by mail service a week later. (Online printing is more expensive than offline since it requires computer time.) Once users have the abstracts and annotations, they can select the relevant ones and decide which of the original documents or journal articles will be most useful. Figure 3 shows the process involved in a computer search.

SUMMARY

The power of ERIC to assist adult learners in retrieving information quickly and accurately has been emphasized in this chapter. It is important to note, however, that the system rewards most richly the user who approaches it intelligently. Primarily, users must have control of the special terminology of their discipline and of the subject they have chosen to search, plus the skills needed to analyze it and coordinate the resulting factors with appropriate ERIC descriptors. According to Cross:

> Few adults, on the job or in their role as citizens and family members, are ever told what they need to know or where the answers will be found. Much more commonly, the learner is required to define the problem, locate appropriate learning materials, and demonstrate not just subject matter comprehension but the ability to apply the knowledge on the job, in the home, or for personal development. These needs call for thoughtful, autonomous learners rather than dependent learners. Moreover they call for people who know how to select and use the multiple resources available in the learning society. They call for discriminating consumers of educational services.[8]

Information retrieval systems, including ERIC, are one of the multiple resources available in the learning society. Through their use, adult learners can achieve a sense of control over their research and learning projects and increase their confidence in their ability to shape them. Information retrieval systems could give an impetus to the increasing practice of encouraging adults to set their own goals and design their own learning projects, as illustrated in the work of Tough. In his words:

> The adult learner of the future will be highly competent in deciding what to learn, and in planning and arranging his own learning. He will successfully diagnose and solve almost any problem or difficulty that arises. He will obtain appropriate help competently and quickly, but only when necessary.[9]

ERIC Clearinghouse Addresses

ERIC Clearinghouse on Adult, Career and Vocational Education
The National Center for Research in Vocational Education
The Ohio State University
1960 Kenny Road
Columbus, OH 43210
(800) 848-4815; (614) 486-3655

ERIC Clearinghouse on Counseling and Personnel Services
The University of Michigan
2108 School of Education
Ann Arbor, MI 48109
(313) 764-9492

ERIC Clearinghouse on Higher Education
George Washington University
One Dupont Circle, N.W.
Washington, D.C. 20036
(202) 296-2597

ERIC Clearinghouse on Junior Colleges
University of California
96 Powell Library Building
405 Hilgard Avenue
Los Angeles, CA 90024
(213) 825-3931

QUESTIONS AND EXERCISES

1. Analyze a continuing education subject of your choice into its concepts and relevant descriptors.
2. If possible, conduct an ERIC search using RIE and CIJE to find references or documents applicable to this subject.

REFERENCES

1. *Lifelong Learning During Adulthood: An Agenda for Research.* New York, NY: Future Directions for a Learning Society, College Entrance Examination Board, 1978. (ERIC Document Reproduction Service No. ED 163 209).
2. Davis, Charles H., and Rush, James E. *Guide to Information Science.* Westport, CT: Greenwood Press, 1979.
3. *Encyclopedia of Information Systems and Services, Fourth Edition.* Edited by Anthony T. Kruzas. Detroit, MI: Gale Research Co., 1981.
4. Feaster, Thelma J.; Peterson, John C.; Lund, Charles W.; and Bina, James V. *Databases and Clearinghouses: Information Resources for Education. Information Series No. 167.* Columbus: The National Center for Research in Vocational Education, Ohio State University, 1979. (ERIC Document Reproduction Service No. ED 184 534).
5. Hoover, Ryan R. *The Library and Information Manager's Guide to Online Services.* White Plains, NY: Knowledge Industry Publications, 1980.
6. Wexler, Henrietta. "All You Have To Do Is Ask." *American Education* 17 (June 1981): 22-27. (ERIC No. EJ 248 164).
7. *Thesaurus of ERIC Descriptors. 9th Edition-1982.* Phoenix, AZ: Oryx Press, 1982.
8. Cross, K. Patricia. *Adults as Learners: Increasing Participation and Facilitating Learning.* San Francisco, CA: Jossey-Bass, 1981.
9. Tough, Allen. *The Adult's Learning Projects: A Fresh Approach to Theory and Practice in Adult Learning.* Second Edition. Toronto, Ontario: The Ontario Institute for Studies in Education, 1979.

Human Resource Development: Expanding Role

Eugene E. DuBois

Professor of Education & Human Development
George Washington University

In recent years the field of adult education has assumed greater leadership and responsibility for the reconstruction of American society. Recent social legislation and the continuing democratization of American society, with its emphasis upon equal opportunity, has brought adult education closer to the threshold of centrality in American educational life.

For years, the adult educator had been a "marginal man" in American education. Often thought of as an ancillary person in the hierarchy of institutional education — bereft of educational theory — the professional adult educator in a few short years has risen to a position of prominence and leadership among his peer educators. The fact that the professional adult educator is increasingly sought out as a consultant for a variety of social systems including industry, hospitals, educational institutions, and religious and governmental agencies attests to this newly-acquired professional status.

The adult educator, solely, as a transmitter of knowledge in Americanization courses or as a teacher of leisure time activities is no longer. The competent adult educator has now acquired skills and an understanding of the behavioral sciences to such an extent that his technology, knowledges, and expertise permeate the total spectrum of modern social institutions. The adult educator today has emerged as a competent scholar and practitioner of the social sciences with evolving specialties of practice.

Basically, the professional adult educator possesses several consistent capabilities for the performance of his skills. Some of these skills are:
1. A belief that most people have potentiality for growth.
2. Imagination in program development.
3. Ability to communicate effectively in both speaking and writing.
4. Understanding of the conditions under which adults are most likely to learn.
5. Ability to keep on learning.
6. Effectiveness as a group leader.
7. Knowledge of his own values, strengths, and weaknesses.
8. Open-mindedness — willingness to accept other's ideas.
9. Understanding of what motivates adults to participate in programs.
10. Strong commitment to continuing education.[1]

These then, may serve as the criteria for the professional adult educator; on the other hand, criteria for the professional, regardless of academic disciplines, raises a more general and overriding set of suppositions. The following criteria apply to professions:
1. It must satisfy an indispensable social need and be based upon well-established and socially acceptable principles.
2. It must demand an adequate professional and cultural training.
3. It must demand the possession of a body of specialized and systematic knowledge.
4. It must give evidence of needed skills which the general public does not possess — skills which are partly native and partly acquired.
5. It must have developed a scientific technique which is the result of tested experience.
6. It must require the exercise of discretion and judgment as to the time and manner of the performance of duty. (This is in contrast to immediate direction and supervision.)
7. It must be a type of beneficial work, the result of which is not subject to standardization in terms of unit performance or time element.
8. It must have a group consciousness designed to extend scientific knowledge in technical language.
9. It must have sufficient self-impelling power to retain its members throughout life. It must not be used as a mere stepping stone to other occupations.
10. It must recognize its obligation to society by insisting that its members live up to an established and accepted code of ethics.[2]

Adult education became academically recognized as a profession in 1935 when Wilbur C. Hallenbeck and William Stacy were the first persons to receive the doctorate in Adult Education at Columbia University.

Adult education has made significant contributions to American life through its Americanization courses, evening schools, and settlement house programs. Often adult basic education courses, offered to the foreign-born or the underprivileged, became the standard equivalent of all adult education programs. Unfortunately or fortunately, this segment of adult education did too good a job, and thus the field has been associated with this elementary level of accomplishment.

Eventually other areas of specialization came under the intellectual purview of the professional adult educator. Human relations training brought the field to new levels of intellectual inquiry with a theoretical base in the social sciences.

The organizational development period isolated the skill and technology of the adult educator who used this skill and technology in effecting systematic organizational change of total systems and thus formed a theoretical base grounded in the behavioral sciences. The National Training Laboratories for Applied Social Sciences is the result of these pioneering efforts. Eventually this skill and technology became common among both practitioners and theoreticians in educational circles.

Human Resource Development as a Profession — The development of human resources has come under the scrutiny of the adult educator and has thus become one of his sub-specialties. According to Leonard Nadler, human resource development (HRD) is: (1) a series of organized activities, (2) conducted within a specified time, (3) designed to produce behavioral change.[3] The Kennedy era of social concern and the Johnson administration brought about a new awareness for the needs of people and a concerted attempt to reconstruct society on a major or significant level through a variety of legislative and policy enactments. The many human resources oriented agencies in government and industry are the result. These tend to be large scale social programs intended to centralize change by building megasystems.

Educational philosophers and curriculum designers have attempted to make clear and distinct differentiations between "training" and "education." Unfortunately, scholars have consistently opted for "education" as a more sophisticated and respectable level of learning experiences, to the detriment of "training."

Adult educators and professional trainers have raised the level of training to that of a legitimate role and function. Organizational development, institutional advancement and other endeavors which have evolved out of the adult education movement have gained intellectual respect based upon social science research.

Viewed in another manner, Lippitt and This have reported the prerequisites of a profession, by professional social workers, in the order of their cited frequency:
1. The profession has a body of specialized knowledge.
2. The profession sets its own standards.
3. The profession engages in activities essentially intellectual.
4. The profession requires extensive preparation.
5. The needed body of specialized knowledge is communicable.
6. The profession places service above personal gain.
7. The profession has a strong professional organization.[4]

An example of just one major organization attempting to emphasize a greater concern for the continuing education needs of its social system is the National Institute of Mental Health (NIMH). In order to implement this new phase of organization development, a reorganization included: (1) a new Continuing Education Branch, (2) added emphasis on training innovations and the training of new types of mental health workers via the Experimental and Special Training Branch, (3) training in special areas of public health significance as part of the new NIMH Centers (Alcoholism, Narcotic and Drug Abuse, Crime and Delinquency, Metropolitan Programs, Suicide Prevention).[5]

Body of Specialized Training Knowledge — Lippitt and This suggest the following as essential areas of professional competency for training personnel:

1. The ability to utilize appropriate findings from the social sciences.
2. The development of a working theory about personality growth and development.
3. The development of concepts of learning based on research findings.
4. The ability to design growth-learning experiences.
5. The ability to accomplish further research on the training process.
6. The development of a philosophy of training related to our present knowledge of the individual, the group, the organization, and the community in which people live.
7. The development of progressive, planned inservice growth opportunities for the individual training director.
8. A good working knowledge of accepted training methods, techniques, and visual aids, and the ability to utilize them effectively in the design of training programs.
9. The ability to sell to, plan with, and work with, the operating people on affective immediate and long-range training programs.
10. The ability to do — to teach — to train — to lead workshops.[6]

Methodology of the Adult Educator

There was a time when the adult educator, the more generalized professional, required a minimum of skills and techniques to perform his practice. Later as the need for new designing techniques became evident, new theories began to emerge with new approaches towards the design of learning experiences for adults.

The fact that adult educators were daring enough to experiment and attempted to create new techniques and designs must attest to their desire to break away from the redundancy of much educational theory or the effect of "education as cultural regression." The previous role of an instructor in an evening high school program or that of a Sunday School teacher was beginning to wane under new social needs.

The contemporary adult educators who specialize in human resource development have organized their professional skills with a host of new learnings from psychology, sociology, human growth and development, and anthropology. A keystone within this new approach towards learning has increasingly been heuristic learning, and more recently "andragogy" as theorized by Malcolm S. Knowles.

Heuristic learning is defined as "helping to discover or learn: sometimes used to designate a method of education in which the pupil is trained to find out things for himself."

Knowles' concept of andragogy has been well established in his writings:

> I am not talking about a clear-cut differentiation between children and adults as learners. Rather, I am differentiating between the assumptions about learners that have traditionally been made by those who practice pedagogy in contrast to the assumptions made in andragogy.

I believe that the assumptions of andragogy apply to children and youth as they mature, and that they, too will come to be taught more and more andragogically.[7]

Andragogy thus becomes "the art and science of helping adults learn."[8] If the definition of learning — that learning is change — is carried further, then change in total social systems or institutions is a form of learning, and thus comes within the purview of the adult educator as a specialist in human resource development.

The assumptions upon which andragogy is based stated succinctly are:
1. His self-concept moves from one of being a dependent personality toward one of being a self-directing human being.
2. He accumulates a growing reservoir of experience that becomes an increasing resource of learning.
3. His readiness to learn becomes oriented increasingly to the developmental tasks of his social roles.
4. His time perspective changes from one of postponed application of knowledge to immediacy of application, and accordingly his orientation toward learning shifts from one of subject-centeredness to one of problem-centeredness.[8]

Andragogy, as presented here, has assisted adult educators in identifying the parameters of the field, and have permitted the role of the adult educator to expand into areas of sub-specializations. This theoretical perspective thus permits the practitioner to:
1. Make rational choices.
2. Be consistent in his/her practice.
3. Test assumptions and revise them if necessary.

With this theoretical base making a distinction between andragogy and pedagogy, and transforming the learning situation to one of collaborative learning from dependent-teaching, human resource developers have expanded their role, and increased their competencies as professional practitioners of applied social science.

The role of the human resource developer has varied greatly: problem solver, change agent, leadership trainer, group process facilitator, conference leader, designer of learning experiences, research specialist, program planner, theoretician, scholar, and administrator. Each of these roles requires a specific set of skills, knowledge, expertise, education, and training.

PROFESSIONAL PREPARATION

Since 1935, the professional preparation of adult educators, and consequently the preparation of human resource development personnel has been at the graduate level. Some of the leaders in the field suggest that the adult educator might find it possible to obtain his/her education preparation much earlier in his/her educational development.

A review of the literature, and an analysis of the role of the human resource development specialist indicates that his/her academic preparation should be divided into two major areas, education and the social sciences. More specifically, the basic foundation courses in education most appropriate are: Educational Philosophy, the Psychology of Adult Learning, Research Methodology, Adult Education Methods. From the social sciences, the disciplines of sociology, psychology and anthropology with their particular emphasis in group learning, change agentry, and human behavior widen and deepen the professional's insights into the nature of man and his world. Obviously, the other integrating disciplines of philosophy, religion, history, economics, and the humanities augment this proposed preparation.

The time is appropriate now for the emergence of a sub-specialty — human resource development — in the field of adult education. Perhaps society and its institutions were not prepared in the past for the systematic and orderly application of the applied behavioral sciences to established institutions and human development.

The fact that continuing education has expanded in recent decades at the graduate level need not necessarily indicate that its future development will remain the domain of research-oriented graduate centers. It is not likely, owing to the history of undergraduate education that experimental research will become a major component of this part of the college curriculum. However, if the baccalaureate curriculum were to include adult education and human resource development, conceivably, a paraprofessional might evolve. The present state of human resource development at this point in time has yet to solidify. The human resource development professional will certainly require the training presently associated with advanced academic preparation to be a competent and professional adult educator.

The emerging role of the human resource developer encompasses much more than that of the traditional adult educator. This professional is a new professional on the educational scene; an adult educator with new and more expansive expertise, cognizant of the dynamics of human behavior and the workings of organizations. Organizations and institutions reflect or mirror the collective behaviors of the human beings who are a part of that organization, and it is this collective behavior; interpersonal relationships, mores, values, and working relationships that establishes a corporate behavior.

H R D professionals must possess skills and expertise, as well as be an integral functioning part of organizations and/or institutions if they are to become more responsive to the needs of the wider social system, their own organizational needs, and the needs of those individuals who look to the professionals for leadership and direction.

QUESTIONS AND EXERCISES

1. Discuss adult education methodology and its relationship to adult learning theory.
2. Design a strategy for institutional change. State a specific institution; desired outcome; develop an evaluation procedure.

3. Prepare an annotative bibliography of human resource development materials.
4. Discuss human resource development as a profession. Include its historical antecedents, philosophical base, learning theory, and significant research efforts.
5. What elements of traditional educational philosophy have influenced human resource development?
6. In what manner has instructional technology affected human resource development?

REFERENCES

1. A.A. Liveright. "The Nature and Aims of Adult Education As A Field of Graduate Education." Gale Jensen, A.A. Liveright, and Wilbur Hallenbeck (eds.) *Adult Education Outlines of an Emerging Field of University Study.* Washington D.C.: Adult Education Association of the U.S.A. 1964.
2. Ibid. pp. 86-87.
3. Nadler, Leonard. *Developing Human Resources.* Houston: Gulf Publishing Company, 1970.
4. Lippitt, Gordon L. and Leslie This. "Is Training A Profession?" *Optimizing Human Resources: Readings in Individual and Organizational Development.* Gordon L. Lippitt (ed.), Reading, Mass.: Addison-Wesley Publishing Co., 1971.
5. Webster, Thomas G. (ed.) *Continuing Education: Agent of Change:* Rockville, Md.: National Institute of Mental Health, 1971.
6. Ibid. pp. 397-398.
7. Knowles, Malcolm S., *The Adult Learner: A Neglected Species.* Houston: Gulf Publishing Company, 1973.
8. Knowles, Malcolm S., *The Modern Practice of Adult Education: Andragogy Versus Pedagogy.* New York: Association Press, 1970.

Organizational Development

Jack A. Sumner

*Professor, Adult & Higher Education,
University of South Dakota*

David C. Wigglesworth

*President, D.C.W. Research Associates of Los Altos,
Los Altos, CA*

Organization Development and its new terminology "Organization Effectiveness" are the buzz words in education today. OD or OE has experienced considerable success in the private sector in large corporations, in the military, and in governmental organizations. It is only logical that OD should eventually come to the attention of educators. OD suggests change. OD practitioners are often referred tp as "change agents." OD is not concerned, however, with change for the sake of change. OD is actually concerned with enhancing the climate, culture, nature of the organization so that it can be more productive. It is based on the belief that people who can relate effectively to their jobs, their colleagues, and to the organization need to be holistically healthy and need to work in a "sane" environment.

Educators have voiced concern about change. While maintaining certain aspects of the status quo, educators, and adult continuing educators in particular, have been actively involved in the change process. OD is process intervention to accomplish effective change. The teaching-learning process involves elements of change. In addition, there is a growing body of knowledge about adult development looking at the effects of adult life changes and program planners assuming the role of change agents.

Progress in the field of adult continuing education requires a clear perspective that program development must have an openness to new concepts that may require a change orientation, and that may help to bring together universal principles about adult continuing education and the change process.

CHANGE THROUGH OD

The concept of change is often challenged as the concept of throwing the baby out with the bath water. Change for the sake of change is not the aim of OD practitioners. Instituting change to effect organizational development requires needs assessments, clarification of goals and objectives, and may involve a variety of processes to accomplish specific tasks or objectives. Among these processes are the Managerial Grid of Blake and Mouton;[1] Reddin's Tri-Dimensional Management Model;[2] Tannenbaum's Leadership Continuum,[3]

Organizational Development

Fiedler's Situational Management,[4] and others. Some of these processes look at tasks, some at the organization, and all relate to people.

Richard Beckhard has said that the challenge of change that faces managers is: "How can we optimally mobilize human resources and energy to achieve the organization's mission and, at the same time, maintain a viable, growing organization of people whose personal needs for self-worth, growth and satisfaction are significantly met at work?"[5]

Utilizing the OD processes in adult continuing education organizations and agencies may provide a change agent strategy that will stimulate the chances for reform in the goals and structure (where necessary) of adult continuing education.

Education, as Cross[6] points out, has to a very large degree been centered around those persons within our society who have yet to attain the age of fifteen. The decline in this population and the growth of the adult population suggests that factors are developing which may mandate the provision of services in the adult continuing education arena. Thus we may be hearing calls for changes in what to all intent and purposes has been a youth dominated system to the structures that will need to be responsive to the requirements of a system to serve adults. The local adult continuing education practitioner may well be at the pivot point of this change.

Thus, OD may be used to implement specific goals in adult continuing education. These could include:

1. The improvement of the local organization and the individuals involved within the organization.

2. The development of the long term capabilities of the local organization to deal with special problems and needs.

3. The improvement of the relationships between the adult continuing education practitioner and the local organization.

4. The enhancement of the potential of the local organization to be an improving provider of adult education programs.

O.D. PROCESS FOR ADULT EDUCATION

Assessment — Planning and Development — Implementation

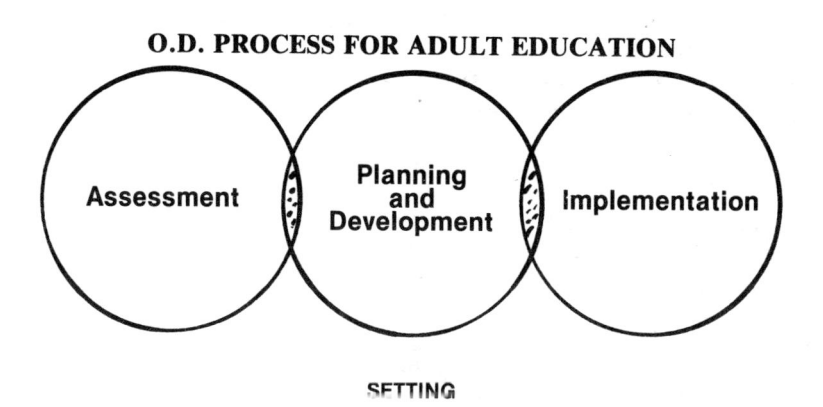

SETTING

FIGURE 1.

THE PROCESS

Figure 1 depicts an Organization Development Process of Adult Continuing Education and presents it as having three major parts or components.

The assessment component is the first part of the application of OD processes to adult continuing education. The focus here is on starting up the communication processes and gathering/generating data. The assessment must start with the goals and objectives of the organization and needs to accumulate the data that provides accurate information and perceptions of both real needs and perceived needs. Often the assessment of the organization's structure which notes the differences and similarities in the substructures may be helpful. The assessment phase also involves a review of problems, potential problems, and the organization's committment to change. The assessment component helps to bring some focus to understanding the problems of the organization and is essential to establishing appropriate guidelines that are concomitant with the goals and objectives of the organization.

The planning and development component utilizes additional data gathering techniques and places emphasis on recognizing the need for possible team building, problem identification and focusing, prioritization, conflict awareness and the types of communication processes that need to be refined and employed.

The implementation component is bringing it all together and making it work. In the implementation mode key aspects are involved that include reorganization, restructuring, relationship building, long range reviews and an ongoing monitoring/feedback system.

This oversimplification of the three part model is not intended to be either all inclusive, or cover all aspects of each component, or definitive. It is presented to place the process in perspective. This perspective needs also to include an awareness of the setting in which the process is to take place. The setting may be the critical factor in any OD process. It is necessary to be aware of the overall status or condition of the setting as well as of similar, competitive or rival groups. And the setting cannot ignore outside political forces and the concerns of society. It may be important to note that the shaded areas in Figure 1 that overlap represent feedback areas which are essential.

Certain underlying assumptions that may be common to both OD and ACE are:

1. Learning and change consist of elements that are interrelated and dynamic in the way in which they operate.

2. The reordering and reorganization of individual and collective experiences are a significant activity of the learning and change process.

3. Meaningful participation and commitment to the outcome of a process are inextricably linked together.

4. The identification and use of organization problems and needs may be focal points and starting points for change.

The OD practitioner must work within the organization context and two categories may be useful for working with procedures. These are the category of "Agency, Institution, and Community OD," and the category of "Program Activity and Instruction OD." These two separate classification clusters provide avenues for listing adult continuing education formats and/or participation patterns. Suggestions for methods for each category are as follows:

1. Agency, Institution, and Community OD — Adult Continuing Education methods that may be suited to this category are: forums, institutes, symposia, colloquy, clinics, charettes, conferences, Phillips 66 method, and participative training sessions.

2. Program, Activity, and Instruction OD — Adult Continuing Education methods that may be suited to this category are: problem solving groups, discussion groups, instruction groups, reaction panels, laboratory and consultation groups, buzz groups, teaching-learning teams, fish bowl techniques, brainstorming, values clarification strategies, committees, dyads and triads, self-diagnostic exercises, and quiet meetings.

The OD processes have promise for different levels and areas. The teaching-learning transaction of the facilitator, resource person, or teacher of adults can be used in selected areas for program, curricula or materials improvement. The process can bear upon the inservice activities of a program, or as Knox[7] asserts as an important aspect of the total staff development program for teachers. Administrative personnel sometimes view organization change as not part of their job or as a nearly impossible task. They may view OD as something that should come from the central office or be done by an outside consultant. Experience has demonstrated that internal OD programs can be positive.

OD may also assume an important role in areas other than administrative. Looking at the assessment component of the process, its utilization by a group or committee organized to select materials, try a new program, develop curricula or plan an event can be helpful.

Adult Continuing Education and OD may develop more effective ways of communicating and sharing through those procedures that are common to both such as buzz sessions, discussion groups, or even written exercises designed to identify common practices, rules, and guidelines within the organization.

Teaching-learning teams, panels, and committee reports can be used to pull together analyses of an organization's structure both formal and informal. Employing facilitators, observers, and recorders can be valuable to the OD processes. In this assessment component, self assessment exercises, logs, diaries may be helpful in relating respective problems and responsibilities to the more global concerns and structures for a more holistic viewpoint. While the assessment component would seem to be largely task oriented, there is also a need to develop a balanced awareness of problems specific to individuals and dyads and triads, values clarification exercises and buzz group work may assume patterns of importance in maintaining a process orientation.

The formats identified are useful in starting and continuing communication. They also can play a role in the critical development of group identity and group maturity so that the participant understands that solutions to problems and completion of tasks are not the sole responsibility of the convenor, supervisor, or any other single individual. The goal is that the group or team will build toward answers and results from both individual contributions and the group process.

The phase-over from the assessment component to the planning and development component is often enhanced by the group's development of a product. This product can be a guide, a position paper, or other document developed by those involved. The creation of this product helps the group to utilize group feedback mechanisms for enhancement of the product that prepares the guidelines for use in the remainder of the OD process. While naturally evolved through the process, they need to be articulated and agreed to by all concerned.

Similar combinations of procedures that are designed to discover and strengthen the best possible approaches are utilized in the remaining two components.

SUMMARY

It can be seen that Organization Development can provide a guide for the Adult Continuing Educator to use in striving toward the improvement of the organization. It is a process that helps individuals to become a part of the organization and to improve themselves and their surroundings. The role of the practitioner may be to understand, introduce, and facilitate the utilization of the OD process. The three major parts of an OD model for Adult Continuing Education (assessment, planning and development, and implementation) are not intended to be a magic formula with a specified panacea. The aim is at helping in the development of the organization and its members as individuals. Obviously, a set of common assumptions that are related to the model and to ACE are essential underpinnings for adaptive application of the OD process for Adult Continuing Education.

In essence, this means that Adult Continuing Education procedures can be combined in ways to facilitate the necessary learning and change. OD offers promise for use by those in administration, as well as those working in direct contact with the adult learner. The success of society's organizations may lie in the degree to which the organization, the individual, and the process for planned change stimulate all aspects of this important concept.

QUESTIONS AND EXERCISES

1. The use of Organization Development as a model for Adult Educators carries with it the risks involved in using any and all models. In your opinion what do you consider to be the biggest risks?
2. How would you apply the Organization Development process to an organization (club, organization, professional association, church) that you are involved with, separate from your main source of employment?

3. In reviewing the other chapters of this book do you see mentioned one or more organizations that are fertile areas for the application of the process? What do you believe to be the most difficult organization?
4. How do you see Organization Development applications differing from other change processes?
5. Please respond to this statement: People are receptive to change, they are required to change every day. They change their ideas, attitudes, values, predisposition toward other points of view, behaviors, their principles. The only thing that does not change are organizations such as bureaucracies.

REFERENCES

1. Blake, Robert and Jane Mouton, *Corporate Excellence Through Grid Organization and Development*, Houston, Texas: Gulf Publishing, 1968.
2. Reddin, William J. *The 3-D Management Style Theory, Theory Paper #6 —* Style Flex, Fredericton, Canada: Social Science Systems, 1967.
3. Tannenbaum, Robert *et al, Leadership and Organization: A Behavioral Science Approach*, New York: McGraw-Hill, 1959.
4. Fiedler, Fred E., *A Theory of Leadership Effectiveness*, New York: McGraw-Hill, 1967.
5. Beckhard, Richard *Organizational Development: Strategies and Models*, Redding, Mass: Addison-Wesley, 1969, p. 3.
6. Cross, Patricia K. *Adults As Learners*, San Francisco, CA: Jossey-Bass, 1980.
7. Knox, Alan B. *Enhancing Proficiencies of Continuing Educators*, San Francisco, CA: Jossey-Bass, 1979.

Join Your Professional Organizations

Wendell L. Smith

*President, Adult Education Association, USA;
Professor, Continuing Education Extension,
University of Missouri, St. Louis*

Gary A. Eyre

*Executive Director,
American Association for Adult & Continuing Education (AAACE)
former Executive Director,
National Advisory Council on Adult Education*

James W. Miller

*President, NAPCAE;
Division of Federal Assistance,
State Department of Education, Ohio*

Professional associations are extremely important to the furtherance of adult and continuing education. They provide critical links with state and national legislatures, standards to uphold our professional status as well as offer professional development opportunities through conferences and publications. Without the total support of adult and continuing educators at all levels (local, state, national), professional organizations would not be able to continue their important work, and the future of the profession would be in severe jeopardy.

HISTORICAL EVOLUTION

A number of factors have affected the historical development of associations serving the adult and continuing education profession, including societal trends in lifelong learning participation, legislative enactments, and most importantly, the changing professional needs of the associations' members.

In the 1978 edition of **Materials and Methods in Continuing Education,** Dr. James Dorland summarized the events surrounding the formation of the associations serving the profession. A recent event in the historical evolution of associations has been the consolidation of the Adult Education Association (AEA/USA) and the National Association of Public Continuing Adult

Education (NAPCAE) into a new association, The American Association of Adult and Continuing Education (AAACE). Many believe this consolidation is a significant milestone in the growth and development of the profession and will serve to stimulate further linkages among allied associations. The AEA/NAPCAE consolidation was voted into effect at the 1981 National Adult Education Conference. The subsequent year involved considerable planning and development of the governing structure that would serve the new association. AAACE came into existence on November 12, 1981, at the 1982 National Adult Education Conference in San Antonio, Texas.

At its inception, AAACE received approximately 6000 charter (carry over) members from AEA and NAPCAE, making it by far the largest association serving the adult and continuing education profession. AAACE was designed as an umbrella individual-membership association that would provide leadership in advancing education as a lifelong process by:
1. Unifying the profession.
2. Serving as an advocate for the field of adult and continuing education.
3. Developing human resources.
4. Encouraging and using research.
5. Communicating with the public and its members.
6. Providing other member services.

The Purposes of Various Types of Professional Associations — Although there are many generic purposes shared among professional associations, the intensity and manner in which the purposes are addressed within an organization have considerable variation; this degree of variation is generally consistent with three typologies. The three types of professional associations are:
1. Individual-membership-based organizations.
2. Institutional-based organizations.
3. Organizational-based associations.[4]

Individual-Membership-Based organizations are typically those associations that derive the majority of their operational budgets from individual member fees and those associations in which individual members are vested with the majority of the governance control.

Typically, individual-membership-based organizations devote a considerable amount of their efforts to services that directly benefit individual members, such as publications, job referral services, and group discounts for insurance and travel.

Institutional-Based organizations are those that obtain their major operational budgets in fees from institutions rather than individual members' dues. Member institutions (colleges, universities, local school districts), typically are entitled to name one individual who is vested with voting rights and who is extended eligibility to hold an office in the organization.

Institutional-based organizations are generally not as concerned with individual member services as they are with the concerns that directly affect the institution. Strategies to enhance the academic credibility of the adult or continuing education program in an institution, effective administrative management procedures, and models for inter-institutional cooperation are typical of the primary concerns of institutional-based associations.

Organizational-Based associations represent the third type of association. These are associations that link several individual and institutional-based associations in order to aid their member associations in more effectively carrying out their respective responsibilities.

Organizational-based associations generally derive their operational budgets through fees that are assessed to their member associations. Member associations designate individuals from their respective membership or executive staff who are empowered to participate in the governance of the organizational-based association.

Professional associations in adult and continuing education exist at three levels: (1) national, (2) regional, (3) local or state. At each level there are:
1. Associations that have broad and encompassing objectives, all of which fall under the adult and continuing education umbrella.
2. Specific associations that concentrate on individual aspects or discipline areas represented within the total profession.
3. Associations that have primary missions in areas other than adult and continuing education, but that have adult and continuing education as one of their areas of interest.

Most local, state and regional associations are affiliates of national associations and serve to complement and localize the concerns that are addressed on the broader national basis. Local, state and regional associations do not generally have an executive staff and provide considerably fewer member services, such as publications, than does a national association.

Opportunities for Leadership Involvement — Professional associations rely heavily on their membership providing voluntary services; this is particularly true with local, state and regional associations that do not normally have a paid executive staff.

Association leadership (members who are officers or Board members) have generally progressed through the ranks, having formerly made significant contributions as members of various task committees and standing committees.

Task committees are temporary committees with a single mission or purpose; these committees are usually expected to accomplish their task within one year or less. The Board of Directors or the President of the association is usually responsible for the creation of task committees and for the appointment of their membership. Standing committees are prescribed in the association constitution or bylaws; often the membership of these committees is elected from ideological or special interest groups within the association.

Many contend that the degree to which individuals are involved in their professional association directly correlates with the benefits that they derive from the association. The member who is actively involved will have more opportunity for greater professional development and personal gain than the member who sits back and watches things happen or who wonders what happened.

There are numerous opportunities to become involved in any professional association; new members or those who are unfamiliar with these opportunities should review the association's governance documents, visit with existing leaders within the association, and volunteer to assume assignments within the association.

Most associations conduct annual elections to select their officers. Typically, a nominating committee reviews who has been active in the association and makes inquiries as to those persons who would like to assume additional responsibilities. Many excellent potential candidates for office decline nomination because of the myth that persons with a strong constituent base (those from states or regions representing large association memberships, or those who are members of the larger special interest areas in the association) are assured of success in winning the election.

A recently reported longitudinal study of voting patterns in the Adult Education Association of the United States reflected that there was no correlation between the size of a candidate's geographical or ideological constituent base and whether or not the candidate won or lost an election. The primary influence on whether or not a candidate won an election appeared to be the extent to which he or she had been involved and contributed toward the profession, and specifically the association, in recent years.[2]

The Future of Professional Associations — The past importance of professional associations to the furtherance of adult and continuing education has been well documented. In a publication entitled **The Decision to Join**,[3] the American Society of Association Executives (ASAE) surveyed 2,000 members and nonmembers of professional associations concerning their perceptions of the future role of professional associations. The study found:
1. There was a positive overall attitude of both members and nonmembers toward associations.
2. Associations have a continued ability to meet member needs.
3. One-fourth of the respondents believe there are too many professional associations in their field.

The ASAE study documents the continued importance of professional associations. As we face an increasingly complex world with more problems and greater pressures, and as the adult and continuing education profession continues to grow, professional associations will have a continued responsibility to determine potential problems and then help solve them.

Based on the successful consolidation efforts of AEA and NAPCAE and the successful interlinkages and collective efforts that have been demonstrated by other professional associations at local, state, and national levels, it appears that the profession is reaching a stage in its life cycle that is conducive to cooperative efforts and that it will continue to move toward further unification.

SUMMARY

Professional associations have had a major role in the growth and development of the adult and continuing education profession. There have been a variety of allied associations serving at local, state, regional and national levels. The profession is reaching a stage in its development when it is increasingly important to foster unity and consolidation among the professional associations that have adult and continuing education as their central purpose. The landmark consolidation of AEA and NAPCAE to form AAACE will likely stimulate further consolidation and cooperative efforts among allied associations within our profession.

As the adult and continuing education profession moves forward in meeting the expanding needs of the lifelong learners of tomorrow, the role of professional associations continues to be of paramount importance. Professional associations link their members with state and national legislatures, provide professional standards and inservice educational opportunities, and help keep abreast of research findings that will aid in solving future problems, many of which are not even considered today.

Adult and continuing educators must continue their financial support and active personal participation in professional associations if the profession is to continue to be successful in the future.

If you are not currently involved in professional associations, join the local, state, regional and national associations of your choice. If you are currently a member of professional associations, continue your participation. Without our professional associations, we would not be!

REFERENCES

1. Dorland, James, "Role of Professional Organization," *Materials and Methods in Continuing Education*, Chester Klevins (ed.), Canoga Park, CA.: Klevens Publications, Inc., 1978.
2. Smith, Wendell L., "President's Letter," Lifelong Learning — The Adult Years, Washington, D.C., AEA, April, 1982.
3. Steel, Robert H., *The Decision to Join*, Washington, D.C., The American Society of Association Executives, 1981.
4. Adult and Continuing Education Associations and Organizations

    (1) American Association for Adult &
    Continuing Education
    1201 Sixteenth St., N.W.
    Washington, D.C. 20036
    (202) 822-7866
    (Formerly AEA/USA & NAPCAE)

    (2) American Association of Community &
    Junior Colleges
    One Dupont Circle, N.W.
    Suite 410
    Washington, D.C. 20036
    (202) 293-7050 Ext. 49 or 50

    (1) American Society for Training &
    Development
    One Dupont Circle, N.W., Suite 400
    Washington, D.C. 20036
    (202) 659-9588

    (2) National Association of Trade &
    Technical Schools
    2021 K. Street, N.W.
    Washington, D.C. 20006
    (202) 296-8892

    (1) American Vocational Association, Inc.
    2020 North Fourteenth St., N.W.
    Arlington, Virginia 22201
    (703) 522-6121

    (1) National Community Education Association
    1030 Fifteenth St., N.W., Suite 536
    Washington, D.C. 20005
    (202) 466-3530

(1) Association for Continuing Higher
    Education
    451 Extension Building
    Knoxville, Tennessee 37916
    (615) 974-6629

(3) Coalition of Adult Education Organizations
    Department of Adult Continuing Education
    Montclair State College
    Upper Montclair, New Jersey 07043
    (201) 893-4353

(3) International Council for Adult Education
    29 Prince Author Avenue
    Toronto, Ontario, Canada M5R 1B2
    (416) 924-6607

(2) National University Continuing Education
    Association
    National Center for Higher Education
    One Dupont Circle, N.W., Suite 360
    Washington, D.C. 20036
    (202) 659-3130

    National Home Study Council
    1601 Eighteenth St., N.W.
    Washington, D.C. 20009
    (202) 234-5100
    (201) 893-4353

(1) United States Association of Evening
    Students
    1016 Tyrus Ct.
    North Merrick, New York 11566
    (516) 489-2011

(1) Individual Membership-Based Organization
(2) Institutional Membership-Based Organization
(3) Organizational-Based Association

Illiteracy Eradication: a Future Model

George F. Aker
*Director, Division of Educational Management Systems,
College of Education, Florida State University*

Jack L. Gant
*Dean, College of Education,
Florida State University*

As with many complex concepts, literacy like democracy, beauty, and truth is not something one arrives at or becomes perfect in — rather it is a goal that one must continuously move toward.

The Ph.D. scientist or postgraduate engineer who spends most of his/her life learning more and more about less and less can easily become less literate than the non-schooled migrant worker regarding the practical affairs of life or the general conditions of the community. And, the civic illiteracy of an increasing supply of highly schooled specialists who tend also to occupy key policy and decision-making posts in our agencies of government and business may well be a larger threat to our survival than the academic illiteracy of that much larger segment of society who have less than a high school education.

THE PROBLEM OF DEFINITION

Illiteracy, or its converse literacy, are vague and ill-defined concepts. Literacy has variously been defined as simply the ability to read and write one's name, as having completed a prescribed number of years of formal schooling, as more elaborate functions involving communication, computational, and problem-solving skills, and as detailed descriptions of performance levels needed to function with a certain degree of efficiency and effectiveness in a variety of social roles in a highly technological, knowledge-based, rapidly changing society.[1][2]

At the risk of oversimplification, literacy is defined as the intellectual, social, vocational and civic skills and abilities expected of a high school graduate who has had a "reasonably good" education. At this level of ability, a person ought to be able to continue his or her education, to retain (though not necessarily find) a job, to calculate the itemized deduction version of the federal income tax form — albeit with considerable difficulty — and to effectively cope with or adapt to most of the routine and ordinary conditions of life and society.

Illiteracy Eradication: A Future Model

The Scope of Illiteracy — Despite our efforts to the contrary, present social and institutional structures tend to operate more to maintain than to reduce illiteracy. This is a strong indictment considering the United States represents one of the most highly educated societies the world has ever known. But look at the facts.

By current Census data slightly more than 50 percent of our population over age 25 have graduated from high school while nearly 60 percent of American adults over age 16 and not enrolled in school have less than a high school level education. Data developed by State Departments of Education show that 66 million of our 16 years of age and over — out of school population — have not completed high school and 24 million of them have not attained an elementary level education. And these data — Census data — are very conservative to say the least. That is because many people tend to remember years of school completed on the high side.

Such data also do not account for the fact that many high school graduates are not literate — cannot read, write or compute at the 5th grade level, cannot pass the adult GED exam or the Army entrance tests. Given such a situation, we submit that the actual state of illiteracy is unknown in this country. Consequently, gross or approximate data is a more helpful way of understanding the scope of illiteracy.

There is a simple and appropriate way of remembering the condition of our illiteracy. Nationally, about half of our adult population have less than a high school level education (50 million). Half of these have less than an 8th grade level of education (25 million); half of these have less than a 5th grade level of education (12.5 million) and are called "functionally illiterate" and approximately three million adults cannot read or write in any language.

In this instance, "functionally illiterate" means that 12.5 million adults cannot read an urban newspaper or listen to a national newscast with good comprehension, or fill out most job application forms, differentiate unbiased reports from propaganda, or readily enter into a job skill development program. So half of the adult population are illiterate by any high school definition, and half of these are illiterate by the USOE definition of functional literacy.

When we examine enrollment in ABE programs and the relationship between cumulative participation in ABE and the magnitude of the target audience, it is clear that present efforts to reduce illiteracy represent a holding action at best. (Figure 1.)

Depending on whose estimate or set of figures one uses, from 700,000 to 1,000,000 youth drop out of our formal K-12 school system each year and our present public programs of adult basic education reach slightly less than this amount or one percent of the target population. And while we continue to increase the percent of high school and college level members of society, in absolute numbers more adults are counted as illiterate each day.

In the mid 1960's, illiteracy was about evenly divided between urban and rural, between non-white and white. That same relative distribution probably remains today. This also means that the rural and the non-white are

Relationship of Populations[3]

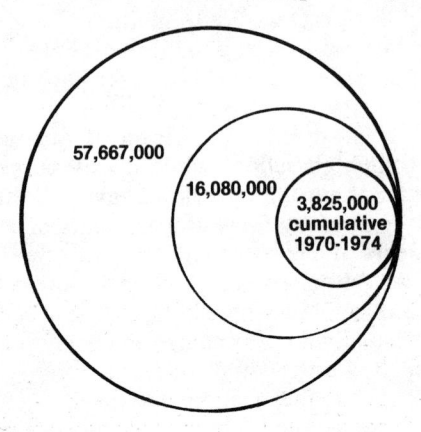

57,667,000 — TARGET POPULATION — 1970 CENSUS. 16 years of age & older. NOT enrolled in school with less than the completion of secondary education.

16,080,000 — Adults over 16 years of age with LESS than an eighth grade education.

3,825,000 cumulative 1970-1974 — ABE Participants. Includes adults living overseas as civilians, armed forces personnel overseas, and individuals in penal institutions.

Figure 1

considerably overrepresented in our illiterate society. And surprisingly, the bulk of those who are illiterate are not the old folks — no, they are between the ages of 16 and 45!

Given sufficient political, economic and educational commitment, this is all avoidable. Illiterate adults want to become literate and they do have the ability to learn.

THE CORRELATES OF ILLITERACY

Given that thousands of illiterate or semi-literate American adults are socially responsible, contributing citizens, illiteracy is still a tremendous handicap — to the individual, the family, the community and the larger society.

Nearly any undesirable human, social, or economic condition one can identify, bears a statistical relationship to illiteracy. In relation to those who are highly educated, persons who are undereducated are more likely to:
1. Have serious difficulty in income maintenance.
2. Be victimized by creditors.
3. Be unemployed or underemployed.
4. Be on welfare.
5. Have inadequate conditions of physical and emotional health — including hypertension, poor hearing and poor vision.
6. Have inadequate nutrition.
7. Live in substandard housing.
8. Lack reliable transportation.
9. Pay more for meeting basic survival needs as well as non-essential items.
10. Have difficulty with the role of parenting.
11. Have children who will face problems much like their own.
12. Have more children than they want.
13. Not vote or engage in civic or political affairs.

14. Have difficulty in obtaining needed social, health and/or economic services provided by the community.
15. Feel helpless or powerless to work the system or control the forces that most influence their lives.
16. Be incarcerated.
17. Not participate in any organized form of continuing education.
18. Experience more accidental injury.
19. Live fewer years.

The message is clear — poverty, exploitation, alienation and related conditions are among those that are highly associated with being illiterate in a highly literate society.

The recent literature of adult and continuing education and related social sciences abounds with conclusive evidence of the interacting and complex relationships that exist between substandard living and substandard levels of education.

And while the condition of illiteracy is as much an urban problem as a rural one, or a white as a non-white one, or a male as a female one, or an old age as a young one, the relationships that exist between undesirable conditions of life and community and illiteracy are even stronger if you are non-white or rural, stronger if you are both.

Yet, in spite of such harsh statistics, the existence of and opportunities for desired human, social and economic development and change are great. We must assume the responsibility for our own destiny and deliberately build toward desired futures — and simultaneously serve as a model for other countries; or we can ignore our opportunities, imitate the historic patterns and have an educational system fit for the 19th century.

To assume leadership, major changes are required in certain political, economic and educational policies and priorities — especially in regard to the development of under-realized sources of tax revenue and gross under-utilization of educational resources for formal and non-formal lifelong learning.

One thing that has been learned from extensive research in world literacy programs is that by itself, literacy education is insufficient as a catalyst to economic development.[4] To be effective adult basic education must be systematically incorporated into a larger, carefully planned design including:
1. Capital and material resource development and utilization.
2. Urban, rural and regional planning.
3. Development of public and private work opportunities.
4. Parent, family, and community-wide education.
5. Effective information delivery and knowledge sharing systems.
6. Widespread participatory involvement of citizens in change processes.
7. Coordinated, cooperative, and in some cases merged social, health, rehabilitative, and educational delivery systems.

All of the above are, of course, predicated on the assumption of on-going efficient needs assessment activities, monitoring of relevant change indices and trend data and scientific evaluation of process and product variables.

Weaknesses and Strengths of Present Activities in Adult Basic Education — Over the past decade adult educators and social scientists have consumed millions of dollars in attempts to improve the efficacy of adult basic education through research and teacher training activities. The response of the private sector in the development of innovative learning materials and effective educational technologies has been phenomenal. As a consequence, we have acquired the knowledge and the technology needed for implementing high quality adult basic education programs. But observations of the practice of ABE in nearly any community reveal that we have utterly failed in our ability to apply what we know. Among the many of our deficiencies can be included:
1. The public is generally unaware of the problem of illiteracy.
2. ABE is by and large a "moonlighting" operation carried on by part-time, short-term day school teachers of children — too tired and ill prepared for the demanding work of adult education.
3. Members of the potential audience for ABE are not attracted to the types of programs offered — and usually are unaware of opportunities that exist.
4. The concepts of practical and functional education based on adult performance levels are for the most part not being operationalized.
5. There is little integration between adult basic, vocational and career education — or with any other facet of adult education.
6. There is no schema for incorporating ABE into an overall plan for social and economic development, no follow-through with former participants, little effort to provide the undereducated with opportunities for or a view of lifelong learning, and no effective coordination between manpower, welfare, and education specialists at any levels of their bureaucracies.

While ABE has not been resoundingly successful, it has not been a failure either. Quite the contrary, since 1966 ABE has significantly contributed to the quality of life of millions of Americans. USOE has documentation on hundreds of thousands of participants in ABE who have gained or advanced in employment, left welfare, paid taxes, increased the educational climate of their homes, initiated participation in civic and political affairs.

Thus far, the academic growth of participants in ABE has exceeded the rates of advancement of youth per units of time and money. And the rates of dropout in ABE have been as low or lower than in our K-12 programs for children! The main problem appears to be one of insufficient commitment of resources, lack of integrated economic-educational planning, and lack of policies and administrative practices necessary for the effective use of already existing knowledge and technology. Given adequate political commitment and appropriate policy, adult education has a key role in creating alternatives to welfare, a viable economy, and a socially healthy democracy.

PRESCRIPTION FOR LITERACY

The challenge to the United States is to begin the development of policies addressed to the following goals:

1. Establish adult basic education as an enterprise having equal priority with youth education — an enterprise that is fully integrated or coordinated with all levels of education and with vocational-technical, career and community education.
2. Establish adult basic education so that its leadership and instructional personnel are employed for full-time service with full-time commitments. ABE should not rely on part-time, day school teachers of children. Rather its staff should represent a blend of educators including: (a) persons especially prepared for adult education, (b) persons with specific skills in technology, agriculture, business, (c) persons who simultaneously work in youth and adult education, (d) persons who are retired or semi-retired who can make significant contributions to part or full-time service in ABE, (e) young persons who are in training for service in education (interns, community college students).
3. Create a system of public education which blends education, working, citizenship and leisuring for all ages so that the ideals of career and community education can be fully implemented. Youth should have sufficient apprenticeship experiences (in both the private and public sectors) so that they are employable should they elect to leave school prior to graduation.
4. Remove the stigma of school drop-out and provide attractive opportunities for recurrent career long, lifelong education so that individuals can combine working and learning at any stage of the life cycle.
5. Establish research priorities to provide useful data on the economic and social benefits of adult and recurrent education.
6. Re-define the concepts of working and welfare so that income maintenance is provided to unemployed members of the work force through their participation in full-time adult education and training activities. This would require collaboration between government, industry and organized labor.
7. Establish priorities and needs for public works and service projects so that public employment and education are addressed to significant community needs and problems.
8. Establish regional training centers, clearinghouses, and demonstration projects designed to further the goals of lifelong learning, economic, and social development.
9. Determine the undesirable and desirable consequences of labor intensive industries and establish relevant goals and policies relating to them. (While the exploitation of "cheap" labor by foreign industry is detrimental to the economic and social growth of the region, there may be opportunities for labor intensive employment through home industries or crafts for retired persons who want to supplement their incomes and who want to find satisfying work.)
10. Re-direct the role of teacher colleges to pre and inservice education for the expanding needs in recurrent and life-long education as the need continues to lessen for teachers of children.

11. Create regional, state and local councils for lifelong education to facilitate integrated economic, social and educational planning in terms of: (a) inter-agency cooperation and coordination, (b) needs assessment, (c) efficient use of the technologies of mass and non-formal education, (d) follow-through opportunities for continuing education as a natural consequence of participation in ABE/APL programs, (e) dissemination of results of research and demonstration activities, (f) continuing program evaluation, (g) effective linkages between the adult and non-traditional education activities of community schools, technical institutes, community colleges, universities, social work agencies, business and industry, the mass media, libraries, most government agencies and organized labor.

SUMMARY

Economic development, recognizing the negative outcomes of a "bigger is better attitude," and concurrent adult education are both crucially interrelated in the development of people, communities, and the quality of life. Adult education that leads to personal and community development should be based on the assumption that a high and continuing priority be given to the elimination of existing patterns of racial and sexual discrimination. Communities in which children are racially segregated between public and private schools and wherein all sorts of discrimination by race, sex, age, religion, income or vocation exists can humanly develop only to the extent that such conditions can be overcome. For in the final analysis, the goal of development — be it economic, social or educational — is human development.

REFERENCES

1. Griffith, W.S. and Cervero, R.M. "The Adult Performance Level Program: A Serious and Deliberate Examination." New York City: AEA/NAPCAE Annual Conference, November, 1976.
2. 1970 Amendments to the Adult Education Act of 1966. P.L. 91-320.
3. *A Target Population in Adult Education*, Report of the National Advisory Council on Adult Education, U.S. Government Printing Office, Washington, D.C. 1974.
4. *The Experimental World Literacy Programme:* A Critical Assessment. Paris: The Unesco Press, 1976.

Career Change: A Never Ending Process

Max E. Jobe

Associate Professor, Vocational Education
East Texas State University

Changing careers has become a way of life. The average worker changes jobs from five to eight times in his life span. These changes often involve career changes. A study by Arbeiter[1] found 36 percent of the population between ages 16 and 65 were in career transition. Job change may be self imposed or may be forced upon the worker by external forces. The career or job change may include changing companies, changing geographical location and/or changing work environments. Adult and continuing education can help workers ease the stress of changing careers. As the mobility of the labor force increases, there is a concomitant need for educational institutions to be aware of and to give attention to workers in career transition.

There was a time when few people changed careers. A person chose a career and stayed with that career for a lifetime and few ever gave thought to the changing of a career. Many adult education students in the process of negotiating the job market for the second time ask themselves the validity of having a single, lifetime occupational role identity.

Economists and others specializing in the study of employment trends believe that they can discern a new pattern of life 20 to 50 years ahead. Instead of going through the cycle of school, work and retirement just once, many people wil need retraining and readjustment to work several times during their lifetime. Changing careers has not only become accepted, but in many instances, is the desirable thing to do.[2]

Not only do the young and the unskilled change careers but the middle aged and older workers, often found in skilled and executive jobs, also change careers. Arbeiter,[1] in a study of college educated subject persons, interviewed 401 adults in career transition and found they were largely female, 20-29 years of age, white, married, and with an annual income in excess of $10,000. This group is typical of many who seek the services of adult and continuing education counseling services. However, as more and more people find themselves needing to make career changes, it is well to recognize that changing careers is a rightful part of the process of continuous growth and development which extends through a lifetime. It is not surprising therefore that the number of adult mid-career persons re-entering some form of post-secondary education or training has increased drastically.

Reasons for Changing Careers — There are diverse reasons for changing careers:
1. Seeking a new career for financial and professional advancement.
2. Skills obsolescence often brought about by technological change.
3. Re-entering the world of work after months or years of absence in rearing children.
4. Re-thinking life goals.
5. Leaving a career because of boredom.
6. Seeking a career that is less demanding — an outgrowth of stress and strain of present job.
7. Retirees seeking new careers.

Money is a key factor in work and career change. Arbeiter found financial need was the major reason for changing jobs. Stern,[3] however, hypothesized that increased awareness of different kinds of work and willingness to risk leaving an occupation as major reasons for changing careers. Thomas,[4] in a study of persons changing careers, concluded — career change by itself is only a rough indication of what is going on in an individual's life during mid-life period. Other factors often involved in career change are the desire for new experiences, new opportunities, and a desire to do something more enjoyable.

When Does Career Change Occur — When in a life span or at what critical point are persons most likely to change careers? Gail Sheehy[5] in her book, *Passages,* indicated that many executives will change careers in their 40's or early 50's. She also indicated that 35 is when the average married woman re-enters the world of work. Heddesheiner[6] in a study of 1000 persons changing jobs found the average age to be 35. Retirement, which may come as early as in the 50's or as late as in the 70's often brings about a career change. The desire for professional or economic gain is most likely to cause career changes among younger persons in their late 20's or early to mid 30's. Technological change and job obsolescence affects all ages and is tied to technical advancement as well as national interest and priorities.

The foregoing studies clearly indicate that career change can affect nearly every group of students in adult and continuing education.

Educational Needs of Those Changing Careers — A career change will demand career information, counseling, guidance, and training. It may mean entry into a new career at a level low in position, skill, and prestige. The acquisition of skills and the acquiring of prestige and position when changing careers often can be a long and painful process involving perhaps years of self examination and exploring of new career possibilities, as well as on-the-job training and/or attending school to develop the skills needed for the new career.

Those persons changing careers most often change companies or employers and have to go back to school to learn new job skills. According to Sheehy, there is often a training or learning period which demands the person to be willing to suffer uncertainty and embarrassment at starting over and being at the bottom once again economically, socially and professionally.

The key question that should be examined is what educational factors may or should be involved in a career change. The study by Arbeiter of adults in the process of career change found most were desirous of career information, counseling, guidance, and training. This training may range from specific performance skills to general conceptual skills and the need for specific and/or general job related information. In addition, there may exist the need for human relations, managerial and life coping skills.

The advent of career change and the mobility of workers and families creates a different educational clientele of adults, often well educated and well informed, with the sophistication to know the kind of education they want and need, and the independence to demand it.[3] This involves a curriculum that is up-to-date and designed to meet the felt needs of the learner. This new clientele also will seek and demand a learning environment that is adapted to the adult learner and different from the customary autocratic classroom. The adult learner expects institutions to provide resources necessary for specific areas of instruction, and to acknowledge the maturity and experiences of the adult student. The instructor must not only be an expert in his/her teaching area, but must have the teaching skills to create a comfortable, convenient, and productive learning environment. This learning environment must be created at a time and location most convenient for the adult student.

CAREER CHANGE CYCLES

As shown in Figure 1, the career change cycle begins when the need for a career change arises and concludes with the satisfactory adjustment into the new career. Milestones in this cycle are awareness of career possibilities, exploring careers, career decision making and preparation for a new career.

CAREER CHANGE CYCLE
Need For Change
Internal   External
Awareness of Career Possibilities

EXPLORING CAREERS
Career Decision Making
Preparation For Career
School   Work   Relocation
Adjustment to Career

Figure 1.

The need for change, either internal or external, can be viewed as the initiating force of the cycle. These forces can be subject to numerous interpretations. Education, specific work adjustment, and/or relocation are outgrowths of a mix of these same internal and external forces. The milestones are crossroads for individuals making a career change.

Awareness of career possibilities is the point at which the need for change is conceptualized into a real, viable, new career. Exploring careers is more than conjecture. It is a positive seeking-out of needs gratifications and the income potential of a new career. Career decision making is the point of "go-no-go" in making a career change. Preparation for a career is the natural result of the preceeding decision.

Career change can be painful from the standpoint of entering a career with low level prestige that can be ego deflating and depressing. This career change involves the entire family and may require a new life style for the family, as well as for the person or persons changing careers. If there are other working members in the family, a relocation of the family will require career or job changes for those persons also. In addition, a career change may necessitate: (1) the family to relocate to a new city, (2) a change in social status, (3) a change in economic status.

Employers need to recognize career problems related to mid-life transition and provide in-house training and counseling.[7] A few employers are moving in this direction. Harvard University started a course for its employees called, "Personal Life Fulfillment." This course was designed for 30 to 50 year olds and will stress second careers. However, a survey of 1300 companies recently found only 10 of those companies providing older employees any help in training for post-retirement occupations. Clearly counseling and instruction must go hand-in-hand in providing training for those in mid-life transition.

Career life planning must be available to all. This is the responsibility of the business world, the educational world, and the world of government. Fulfilling this responsibility will include identifying educational needs of adults as well as providing for educational and explorational opportunities before the change of career and after the career change is made. In fact, some specialists contend that self-assessment is the key to a successful career. As pointed out by Stubblefield,[9] persons considering career changes may try out the new career through participation as a volunteer. Providing career life planning for adults changing careers is a major responsibility for adult educators.

Planning Needs — The activities of educators and educational institutions for assisting persons in the process of changing careers should range from conducting research to providing specific on-the-job training. There is need for conducting studies of persons as they contemplate and enter into career change. These studies should identify needs and problems of the worker and the family of the worker. Studies need to be conducted of adults in transition to identify their learning abilities, learning habits, and desires. Research is needed that will identify specific skills needed by teachers and others who will work with adults in preparation for career change. Counseling centers need to be developed in business and industry as well as in education. These centers should provide adults with information on career opportunities, educational opportunities, and other related information. In yet another area, specialized training must be provided for those educators who will be working with adults. This specialized training should be offered to the total staff of educational institutions. Lastly, adult educators should continue to intensify their cooperation with business and industry, especially as it relates to career changing needs.

SUMMARY

The great American dream of choosing a career and pursuing it until retirement is destined never to be as it was in the past. Perhaps it should never have been in that life's challenges can make one's life more fulfilling and rewarding — if these challenges are met. With the rapidly growing life expectancy and increasing technological advancements, it is perhaps undesirable to have so many skilled people not working at that kind of work which they would prefer to do. Assisting persons in preparing for and changing careers whether in youth, at mid-life, or upon retirement is a responsibility and challenge for our nation and especially for our adult educators.

Questions & Studies

The adult vocational counselor profiled four adults seeking assistance in changing careers. They are:

Case 1: is a female, 42 years of age, married and the mother of three children. Her husband is a construction supervisor working long hours and often away from home. All of her children are living away from home. She worked for one year as a typist after graduation from high school. She has not worked since nor attended college except for taking a community service course in aerobics. She wishes to find work in the public service area but not at the clerical level.

Case 2: is a male, 52 years of age, married and has two grown children. He has been with a large industrial firm and is now manager of procurement. It is obvious he will progress no higher in the firm and has grown weary of the pressures his job brings. He would like to change careers and find a low pressure job in something that will allow him to be creative, and would allow him to work alone.

Case 3: is a male, 38 years of age, married and has one child at home. He works on an assembly line and has been told the plant is closing in six months. His company has nothing for him after that. He has worked for this company for 10 years and prior to that held odd jobs such as delivery routes for bread and soft drink firms. He would like to move into a craft and become a journeyman but has been told he is too old.

Case 4: is a female, 61 years old. She is retiring in a few months after 20 years with one company as a salesperson. Her husband died several years ago and she has two grown children. She wishes to continue working part-time to supplement her retirement income and social security. However, her primary interest is to have something to do and to feel she is making a contribution.

Questions: 1. What additional information would you need from each of the above to provide career counseling? 2. Based on the information you have what suggestions would you have for each in regard to: (1) further education, (2) types of work? Visualize using Figure 1 in arriving at these suggestions.

REFERENCES

1. Arbeiter, Solomon. "Career Transitions the Demand for Counseling." *Journal of College Placement*, 38, 1976, 54-58.
2. McMillan, Robert L. "Second Careers and the Adult Student." *Adult Leadership*, 25, 1977, 201-203.
3. Stern, Barry E. *Toward a Federal Policy on Education and Work*, U.S. Government Printing Office, Washington, D.C., 1977.
4. Thomas, L. Eugene. "Mid-Career Change: Self-Selected or Externally Mandated?" *Vocational Guidance Quarterly*, 26, 1977, 320-328.
5. Sheehy, Gail. *Passages*. New York: Dutton, 1976.
6. Heddesheiner, Janet C. *Vocational Education and Mid-Career Change*. Ohio State University, Columbus, 1980.
7. Golembiewske, Robert. "Mid-Life Transition and Mid-Career Crisis: A Special Case for Individual Development." *Public Administration Review*, 30, 1978.
8. Montana, Patrick J. and Margaret V. Higginson. *Career Life Planning for Americans*, AMACOM, New York, 1978.
9. Stubblefield, Harold A. *Leisure and Career Development in Mid-Life: Contributions of Continuing Education*. Virginia Polytechnic Institution, Blacksburg, 1977.

The External Degree: A Viable Alternative

Eugene E. DuBois

Professor, Education & Human Development
George Washington University

Education today and its delivery system has been under attack from both the conservative and liberal schools of eduational theory. The economics of today's society call for measures which will focus upon quality education and realistic means for bringing about desired results.

One approach in responding to the attack is to combine the two elements of quality and economy in the external degree. For many people the external degree is a phenomenon of the twentieth century United States; they do not realize its actual origin was in Europe during the last century. Unfortunately, in their enthusiasm to be critical, many scholars have often failed to note the historical antecedents of this departure from the traditional educational delivery system and have thus erroneously assailed this increasingly acceptable teaching-learning practice as being novel or untested.

The external degree program may be the most controversial of all alternatives to traditional education. Many institutions have designed programs of study which provide alternative learning designs towards meeting learning needs of a diverse student body. While many alternative programs have been designed in both the United States and in Europe, the successes and failures tend to substantiate either the philosophical positions of those who differ with or agree with the external degree and other alternative higher education programs.

Historically speaking, the external degree has reflected changing needs in providing higher education to an increasingly bifurcated, mobile and technical society. Viewed from another stance the external degree reflects expanding concepts of the nature and function of higher education. The historical development presents a clear picture of educational vitality.

U.S. Experimentations in Non-Traditional Adult and Higher Education —
The year 1837 might easily be considered the beginning of the modern-day women's movement in the United States. It was in that year that four women were admitted to Oberlin College in Ohio. The women were permitted to study for the traditional B.A. degree as well as a special *Ladies Course* which culminated with a diploma.

In 1874, Harvard agreed to give examinations to women for work they had taken elsewhere, and then award them certificates. However, this did not admit them to the institution for study.

In 1879, a group of Harvard professors began to offer courses to women outside of the university under the auspices of "The Society for the Collegiate Instruction of Women." These courses became popularly known as the Harvard Annex. It was not until 1898 that the Annex achieved full status as Radcliffe College, Harvard's coordinate college for women.

The German Model — The University of Chicago was reorganized under the leadership of William Rainey Harper. Dr. Harper was much impressed by the German university system and its reliance on research and graduate study.

The division of the University into undergraduate, graduate and professional schools and colleges, the creation of a junior college within the University structure, correspondence education and the conscious attempt of articulation of secondary schools and higher education, all helped to create the University of Chicago as a leader in alternative higher education.

Two-Year Colleges — The German university design as established at the University of Chicago was an innovation in higher education and contained many other features heretofore not known in the United States. One of these innovations was the 1892 creation of a bifurcated undergraduate division, the Academic College and the University College. The former enrolled the freshmen and sophomores and the latter the upper division.

The Academic College became the Junior College in 1896. The success of this model led to the creation of other alternative colleges; Lewis Institute was established in Chicago in 1897, and there was an addition of two years of study to the high school program in Joliet, IL in 1901. This latter program became Joliet Junior College, the oldest public junior college in the United States.

The cessation of World War II brought about a need for expanded educational facilities and new programs for an increasingly technical and industrial society. It was during this period that junior colleges began to assume greater responsibilities, higher visibility, and prestige.

The 1200 publicly sponsored community colleges and technical institutes and private junior colleges are the direct result of the German model experimentations begun in Chicago in 1892.

Cooperative Occupational Education — Cooperative Occupational Education (Co-op) is uniquely American. Co-op is designed in such a way that the students' studies are coordinated with a work experience. This should not be confused with summer employment or part-time employment. Cooperative Occupational Education is coordinated by an official of the educational institution, and designed to provide the student with hands-on experiences, as well as an introduction to the world of work.

Dean Herman Schneider of the University of Cincinnati introduced cooperative education in 1906. Schneider's plan began in the College of

Engineering, and until 1921 remained in that field. When President Arthur E. Morgan reorganized Antioch College, that institution transferred the concept to the liberal arts.

Since co-op education's early success was in the field of engineering, those institutions specializing in this area began adopting "co-op," thus, institutions such as the Rochester Institute of Technology in New York and Northeastern University in Massachusetts became leaders in the field. Soon community colleges, junior colleges, and two-year technical institutes followed their lead.

The advantages of cooperative education are four-fold: (1) it assists the student in maintaining relevance by correlating studies with the world of work, (2) it keeps the cost of education within reason for many students by providing an income, (3) it keeps the faculty abreast of the work-world, (4) the local community is assured of a cadre of skilled manpower.

St. John's College, founded in 1786, is the third oldest American college, and in 1937 it became the leader in developing alternative higher education. In 1937 the economic and academic conditions of the institution caused its administration to realize that a total reorganization was necessary. Under the leadership of Stringfellow Barr and Scott Buchanan a new curriculum was designed departing from the traditional American system of higher education. The focal point was a bi-weekly evening seminar in which two or three tutors would meet students usually in groups of fifteen to twenty to discuss the Great Books of the World. The works of Homer and literature of the Greek, Roman, and Medieval periods extending to the present day were selected as the basic curriculum as they are purported to be answers to the serious questions of human existence.

Tutorials were conducted for one hour on four days weekly. Greek and French were studied for two years to satisfy graduation requirements. Laboratory work and formal lectures (Friday evenings) were included in the curriculum.

Certainly the St. John's program of undergraduate study is atypical of the contemporary American institution and presents a significantly different learning design.[1]

OPEN UNIVERSITIES

During the 1960's American educators began to recognize three very serious facts of life: (1) a new kind of student was beginning to appear, (2) the economic cost of education was increasing rapidly, (3) more was learned about the psychology of adult learning.

Out of these three factors new designs were developed and two in particular have been most effective in opening the educational world to innovation and experimentation — The University Without Walls (UWW) and the free university.

The University Without Walls was developed as a program of Antioch College with a consortium of 25 institutions to conduct experimental research. UWW began with a grant of $415,000 from the U.S. Office of Education.

Later other grants were received from the Ford Foundation and UNESCO.

The University Without Walls is based upon self-direction with the student accepting broad responsibility for his education. Each member institution agrees to the basic principles of adult learning theory which includes: (1) no fixed curriculum, (2) programs planned and designed for each student in consultation with an adviser, (3) no fixed time schedule for the completion of degrees.[2]

Another alternative, free university, is an organization which is community-based and offers non-credit courses for all. The often quoted motto is "anyone can teach and anyone can learn." This is fully accepted by those participating in this alternative learning program.

Founded in protest to the traditional university with its organized classes, fixed schedules, prerequisites and requirements, the free university views those restraints as alien to learning, and places the professor rather than the student into the centrality of the learning design.

Known as open education exchanges, "communiversities," and experimental colleges, these programs perhaps represent the broadest and most varient opportunities for learning. The educational programs are heterogeneous, and reflect the entire community through age, race, sex, occupation, and previous educational experiences.

Originating in the free speech movement at the University of California at Berkeley in 1964, the concept quickly spread across the country to colleges and universities. However, as that generation left the campuses and some of the traditional institutions nominally made changes in order to meet the needs of these students, free universities became less activist and undergraduates became oriented again to the more traditionalist adult education movement.

Presently, there are two hundred (200) free university centers serving over 300,000 adults. These centers are serviced by the Free University Network located in Manhattan, Kansas.[3]

THE EXTERNAL DEGREE

The Modality — No responsible educator would abdicate his control of the quality of educational services. Thus a control system, whether in a traditional campus-based program of studies, or in an alternative program of studies must be continually present. However, economics continues to affect the learning modality.

The external degree, or field-based program, transfers the site of the learning experience from the institutional campus and places it near the constituent student population. Thus rather than the student traveling to the traditional campus, the instructor travels to the student, providing him or her with the same expertise, learning designs and experiences he/she would have received on the campus.

The modalities of delivery vary with the institutions, degrees, and programs. However, it is possible to discuss here the commonalities of the

external degree field-based program and thus place it in perspective.
One of the major difficulties of the external degree program is it is often perceived in terms of the traditional designs, categories and terminology of education. This perception is often a teacher lecturing to a mass of students, answering questions, administering quizzes and examinations, and possibly assigning a term paper.

While the external degree may be part or whole of these elements its modality is much larger and more expansive. Since most of the students studying in external degree programs are employed professionals, the learning experiences are of immediate use or related to the job experiences and are directly applicable to real life situations.

The Support System — Every educational experience requires a support system. Learning materials, books, periodicals and other instructional aides are necessary to supplement lecturing, discussions, and cognitive analysis.

The external degree program relies upon other persons and institutions for the support of their learning activities. Learning resources may not always be the instructor for the resources of the local community may support the expanded instructional design. Recent revolutionary experiences in the area of information retrieval systems are perhaps the most significant contributions to the external degree program support system. The various federally funded research clearinghouses, the use of microfiche, microfilming and hard copy information retrieval systems make the traditional concept of libraries almost obsolete. This is not to say that libraries are inappropriate for learning, but new technology offers convenient alternative methods of information retrieval for the mobil student who is not campus-based.

One additional advantage to the external degree program is the opportunity for students to be exposed to the expertise of the leadership in the various disciplines. Few traditional institutions of higher education can maintain the high quality professional personnel that external degree programs may maintain. Through these adjunct faculty members, from a variety of institutions, the students meet and often maintain professional relationships with the leadership of their disciplines.

Logistical Concerns — Admittedly, the external degree program presents many logistical problems. The first is the recruitment of potentially qualified students, processing applications, collecting fees and scheduling. The local on-site coordinator who usually performs these functions becomes the crucial link in this phase of the program.

The location for instruction is usually through a host institution or conference center. At this location the basic learning materials must be catalogued, stored, and circulated to the students through the coordinator.

SUMMARY

Withstanding the problems of: (1) unacceptance, (2) ignorance of the external degree program, (3) historic antecendents, (4) experimentation and research, (5) logistics, the years have proven that the external degree program is a viable alternative to campus-based programs.

Sound academic planning and an educational philosophy which is concerned more about learning than merely teaching has brought about this alternative to traditional education.

By all indications the next expansion in education will be in adult education; primarily in educating adults for technological and societal change. By altering the educational delivery system the learning needs of this expanding adult population can be met. It may be virtually impossible to meet these burgeoning needs with the present delivery system.

Economics, time and the explosion of knowledge all attest to the need for alternative learning designs. The end-product, perhaps not the process, should be the keystone of evaluation. Criticism of the external degree will be helpful in that it will refine this new thrust. It will allow program planners and instructional facilitators to test theory, to evaluate programs and to construct new designs for the new learners. However, the thrust is there, the need is the present and the mechanism *can* be utilized.

QUESTIONS AND EXERCISES

1. Research the contemporary literature, and prepare a paper supporting the external degree.
2. Survey special degree programs for adults and write a paper analyzing their strengths and weaknesses.
3. Often institutional innovation includes smaller, although significant, creative instructional designs, for example, the seminar in the German model, or programmed instruction in the two-year college, or the use of information retrieval technology in external degree programs. Discuss these and other instructional designs, and their significance for the adult learner.

REFERENCES

1. Barbeau, Joseph E. and Eugene E. DuBois. "Cooperative Occupational Education: A History and An Assessment" *Community College Review.* Vol. III, No. 3, January, 1976.
2. *The University Without Walls: A First Report.* Yellow Springs, Ohio: Union for Experimenting Colleges and Universities, 1972.
3. Draves, Bill. *The Free University: A Model for Lifelong Learning.* Chicago: Association Press/Follett Publishing Company, 1980.
4. Brower, H. Terri. "The External Doctorate" *Nursing Outlook,* September 1979.
5. DuBois, Eugene E. and Frederic A. Ricco. "Nontraditional Study: Emergence Through Social Change." Phillip J. Sleeman and D.M. Rockwell eds. *Instructional Media and Technology: A Professional's Resource.* Stroudsburg, Pa.: Dowden, Hutchinson and Ross, Inc. 1976.
6. Gleazer, Edmund, J. Jr. *The Community College: Values, Vision, and Vitality.* Washington, D.C. American Association of Community and Junior Colleges, 1980.
7. Houle, C.O. *The External Degree.* San Francisco: Jossey-Bass. 1973.
8. Scigliano, John and Eugene E. DuBois. "Staff Development: Nova Style" *Junior and Community College Journal* Vol. 47; No. 2, Oct., 1976.
9. *University of San Francisco External Degree Programs.* San Francisco: University of San Francisco, 1976.

Technology & the Future

David C. Wigglesworth

President, D.C.W. Research Associates of Los Altos

David G. Gueulette

Associate Professor, Dept. of Leadership & Educational Policy Studies, Northern Illinois University

"Education which is not modern, shares the fate of all organic things which are kept too long." — Alfred North Whitehead

Educators in the United States, by and large have ignored the possibilities of educational technology and its positive potential for meeting some of the real challenges of this and future generations. Evidence of serious attempts to develop a "teaching machine" can be traced to the works of Sidney L. Pressey and B.F. Skinner, early educational entrepreneurs of the 1920's and 1930's. These first "teaching machines" were clumsy and crude affairs that were primarily directed to testing and later actual drill and instruction with some means for recording students' efforts.

Skinner became the best known of these "teaching machines" pioneers and espoused behavioral management techniques based on "program of instruction." While interest in programmed instruction was maintained and utilized in language, mathematics and some vocational training, "teaching machines" *per se* have fallen by the wayside. Relating technology to education found no widespread acceptance.

However youth born in today's world will need, by necessity, an education emphasizing technology to a preponderant degree. True, there will still be great teachers and a need for the Humanities, but adults not skilled in the language and methodology of technology will be as disadvantaged as those who cannot read or write.

Now, it is not the intent to suggest that educational technology (no matter how defined) can be viewed as providing instant panaceas to the complex problems of education in today's world. Rather, educational technology must be viewed as one of a number of potential strategies for effecting positive change within education to best meet the needs of our society.

For this change to occur, the overriding determinant governing the utilization of educational technology is the nature of the "fit" between the competencies and desires of the user group and the threats and opportunities presented by the environment. Furthermore, as the costs of education rise and as the sources of financial support diminish, educators will be reluctantly forced to utilize educational technology to meet the demands of their constituencies. For, in fact, continuing education students often through their employment have some knowledge of technology, to a greater or lesser extent than their instructors. They will create a demand for technologically relevant instruction as their needs are assessed and programs are built upon those needs.

Looking at American education, it is clear from what has recently been written that a large number of educators are not totally supportive of educational technology in its new and present form. Often this is because of an insecurity as to the uses of technology and the lack of skills needed to perform technological tasks. It is true that some educational technology such as overhead projectors, films, video-tapes, and even audio-tape recorders have finally become recognized as "safe" tools. However, a recent journal raised the question if teachers were prepared for the invasion of microcomputers into their classroom.

At a Computer Conference (COMCON '82) in San Francisco, a number of educational speakers were less than enthusiastic about the utilization of computers in education (other than for recording grades and maintaining attendance records).

The Council for Education Development and Research (CEDaR) published (1982) "A Bright Promise But A Dim Future, Researchers Examine Potential of Educational Technology." In this article the Council recognized that educational technology holds promise but they seem to indicate that educators will become confused between gadgetry and technology and that educators are not capable of evaluating either educational hardware or software.

For years, educators have been evaluating everything from school furnaces, furniture, and food to filmstrips, financial packages, and finger paints. It is clear that they can learn to evaluate the hardware of the new technologies and should have little difficulty in assessing the comparative values of educational software — promulgated by the same educational publishers who have been providing them with materials throughout their careers.

If present projections are realized by 1985, 100,000 American schools (K-12) will contain microcomputers. Teachers have been notoriously "futuristic-dreaming" of when the computers arrive twenty (20) years hence. They may be upon them now.

THE COMPUTER AND ITS COMPONENTS

The key to making the computer a useful tool is the program and programs are simply a list of instructions organized so that the computer will do intelligible things. The problem for students and educators alike is that the computer "talks" its own language. Thus, to use a computer wisely, the language must be mastered. Like their predecessor (the large memory rapid computer), microcomputers lack the extensive instructional programs necessary to allow them to become truly integrated into total educational programs. Some programs developed in certain fields such as medicine and engineering cover major portions of their fields, but these are exceptions. There are currently few computer programs for either large or micro computers that cover substantial areas of disciplines or grade levels.

One reason this technology is not more widely utilized is that it requires three skills in order to operate a program. They are:
1. How to read.
2. How to type.
3. How to speak "computerese."

The effort and time it takes to learn these three skills often makes it not worth the effort for the average harrassed and busy school administrator and teacher.

The advent of simple pre-programmed software designed by competent educators and computer experts will open up vast opportunities for professionals. Despite the problems, the microcomputer will become a powerful educational tool when it is fitted into current educational methodology and matched to present desired outcomes.

Most computers — whether micro or not — have several components:
1. A central processing unit.
2. Memory.
3. A clock.
4. A bus.
5. Interface.
6. Power supply.

The heart (or brain) is the "chip." This chip allows for storage of "bits" of information. In fact, some highly sophisticated computers can hold more than one million "bits" of information. The chip is a miniature electronic information storage and processing board that replaced the larger more expensive transistor or circuit board thus revolutionizing the information processing world. Perfected in the late seventies, the chip encouraged the development of cheap and effective small computers.

THE NATURE OF THE FIT

What is the "nature of the fit"? There are six (6) elements the adult educator should look at:
1. Teaching/problem solving.
2. Graphic representations.
3. Individualization.
4. Interactive dialogue (computer literacy).
5. Programming: cognitive development.
6. Communication: socialization.

Problem Solving — More and more educators hold that developing problem solving skills is the best educational teaching method, and less attention should be given to rote memorization or even learning by repetition. Computers can create environments (simulations) where complex problems may be solved by either conventional or non-conventional means. This methodology is applicable from elementary school through graduate school: children can play games with non-existent extra-territorial beings, continuing education students can analyze budgets of a dynamic nature, returning nurses can diagnose and treat a progressively debilitating disease.

Graphic Display — Much information is more readily understood when presented in a graphic or pictorial fashion. For example, students in drafting and other similar subjects can through the use of computers see what the "finished" product will look like. The "fit" here is between abstraction and a simulated reality. The challenge will be to determine what curricula assignments, projects, or instructional aids can be transferred or translated from book prose and static drawings to dynamic graphic displays.

Individualization — More and more attention is being directed toward exceptionality as the spectrum of adult students broadens. Uniqueness as a factor of student background, divergence as a factor in needs assessments, multiplicity in terms of individual and social goals, all require differentiation of instructional method and instructional outcome. Computers can be the ultimate "individualizer." Programs may be adjusted to fit individual learning needs, individual learning programs, individualized pacing, and individual remediation.

Interactive Dialogue (Computer Literacy) — The classroom with six rows of eight seats — a museum relic — used verbal instruction by the instructor and silent regurgitation on paper by the student. The computer allows for keyboard, voice, and now recently, tactile response or any combination of the three. This has required a new form of instructional communication. Some of this communication will be in the nature of student responding to computer cues. Some of it will be translating present data into computer managed data, still others will require verbal response stated in grammatical or code languages. The word processor has already revolutionalized the clerical/stenographic field, even more revolutionary will be advances in telecommunication utilizing the inter-active video (more widely used in foreign nations).

Microcomputers can be linked via telephone or cable television lines or even satellites to tie together the participants in a gigantic interactive information and instruction network. Or it may be possible to link home television sets with microcomputers via cable television networks to central switching and memory systems. The configurations are many. Even now in Columbus, Ohio, there is in operation a prototype system of television subscribers with sets and responders that can interact with the central computer to express opinions, answer questions, and provide a participatory learning experience for the viewers. The computer may make language encompass seeing, feeling, hearing, speaking, and doing.

Programming: Cognitive Development — As skill develops in writing and devising programs, students may begin to develop their own learning curricula, programming personalized learning tracks and formulating novel courses. At Stanford University a computer has been programmed to teach singing. A good deal of the problem of the "fit" has been to decide what responsibility the student has for not only learning the material but deciding what material is to be learned. If learning is internalized knowlege and cognitive patterns, then the challenge the computer holds is how to best internalize the plethora of knowledge and how best to strengthen cognitive ability.

Communication: Socialization — Arguments against the widespread use of educational computers generally suggest that the machine is dehumanizing, easily controlled by a ruthless autocracy and not appropriate for the ideal education that should be dealing with morals, ethics, values, human relations, or aesthetics — the electronic machine is a threat to the best teaching done through human interaction and discovery.

Strangely enough, the computer may usher in the age of socialization. Computer critics have held that computer use is atomistic. Yet, through universal computer literacy peoples of all nations can begin to communicate. The use of computers to maintain dialogue can further reduce isolation in rural or remote places, can bridge enormous socio-economic differences, and can begin to provide a means of enhancing true empathetic understanding of different cultures and mores.

The National Institute of Education has monitored various foreign nations in their development of technologically relevant curriculum. It has reported that in Japan science is treated as a universal skill. Other countries have begun to look upon the computer as an integral part of all educational curriculum.

In Japan, interactive television, computer based instruction, and systems approaches to learning are gaining wider acceptance. In fact fifty percent (50%) of Japanese managers in training have a strong computer background.

In Canada, there are varying uses of computers in general education. In Ontario, for example, some high schools have eighteen to twenty-seven microcomputers each! Also, in Canada, microcomputer based instructions for musical performance is being pursued as an area of research.

The U.S. military is utilizing educational technology rather widely and is experiencing success. U.S. industry is rapidly moving into interactive learning through educational technology. The community colleges are also taking important steps in this direction.

By 1981 close to 100,000 microcomputers had been sold to educational institutions within the United States. A large portion of these appear to be utilized in two major areas: (1) teaching computer languages and skills for career training purposes, (2) providing basic skills instruction with emphasis on rote learning and remediation.

Continuing education is ideally suited to educational technology for it can deliver appropriate instruction at times suitable to the needs of the student. Computer-based instruction, interactive video, and systems approaches to learning offer new and challenging opportunities to provide cost effective delivery systems to continuing education students in their homes, at work, in community facilities, as well as in traditional school buildings.

The utilization of new technologies requires greater involvement of teachers. They become managers, facilitators, tutors, diagnosticians, and have an opportunity to relate one-on-one with students to meet individual needs. At the same time educational technology offers the potential of relieving teachers of the drudgery of testing, grading, providing repetitive reinforcements; and of trying to reach all students at one time.

COMPUTER CHALLENGES

Some challenges presented by the computer are:

1. **Teacher inservice training** — When new educational technology is introduced, previously established patterns of activity are disrupted. The question will be: Can inservice training for teachers be devised that will modify teacher behavior with a minimum of disruption or will the "machine be banned!"?

2. **New learning materials** — Presently, computer "set-up" often requires 15-20 minutes before the student begins to use the program. Learning materials will need to be developed that provide easy access and written in a language easily understood.

3. **Expanded curriculum** — Often software does not take into consideration grade level or scope and sequence. There have been examples of third grade arithmetic facts written at a sixth grade reading level.

4. **Financial incentives (pay differentials)** — As teachers become more proficient in the use of computers, some means must be devised to keep them in education and not let them be recruited by industry.

5. **Credits for open-ended learning** — Adults will use computers at home, at work, and at the learning center. Many will prefer to use a home computer rather than travel to a learning center and they will request credit for their accomplished tasks.

6. **Intra and extra mural instruction** — Industry, clubs, and private groups will begin to offer instruction through university and school computer networks. Problems of financing, time sharing, and student monitoring will be encountered.

7. **Action oriented learning projects** — How can the plethora of new learning modes by contained in a curriculum — static and rigid — when the versatility of the computer will encourage students to explore new ways to solve problems?

Another complete dimension of Continuing Education involvement with technology is to provide opportunities for adults to explore and learn about the world of computers. Non-credit classes, demonstrations, lecture series, and simply "play-with-me" classes in technology can reduce the average American's fear and trepidation about computers. To overlook the socializations that can be obtained through interaction with technology would be overlooking a new realm of adult education instruction.

SUMMARY

While microcomputers and similar technologies like central large computers with cable television hook-ups could provide twenty-four (24) hour, home-based and lifelong teaching possibilities, it is probably unlikely and inappropriate that they should. Isolated and inert learners would learn only the world as mediated by the technology of the computer and already excessively pervasive television. A totally simulated world could encourage only imitation lives.

The transition from the traditional ways of teaching and the traditional perceptions of the public of what constitutes education to a new computer-based approach will not necessarily be easy. Continuing Education offers a way to bring educators, students, and the general public into an appreciation of the value of educational technology.

The overriding determinant governing the utilization of educational technology is the NATURE OF THE FIT between the competencies and desires of the user group, and both the threats and opportunities presented by the environment. This is indeed the bright promise of a brighter future!

REFERENCES

1. Beder, Hal, "In-Home Educational Technology. What is the Future?" *Lifelong Learning*, Washington, DC. AEA, Dec. 1981.
2. *PDK Newsletter*, Bloomington, IN. PDK, June 1982 Vol. 4, No. 4.
3. *Today's Education*, Washington, DC. NEA, April-May 1982.

Index

Administrator
  advisory committees, 66-73
  decision making techniques, 317-322
  Dept. of Defense, 56, 57
  evaluation, 335-345
  function in program planning, 102, 103
  human resource development, 371-377
  information retrieval systems, 360-370
  keep your ADA, 284-290
  lobbying, 35-39, 41-42
  needs assessment, 61-64
  political process, 33-42
  problems of the non-literate, 328-334
  use non-paid professionals, 299-307
  use volunteers successfully, 278-283
Adult basic education
  back to basic skills, 197-204
  Dept. of Defense, 59
  functionally non-literate, 16
  GED, 3
  holistic learning model, 235-245
  identify & teach the non-literate, 328-334
  illiteracy eradication, 390-396
  programs, 2
  reading, 155-167
  statistics, 2
  use non-paid professionals, 299-307
  use volunteers successfully, 278-283
Adult education
  Act (P L 91-230), 1
  adult instructional model, 222-234
  aging, 113
  changing support, 6
  competency-based, 21, 74-77
  computer based revolution in, 151-154
  definition, 23
  Dept. of Defense, 52
  expansion, 1, 18, 19
  goals & roles, 18, 19, 24
  history of, 1, 20-23
  impacted by economy, 11
  life skills, 132-143
  new Federalism, 6, 7
  occupational needs, 123
  ongoing, 15
  participants, 4
  philosophy, 17, 19, 24
  research, 13
  societal assumptions, 13, 53-54
  statistics, 1, 2, 34
  status of, 1-10
  strategy, 9, 10

  vocational, 123-130
  voluntary, 52
  women in, 43-49
Adult educators
  advanced degrees, 2
  be a better teacher, 323-327
  be aware of reading problems, 155
  beliefs, 25-31
  decision making techniques, 317-322
  democratic philosophy, 67
  evaluation, 335-345
  feedback, 247-259
  keep your ADA, 284-290
  legislators view of, 35
  lobbying, 34, 35-39, 41-42
  model, 30
  New Federalism, 7
  new goals, 9, 10, 17-19
  philosophy, 17, 18
  practitioner, 12
  priorities, 8
  teaching handicapped, 110, 111
  use non-paid professionals, 299-307
  use readability measures, 158
  use volunteers successfully, 278-283
  women, 43
Adult instructional model
  AID model, 224-233
  evaluation, 232-233
  guide for teaching/learning, 223-233
  instructional (lesson) plans, 230-232
  needs & objectives, 226-228
  organizational process, 224-226
  positive direction, 224
Adult learning patterns
  individual, 205
  large formal group, 209
  mass, 210
  organization, 205
  patterns of learning, 205
  small groups, 207
Adult Performance Level (APL)
  definition, 75, 80
  functional competencies, 75-77
  life skills, 78
  model, 76
  objectives, 75
  project, 3, 75
Advisory committees
  characteristics, 68
  community involvement, 67
  competency-based, 74, 75

Index

evaluation, 71
meetings, 70
membership, 68
orientation, 69
purpose, 66
role, 66-67
selection, 69
utilization, 70-71
Aging
  educational needs, 115-118
  educational wants, 118
  gerontology, 114
  history, 113
  learning ability, 119
  new force in society, 113
  participation in education, 114-115
  statistics, 113
Alternative delivery systems
  one to one, 201
  handicapped, 202
  homebased, 201
  T V, 201
Andragogy, 23, 127, 130, 175, 374, 375
Basic skills
  alternative delivery systems, 201-203
  APL, 198
  GED emphasis, 197, 198
  larger programs advantageous, 200
  life skills, 197, 198
  technology, 197
  voc-ed, 197, 199, 200
Be a better teacher
  adaptive techniques, 323
  be a better teacher, 323-327
  cardinal rules, 327
  lesson plan, 324-325
  review objectives, 325
  rules of first class, 323-324
  students' needs, 323
  students' success, 326, 327
  test taking tips, 326
Behavior
  cultural, 187-188
  culture, 215
  individual & group, 194, 195
  job getting mind set, 297
  learning, 216
  learner, 254
  life style concepts, 127-131
  objectives, 218
  problem solving, 132, 134, 138
  response—cognitive, affective, psychomotor, 133, 137-138
  space, 192
  teacher, 252
  terminal, 221

Beliefs
  about learners, 27, 28
  bases of, 30, 31
  democratic philosophy, 67
  help programming, 25
  identify, 31
  learning, 30
  orders of, 26-27
  purposes of C.F., 29
  role of educator, 30
Bell, T.H., 23, 77
Career change
  a never ending process, 397-402
  adjustments, 400-401
  career transition population, 397
  cycles of, 399
  educational needs for, 398-399
  history of, 397
  reasons for, 398-400
Career counseling
  behavioral changes, 148
  career planning, 308-316
  careers, 144-150
  clientele, 144
  conceptual model, 144-147
  counseling model, 141
  life concepts, 144-147
  life skills, 135-136
Career planning skills
  career planning & job getting skills, 308-316
  ideal job, 308-314
  ideal job description, 312
  ideal job model, 309
  job getting skills, 314-315
  life career planning, 310-313
  process, 310-312
  research, 308
  strategies for job getting, 314-315
Carnegie Council Report
  higher education, 43
  Three Thousand Futures, 54
College Level Examination Program (CLEP), 59, 177
Colleges
  Carnegie report, 54
  concerns, 49
  counseling, 47
  Dept. of Defense, 57-59
  institutional obligations, 45-46
  recruiting, 46-47
  statistics, 2, 44, 45, 54
  special curriculum, 48-49
  special support, 4, 5
Community based organizations
  budget, 90, 91

challenges, 84, 85
continuing evaluation, 89, 90
cooperation, 85
define goals, 87-88
history, 83
implication for communities, 176-178
industry and, 84
needs assessments, 85
network, 89
plan program, 85-89
purpose, 82
scope, 82
Competency-based education
concept, 74
future, 80
history, 74
philosophy, 75
practice, 75-78
Computer based training
computer-aided learning systems, 151-152
computer assisted testing (CAT), 152
computer assisted learning (CAL), 152
computer managed instruction (CMI), 152
Dept. of Defense, 151
industry activity, 151
interactive video, 152, 153
massive changes, 151-154
simulation, 153, 154
training industry & military personnel, 151
Conceptual approach
behavioral change, 216-217
change, 214
cognitive mapping, 212, 214
concept, 212, 213-216
development of program, 217-218
experience, 216
individualized strategies, 212
need, 215, 218
organizing system, 213, 216
program development, 212
Council for the Advancement of Experiential Learning (CAEL), 49, 177
Cross cultural education
changeable, 187
communication, 190, 191
cultural behavior, 187
cultural skills, 188-189
definition, 187
language, 189-190
learning—experiential, 195
micro-culture, 188, 189, 196
space in culture, 191, 192
time in culture, 192, 193
women's liberation, 193, 194
Curriculum
APL, 76-79
defined, 99-100
designs, 127-131
life skills, 132-143, 198
modification for handicapped, 109-109
pictures to passages, 199-200
program development, 101
special, 48, 49
vocational, 125-130
Decision making techniques
alternatives, 318-319
decision strategies, 317-318
defined, 317
examples of, 321-322
how to choose, 319, 321
process for, 317-322
Department of Defense
education fact sheet, 58-59
evaluation, 52, 53, 55, 56
future plans, 55, 56, 57
largest educational program, 55
policy revisions, 53
quality control, 52, 56
voluntary education, 52, 53, 54
Education
cross-cultural, 187-196
Dept. of, 6
Dept. of Defense, 52-59
for the aging, 118-122
for the handicapped, 106-112
of returning women, 43-50
new Federalism, 7
success story, 8
vocational, 123-130
Evaluation
as accountability, 338
continuous, 97, 338
evaluation as learning, 343
evaluation techniques, 344-345
feedback, 89, 250-256, 336-337, 340
formative, 94, 97, 98, 335, 337, 343
instructional model, 232, 233
life skills, 136, 137
objectives, 342
program, 342-343
recognition, 338
staff interactive process, 339, 341
student of teacher, 335, 336, 339
summative, 94, 97, 98, 335, 337, 338, 341, 343
summative to improve learning style, 337
total educational evaluation, 335-345

Index 419

External degree
  a viable alternative, 403-408
  cooperative occupational education, 404
  external degree, 406-407
  non-traditional programs, 403-407
  support systems, 407
  tutorials, 405
  two year colleges, 404
  University Without Walls, 406
Feedback
  effective teaching, 247-259
  evaluation, 89, 90
  life skills, 136, 137
Free Library, 21
Freire, Paulo, 83, 181, 198, 199
Functionally illiterate
  CBE, 74
  Right to Read, 74
  statistics, 3
General Educational Development Test (GED), 3, 77
Get/hold job skills
  correctly prepare application, 291-292
  interviews, 293, 294, 295-296
  job getting mind set, 297
  job getting strategies, 291
  resume, 294, 295
  role play, 293, 295, 298
  techniques of getting/holding job, 291-298
  where to look, 292, 293
Hall, 179, 181
Handicapped
  behavior modification, 108
  defined, 106
  individualized learning, 111
  new terminology, 107
  programs, 107
  removal of physical barriers, 110
Holistic learning
  back-to-the-basics, 235
  basic skills program, 238-242
  holistic education, 235-245
  listening, 243, 244
  notemaking, 241, 242
  reading, 244-245
  screening devices, 237
  student, 236
  teachers, 236
  total language program, 238-245
Human resource development
  adult educator role change, 371-377
  andragogy, 374-375
  criteria for professional, 372
  growth in skills performance, 371
  heuristic learning, 374
  history of growth of, 371-372
  HRD, a profession, 373, 374
  professional competency, 374, 395, 376
Identify & teach the non-literate
  characteristics of, 330
  culture, 328
  defined, 330
  English as a Second Language (ESL), 328-329
  identify & teach the non-literate, 328-334
  other causes of, 331-332
Individualized instruction
  CAI, 152
  CAL, 152
  interactive video, 152, 153
  learning patterns, 205
  simulation, 153, 154
Illiteracy eradication: a future model
  ABE programs, 391, 393, 394
  correlates of illiteracy, 392, 393
  definition, 390
  design for change, 393
  illiteracy eradication model, 390-396
  illiterate youth, 392
  message of illiteracy, 393
  Natl. Advisory Council on Adult Education report, 392
  prescription for literacy, 394, 395
  relationship of populations, 392
  scope of illiteracy, 391
  weaknesses & strengths in ABE, 394
Information retrieval systems
  abstracts Resources in Education (RIE), 362
  comprehensive references, 361
  computer search, 366, 368
  Current Index to Journals in Education (CIJE), 362
  define subject, 364, 365
  descriptors from Thesaurus, 366
  Educational Resources Information Center (ERIC), 362
  ERIC (ERIC/ACVE), 362
  identify concepts, 365
  information retrieval systems, 360-370
  manual search procedures, 266, 267
  reference tools, 363, 364
  searching ERIC, 364-370
  storage of data, 361
Join your professional organizations
  Adult Education Association (AEA/USA), 384

American Association of Adult &
  Continuing Education (AAACE),
  385
consolidation, 384-385
future of our associations, 387
leadership involvement (you), 386
history, 384-385
list of adult education associations,
  388, 389
memberships, 385-386
National Association of Public
  Continuing Adult Education
  (NAPCAE), 385
national, state, local, (join), 386
professional associations, 384-389
purpose of, 385
Keep your ADA
ADA (average daily attendance), 284
dropout defined, 284, 285
dropout descriptors, 286, 287
first class meeting, 288
how to prevent dropouts, 287, 288
instructor's role, 289, 290
reasons for dropout, 285
research, 285, 286
Knowles, 127, 130, 171, 175, 222, 374,
  375
Laws
Adult Education Act, 77, 82
Educational Consolidation Act—
  1981, 6
legislation, 22-23
Learning
abilities of aging, 119
APL, 77
associate, 261
attendant, 261
behavioral modification, 108, 142
CAI, CAL, CAT, 152
cognitive, 96
computer-aided, 151
concept, 15
dimensions—content, group,
  problem solving, 133-135
experiential, 49
goals, 18, 263
Kolb inventory, 96
lifelong, 1, 2, 15, 16, 17, 18
life skills, 132-143
modes, 96
motivation, 95
primary, 261
skills, 77
systematic, 216
style, 95
techniques, 96, 97

Learner feedback
benefits of self-made, 249-251
commercially prepared vs self-made,
  248, 249
course qualities, 253
creating stems or questions, 256-258
environmental qualities, 255
evaluation, 250-256
feedback, 247-259
improves instruction, 247
learner behavior, 254
pros & cons of, 247-248
sources, 247
teacher behavior, 252
Learning through discussion
criticism, 260
definition, 261
develop patterns of thought, 261
discussion leader, 262-263
participants responsibilities, 262, 266
process, 262-266
solve problems, 260
teaching/learning discussions,
  260-267
topic, 264
Lifelong learning
act, 15
concept, 15
essentiality, 16, 17
learning society, 18
way of life, 2
Life skills
behavior, 132
cognitive science, 137-138
conceptual growth, 139
defined, 132
model, 135-137, 140
objectives of, 142
process, 132
product/process objectives, 140-142
use of choice, 134
use of dimensions, 132-135
Materials
designing, 127-131
level of reader, 156
use of library, 202, 203
V-Tecs, 127
Methods
aware of students neds, 323
individualize instruction, 327
individualizing teaching strategies,
  219, 323
learner's responsibilities, 220
learning patterns, 205-210
lesson plans, 324-325
review methods, 323

Index

review objectives, 325
use media, 325, 326
vary techniques, 325
National Advisory Council on Adult Education, 16, 392
National Center for Educational Statistics, 1
National Center for Research in Vocational Education, 126
Needs
  ascribed, 60
  contributive, 117
  coping, 116
  expressed, 95
  expressive, 116-117
  felt, 60, 95
  growth, 95
  influence, 117
  real, 60
  transcendence, 118
Needs assessment
  data gathering techniques, 62
  definition, 60
  models, 62
  purposes, 60
  planning, 61-62, 95
  use of data, 63-64
Non-literate
  back to basic skills, 197-204
  identify & teach the non-literate, 328-334
  illiteracy eradication, 390-396
  language experience approach, 160-165
  MOBRAL, 199
  pictures to passages, 199-200
  use of library, 202, 203
Non-paid professionals
  defined, 299
  evaluation of, 306
  placing of, 305, 306
  problems of, 300-302
  program coordinator, 303-304
  recognition of, 306
  recruitment of, 304-305
  strengths of, 302-303
  termination of, 306
  use non-paid professionals, 299-307
  volunteers, 299-307
Objectives
  educational terms, 86, 87
  skill, 135-136
Organizational development
  assessment, 380
  assumptions common to OD & ACE, 380-381

change agents, 378
  implementation, 380
  organization effectiveness, 378-383
  planning & development, 380
  process intervention, 379, 380
Participatory modes
  action education, 183-186
  concept, 179, 190
  conferences, 183, 184
  decision-making, 179, 180, 181
  Hall, 179
  knowledge base, 181
  participatory research, 179-186
  practitioners, 181
  self-determination, 179-180
  traditional research, 182
  UNESCO, 181, 182, 183
Philosophy
  ABE, 75
  adjustments, 18
  basic assumptions, 17-18
  conceptual approach, 212
  democratic, 67
  handicapped, 108
  learning society, 18
  strategy, 9, 10
Political process
  coalitions, 40
  lobbying, 35-39, 41-42
  national, state, local, 34
  non-involvement of educators, 33
  organizations, 14, 35, 40
  participation, 35, 36
  political action, 15, 16
  rules of, 35, 36
Preferential style: cognitive mapping
  alternative approach, 268
  assessing, 269
  auditory learner, 270, 271
  CARE techniques, 274, 275
  cognitive mapping, 268, 273, 274, 276
  differential profiles, 269
  holistic learning, 276
  identifying style, 270
  kinesthetic learner, 272
  methods, 270, 271, 272
  preferential inventories, 272, 273
  preferential method, 275, 276
  preferential style, 268-277
  visual learner, 271
Professional Associations
  adult voluntary, 14
  change, 11
  contributions, 11
  join your professional organizations, 384-389

Program development
  conceptual framework, 99-101
  interactive model, 92, 94
  planning process, 92-94
  primary distinctions, 101, 102, 104
  procedural steps, 95-97
Programs
  a model, 92-97
  APL, 3, 75, 78
  career planning & job getting skills, 308-316
  CBOs, 82
  competency based, 130
  conceptual approach, 212-221
  conceptual framework, 99
  decision making techniques, 317-322
  define goals, 99
  defined, 99-101
  Dept. of Defense, 52, 53
  designs, 127
  development, 99
  for the handicapped, 106-107
  holistic learning, 235-245
  identify & teach the non-literate, 328-334
  instructional goals, 129
  life skills, 132-143
  needs assessment, 60
  open learning, 2
  options, 46
  participatory research, 179-186
  planning, 85-89
  post-secondary support, 5
  reading, 155-167
  reentry women, 43-50
  Right to Read, 74, 83
  self-directed, 171-178
  use of advisory committees, 70-71
  use non-paid professionals, 299-307
  vocational, 125-130
Reading
  comprehension, 167-168
  definition of readability, 156, 158
  develop lessons, 162-165
  formulas, 156-157
  ideolect, 161
  implementing & evaluating, 155-167
  language experience approach, 160-161
  reading prescriptions, 169
  segmented, sequential, merged details, 158-159
  skills, 157-160
  statistics, 155
Research
  advisory committee, 68
  APL, 76, 77, 79
  career planning, 308
  CBAE, 79
  dropouts, 285
  functional literacy, 75
  information retrieval systems, 360-370
  learning styles, 269
  life skills, 138
  Institute of Defense Analyses, 151
  participatory, 179-186
  reliability, 673
  self-directed learning, 171-174
  validity, 63
  vocational education, 124, 126
Right to Read, 74, 83
Self-assessment
  history, 346
  inventory of skills, 347-349
  inventory scale, 347
  skills to improve teaching, 346-359
  strengthen your skills, 349-358
Self-directed learning
  defined, 171, 176
  future research, 174, 175
  history, 171
  implications for institutions, 176, 177
  implications for learners, 175
  implications for practitioners, 175, 176
  Knowles, 171
  readiness, 173
  research, 171-174
  self-directed learning readiness scale (SDLRS), 173
  Tough, 171, 172
Teaching/learning
  career planning & job getting skills 308-316
  conceptual approach, 212-221
  cross cultural, 187-196
  decision making techniques, 317-322
  discussion, 260-267
  evaluation, 335-345
  feedback, 247-259
  get/hold job skills, 291-298
  guide for teaching/learning, 223-233
  holistic learning, 235-245
  how aged learn, 119-120
  how handicapped learn, 106, 111
  identification of learners, 102
  identify & teach the non-literate, 328-334
  information retrieval systems, 360-370
  learning patterns, 205-211
  participatory modes, 179-186
  preferential styles: cognitive mapping, 268-277

Index

program planning, 103, 104
reading, 155-167
self-assessment, 346-359
self-directed, 171-178
use volunteers successfully, 278-283
Technology
  advancements, 1, 7, 8, 151-154
  CAI, CAL, CAT, 152
  computer-aided learning, 151-154
  computer based training in industry, 152-154
  interactive video, 152
  media, 5
  simulator, 153
Technology & the future
  challenge to educators, 414
  computers, 410, 411
  educators & technology, 409, 410
  history, 409
  nature of the "fit," 409, 411, 415
  purpose of, 409
  technology, 409-415
  uses of computer in education, 411-414
Tough, 171, 172, 206
Urban league, 84
Use volunteers successfully
  community support, 278, 279
  coordinator, 279
  defined, 278
  evaluation, 281, 282
  history, 278
  in ABE, 279
  matching, 280
  orientation, 279, 280
  planning program, 279
  recruiting, 279
  staff support, 279, 280, 281, 282
  support of, 280, 281
  training, 280
  use volunteers successfully, 278-283
Vocational-technical education
  CBAVE plus API, 129
  changes in, 124
  computer-aided learning systems, 151-154
  comprehensive view, 123, 124
  definition, 123
  fundings, 126
  future changes, 131
  handicapped, 109
  learning designs, 127-131
  model school, 129
  occupational needs, 123
  prevocational guidance, 126
  programs, 125
  reason for attending, 125-126
  statistics, 124
  typology, 125, 126
  unemployment problems, 123
Women
  counseling, 47
  institutional obligations, 45-46
  reentry program, 43
  special curriculum, 48-49
  special programs, 49
  statistics, 44
  status of, 43

DISCHARGED
MAR 2 8 1995
DISCHARGED
DISCHARGED

DEC 8 1988

DISCHARGED
JAN 19 1988

DISCHARGED
JUL 2 0 1985

DISCHARGED
APR 0 3 1987

MAR 1 8 1987

APR 2 1 1987

DISCHARGED
NOV 3 0 1987

APR 2 4 1987

NOV 1 8 1987

DISCHARGED
MAR 1 1 1988

MAR 0 5 1994
DISCHARGED

MAY 2 1 1994

MAR 0 1 1996

MAR 1 8 1999